CULTURE *of*
PREJUDICE

CULTURE OF PREJUDICE
Arguments in critical social science
::
Judith C. Blackwell, Murray E.G. Smith, & John S. Sorenson

broadview press

NATIONAL LIBRARY OF CANADA CATALOGUING IN PUBLICATION

Culture of prejudice : arguments in critical social science / edited by Judith C. Blackwell, Murray E.G. Smith, and John S. Sorenson.

ISBN 1-55111-490-9

1. Prejudices.   2. Culture.
I. Blackwell, Judith C., 1944-
II. Smith, Murray E. G. (Murray Edward George), 1950-
III. Sorenson, John, 1952-

HM1091.C84 2003   303.3'85   C2003-902052-5

BROADVIEW PRESS, LTD. is an independent, international publishing house, incorporated in 1985. Broadview believes in shared ownership, both with its employees and with the general public; since the year 2000 Broadview shares have traded publicly on the Toronto Venture Exchange under the symbol BDP.

We welcome comments and suggestions regarding any aspect of our publications—please feel free to contact us at the addresses below or at broadview@broadviewpress.com. Broadview Press gratefully acknowledges the support of the Ministry of Canadian Heritage through the Book Publishing Industry Development Program.

North America
Post Office Box 1243,
Peterborough, Ontario, Canada K9J 7H5

3576 California Road,
Orchard Park, New York, USA 14127
TEL (705) 743-8990; FAX (705) 743-8353

EMAIL customerservice@broadviewpress.com

UK, Ireland and continental Europe
Plymbridge Distributors Ltd.
Estover Road, Plymouth PL6 7PY, UK
TEL (01752) 202301; FAX (01752) 202333;
E-MAIL EMAIL orders@plymbridge.com

Australia and New Zealand
UNIREPS University of New South Wales
Sydney, NSW 2052
TEL 61 2 9664099; FAX 61 2 9664520
EMAIL infopress@unsw.edu.au

♻ This book is printed on acid-free paper containing 20% post-consumer fibre.

Cover design by Black Eye Design.
Typeset by Liz Broes, Black Eye Design.

Printed in Canada

10 9 8 7 6 5 4 3 2

CONTENTS

acknowledgements

The authors wish to thank June Corman for helping us to formulate many of the themes of this book as well as for her continued support and advice while we wrote it. We also wish to acknowledge the thoughtful comments of the anonymous reviewers of the manuscript. Thanks are also due to Linda Landry for the gift of communication when our electronic incompatibilities confounded us. Judith Blackwell thanks a number of supporters for their insights and assistance: Ed Borowski, Jane Helleiner, Viola Shuart, Michelle Webber, and the "Ladies of the Lake." Murray Smith thanks Tom Reid, Ken Campbell, John McAmmond, and Joe Colangelo for many useful comments on his chapters. John Sorenson thanks Atsuko Matsuoka for her suggestions and support. Finally, the authors would like to thank *each other*, for being stimulating colleagues and working so well together. Murray Smith and John Sorenson put a great deal of work into the "front end" of the project, preparing and circulating our book proposal. Judith Blackwell pulled it all together at the end, preparing the manuscript for submission for review and then again for publication. Many thanks to the wonderful people at Broadview Press who assisted us during the production of this book.

PART ONE

introduction to the Book & its Authors

Introduction to the Book and its Authors

CULTURE: "...the complex everyday world we all encounter and through which we all move. Culture begins at the point at which humans surpass whatever is simply given in their *natural* inheritance."[1]

PREJUDICE: "A previous judgement; *esp.* a judgement formed before due examination or consideration; a premature or hasty judgement; a pre-judgement."[2]

The great majority of people in the Western world have every reason to be grateful that they are alive today rather than in some long-past historical era. An obvious reason is that average living standards in the West are much higher than they were in feudal Europe, ancient Rome, or Victorian England. However, an equally important and perhaps even more compelling reason is that those alive today are the beneficiaries of titanic social struggles that succeeded both in expanding the scope of human freedom and thereby also succeeded, in some measure, in dismantling some aspects of what we call the "culture of prejudice."

The culture of prejudice is the antithesis of human freedom and the mortal enemy of human self-realization. It is a system of ideas and values that is rooted in the impulse of some segments of humanity to improve their condition at the expense of other humans, non-human life forms, and the health of the planet. As such, the culture of prejudice is a mainstay of social oppression and exploitation—a fount of selfish and ill-founded judgments and attitudes that are disseminated by the socially privileged and often uncritically accepted by those who are its victims. Its chief function is to discourage the kind of critical, rational thought that might inspire collective action to achieve social justice, human equality, and genuine social progress.

---

1. A. Edgar and P. Sedgwick, *Key Concepts in Cultural Theory* (London: Routledge, 1999) 102.

2. *Oxford English Dictionary* (Compact Edition).

In the Western world, the culture of prejudice of five hundred years ago maintained that there was but one legitimate religious authority, the Roman Catholic Church. Four hundred years ago, the idea of the "divine right of kings" was still widespread and democratic ideas were regarded as treasonous. Three hundred years ago, the few parliamentary democracies in existence still limited the right to vote to men with substantial claims to property ownership. Two hundred years ago, chattel slavery was still a thriving institution in much of the world, including the Western hemisphere. One hundred years ago, in virtually every country in the world, women were still deprived of the right to vote and of many other citizenship rights enjoyed by their fathers, brothers, and husbands. Over the course of the past century, epic struggles have been waged against colonialism, national oppression, sexual oppression, racial oppression, and class exploitation, and the ideas that justified these iniquities are now widely understood to be unacceptable and retrograde. *Some* progress, it would seem, has been made in replacing "backward" ideas with "enlightened" (or what some choose to call "politically correct") ones.

Yet it is common these days for intellectuals to be suspicious of such claims. The postmodernist trend in contemporary social theory and philosophy has provided new grounds for skeptical attitudes toward such traditional Enlightenment values and aspirations as "critical reason" and "human progress." In distancing themselves from the legacy of eighteenth-century Enlightenment thought, postmodernist thinkers have pointed to the dangers of "grand narratives" of the human condition or human history which "privilege" science over religious faith or which value "modern society" over traditional ways of life. Their skepticism toward Enlightenment or modernist projects arises from disillusionment with the results of those projects, which, to be sure, have been a mixed blessing at best. The progress of modern science has not been unequivocally beneficial, for the fruits of that progress have typically been harvested by the socially privileged and powerful to fortify their positions. Furthermore, the extent to which technological innovation has encouraged genuine progress in the sphere of human morality and ethics remains highly arguable.

It is easy to affirm agreement with many of these postmodernist propositions. However, we must part company with the postmodernists in any case. In our view, the problem with the Enlightenment project was not the "faith" that it placed in critical reason and scientific method, but the *insufficiently radical* nature of its break from more traditional forms of thought. Enlightenment thought challenged dogma, superstition, and intellectual intolerance; it undermined the claims of hereditary privilege and rigid social hierarchies; it popularized the idea of human equality. In doing these things, it contributed tremendously to the demolition of the cultures of prejudice that characterized European feudalism. Nevertheless, it failed to see that the scientific rationality that it was championing— both in the natural and social sciences—was not a socially neutral engine of human progress but a weapon in the service of new forms of class domination, exploitation, and oppression, specifically the forms associated with capitalism. While many postmodernists would agree with this last point, most are nevertheless unwilling to look beyond the horizon of capitalism to a new form of society, and they are reluctant to acknowledge that the "modernity" that has disappointed them so profoundly may be best seen as a *transitional* chapter in the story of human progress. For this contradictory episode in human history to be surpassed, we believe that champions of human progress should neither dispense with critical reason and appeals to universal values nor abandon a commitment to disclosing "objective truths" as a guide to resolute forms of social action. Rather, the "science" that has been such a key element in the success of modern capitalism must be transmuted into an instrument of human emancipation. Natural science, the fruits of which are embodied in modern technology, can be harnessed for such a goal only in the context of radically new forms of social organization. It is the goal of an emancipatory and critical social science to illuminate the shape of those new social forms and to propose the means by which they might be realized.

One of the tasks of such a social science today is to expose the deepest roots of the contemporary culture of prejudice. For example, openly racist remarks are no longer tolerated in most of the western world; yet racism remains a pervasive reality. Indeed, its pervasiveness goes a long way to explain the equanimity with which the predominantly white populations of North America and Europe accept the appalling poverty of billions of people living in the Third World. Racism is that component of the culture of prejudice that encourages the belief that people of colour are less deserving of a decent quality of life than people with paler complexions. Consider a second example. Declaring that the "proper place" of women is in the home, attending to the needs of their husbands and their children increasingly raises eyebrows, if not eliciting incredulity or downright anger. Nevertheless, sexism remains alive and well in the "family values" rhetoric of mainstream politicians, as well as in the day-to-day practices of billions of people.[3] Sexism and heterosexism are those components of the culture of prejudice that encourage working people to believe that a gendered division of labour is "natural" and that "life styles" that are presumed to depart from the needs of private capital for properly socialized wage labour are to be deplored. While there is certainly more to women's oppression than the economic requirements of capitalism, a great deal is missed about the sources of "sexist attitudes" if one fails to appreciate that a governing maxim of capitalist society is this: "Ask not what the economy can do for you, ask what you can do for the economy."

---

3. See the Postscript to Chapter 26, which elaborates on how the logic of a ruthlessly competitive economic system geared toward private profit maximization is to continuously reduce costs of production of privately owned enterprises, regardless of the social cost of this activity. This means that such a system must preserve the nuclear family unit in order to ensure the cheapest possible "reproduction" of human labour power as a critical input to production. (M.E.G.S.)

HUMAN CONSCIOUSNESS, CULTURE, AND SOCIAL RELATIONS

Why do we believe the things that we do? The answer to this question is at once disarmingly simple and dauntingly complex. As individuals, we believe in much of what we do because we are all subject to processes of socialization through which *culture* is transmitted to us. This simple answer, with which almost all social scientists would agree, immediately invites a series of further questions concerning the meaning of "culture." Everyone knows that our involvement in human social life decisively shapes our views of the world and of our position within it. Nevertheless, social life is woven from the strands of many different cultural traditions. Depending on the time and place of our birth, we may be devoutly religious in our outlook or resolutely secular. Over the course of our own lives, exposure to different cultural influences may cause us to rethink our views and perhaps even to alter them radically.

During the 1960s and 1970s, many members of the baby boom generation who had grown up in the conservative climate of the Western world in the 1950s abandoned many of the commonplace notions that they had learned from their parents, teachers, and other authority figures. They became involved in the struggle of African Americans for civil rights and social emancipation, the Vietnam anti-war movement, the rejuvenation of women's liberation, and the growth of many other social movements that challenged the *status quo*—the "power structure." These developments both demonstrated and stimulated the willingness of large numbers of young (and some not-so-young) people to rethink some of their most cherished beliefs about "democracy," "human rights," "the family," "patriotism," "free enterprise," the role of their countries in the larger world, and the relation between human beings and their natural environment. Many carried this rethinking so far that they were willing to consider and embrace the ideas and values of cultural traditions that had decidedly "foreign" roots. For a period of at least ten years in the English-speaking world, huge numbers of young people, who had grown up with Walt Disney movies and a belief in the essential goodness of the way their democratic countries were being run, rallied to the ideas of Mao Zedong, Ho Chi Minh, Che Guevara, Fidel Castro, Vladimir Lenin, and Leon Trotsky. This youth radicalization had a still greater and more enduring impact in many European countries. The "late-sixties" are often treated as merely youthful "sex, drugs and rock 'n' roll," but this representation falls far short in its neglect of the serious political analysis and desire for a more egalitarian social system that engaged so many young people at this time.

How can this "cultural revolution" be explained? At one level, once again, the answer is straightforward. People tend to believe things that they find useful, and they begin to question certain ideas when their usefulness is found wanting. For increasing numbers of young people in the 1960s and 1970s, the ideas they had been led to believe in no longer seemed adequate to the understanding of a rapidly changing world. In fact, many of these ideas seemed hopelessly wrong-headed.

Was the American intervention in Southeast Asia really a matter of stopping "Communist aggression"? This simple-minded way of articulating US policy in Vietnam fairly reeked of prejudice, not to mention willful ignorance. Whose interests were served by such a prejudice? If American policy in Vietnam was manifestly wrong and immoral, if it amounted to a war of aggression against a whole people's right to determine their own destiny, and if this policy was justified in the name of anti-communism, then perhaps this anti-communist prejudice deserved some serious critical scrutiny.

During the 1950s and early 1960s, at the height of the Cold War, North Americans were warned that communists were masters of "brainwashing." Not only were they the master puppeteers and "outside agitators" of trade unions and civil rights movements, but once in power they were also supremely adept at forcing people's thoughts into a common totalitarian mould. Against this mythology, a new generation of independent thinkers began to consider whether the truly "brainwashed" might not be the complacent citizenry of North America. What if anti-Communism was a weapon aimed not only against the Soviet Union and its allies, but against civil rights, freedom of speech, unions, kindergartens, public libraries, women's equality, anti-racism, and social welfare programs benefitting the working class and the poor? Such were the questions that had propelled many young people, by the late 1960s, to entertain and sometimes embrace the "forbidden" ideas of the "Far Left."

The radicalism of the 1960s did not produce a genuine *social* revolution—a qualitative transformation in economic structures and social institutions. Nevertheless, its questioning of authority and of deeply entrenched prejudices produced a significant cultural shift, one characterized by a host of social movements ("second wave" feminism, environmentalism, and Third World solidarity movements, for example), by a rhetorical commitment to "human rights," and by opposition to overt expressions of racial, sexual or gender discrimination. During the 1990s, this cultural shift came to be characterized by right-wing commentators as "political correctness," and its fragility and reversibility in a social order still shot through with profound antagonisms were starkly revealed by the campaign that was waged against it over the course of that decade.

In the United States and elsewhere, the right-wing assault on "political correctness" signified a new self-confidence on the part of conservative forces in the wake of the "collapse of Communism." With the Cold War over, the powers-that-be in the Western world became much less indulgent toward social movements campaigning for social justice. At the same time, the *usefulness* of racist and sexist attitudes in deflecting attention away from issues of social class and economic power was once again manifest. The champions of a crisis-prone capitalism, no longer concerned about the spectre of communism, could now ridicule the liberal attitudes of the "politically correct crowd," whose influence and power to destroy hallowed traditions of thought were exaggerated to a ludicrous degree. The way was thus prepared for the authoritarian and repressive climate that would follow September 11, 2001. Hence, the fate of the cultural revolution that began in the 1960s demonstrates that ideas are not independent of social, economic, and historical context. Cultures of prejudice will forever renew themselves so long as the governing social relations among human beings remain *antagonistic* in character, that is, so long as extreme social and economic inequalities persist.

THE CULTURE OF PREJUDICE AND MODERN SOCIAL SCIENCE

While human culture has many dimensions, its *foundation* is a material one. It shares, with all life forms, the struggle to secure and enhance the necessities of life. In this sense, humans are similar to the other animals and, indeed, to the flora that have succeeded so far to live and breed on our planet. Without basic sustenance and shelter, the human aspiration to engage in activities with a "higher meaning" could not be entertained, much less achieved. The patterns of social organization that prevail in a particular time and place furnish the *social forms* assumed by human culture. In some cultures, cooperation is the governing principle and competition is virtually unknown. In others, competition and cooperation are both critical features of the social division of labour and the culture it sustains. Whether a particular social formation is more or less egalitarian, more or less democratic, or more or less open to outside influences has a profound effect on the consciousness and the mentality of the individual human beings who comprise it.

The values, ideals, and cherished beliefs of individuals within particular cultures often appear to have a mysterious, transcendent or even supernatural origin that endows them with a meaning and significance that defy "mundane" considerations. Yet, in principle, there is little reason to believe that these elements of "high culture" (distilled most potently in religious doctrines and political ideologies, and often given powerful aesthetic forms through works of art and literature) are not themselves the products of historical processes in which humanity's struggle with nature and the social relations among human beings have played the dominant roles.

To locate the origins and sustaining mechanisms of particular ideas within the social practices and institutions that they help to perpetuate is one of the most difficult but also one of the most important tasks of social science. Why do "bad" ideas exist? Why do ideas that are clearly hurtful, discriminatory and oppressive to large numbers of people persist? Do the existence and persistence of such ideas simply reflect a fatal flaw in an unchanging "human nature"? Conversely, are there grounds for believing that progress has been made in overcoming these backward ideas, and that much more progress can still be made? In overcoming these ideas, is it possible simply to reform the institutions that have historically relied upon them? Or is it necessary to abolish those institutions and replace them with new ones? If the latter, is this feasible, and will the cost of social reconstruction be an acceptable one? These are some of the most important questions that modern social science is obliged to confront. No agreement exists as to how they should be answered. Indeed, a great many social scientists would even disagree with the way in which they have been posed here.

From its inception some two to three centuries ago, modern social science has been divided into two distinct camps: one that has sought to legitimate and treat as "natural" the myriad forms of oppression, exploitation, and social injustice, and another that has sought to promote social equality and the project of human emancipation. The former approach has seen the task of social science as one of producing knowledge that is chiefly useful in refining the techniques of domination and social control, while the second has sought to assist the dominated in their struggles for a society free of invidious competition, oppression, and bigotry. This book is a celebration of the second approach to social science, one that is characterized by a many-sided challenge to the culture of prejudice—an intricate system of prejudicial beliefs, attitudes, and practices which reinforces the manifold forms of social oppression and which is itself sustained by ignorance and fear of the unknown and the unfamiliar.

For us, "prejudice" refers to unreasonable, injurious, and hateful attitudes and actions directed against specific groups of perceived "outsiders" and based on ill-informed judgments.[4] This is a broader definition of the concept than the one that is generally employed in popular discourse or the social-scientific literature. For while it is commonly accepted that racialized and ethnic minorities, women, disabled people, gays and lesbians, and immigrants are frequent victims of prejudicial attitudes and behaviour, it is seldom appreciated that people who place themselves "voluntarily" outside of the social mainstream—by resisting some of the dominant cultural values and ideological presuppositions of their society—are also subject to forms of ostracism and discrimination characteristic of the culture of prejudice. Indeed, the bigotry, scorn, and repression visited upon communists, anarchists, socialists, radical democrats, union organizers, anti-authoritarians, pacifists, religious non-conformists, and animal-rights activists can be just as virulent as that experienced by those possessing the "wrong"

---

4. John Sorenson would add to this, arguing that prejudice extends beyond the boundaries of our own species and that our domination and exploitation of other animals comprise one of the most fundamental forms of prejudice. Certainly non-human animals have suffered from actions that are "unreasonable, injurious and hateful" as they have been deprived of habitat, hunted to extinction, enslaved in factory farms, subjected to torture in gruesome and pointless "experiments," invested with imagined characteristics (e.g., wolves as agents of the devil), and so on.

skin colour, sexual orientation or mother tongue. If it is true, as we believe it to be, that bigotry and prejudice are nurtured from a common fount of ignorance, and that all forms of oppression are interrelated, then issues of *ideological intolerance* must necessarily be addressed in connection with the effort to critically confront the culture of prejudice.

Ideology is a bedrock of the culture of prejudice and, like prejudice, has a great many possible definitions and connotations. When we use the term "ideology" in this book, we mean *thought that serves class or group interests, and especially the interests of those in dominant positions within society*—a system of beliefs that exists in a somewhat uneasy and even contradictory relationship to science. In the words of one critic,[5] ideology is "the cuckoo in the nest of science"—limiting the scientific enterprise to questions that interest the powerful, while dismissing those of concern to the dominated. The one-sidedness of dominant ideologies puts a severe constraint on science—one that can be removed only by according serious attention to perspectives that aim to promote the interests of working-class people and victims of "special oppression," such as women, racialized minorities, and non-human animals. Accordingly, while the arguments in this book are not free of what some people might consider to be "ideology," we believe that by examining society from the standpoint of the dominated, the exploited, the excluded, and the oppressed, they serve the cause of both human emancipation and social science.

PREJUDICED OR BIASED?

This brings us to the question of whether we, as the authors of this book, are "prejudiced" or "biased." The *Oxford English Dictionary* defines "bias" as "... inclination, predisposition (towards), prejudice, influence ..." and defines "prejudice" as "preconceived opinion, bias (against, in favour of, person or thing)...." On the basis of these two definitions, it would seem that the two words mean much the same thing. However, a cursory search of the Internet revealed an interesting contrast. The word "bias" produced a host of discussions on the mass media, with both conservatives decrying left-wing bias and others arguing that the media are inherently conservative. Everyone seems to think reportage always has a "slant" against his or her favoured view of the social world. The internet search on "prejudice," in contrast, produced links to concerns about discrimination and the negative stereotypes which in turn produce behaviour that denigrates, stigmatizes, and oppresses groups identifiable by social class, gender, skin colour, sexual orientation, and so on. Here we find arguments that "prejudice" produces violations of the human qualities of reason, of tolerance, and of social justice. It seems, therefore, that as they are used in con-

---

5. Joe Carney, "The Theory of Ideology," *Radical Philosophy* (Spring 1976): 31.

temporary language, there are differences between the two words which speak to a core question: "Is it possible to be an unbiased observer of our social world?"

Critical social scientists will argue that the completely objective observer is an impossibility, a fiction promulgated by social philosophers who hoped to pattern their research and theory on the model of the physical sciences. According to this model, there were hypotheses to be constructed, social "facts" to be observed, and scientific conclusions to be drawn. In cases of conflicting opinion, social scientists could be trained to be "neutral" observers, presenting controversies or opposing political positions in a "balanced" fashion. In other words, by becoming a social scientist one could unlearn or repress all those attitudes, beliefs, and predispositions that make us all individual human beings and colour our perceptions of the world around us. The paradox of this position is the assumption that the more we study and think upon social issues, the less caring we should become about their implications for the future of humankind.

The impossibility of this project became increasingly evident in the latter decades of the twentieth century. Accordingly, many social scientists, like some journalists, decided to examine their own predispositions and biases on certain issues, and they vowed to do their best to declare them in their publications. According to this view, we may not be able to turn ourselves into unbiased observers and reporters, but *we can declare our biases*. The logical corollary to this is that if no one can be unbiased, to assume someone is biased because of self-declared theoretical orientation or political stance is a meaningless statement. Humans who think rationally and systematically about issues become biased. To be unbiased is to be brain dead.

Nevertheless, we still hear dismissive accusations of "bias" hurled about in reference to theorists of both the left and the right. The implication underlying these statements is, in fact, that the arguments presented are not to be taken seriously. Indeed, they should be rejected out of hand, simply because the person is a feminist or a Marxist or can be given some other label, no further discussion needed. Presumably, "biased" writers are too "prejudiced" to be believed.

To clarify our objection to such dismissiveness, let us return to the beginning of this chapter and the definition of "prejudice" we provide there. It includes the words "premature or hasty judgement." In other words, prejudice involves a kind of "knee-jerk" reaction, a response based on *unconsidered* assumptions about other people's unworthiness to be taken seriously or their inherent inferiority. We argue that "bias" can develop out of months or years of deep consideration and intensive research. Indeed, it often involves honest self-examination, as well as voyages into the minds of others, both the powerful and those who are excluded from power, with a view to understanding their worldviews. Instead of summarily dismissing people's thoughts or arguments on the grounds of bias, the accuser should be obliged to work through the thought processes which brought the other to certain conclusions. If these are discovered to be ill-founded, illogical, mean-spirited or self-serving, a case can be made simply for prejudice.

In this book, our stated and unswerving intent is to argue against the prejudicial attitudes, behaviours, and social policies which are so abundantly observable in our social world, that is, in the culture of prejudice. We wish to demonstrate how critical social scientists can deploy their analytical skills to craft arguments that undermine the culture of prejudice. We make no claim to being comprehensive, either in terms of the variety of prejudices that exist in the contemporary world or in terms of the methods that can be employed to counter them. The reader will undoubtedly disagree strongly with some and perhaps many of the arguments presented here. We welcome expressions of disagreement, as long as they are based on reason and evidence rather than on appeals to a specious "common sense" that is often a mere cover for prejudice.

Our principal assumption in this book is that social science is at its best, and most exciting, when it *challenges* the culture of prejudice. Such a *critical* social science, we believe, has an indispensable role to play in promoting human freedom and extending human capacities. Accordingly, while the book is primarily addressed to undergraduate social science students, we hope that it will also appeal to a much broader audience, including social and political activists interested in a provocative survey of contemporary social issues.

THE BOOK AND ITS AUTHORS

We have arranged the book in a series of short chapters grouped into sections dealing with nationalism, racism, fundamentalism, and terrorism; colonialism and globalization; poverty and social dispossession; social class; feminism and the women's movement; health, sexuality, and reproduction; policing the culture of prejudice; ecology and animal liberation; the economy; and politics and ideology. Each part ends with a list of suggested readings; as a supplement to the footnoted references in each chapter, we have included lists of resources that we think are "classics" in the field or a good start for further research on the issues discussed in this book to help readers whose interest has been piqued. Each chapter begins with an aphorism, anecdote, or quotation illustrating a particular aspect of the culture of prejudice. Its author attempts to subject the issue under consideration to a concise, critical discussion, drawing upon some of the best research and thought in the social scientific literature (and beyond). Authorship is indicated at the end of each chapter. We have included a glossary at the end of the book in the event that some readers may not be familiar with some of the terminology we use.

Here now are the authors' own self-introductions.

judith c. Blackwell:

I identify myself as a critical social scientist whose primary intellectual and personal concerns focus on issues of social equality and justice. I operate on the principle that most human beings—whatever their culture or class, whatever misfortunes have been visited upon them—are potentially capable of advocating for and endorsing programs and policies which promise to lead to greater societal good, social justice, and righting the wrongs perpetuated by social inequality. For this ideal to be realized, however, it is important for people to make up their minds in an atmosphere of sound information, clear-sighted evaluation of the costs and benefits of decisions to be made, and self-insight into personal biases. Well-informed, well-educated human beings can make sound decisions in the interests of the common good, but they will not be able to do so if their minds are crammed with misinformation, half-truths, and the downright lies which are passed off as "common knowledge." As a social scientist, I have a lifelong interest in how tenaciously people are encouraged to abide by the myths supporting their prejudices, and how in doing so they become servants to the interests of the power elite.

To varying degrees, every thinking person is a social scientist. It is my contention that this should be much more than being "just curious" about social events or "having an opinion." It should also entail putting information in context, critically analyzing the biases of information providers, and paying constant attention to the common good. Furthermore, the common good is not just the interests of one's own class and culture, but also the welfare of all humans and the health of the planet on which we live. I view critical social science as a life project, a perspective that must not only inform academic research and theorizing, but also be woven into the intellectual fabric of all those who consider themselves to be serious observers of their social world and responsible citizens.

Murray E.G. smith:

My approach to challenging the culture of prejudice is shaped by the firm conviction that the elimination of class exploitation and division is a necessary, though by no means the solely sufficient, condition for the eradication of all forms of oppression and social injustice. In the chapters that I've contributed to this book, I've sought to demonstrate the centrality of class analysis, and more specifically Marxist social theory, to a social-scientific enterprise whose goal is human emancipation.

In my view, the goal of human emancipation involves progress in two distinguishable but intimately interconnected sets of relations: the relations of human beings to non-human nature, and the relations of human beings to one another. The former set of relations encompasses the capacities that human beings develop in order to satisfy their material needs and reduce their burden of physical toil by subduing the forces of nature, pre-eminently by extending their natural-scientific knowledge and fashioning ever more sophisticated technologies. The latter set of relations encompasses the forms of social organization that structure social interaction and that mediate the relation of the human community to nature. Progress in the humanity-nature relation can be measured in terms of the development of the *productivity* of human labour—our ability to create more and more output with progressively less labour input. Progress in human social relations can be measured in terms of the extension of human *freedom* —defined as the capacity of individual human beings to realize their talents and capabilities in an "all-round" fashion.

Throughout recorded history (that is, the history of class-antagonistic "civilized" societies), human freedom has been purchased for a privileged few at the expense of the great majority of the population. A ruling class of "appropriators" has confronted a class of "direct producers," and the lion's share of the social surplus product has been put at the disposal of the ruling class. I share Karl Marx's view that the modern capitalist mode of production sponsors an ongoing technological revolution that dramatically increases the productivity of labour and that in so doing it creates the material conditions for a vast expansion of the social surplus product. Moreover, by developing the "forces of production" so powerfully, capitalism creates the *potential* for a tremendous extension of human freedom to the whole of the population. This potential, however, cannot be realized within the framework of the class-antagonistic social relations of capitalism. The *contradiction* between the productivity-enhancing dynamic of capitalist production and its structural logic of putting the private profit of the few before the needs of the many makes the struggle for a new social order mandatory. Only a planned socialist economy can extend the benefits of modern labour-saving technology to the labourers themselves. And only a democratically administered socialist society can fulfill the age-old dream of all-round human emancipation.

john s. sorenson:

Many academics claim that they are engaged in objective, value-free social science and that this is reflected in their publications and teaching. In my view, such claims are practically impossible to believe. Most people have an opinion about minor changes in the weather, so it is likely that they have opinions about important social issues as well. In fact, it would seem extremely odd and an abdication of responsibility for one not to have an opinion about such facts as that a tiny percentage of the world's population enjoys fantastic wealth while the bulk of humanity lives in desperate poverty, that the planet is being choked with pollution, that our society is based upon the abuse of billions of animals who endure lives of agony before being horribly slaughtered, and so on. Those intellectuals who claim to be objective or neutral about these issues virtually always produce material that endorses the *status quo* (although there are also those intellectuals who do not claim neutrality but explicitly place themselves in the service of repression). Oddly enough, it is only material that challenges the *status quo* that is considered to be "political" or "partisan" scholarship and never that which acts to maintain existing relations of power and domination. The attempt to establish one's own voice as the voice of reason is a standard technique in the struggle to maintain hegemony, to define reality, and to change the minds of others.

There is no neutral position for critical scholars. Critical scholars should take a political stance that supports those who have been victimized by the various power-wielding elites who perpetuate various forms of social injustice, whether these injustices are carried out along the lines of species, class, gender, phenotype or other hierarchies. Critical scholars should declare their solidarity with those who suffer most from social inequalities. We should also recognize that our contributions are usually marginal and that change is mainly accomplished through resistance on the part of those who are most directly affected by forms of domination.

Obviously, critical or partisan scholarship does not mean the intentional falsification of data or the distortion of others' arguments. As Noam Chomsky says, "it is the responsibility of intellectuals to speak the truth and to expose lies."[6] Critical scholars make their position clear from the beginning, indicating their point of view and their aims. Knowing an author's position and intentions can help readers judge for themselves the worthiness of his or her argument.

My own biases should be evident in the chapters I've written for this book. My approach is interdisciplinary, although my academic background in anthropology provides me with an awareness of the plight of indigenous peoples around the world. My ideas have been shaped by my own work in solidarity activism with various Third World struggles. In particular, I have had a long association with the Eritrean nationalist movement and through my work over a decade with the Eritrean Relief Association I learned a great deal about the meaning of solidarity and the commitment to revolutionary social change. My work as an activist intersected with my academic interests and led me to write a PhD thesis and to produce several books on the Horn of Africa. Also, through my contacts with government officials, NGO[7] representatives, and academics interested in the region, I came to understand that, despite many claims of neutrality, virtually everyone who had any involvement also had a partisan position. Indeed, some of the most partisan statements, policies, and actions came from those who made the strongest claims of detached objectivity.

In the chapters that I have contributed to this book, I touch on a variety of topics that are central to the culture of prejudice: colonialism, imperialism, nationalism, racism, religious fundamentalism, and corporate globalization. I have drawn on insights from a variety of anarchists, libertarian socialists, and left-wing Marxists,

6. Noam Chomsky, *American Power and the New Mandarins* (New York: Pantheon, 1967) 325.

7. Non-governmental organization

feminists, ecologists, and animal-rights philosophers. I am particularly happy to have drawn these issues together in this book on social justice where I have also contributed several chapters on issues related to animals. Too often, those who are concerned about other important matters of social justice overlook the issue of animal rights. However, animal rights should be a matter of special significance to those who see themselves as enlightened and progressive people. At the most basic level, one would have to be skeptical about the sincerity of those who claim to be concerned about social justice if those same people choose to contribute to a system of horrible exploitation of animals simply because it is convenient or because they enjoy the taste of flesh. But beyond this basic point, we should also recognize that rejecting speciesism almost necessarily means rejecting other forms of prejudice, for no one who has followed and understood the arguments against this form of prejudice could be in support of comparable structures such as racism and sexism. Far from detracting from social justice for underprivileged people, concern for animals is part of the solution: replacing animal-based agriculture would have a profound and positive ecological impact. Thus, those who advocate animal rights are also part of a broader struggle to improve the lives of the majority of human beings.

suggested readings

Allport, Gordon. *The Nature of Prejudice*. Cambridge, MA: Addison Wesley, 1954.

Gioseffi, Daniela, ed. *On Prejudice: A Global Perspective*. New York: Anchor Books, 1993.

Hall, John R., and Mary Jo Neitz. *Culture: Sociological Perspectives*. Englewood Cliffs, NJ: Prentice Hall, 1993.

Harris, Marvin. *Cultural Materialism: The Struggle for a Science of Culture*. New York: Random House, 1979.

Levin, Jack. *The Violence of Hate*. Boston: Allyn and Bacon, 2002.

Palmer, Bryan D. *Cultures of Darkness: Night Travels in the Histories of Transgression*. New York: Monthly Review Press, 2000.

PART TWO

Nationalism, Racism, Fundamentalism, & Terrorism

CHAPTER 1

"My country, right or wrong"
Notorious motto of nationalistic jingoism

The end of the twentieth century was characterized by two dominant phenomena: the triumphalism of corporate globalization and the resurgence of ethnic nationalism. Despite the apparent contradiction, much of the idealization of traditional cultures often came as a response to the disruptions brought by the spread of the free market. Previously existing hierarchies became destabilized and many people experienced changes to traditional patterns of behaviour while facing economic futures that seemed uncertain or bleak. In these circumstances, nationalism provided some with a sense of community and identity while promising to pave the way for a better future.

Nationalism is necessarily an imaginative commitment, not only requiring that people construct a sense of community, kinship, and shared identity with large numbers of other people whom they will never meet, but also involving fantasies of belonging and history.[1] Nationalism suggests shared identity: while every nation is multicultural, nationalists emphasize the boundaries that separate the national family from others while exaggerating common identity and minimizing differences that exist within those boundaries. Nationalism can evoke sentiments of public responsibility, and the commitment to community may often encourage noble acts. However, these commitments to the nation are often uncritical ("My country, right or wrong") and the sense of community too narrow; rather than recognizing common interests of humanity as a whole, one gives loyalty only to one's national group. The importance and intensity of such attachments are rather surprising when one considers that modern nation-states are relatively recent developments, mere ephemera when seen in the broad context of human evolution. Furthermore, while operating with a rhetoric of family and inclusion, nationalism is always exclusionary and readily succumbs to the same violent urges found in racism and religious zealotry.

---

1. See Benedict Anderson, *Imagined Communities* (London: Verso, 1983) and Jacqueline Rose, *States of Fantasy* (Oxford: Clarendon Press, 1996).

Nationalism proposes that the world is composed of various distinct populations, each one of which is characterized by a certain unique culture and identity. Individuals within the nation reflect and embody these characteristic traits, so that just as each nation is imagined to have its own distinct soul so do all members of the nation share certain essential aspects and behaviour. There is usually strong pressure for obedience and conformity, and measures are taken to ensure that proper attitudes and behaviours are present. Solidarity with the group becomes the primary value and there is increased control over individuals, who consequently have limited choice. Allegiance to the state becomes the basis of identity, and along with this comes a hostility toward strangers. It is usually assumed that the nation is culturally unified and that members of the nation have more in common with one another than they do with members of other nations, despite internal injustices based on class, gender, and race. By suggesting these essential similarities between all members of the nation in contrast with the striking opposition that is proposed between nations, nationalism serves a useful function in deflecting criticism of internal hierarchies and helping to present them as normal, natural, and good.

In the usage of the time, Marx observed the essence of nationalism in his famous statement that "working men have no country": while no country exists where workers have political power, capitalism has eroded significant cultural differences, and workers have more in common on the basis of their class than they do as members of different nations. Instead of embracing nationalist propaganda that leads them to subordinate themselves to the ruling classes of their nation, workers should form international alliances and abolish the very ideas of nations and countries. However, in practice, it has often been the case that groups defining themselves as Marxists have opposed nationalist struggles simply to maintain an ethnic *status quo* from which they derived benefits, as exemplified in the case of Ethiopia. Anarchists have sometimes supported nationalist movements as struggles against oppression, as in the cases of East Timor and Eritrea, for example, but they have been critical of the limited goals of nationalist groups who merely seek to attain the power of the state for themselves; many anti-colonial struggles organized to overturn the domination of foreign invaders have degenerated into dictatorships. Anarchists are internationalist almost by definition, for they see the state as oppressive and reject the patriotic ideology of nationalism simply as a tool used by ruling classes to maintain their hegemony.

Nationalism provides a means to mobilize people in pursuit of certain political goals. Nationalist propaganda often asserts the existence of a previous Golden Age in which national culture flourished, and nationalist activists may promise a renaissance if certain conditions are met. Usually it is assumed that in order for the nation to collectively realize its destiny and for the individuals who belong to the nation to reach their full potential, nations should control a distinct territory. Thus, nationalism provides useful ideological support for conquest. It also provides a rationale for genocide. Those who do not share the selected characteristics are considered obstacles or threats to the health of the nation and can be expelled or killed. For example, in Nazi Germany Jews and Gypsies, along with communists, homosexuals, and the disabled, were murdered on an immense scale, ostensibly to preserve Germany's racial health. More recently, Serbian nationalists agreed that it was necessary to create ethnically cleansed zones in Bosnia-Herzegovina in order to achieve their glorious destiny. Convinced of their duty to the nation, they set about the slaughter and expulsion of hundreds of thousands of Muslims. Other ethnonationalist leaders competing for power in the rubble of the former Yugoslavia shared this outlook and engaged in their own projects of murder and terrorism.

Even more terrible acts of ethnic cleansing took place in Rwanda. The two major ethnic groups, Hutus and Tutsis, share the same language but have been categorized according to the racial stereotypes of European colonialism: Hutus were believed to be shorter and more thick-set than the tall, thin Tutsis. Colonialism intensified the differences between the two categories and elevated Tutsis above Hutus, creating resentment and distrust that were used by a small activist group to mobilize Hutus in 1994 to slaughter a half-million or perhaps more Tutsis, along with Hutus thought to be too sympathetic to them. Hutu propaganda stressed the danger to the nation posed by the Tutsi "cockroaches" and persuaded much of the population to attack their neighbours with clubs and knives, burn families alive in their homes or slaughter crowds of terrified people in the churches where they sought sanctuary. Although the United Nations and foreign governments were fully aware of what was happening and had been warned in advance, they made no effective intervention; Canadian peacekeeping forces say they could have prevented some of the murders but were ordered by the UN not to act.

As the examples of Germany, Yugoslavia, and Rwanda demonstrate, nationalism is closely linked to latent forms of ethnic consciousness that can be used by small activist groups to mobilize a broader population. The glorification of ethnic affiliations becomes especially attractive to those experiencing a sense of alienation and powerlessness. Nationalism is closely linked with ethnocentrism, xenophobia, and racism and, like these, encourages scapegoating of "foreigners." For example, during World War II, thousands of American and Canadian citizens were imprisoned in concentration camps solely because of their Japanese ancestry, which allegedly made them a threat to national security. Confiscation of their homes, businesses, and property proved extremely profitable to their white-skinned fellow citizens. During the 1998-2000 war between Eritrea and Ethiopia, Ethiopia followed the North American example by deporting approximately 70,000 Eritreans and Ethiopians of Eritrean descent. The deportees included elderly people and children; many had lived in Ethiopia their entire lives. Ethiopian President Meles Zenawi responded to international criticism by asserting that his government had the right to deport anyone merely because "we do not like the colour of your eyes."[2]

Throughout the 1980s and 1990s there was a resurgence of fascist groups across Europe, such as the Vlaams Blok in Belgium, the Front National in France, and the Freedom Party in Austria. These groups were founded by surviving Nazis or their neo-Nazi descendants and their rhetoric was a mixture of racism, Holocaust denial, and xenophobia, as they called for controls on immigration in order to preserve "Germany for the Germans," and so on. In every European country these fascist groups won a sizable percentage of the vote in local and national elections. Their narrow and exclusivist demands and the call to expel or kill the aliens amply demonstrate the ugly face of nationalism. Nationalist appeals encourage such hatreds and essentialist feelings that "we" have certain laudable characteristics while "they" do not. Taken to extremes, this discourages any empathy or identification with others and makes other groups seem misguided, bizarre or even demonic.

Often, nationalist ideologues propose a mystical attachment with certain territory. Where nationalism is aligned with or defined by religious identity, it may even be asserted that the group has been given the right to this territory by the authority of a supernatural being. Thus, a Chosen People will need to inhabit its Holy Land in order to fulfill its divine covenant, with unfortunate consequences for any other populations who may inhabit the territory but who are not considered part of the nation. For example, European invaders and their descendants imagined they had a Manifest Destiny to acquire the Americas and nearly exterminated the indigenous population in the course of taking possession. More recently, supernatural sanctions have been invoked by Israelis who violently dispossessed the population of Palestine. As Israel came to be defined as a Jewish state, promised to them long ago by a supernatural being, most of the Palestinian population was expelled; approximately 4.5 million still live there as refugees. Millions of Palestinians remain under military occupation, under constant surveillance and regular attack by Israeli forces, including tanks, fighter planes, and helicopter gunships. Their houses and land have been destroyed or expropriated and given to hundreds of thousands of armed settlers. Former Israeli prime minister Golda Meir simply dismissed their suffering by asserting that "Palestinians do not exist." While international media audiences are well informed about the dreadful attacks by Palestinian suicide bombers, the far higher rate of Palestinian deaths and casualties is defended as retaliations or self-defence. The 1993 Oslo peace process simply gave an extremely constrained form of power to Yassir Arafat's corrupt regime, while allowing the occupation to continue.

Often, nationalist rhetoric presents the nation as being under threat, requiring mobilization to preserve endangered traditions. This often reflects the precarious position of the nationalists themselves. Nationalism is often a project of small, elite classes

---

2. Heard on Radio Ethiopia, 9 July 1998.

and disenfranchised intellectuals whose own position is tenuous and who seek to advance their own interests through promotion of nationalist projects. By presenting themselves as leaders in the movement to restore national pride and by demanding the replacement of existing structures of political control, they seek to guarantee themselves positions of authority and power. Often, a great deal of support for nationalist projects comes from exile populations for whom the restoration of their distant homeland becomes an all-encompassing obsession.[3]

As a social construct, nationalism is also gendered: nations are characteristically imagined as fatherlands or motherlands that demand filial piety from their subject-children who should unselfishly serve them. Typically, narratives of national identity depend on stereotyped images of masculinity and femininity: male warriors preserve the honour of women who reproduce the nation and guard its traditions. (Yet, once again, divisions based on class and ethnicity ensure that not all women are considered worthy of such treatment, as exemplified by the forcible conscription of ethnic Koreans or Chinese and poor Japanese women as sexual slaves, "comfort women," by the Japanese military in World War II.) Nationalist ideologies typically construct women as breeders whose task it is to produce large numbers of children to present to the nation.

While women are celebrated as the bearers of tradition and symbols of pure culture, they are regarded as the property of the patriarchal nation (and of men) who must be policed and controlled and punished for infractions. Although women are often vigorous supporters of nationalist projects, it is men who assume the authority to control appropriate behaviour, and masculinity comes to be defined through the domination of women's behaviour. Just as nationalists see it as a duty to protect "their" women, the bodies of "other" women become the site of nationalist struggles. For example, mass rapes in Bosnia were conducted against women as symbols of the opposing nation; they were targeted by soldiers who not only felt that they could prove their virility through rape but sought to inflict humiliation on the enemy men who could not defend "their" women. In many cases, the women who were impregnated in such attacks found that they were shunned by the men of their own ethnic groups, who regarded them as tarnished and impure.

Although some nationalist movements have promoted women's emancipation, especially in the context of anti-colonial struggles, many of these commitments were quickly abandoned or reversed after independence was achieved. Men assumed that once the goal of national liberation had been achieved, a return to traditional forms of domestic hierarchy would be in order. In other cases, nationalists have been explicitly opposed to women's rights, often deriding what they call "feminism" as a foreign ideology that threatens the cherished traditions of true indigenous culture. According

---

3. Atsuko Matsuoka and John Sorenson, *Ghosts and Shadows: Construction of Identity and Community in an African Diaspora* (Toronto: University of Toronto Press, 2001).

to such views, the proper place for women is in the domestic sphere and women who venture beyond this are often attacked for their transgression of cultural values. For example, in Afghanistan the Taliban regime prevented women from attending school and some Afghan refugee women who attended school in Pakistan were punished by fundamentalist men who threw acid in their faces. Religious ideologies often provide justifications for these attitudes and claim supernatural sanctions for repressive relations. Nationalism often concerns itself with policing individual sexual behaviour so that the nation will not be defiled by degenerate practices. Thus, just as nationalist ideology frequently maintains that women should remain in the home and busy themselves with the reproduction of pure offspring to carry on the nation's glorious traditions, so is homosexual and lesbian behaviour considered a violation of the moral community. For example, in Colombia, police, paramilitary groups, and business organizations are responsible for daily executions of those who are considered detrimental to national health: homosexuals, thieves, homeless people, drug addicts, sex workers, transvestites, street children, Jews, and ethnic minorities.[4] Those who commit the murders justify their activities on the grounds of public safety, security, morals, and economics; there is little protest because the victims are widely considered to be social "scum." In Argentina, Brazil, Chile, El Salvador, Guatemala, and Uruguay, fascist regimes explicitly appealed to a patriotic duty to save the nation as they directed the disappearance, torture, and murder of those they considered subversive elements: unionists, students, teachers, journalists, communists, liberals, social workers, priests, indigenous people, and peasants. Throughout Central America, death squads busied themselves with saving the nation by murder, torture, and mutilation. Rather than being aberrations, such practices are more often the characteristic achievements of nationalist ideologies.

Nationalist slogans such as "My country, right or wrong" are enticements to turn a blind eye to everything from mistaken beliefs to the most appalling horrors inflicted on those who are seen to stand in the way of nationalist agendas. Nationalism is yet another example of how the culture of prejudice encourages people to uncritically adopt whatever attitudes, beliefs or norms of behaviour are dispensed from on high. As such, it is anathema to the critical social scientific perspective advocated in this book.

John S. Sorenson

---

4. Colombia Human Rights Committee, Proyecto Dignidad, "No Human Being is Disposable" (San Francisco: International Gay and Lesbian Human Rights Commission, no date).

CHAPTER 2

"Everybody is a racist; it's part of human nature"

Fatalistic belief condoning the perpetuation of racial oppression

The final decades of the millennium constituted a New Dark Age, a period of barbarism, ignorance, and bizarre superstition that grew from one of the most violent centuries in human history. Globalized inequality and social decline promoted cultures of prejudice in supposedly sophisticated Western metropolitan centres. Diverting attention from how the world is structured in political and economic terms, the culture industries created a steady flow of propaganda and entertainment promoting simplistic interpretations, celebrating greed and aggression, and creating desire for luxury goods. As unemployment soars and social programs are eviscerated, people feel that they have been cheated out of what they deserve. In this context of heightened desires and diminished attainments, fundamentalist mythologies and muddled thoughts proliferate; enemies are identified, heretics are punished.

One of the shibboleths of the New Dark Age is a resurgent interest in "race." "Race" is an utterly meaningless concept: it is inaccurate, lacks consistency, and has no scientific reality whatsoever. "Races" cannot be sharply defined, as there are always people who do not fit neatly into proposed categories, either falling between them or combining whatever features are selected as markers. There is no agreement on the number of "races" that exist or how to define them. The term mixes social and biological categories and classifications in meaningless ways. Although physical differences do exist, these are not the same as "race." This is a concept that seems inseparable from the muddled thinking, injustice, and oppression that have created it; it is best abandoned.

Although "races" do not exist, racism certainly does. Racism is the belief that races exist, that physical characteristics determine cultural traits, and that racial characteristics make some groups superior. This ranking allows some groups to have more wealth and power and justifies unequal treatment: those at the bottom are there because of genetic characteristics, not because of social and political conditions. Racist ideology says that although races are permanently fixed, they must be kept apart, usually to avoid degeneration of the superior beings. Racism can be directed against any group that can be identified by physical features or by cultural characteristics. It is unnecessary for real physical differences actually to exist; they may be invented and racists will then observe them with regularity.

Although distrust and animosity toward strangers are widespread (although not universal) phenomena and physical differences are often used to identify strangers, racism is not part of every human society or an innate part of human consciousness that would justify a claim that "everybody is a racist." The ideology of "race" is different from generalized distrust or xenophobia. Contemporary ideas of "race" involve a complex of beliefs existing in systematic form that developed in association with European imperialism over the last five hundred years. As Europeans began to conquer the world and came into greater contact with people of different appearances, they were originally concerned with religious differences; ideas of "race" developed later. There was growing recourse to Aristotle's notion that some people are "natural slaves" and to notions that life was arranged in a hierarchy that placed some people closer to a supernatural being. Scientific racism developed in the eighteenth century in various disciplines such as medicine and anthropology; later, scientists influenced by Darwin's evolutionary studies explored the origins and nature of human beings. Although Darwin regarded physical differences among humans as superficial, others believed these indicated more significant differences such as separate origins and lines of development and different qualities.

These ideas proved useful in the context of colonialism: other groups were seen as primitive and inferior and thus could be exterminated or "civilized" as required. The particular policy depended on European goals at the time: if resources but not the population were desired, the natives should be exterminated and their resistance merely proved their savagery; where people might be useful, some possibility of uplifting them could be expressed. For example, Europeans usually did not regard Africans as sub-human before the need arose for labour in colonial plantations. New representations emerged of Africans as less-than-human, brutes, animals or children. They were defined as something very different from Europeans and were sometimes said to have been created separately in a process of polygenesis (the belief that various "races" were created separately and at different times by a supernatural being). The idea that Africans were similar to apes was very popular and sometimes apes and African people were placed together on public display in Europe. In the context of a dominant view that nonhuman animals existed for human use, equating apes and Africans provided justification for exploitation. Opponents of exploitation also recognized this: "the overlap between leaders of movements against the oppression of blacks and women, and leaders of movements against cruelty to animals, is extensive; so extensive as to provide an unexpected form of confirmation of the parallel between racism, sexism and speciesism."[1]

Racism grows in a specific climate and its resurgence in the New Dark Age feeds in this context: frustration, resentment, and xenophobia are channelled into a system of racist thought and action. The culture of prejudice spawned in this period is characterized by a resurgence of right-wing forces. With the appearance of neo-conservatives and neo-fascists, the "mainstream" has moved farther to the right and extremist statements have become more acceptable while cults of every description proliferate in a context of irrationalism. Racist groups mobilize in this context by appealing to a sense of identity and group membership, while offering simple solutions.

Loss of colonial power offended the sense of superiority that Europeans had felt toward people from former colonies. In the 1980s a vogue of colonial nostalgia emerged in films, novels, and fashion. As social conditions declined with unemployment and cuts to social programs, frustration increased among working classes, who feel themselves threatened by immigration. In France, Jean-Marie Le Pen, leader of the Front National, gained popularity in the 1980s through racist appeals, playing on anti-Arab sentiments by calling for restrictions on immigration and anti-Semitic views in his expressed doubts about the Holocaust. His anti-gay statements and opposition to abortion drew support from religious fundamentalists. Although his own record was repellent (accusations of torturing prisoners during army service in Algeria, support for French imperialism in Vietnam, a business selling recordings of Hitler's speeches and Nazi songs), Le Pen received support from industrial areas whose residents interpreted economic instability as the result of invasion by foreigners. Le Pen pandered to these sentiments through his extreme statements, helping to make those sentiments seem acceptable.

Similar sentiments surfaced in Germany. After the Nuremberg trials, forces that had initiated major wars and engineered the slaughterhouse-style execution of millions of Jews, gypsies, homosexuals, and communists were reinstated. Corporations that had serviced the Nazi war machine with slave labour continued to operate and many Nazis retained their wealth and power in high-level government posts. They encouraged neo-Nazis to organize, obtain weapons, and engage in racist attacks. While police blocked anti-fascist rallies, large demonstrations expressed open support for Nazism and racist violence. After unification in 1990, economic crisis boosted neo-Nazi attacks on immigrants and refugees, gays, the homeless, Jews, and other "undesirables." This included assaults and murders in several cities; in Rostock, for example, Nazi skinhead mobs spent five nights in 1992 attacking a refugee housing project. Local residents applauded while police allowed skinheads to torch the buildings. Although some terrorist groups such as German Alternative and the Nationalist Front were banned, other Nazi groups issued anti-Jewish propaganda

---

1. Peter Singer, *Animal Liberation*, rev. ed. (New York: Avon, 1990) 221.

and Holocaust denials, and the Republikaner Party, led by former SS officer Franz Schonhuber, won seats in the European Parliament by promoting "family values" and opposing immigration.

Canada has a long tradition of institutionalized racism. The indigenous population has been marginalized in reservations and brutalized in indoctrination centres ("residential schools") designed to smash their cultures. During World War II, Canadians of Japanese descent were imprisoned in concentration camps and their property was stolen by white Canadians. Although Japanese Canadians finally received an official apology and partial compensation, indigenous people in Canada still struggle for their rights and, at places such as Kanehsatake (Oka) and Ipperwash, have faced direct violence from state repression. Canadian police and military forces are notorious for their racism, exemplified in the exposure of a network of Nazis and Ku Klux Klan (KKK) members in the army after the torture and murder of Somali prisoners in 1996.

In addition to the institutionalized racism of the Canadian state, privatized hate groups have mobilized. The main white supremacist group is the Heritage Front, led by Wolfgang Droege, a KKK organizer who spent seven years in prison for drugs and weapons charges and his involvement in a failed coup attempt on the island of Dominica with US Nazis. Droege provided guards for Reform Party (now the Canadian Alliance party) meetings in southern Ontario in the early 1990s and fought violent street battles with anti-racists in Ottawa. His group targets young people, exploiting their sense of alienation and disenfranchisement and presenting racism as simply pride in one's heritage. Another activist is Ernst Zundel, a major international source for Holocaust-denial material, delivered from his fortified Toronto home until his move to the southern US.

The US was founded upon the genocide of indigenous people along with centuries of oppression of the black population and imperialism abroad. More recently, state repression and racist violence continued in COINTELPRO, the FBI's campaign of disinformation, surveillance, false charges, and violent attacks against enemies of the state. This included the assassination of Black activists such as Fred Hampton and Mark Clark of the Black Panther Party. Another target was the American Indian Movement. The threat of land claims and the presence of large deposits of oil, uranium, and other strategic minerals led to a war on activists such as Leonard Peltier, framed for the murder of two FBI agents in 1975 at Pine Ridge, South Dakota. He was extradited from Canada on evidence that the US government later acknowledged to be fabricated and remains in prison despite an international campaign to overturn his unjust conviction.

Hate groups have also organized international networks. In the US, anti-Semitic propaganda is produced by the Liberty Lobby led by Willis Carto, who has a long involvement in racist, right-wing politics and links to Nazis and white supremacists.

Carto funds many racist and fascist publications and groups, such as the Institute for Historical Review, which publishes Holocaust-denial material. He supported David Duke, a Nazi, a KKK "Grand Wizard," who was elected as a Republican in the Louisiana state legislature and sought the Democratic presidential nomination. Carto also supported the World Anti-Communist League, founded in 1966 by the governments of Taiwan and South Korea, whose luminaries included Italian fascists, death-squad leaders from Central America, and former German SS officers. Ideologies of anti-communism and racism are frequently allied and provide interchangeable terminologies. Racists and fascists find each other's company congenial; for example, Ernst Zundel formed links with European racist groups while KKK leader Dennis Mahon from Oklahoma joined cross-burning parties with German white supremacists on a 1991 European tour.

While state repression and racism remain strong at the start of the twenty-first century, new forms of populist racism have also emerged. Fuelled by a heady mix of conspiracy theories, groups of vigilantes opposing the federal government armed themselves across the US. Known as the militia movement, these groups share racist beliefs as well as homophobia, misogyny, and religious fanaticism. They emphasize two events as symbols of federal oppression: a 1992 shoot-out in Ruby Ridge, Idaho, in which the wife and son of Aryan Nations white supremacist Randy Weaver were killed as the FBI tried to arrest him on weapons charges, and the 1993 death of David Koresh and his Branch Dravidian cult followers in Waco, Texas, as federal agents stormed their compound. Militia members consider gun control a plot to disarm the population in preparation for a take-over by the UN, which has secretly stationed foreign troops in the US to establish a world socialist government. Mobilized by such fantasies, militia member Timothy McVeigh bombed government buildings in Oklahoma City, killing over one hundred people, including children in the day-care centre he destroyed.

The militia movement draws fanatics from different groups, including survivalists, anti-abortionists, game hunters, anti-environmentalists such as the Wise Use movement, and anti-Semitic groups such as Posse Comitatus, who believe the federal government imposes taxation to support an international Jewish financial conspiracy. Many are Identity Christians, white supremacists who claim they are the Chosen People, while Jews are Satan's offspring and minorities are sub-human "mud people." Popular among the Ku Klux Klan (KKK) in 1940s, the ideology was later adopted by the Aryan Nations, a Nazi group led by Richard Butler which established "God's kingdom" in its compound at Hayden Lake, Idaho, a racially pure nation with its own army opposed to what it calls the Zionist Occupation Government. Many fundamentalist Christians think we are in the "End Times" predicted in the book of Revelation and detect magical signs of this in supermarket bar codes and currency notes. They espouse dominion theology, saying Christians must prepare for Christ's return by forming armed communities to conquer secular society. Opposed to feminism, homosexuality, and sex education, they seek a theocracy based on the Old Testament, in which Christians would have total power and could impose the death penalty for murder, incest, adultery, and homosexuality.

Fueled by zealotry and fanatical hatred, many of these groups are extremely violent. For example, since the 1980s Christian Identity groups such as the Order, the Aryan Republican Army, and the Phineas Priesthood have robbed banks and stolen armoured cars to finance Nazi groups and launch an apocalyptic race war, inspired by a white supremacist fantasy novel *The Turner Diaries*.[2] In 1984, the Order murdered Alan Berg (a Denver radio announcer who criticized white supremacy) and in 1988 racist skinheads from White Aryan Resistance in Portland beat Mulageta Seraw, an Ethiopian man, to death with baseball bats; racist skinhead activity increased in the area after the murder.

Many members are "angry white guys" for whom the American Dream has failed. Global restructuring has automated their jobs or sent those jobs offshore to even-more-exploited Third World workers. The relative privilege they had gained from imperialism is now threatened. Poor, alienated, and powerless, they see their future as burger-flippers while staring at spectacles of awesome wealth. Recognizing that the political system is run by elites for their own benefit, they nevertheless cling to an ideology of individualism and rage at those who threaten their power and identity: employment equity, immigration, welfare, environmentalists, gays, minorities, feminists. Right-wing groups manipulate this anger by providing scapegoats: women, immigrants, minorities. To the downwardly mobile who see their future threatened by declining economic prospects, the extreme right wing provides simple explanations and identifiable enemies: global restructuring is a Jewish financial conspiracy; domestic restructuring is a feminist plot. Racist messages blend with conservative appeals to the work ethic and attacks on welfare or employment equity programs: minorities should stop complaining and work hard. Thus, during social crises, small racist groups gain wide support by offering simple explanations for complex problems.

While the bizarre ideas of these groups would be laughable if it were not for their violence and widespread appeal, it is important to note that such attitudes are not simply the result of a lack of education. These ideas are cultivated and well funded by corporate support. Major corporations strongly oppose unions and any policy to redistribute wealth more fairly. The Rockefeller family and beer executive Joseph Coors gave millions to evangelical and right-wing groups that would advance their interests. Through various foundations, corporations and individual billionaires funded thousands of anti-communist radio and television broadcasts, spending millions annually to indoctrinate the population. Corporations funded the John Birch Society and other right-wing groups with racist ideologies because they also promoted a pro-

2. Andrew Macdonald (William Pierce), *The Turner Diaries* (Washington: National Alliance, 1978).

business, anti-communist agenda and because "race" divided the working class. These groups shared an ideology that was pro-capitalist, individualistic, militaristic and patriarchal.

In this context, there is renewed support for previously discredited forms of scientific racism. In North America and Europe, the most extreme right-wing political statements and expressions of virulent racism are accompanied by more "respectable" academic endeavours running the full gamut of revisionist history, from Holocaust denials to renewed efforts to link "race" and intelligence. In this endeavour, intellectuals play an important service role: if "racial" qualities can explain differences between groups, then declining social conditions for most of the population can be presented as the outcome of unrealistic efforts to impose equality based on refusals to accept scientific facts. Right-wing ideologues can present themselves as clear-headed exponents of rationality in efforts to reverse liberal immigration policies, employment equity or "race mixing." If scientific racists can prove that IQ differences exist, there is justification for differential social spending to avoid wasting resources on those argued to be genetically incapable of improvement. Thus, service intellectuals present specious correlations between "race" and qualities such as intelligence, and provide support for policy recommendations based on such correlations. For example, J. Philippe Rushton, psychology professor at the University of Western Ontario, is notorious for his claims that Orientals have bigger brains and are smarter than whites, who in turn have bigger brains and are smarter than blacks. Rushton also claimed that "criminality, morality, love of children, penis length and a host of other traits also could be fit into a racial hierarchy."[3] Although he had been threatened with prosecution under Canada's hate laws and Ontario premier David Peterson had called for him to be fired, Rushton (along with University of Western Ontario zoology professor C. Davison Ankney), reiterated his claims in 1996 at the Baltimore conference of the American Association for the Advancement of Science. Rushton operates with notions that most anthropologists rejected long ago, such as the notion of "race" itself or connections between head size and intelligence; his fascination with penis size recalls European obsessions about the sexuality of various exotic "Others" in the colonized world.

Rushton was an important source for the best-selling book *The Bell Curve*,[4] which sought to link "race" and intelligence. Authors Richard Herrnstein and Charles Murray argued that the US is stratified by intellectual ability: a small, intelligent elite governs the plodding masses. Hailed as ground-breaking, their book simply reasserts old arguments about "race" and intelligence, basically restating the Social Darwinist theme that the wealthy are rich because they are smarter while the poor are stupid. Personal qualities, determined by genetics rather than social or eco-

---

3. *The Globe and Mail*, 12 Feb. 1996: A6.

4. Richard J. Herrnstein and Charles Murray, *The Bell Curve* (New York: Free Press, 1994).

nomic factors, explain stratification and this is reflected in racial differences. The book's major flaw is its premise that the two obscure categories of "race" and "intelligence" can be measured and meaningfully correlated in terms of causal connections. As noted, "race" is not a biological entity with actual existence. There are so many different definitions of "race," so many conflicting measurements, and so many different estimates of the number of actual "races" (three? or thousands?) that the term is meaningless and should be abandoned. Similarly, the notion of "intelligence" is vague and the suggestion that it can be measured and represented by a number is dubious. Not only did Herrnstein and Murray ignore the social and political construction of intelligence, they made numerous other errors that have been widely noted and criticized. They confuse correlation and causation (i.e., because many black people score lower on IQ tests it must be because they *are* black although there is no evidence why that would be so). Their work has been criticized for their misuse of statistics: e.g., blacks score lower on IQ tests, but their scores have been continually rising; this must be due to better education rather than to any genetic change.

In addition to conceptual and methodological problems, the sources they use and their political objectives and affiliations are significant. Herrnstein and Murray rely heavily on material from *Mankind Quarterly* and other publications associated with the journal, which is widely criticized as white supremacist and for disseminating pseudo-scientific racist material. Many contributors and editors have fascist and Nazi connections, anti-Semitic views, and support apartheid and other ultra-right issues. The journal publishes articles by academics who argue for connections between "race" and intelligence: Richard Lynn, Arthur Jensen, William Shockley, J. Phillippe Rushton. This work has been shown to be flawed and misleading, although Herrnstein and Murray ignore the critiques. These researchers form a small, self-confirming circle. Many are financed by the same foundations, especially the Pioneer Fund, started by a US textile tycoon with Nazi sympathies and an interest in eugenics. The Pioneer Fund has a clear political agenda and finances only those who will provide "scientific evidence" to support this agenda.

The Bell Curve was presented as ground-breaking and the authors depicted as brave challengers of the political conformity alleged to have been imposed by liberals or even left-wingers. This supposed conformity was identified by the term "political correctness." In universities, right-wing academics raised the alarm that Western civilization was threatened by non-Western and alternative perspectives, and advanced a preposterous claim that universities were being run by feminists and minorities promoting a radical agenda. Corporate media seized the torch; *Newsweek*[5] announced the threat of "Thought Police" on university campuses, suggesting a tightly controlled world where radicals determine everything that can be said. Although the suggestion itself is ludicrous, the ability of the corporate culture industries and

---

5. *Newsweek*, December 1990.

propaganda machines to construct such a total reversal of reality is impressive. By repeating the term endlessly, corporate media injected it into popular discourse, using it as one element of ideological warfare intended to ensure complete hegemony by depicting any dissent as a rigid left-wing attack not only on freedom of expression but on fun itself, since the "politically correct" were depicted as humourless people unable to take a joke. In fact what is really involved in media attacks on "political correctness" is an attempt to caricature and reverse progressive achievements in human rights attained over decades. Anyone who opposed racist, misogynist or homophobic stereotypes, raised human rights concerns about unrestrained capitalism or sought to protect the environment against corporate polluters could be instantly marginalized through application of the term, while concerns about exploitation of non-human animals were simply off the scale. Brandishing the fetish term of "political correctness" served to stifle any criticism of established systems of power.

The Bell Curve is more properly seen in this context, as an attack on liberal ideas and as a means of naturalizing inequality. The general context is the growing gap between rich and poor, economic disaster for the majority while a small elite basks in profits. A resurgent right wing attacks the poor by slashing welfare, and they are applauded by a working class befuddled by their own misdirected resentment. Religious fundamentalists promote narrowly defined "family-values" and anti-gay propaganda. In a general atmosphere of ignorance and hatred for intellectuals, heretics are dismissed as "politically correct" while pseudo-scientists propose theories of "race" and intelligence. In its effort to naturalize inequality, *The Bell Curve* is an exemplary text of the Culture of Prejudice.

John S. Sorenson

CHAPTER 3

"I'm not a racist, and nobody I know is either"

A worthy statement which invites discussion of "colour-blindness"

We will misunderstand the culture of prejudice if we think its racist dimensions are limited to the activities of the extreme right-wing groups discussed in the previous chapter. Analyzing our contemporary culture of prejudice requires an examination of the social construction of whiteness. Like other racialized identities, whiteness has been invented and its meaning has varied over time. Over the last 500 years, a system of white supremacy developed and spread throughout the world. All white people benefit from this system, although not all to the same extent. Prejudices of class, gender, ethnicity, and religion limit opportunities among white people; however, they are freed from the additional hardships created by white supremacy (and from the ways in which other prejudices act in tandem with this form of racism). This system has become so pervasive, institutionalized, and embedded in our culture, so much a part of its taken-for-granted "common sense" that many who benefit from it do not consciously recognize its existence. Indeed, one of the pernicious aspects of this system is that whiteness is privileged in such a way that it becomes obscured, allowing white people to say they are "colour-blind" and do not think about "race," luxuries denied to those who must suffer the direct effects of racism.

Our culture of prejudice operates in such a way as to normalize whiteness. Within this system, whiteness is both all-pervasive and invisible. It is the standard for judging all other experience. Within this system, white people, independent of any actions or accomplishments on their part, enjoy certain freedoms, privileges, and opportunities that are routinely denied to others. White people can count on certain things: they are not routinely intercepted by the police while going about their business or stopped for "driving while black"; vacancies do not suddenly disappear when they seek housing; their bad behaviour is seen in individual terms rather than as a reflection of their group identity; they are not regularly asked to explain "the white view" of things or to speak on behalf of their "race"; they regularly see people like themselves represented in media, in professions, and in positions of authority; they do not need to make special efforts to find children's literature, dolls or toys that feature people who look like themselves; the "flesh-coloured" pencil or crayon in the box actually resembles their own skin tones; they are not routinely followed by store clerks watching that they do not steal; they do not need to wonder if the obstacles they face are based on racism or if their appearance will count against them if they seek legal or medical aid. Within this system of white supremacy, whiteness becomes the never-directly-stated-but-always-understood standard of behaviour, beauty, and belonging. The artistic and philosophical productions of white people are praised as timeless masterpieces of human civilization while those of other groups are presented as mere entertainment or exotica.

Whiteness is conflated with national identity so that those classified as not-white are always outsiders. For example, while doing research for our book *Ghosts and Shadows*, Atsuko Matsuoka and I interviewed an Eritrean immigrant in Winnipeg who stated, "My son will be born here but he won't be one hundred per cent Canadian. Because he's black, they'll treat him differently."[1] Similarly, people born in Canada but who do not have white skin are frequently asked how long they have been in the country or are complimented on how well they speak English. Despite the fact that apart from the small indigenous population (who are themselves excluded from "mainstream" society) Canada is a nation of immigrants, some groups are considered "real Canadians" because of their appearance while others are always marked as intrusive newcomers who are, paradoxically, either unwilling to work or bent on stealing "our" jobs. While whiteness confers a confident sense of belonging, those who are not included in this category are continually confronted with subtle (and sometimes not-so-subtle) reminders of their outsider status.

Certainly, the culture of white supremacy has changed over time. Segregation and miscegenation laws have been abolished in North America, Ku Klux Klan rallies attract fewer supporters than they once did, and hate crimes are sometimes punished. These advances may lead some white people to feel that because they are not members of an explicitly racist organization and because they do not personally discriminate against others, they are therefore not affected by racism or that they do not participate in its operations. Convinced that they live in a meritocracy where individual effort is always rewarded, they do not recognize that their whiteness is a racialized identity that bestows certain privileges upon them and deprives others of the same advantages. Racism operates not only through individual acts of violence, but also through institutionalized systems and structures that confer advantages to one group over others and, through ideology, provide cultural attitudes that elevate one group over others. Thus, while we can acknowledge that individualized racism also exists among people of colour, it is important to distinguish this from the globalized, institutional power of white supremacy.

---

1. Atsuko Matsuoka and John Sorenson, *Ghosts and Shadows: Construction of Identity and Community in an African Diaspora* (Toronto: University of Toronto Press, 2001) 210.

"Common sense" white supremacy makes whiteness the standard of civilization, beauty, and normal behaviour. It allows racist slurs, jokes, and stereotypes to flourish and to be understood. For example, Ontario's finance minister Jim Flaherty complained that the federal government was only concerned with the health care of Aboriginal people while the provincial governments deliver care to "real people in real towns."[2] Similarly, as Toronto mayor Mel Lastman prepared to visit Mombasa as part of an effort to win the city's bid to host the Olympic Games, he joked to reporters, "Why the hell would I want to go to a place like Mombasa? ... I just see myself in a pot of boiling water with all these natives dancing around me." Although Lastman apologized after it was pointed out that Mombasa is a major city and its residents might be offended by a characterization redolent of the worst stereotypes of nineteenth-century imperialism, the incident did not seem to substantially reduce his popularity. A *Toronto Star* poll found that 73 per cent of Toronto residents felt that Lastman was doing a good or average job and pollsters suggested Lastman had a strong chance of re-election.[3] Indeed, as Kofi Ellison noted in Ghana's *Accra Mail*,[4] Lastman's idiotic remarks are not unusual among political figures. Andrew Natsios, head of the US Agency for International Development, told the *Boston Globe* that antiretroviral drugs should not be provided to AIDS patients in Africa because "many Africans don't know what Western time is" and would therefore not take their medicine regularly as required. Natsios repeated his ethnographic insights into African cultures to the House International Relations Committee: "People do not know what watches and clocks are, they do not use Western means for telling time. They use the sun." Ellison also noted how US president George W. Bush's comments that "Africa is a nation that suffers from incredible disease" required his National Security Advisor to go into damage-control mode and reassure media that Bush was aware that Africa is a continent.

These comments do more than illustrate the intellectual impoverishment of clownish bureaucrats. They are indicative of the fundamental attitude of the culture of prejudice, a conviction that it is those in the West who matter while the bulk of humanity, who live in what was once called the "Third World," are of utter insignificance. To us, in general, their lives are as "invisible as dust."[5] Many people who benefit from white privilege find it necessary to assert colour-blindness ("I don't see colour, I treat everyone the same"). While this may seem well intentioned, it

---

2. *Toronto Star*, 22 Jan. 2002: A1.

3. *Toronto Star*, 20 Jan. 2002: A1.

4. *The Daily Accra Mail Online*, 23 July 2001. Vol. 2(184). < http://www.accra-mail.com>.

5. Leigh Binford, *The El Mozote Massacre: Anthropology and Human Rights* (Tucson: University of Arizona Press, 1996) 4. This view characterizes white supremacy but is not limited to white people. For example, while Afrocentric philosophies have correctly critiqued Eurocentric distortions of African history, they often romanticize an ancient Africa populated entirely by kings and queens and free of all internal inequalities; many African-American cultural critics are satisfied to invoke a glorious African past but are uninterested in the complexities and contradictions of contemporary African cultures.

ignores the fact that a white-supremacist culture of prejudice does exist and that people have different experiences based on their position in that system. While offering a comforting fiction to those who are privileged by this system, it simultaneously denies the pervasive effects of racism and negates important aspects of other people's identities. To suggest that one does not see colour is to claim that institutionalized racism has no effects.

The culture of prejudice sometimes advises "tolerance" for the presence and behaviour of other groups. Yet "tolerance" seems to be a strange goal. To tolerate is to endure, to put up with what one does not like. Rather than understanding and mutual respect, tolerance implies a precarious and perhaps only temporary abeyance in hostilities. Indeed, "tolerance" can rapidly degenerate into hostility. For example, following the September 11th terrorist attacks on New York and Washington, hate crimes more than doubled in Toronto. Although the terrorist attacks took place in another country and those targeted in Canada had no association with them, the police hate crime unit stated that the incidents were "misguided efforts to imitate, repeat and retaliate against the terrorist activities." The main targets of the racist attacks were "anyone who appeared Middle Eastern or East Indian."[6] State action, involving "racial profiling" and detentions without charges or trial, was hardly less racist. Of course, the military response simply ignored any interests on the part of "inferior beings": rather than attempting to bring terrorists to justice, the US simply attacked Afghanistan, killing thousands of civilians and uprooting millions of others, who then faced the possibility of starvation. Thus, those who suffered most directly from the attack on the Taliban were those who previously had been the main victims of its repressive regime. Since the Afghan population is "invisible as dust" to those who matter, this arrangement was entirely acceptable to the civilized world.

Recognition of the social construction of whiteness has led some academics, especially in the US, to focus on white identity as essential for anti-racism work. Certainly, it is useful to recognize that "race" is an issue not just for people of colour but for white people as well. However, the focus on whiteness sometimes tends to fix this as a timeless, unchanging essence that is outside historical and social processes. Yet Marxists have argued that racism is a useful tool of capitalism, developed as a means of splitting the working class through use of biological markers and offering special privileges to one group of workers. Like all racialized identities, whiteness is socially constructed and has its own history: certain immigrant groups have become "whiter" over time as they have been able to consolidate their position within North America's racialized hierarchy (this provides further proof that "race" is an illogical and misleading term). Stereotypes of savagery that European colonialists applied to indigenous peoples of North America and Africa had been previously applied to the local population of Ireland by the English who conquered them. Indeed, geno-

6. *Toronto Star*, 26 Feb. 2002: B3.

cidal assault on Native Americans was preceded by similar acts of slaughter in Ireland, and the same ideology justified both. The Irish were considered wild people who were incapable of being civilized and should be exterminated. As racist ideology developed and skin colour was selected as a primary marker of inferiority, efforts were made to detect physical characteristics among the Irish that distinguished them from their English conquerors. Ignoring empirical realities, some "race scientists" did manage to observe darker skin. As they gradually improved their situation among successive waves of immigrants to North America, the "black Irish" were able to shed this identification and were recognized as white. At various times, "race scientists" have claimed that other groups of immigrants (Italians, Jews, Eastern Europeans) had darker skin, once again in the absence of actual physical markers. Of course, where actual physical differences did exist, the system of racist domination readily deployed them as signs of degeneracy and inferiority.

So what role exists for white people in such a culture of prejudice? Are white people doomed to be racists? Is it true, as Anne Bishop claims, that because the system is so all-pervasive "a white person never becomes non-racist"?[7] Assertions that whites can never overcome racism (or that men can never overcome sexism) are defeatist, paralyzing, and counter-productive; they also help to create romantic stereotypes of people of colour and overlook other forms of racism besides white supremacy. Bishop's book is well intentioned, but in making racism seem inescapable it closes off possibilities for those who do not wish to perpetuate the culture of prejudice.

In contrast to the argument that racism is unavoidable for white people, the editors of the journal *Race Traitor* seem to suggest that becoming non-racist is a fairly straightforward matter.[8] They say white people who wish to overturn this racist system should detach themselves from white identity and identify themselves as black. They assert that whiteness should be abolished and they seem to think this can be accomplished through a simple declaration. It is as if white people can simply reconstitute themselves by choice. *Race Traitor* correctly points out that in a system of white supremacy, racism is not only a problem to be solved by those it targets; it is also the responsibility of white people who benefit from this system to reject it. However, ending white supremacy will not be accomplished by mere declarations. Active solidarity is required to restructure our culture of prejudice. White people need to work collectively with others, listen, empathize, and create a more progressive identity for themselves. Furthermore, we may note that this renunciation of racialized identity recommended by the *Race Traitor* group is a privilege open to only a few. Also, simply denying white identity is an evasion of responsibility: "no matter how vociferously they may renounce their whiteness, white people do not lose the power

7. Anne Bishop, *Becoming an Ally: Breaking the Cycle of Oppression* (Halifax: Fernwood, 1994) 97.

8. John Garvey and Noel Ignatiev, "Toward a New Abolitionism: A Race Traitor Manifesto," *Whiteness*, ed. Mike Hill (New York: New York University Press, 1997) 346-49.

associated with being White. Such a reality renders many white renunciations disingenuous. It is as if some race traitors want to disconnect with all liabilities of whiteness (its association with racism and blandness) while maintaining all its assets (the privilege of not being Black, Latino, or Native American)."[9]

While solidarity with oppressed groups is essential for those who seek to subvert the culture of prejudice, the *Race Traitor* position seems rather limited and naive. Not only is it narrowly focused on the situation in the US, but it also oversimplifies that situation into the polarized binary of black and white, ignoring a multiplicity of other racialized identities and sometimes seeming to minimize their experience of racism. Furthermore, "it implies that the romantic stereotype of the eternally resisting, victimized 'black community' is required to be further strengthened in order to create a suitable location for escapees from whiteness. Thus black people are condemned to racial stereotype as the price of white people's liberation."[10]

Just as men are not inescapably sexist, white people are not doomed to play only oppressive roles. It is not impossible for those who have lived a privileged isolation within a system of white supremacy to work together with others to make a better world. However, in order to do so, they must make an effort to understand the culture of prejudice and their place within it and then accept their share of responsibility for changing it.

John S. Sorenson

---

9. Joe L. Kincheloe and Shirley R. Steinberg, "Addressing the Crisis of Whiteness," *White Reign*, Joe L. Kincheloe et al., eds. (New York: St. Martin's, 1998) 22.

10. Alastair Bonnett, *Anti-Racism* (New York: Routledge, 2000) 141.

"immigrants are threatening our way of life"

centuries-old fear expressed about every new wave of immigration, even by members of the last wave of immigration

After the September 11, 2001, attack on the World Trade Center and the Pentagon, anti-immigrant prejudices experienced a resurgence across North America as "suspicious-looking foreigners" came under the scrutiny of governments and of their neighbours. These prejudices, however, have never been far from the surface in normal times and have been intensifying under the impact of corporate globalization. Right-wing groups have flourished all across Canada and all of them produce anti-immigrant propaganda, almost all of it selective and dedicated to the goal of "keeping Canada white"; therefore, calls to limit immigration are almost always based on racism.

Apart from indigenous peoples, Canada is, of course, a nation of immigrants. Anti-immigrant sentiments should thus be seen in the context of a process in which those who are themselves fairly recent arrivals have come to claim the status of "real" Canadians and, in an act of social and political magic, the indigenous population is made to disappear. (Canada's identity comes to be seen, then, as the unique creation of "two founding peoples," English and French, and national history is interpreted in terms of their "two solitudes," rather than as a story of the displacement of indigenous peoples by various waves of immigrants.) While immigration has been the basis for Canada's development as a nation, it is equally necessary for its survival. Canada, the United States, and most European countries have falling birth rates and a declining population of working-age people.[1] In all of these countries, greater numbers of immigrants are necessary to replace and support an aging population. Although policies determining who can come to Canada largely have been decided on the basis of labour recruitment rather than any humanitarian largesse, it is widely assumed that Canada accepts immigrants with open arms, that all immigrants want to come here, and that they should be grateful for the opportunities they receive here. In fact, Canadian policies have been very selective, focusing on the best-

---

1. Health and Welfare Canada, *Charting Canada's Future: A Report of the Demographic Review* (Ottawa, Health Canada, 1989).

educated and most politically suitable immigrants. However, in many cases, even these highly skilled immigrants find that their qualifications do not count in Canada and the "opportunities" they have consist of the chance to work in low-status, low-paying jobs that others do not want.

Canada's immigration policies have been based on varying demands for new workers, but these policies have not been determined solely on economic criteria. Ideological objectives have contributed as well, and historically these policies have been explicitly racist, with great emphasis placed on the need to protect Canada's "white" identity and character from the undesirable influence of Asian immigrants in particular. Historically, immigration policy has favoured newcomers from northern Europe, with southern Europeans coming in as a poor second choice. Immigration from Africa, Latin America, and the Middle East has been minuscule, although some people from these areas have been allowed in when their labour was required. When thousands of Chinese workers were recruited to meet Canada's labour requirements in the late nineteenth century, the European population seethed with racist outrage, and as work was completed on the Canadian Pacific Railroad the federal government imposed the *Chinese Immigration Act* in 1885, the first of a series of discriminatory immigration laws. Later, the *Chinese Exclusion Act* banned Chinese immigrants entirely from 1923-1947.

Immigrants from other Asian countries were similarly targeted. In 1910 the *Immigration Act* provided a means to exclude a wide range of immigrants who could be deemed undesirable because their customs allegedly prevented assimilation into Canadian society; others could be excluded if they came from tropical areas because they would be unable to adjust to Canada's climate. The *Alien Land Act* of 1913 prevented Japanese immigrants from purchasing or leasing land for more than three years. As newspapers in British Columbia openly advocated violence against Japanese immigrants, citizens responded by forming the Asiatic Exclusion League to stop immigration from Asia. In September 1907, racist mobs rampaged through the streets of Vancouver attacking Chinese and Japanese homes and stores as the police looked on and religious leaders cheered their Christian efforts. Anti-Asian racism continued into World War II; in 1942, 23,000 Japanese Canadians, including those who were born in Canada or who had become citizens, lost all their civil rights as they were rounded up and sent to concentration camps as security risks, despite the total absence of any evidence against them. While the men were sent into forced labour, the houses, property, and businesses of the Japanese Canadians were appropriated and sold for far less than their value; this was a highly profitable arrangement for their white neighbours. Released from their prisons in 1947, Japanese Canadians only received compensation and an official apology in 1988.

Openly racist immigration policies continued throughout World War II, when Jews fleeing Nazi extermination efforts were barred from entering Canada.

Immigration and refugee policies for the second half of the twentieth century favoured Eastern Europeans and those who opposed communist regimes. As a result of this selectivity, a number of fascists and war criminals found a congenial home in Canada. Refugees from murderous right-wing regimes, many of which were political allies and good business partners of the Canadian government, were far less welcome.

Despite the significance of immigration for Canada's economic future, some Canadians believe that immigration is a threat to national security, not because a few terrorists might slip in, but because it is feared that immigrants will take away jobs from Canadians or that they will be a drain on social services. In fact, many immigrants do not gain access to social programs that might benefit them (such as English language training), but find themselves pushed into low-paying jobs that few Canadians would want for themselves. Newcomers and illegal immigrants are very vulnerable to exploitation because of their uncertain status, and employers can use their fears to pay them lower wages and block unionization efforts. Even educated professionals find themselves driving taxis because their qualifications are not recognized in Canada. Furthermore, at least some of the immigrants who are often condemned as a burden on Canadian social services actually bolster such programs. For example, the Mexican "guest" workers who come to pick tomatoes in southern Ontario pay Canadian taxes on the money they earn, but since they are only in Canada temporarily very few of them have any opportunity to benefit from all the programs their taxes support.

Many alarms are raised about a "flood" of illegal immigrants being smuggled into Canada and other developed countries. This has encouraged the political "mainstream" to shift even farther toward the right. For example, Australia's Conservative prime minister John Howard received enthusiastic public backing for his policy of blocking ships full of Iraqi immigrants from entering Australian territory; Pauline Hanson, leader of the racist One Nation party who received widespread support in Australia's 1998 elections, boasted that the Conservative government was merely following the policies her group had put forward. The same racist backlash exists in North America, where the United States has created a militarized border to repel an "invasion" from Mexico. Police agencies have benefitted from the sense of panic in terms of major budget increases, hiring of more personnel, more technological resources, and an inflated sense of their own importance.

Global trafficking in human beings has become a major industry, worth billions of dollars to the organized criminal gangs who control the trade. Millions of women are being sold throughout Asia as prostitutes and sweatshop factory workers. Many immigrants face extremely dangerous conditions in their quest to achieve better lives. For example, in October 2001 a boat carrying Iraqi immigrants to Australia sank and 350 people drowned. In Europe, immigrants have been found suffocated or dead of thirst in sealed containers. Between 1994 and 1997, 1,185 people died, as a result of drowning, exposure, dehydration or being struck by automobiles, while attempting to cross the Mexico-US border.[2] In 2000, the US Border Patrol reported 366 deaths of migrants attempting to cross into Arizona, California, and Texas, a significant increase from the previous year.[3] Over the last few decades, bloated bodies of drowned Haitians have regularly washed up on Caribbean beaches. Although they were fleeing slave-like conditions under brutal repression and government death squads, Haitians were not welcomed as political refugees to the US but were dismissed as "economic migrants." Those who survived the risky ocean crossing and were captured in the US were imprisoned in concentration camps before being deported after cursory hearings. Their experiences provided a stark contrast with the treatment of anti-communist Cubans who arrived in the US and were welcomed as heroic refugees fleeing oppression.

Too often, people fail to look beyond the sensationalized reports and images of "boat people" landing on Canadian shores. Those who do look more carefully will understand that these "waves" of desperate illegal immigrants are in many cases the product of policies made at home. As the North has enriched itself by exploiting the South, this has created the impoverishment, repression, and violence that create the desire for immigration. Neo-liberalism and corporate globalization have established new levels of poverty throughout much of the world while providing even greater benefits to those who are already wealthy.

Since the 1980s, the World Bank and the International Monetary Fund have forced cuts to government subsidies on basic food items, slashed social programs, reduced wages, forced open markets to foreign investment, devalued currencies, and privatized state enterprises. The ostensible goal has been to increase "efficiency," but the effect has been to make life unbearable for the wretched of the earth. Globalization has intensified environmental degradation and reduced people's opportunities to make a living in their own communities. Peasants are evicted from their land as industrial-style agricultural projects move in. While transnational corporations make fantastic profits, the poor face desperate conditions, unable to feed their children as much-needed food subsidies are removed.

Displaced rural populations can no longer support themselves and must migrate to find work. These migrant workers are among the most exploited. Some become seasonal workers or seek jobs in *maquilladora*-style factories in export zones. Millions of women are conscripted into the global trade in sex workers, many of them unknowingly; they are promised jobs as factory or domestic workers and then find themselves imprisoned as sex slaves. Other women migrate as domestic workers for middle-class families in North America. As child care is privatized in North America, middle-class parents are eager to hire foreign women as nannies. These women are very vulnera-

---

2. *New York Times*, 24 Aug: A1.

3. American Friends Service Committee Mexico-US Border Program <http://www.stopgatekeeper.org>.

ble to exploitation because of the strict conditions of their work visas, and many are afraid to complain of mistreatment. Knowing this, and the fact that the women's relatives are dependent on remittances, their employers are able to pay very low wages and demand long hours and extra tasks from these women. For example, in Los Angeles, 90 per cent of the workers in garment factories and other sweatshops are immigrant women and children who exist on subsistence-level wages, sometimes earning just $50 for a 60-hour week.[4] Many Filipina women who have migrated as domestic workers to serve wealthy families in the Middle East have reported sexual abuse.

Immigration and other types of international movement are gendered in other ways as well. For refugees, the risks are particularly acute. Women refugees face other gender-specific dangers of rape and other forms of sexual violence in addition to all of the problems endured by refugee men. Those women who emigrate with their immediate families may find themselves in particularly vulnerable positions because of their status. In the stressful situation caused by adapting to new conditions and roles, women are frequently transformed into targets of male violence inside the home. Those women who are dependent on their husbands' immigration status may be reluctant to complain, while those who speak only their own language or who have little knowledge of their rights may find themselves isolated without help.

Capitalism uses borders to its advantage, opening them when workers are needed and closing them when too many are available. Neo-liberals and boosters of globalization have called for deregulation and open borders but only in a selective way: capital is to be fluid and to cross borders easily, but migrant people are not to be deregulated by allowing them to move at will. Instead, the state is expected to step in and police their movements. New policies of globalization enlist the state as the enforcer of rules on labour movement rather than as the protector of populations. Why should the freedom to move across borders be possible for elites (and their money) but not for poor people who seek opportunities to save or improve their lives?

John S. Sorenson

---

4. Joy James, *Resisting State Violence* (Minneapolis: University of Minnesota, 1996) 118.

CHAPTER 5

"God is on our side"
common belief, usually held by "both" sides in armed conflict

Religion is often viewed in a benign way, as a belief system that unites people spiritually and allows them to form moral communities. By establishing standards of behaviour, offering a sense of purpose and meaning to life, and giving explanations for unsettling events, religions provide cohesion and stability and help people to live without despair. However, religion involves not only beliefs but also social actions shaped by those beliefs, actions that acquire particular force because they are assumed to reflect supernatural authority. These actions and beliefs always involve issues of power. Some individuals and institutions are thought to have special contact with supernatural forces and the beliefs and actions of others are subject to their control. For example, during the medieval Spanish Inquisition the Catholic Church tortured and executed thousands of suspected heretics, acquiring their property and enriching itself in the process. In many cases, religions offer narratives that mirror existing social relationships, with mythological stories that help to legitimize inequalities of power.

Marx viewed religion as illusion and ideology, the "opium of the people," offering fantastic dreams that obscure real conditions, a dysfunctional system for all but the rich and powerful. Rather than integrating society, religion is a mechanism that aids exploitation. Religion distorts actual conditions by invoking supernatural explanations to legitimize and justify social oppression and diverts resistance by offering compensation to oppressed groups: by accepting injustice in this world, they will be rewarded in heaven. Focused on the afterlife, the oppressed remain blind to the real reasons for their oppression. In many cases, religion has played not only an obfuscatory role but a repressive one as well.

For example, in the Philippines, right-wing Christian fundamentalist groups promote anti-communist ideology by distributing propaganda against the insurgents of the New People's Army and actively encourage vigilante death squads to kill anyone identified as a "communist," a category that not only includes labour activists and union leaders but also extends to more liberal religious leaders. Repression by

Christian fundamentalist groups has been even worse in Latin America. For example, in 1982 a coup in Guatemala brought to power Efrain Rios Montt, a spectacular killer associated with a right-wing evangelical organization in the US. Trained by the US military, Rios Montt surpassed the brutality of previous regimes by destroying workers' organizations and murdering labour activists, escalating counter-insurgency attacks and implementing a scorched earth policy against the indigenous population, killing thousands of civilians and herding survivors into concentration camps. His evangelical supporters applauded the slaughter, since the victims were regarded as communists, virtually interchangeable with demonic forces. Throughout Latin America, repressive right-wing dictatorships received enthusiastic support from religious groups in the US as they established astonishing records of carnage and corruption.

Another repressive Christian fundamentalist movement is the Lord's Resistance Army (LRA), which has terrorized northern Uganda from across the border in southern Sudan, fighting the government and seeking to create a society based on its interpretation of the ten biblical commandments. Headed by Joseph Kony, a former altar boy who became the prophet-leader of a guerrilla army, the LRA was created in 1988 from remnants of the Holy Spirit movement led by Kony's aunt, Alice Lakwena. (Among her other accomplishments, she advised followers that spreading nut-oil on their bodies would deflect bullets.) The LRA rules through terror, attacking villages, mutilating people, and capturing children to use as soldiers. The LRA has kidnapped thousands of children, beating, threatening, and subjecting them to psychological torture by forcing them to watch executions or kill other children themselves. Girls are used as sex slaves and, due to the ready availability of small arms, boys are turned into soldiers. By turning children into killers, the LRA severs them from their communities and secures their loyalty by convincing them they have nowhere else to go. Those who do escape are traumatized and isolated. The LRA closed down much of northern Uganda, attacking schools and clinics and mining the roads so that the local population was trapped and forced to live under the LRA's bizarre rules (for example, anyone with a white chicken or pig was killed). Recently the LRA intensified its attacks. By September 2002, 552,000 Ugandans and 24,000 Sudanese refugees in Uganda had been forcibly displaced, with thousands more displaced in Sudan.[1]

The Filipino death squads and the LRA provide striking examples of prejudice taken to violent extremes and justified with religious ideology. On the other hand, religions sometimes play a progressive role by challenging the existing relationships of power. For example, liberation theology developed within the Catholic Church in Latin America as a response to imperialism, fascism, and the ruthless dictatorships that enforced poverty and political repression through brutal violence. Influenced by

---

1. LRA Conflict in Northern Uganda and Southern Sudan, 2002. Human Rights Watch <http://hrw.org/press/2002/10/Uganda-1029-bck.htm>.

Marxist sociology, as well as by their religious beliefs, priests and nuns tried to create a more just society for the dispossessed. They became human rights activists in support of peasants oppressed by large landowners, the military, and transnational corporations. Many were tortured and murdered for their actions. In Canada, as well, some churches take a progressive role, not only by providing aid to the homeless and working for refugees, but also by organizing and participating in protests (for example, against the Conservative Harris government in Ontario that slashed social and environmental programs and promoted privatization).

Yet such commitment to social justice created controversy among Christians; many joined a backlash against this activist role and demanded that religion should be concerned only with spiritual and mystical matters, such as divine judgement, miracles, and the afterlife, instead of being committed to social justice. This concern for social justice is cited as a reason for declining church attendance. Furthermore, many people assume that growing secularization and greater concern with worldly rather than spiritual matters will lead to the end of religion. They assume that the development of science and a rationalistic outlook, along with the complexity and diversity of contemporary societies is incompatible with religious beliefs. Many religious leaders and believers worry about secularization and see it as a dangerous trend. However, religion remains a strong force in Canadian society. In Canada, those without religious affiliation constitute less than 15 per cent of the population, although their numbers are growing. Religion remains a significant force and so Canada cannot be said to be a secular society. In the US, religious beliefs and affiliations are even higher. Forty per cent of Americans describe themselves as "born-again" Christians. Almost the whole population believes in a supernatural being and thinks religion offers viable solutions to contemporary problems. This situation has remained constant throughout the century and various new religious cults have proliferated throughout the country. Thus, the idea that Western societies are completely secular is exaggerated.[2]

The phenomenon of fundamentalism is one form of revival. Fundamentalist movements want to establish what adherents consider more "pure" ways of life based on religious ideas. The term "fundamentalism" often makes people think of "Islamic fundamentalism," but revivals also have occurred among other religions, such as the Christian groups mentioned above, Hinduism, and Judaism. Many supporters of Zionism and the Israeli state believe that Jews have a supernaturally guaranteed right to live in Israel and that this supernatural sanction justifies the expulsion and oppression of the Palestinians and the expropriation of their land.

---

2. We should also see this in the context of other beliefs about the supernatural: astrology, healing crystals, and assorted New Age therapies have gained unprecedented popularity, and much of the US population believe they have been visited by UFOs or abducted by aliens. These deeply irrational beliefs exemplify a strong tendency opposing secularization. Along with the innovation of new cults are efforts to rejuvenate existing religious traditions.

Fundamentalism generally implies narrow-mindedness, backwardness, and anti-intellectualism, despite the fact that in North America many fundamentalists are well educated and come from middle-class backgrounds. Typically, believers think they are under attack and feel a sense of loss of identity and meaning; they are threatened by modern life, which they experience as being corrupt and lacking value. The notion of moral decay has been a strong component of Christian fundamentalism, shared by the so-called "Moral Majority," the new Christian Right. From the 1970s, new fundamentalist and evangelical movements became influential. Partly, this was a reaction to the feeling that "mainstream" churches had become too liberal. Many believers became alienated from churches that supported social action in support of women and homosexuals. Today's Christian fundamentalists still oppose liberal theologies, cultural and religious relativism, and secular humanism. This view is shared by conservative intellectuals who oppose legal amendments for the rights of women and gays, deplore multiculturalism in universities, and seek a return to the so-called "basic values of civilization" embodied in a few selected texts written by white men.

As an antidote to this dangerous social breakdown, fundamentalists offer a return to fundamental principles of religion. They believe in a sacred text that provides all answers to life's problems; this text must be interpreted literally and followed without question. Christian fundamentalists believe the Bible is the ultimate authority, not only on spiritual matters but also in relation to history and science. Believers insist that the Bible's assertions are literally true. They reject the theory of evolution in favour of a belief in divine creation. They believe the world is sharply divided into forces of good and evil: those who follow the text are the "chosen people," deserving supernatural rewards, while those who do not are damned to eternal punishment. And fundamentalists do not leave punishment for a supernatural afterworld: unbelievers are considered less valuable, people to be avoided, controlled, expelled or exterminated.

Convinced that modern society is corrupt and that their children are threatened by evil influences, fundamentalists take active roles in politics, voicing their opposition to abortion, equal rights amendments and affirmative action, feminism, gay rights, limits on school prayers and pornography, as well as seeking to expunge from school libraries any books that might challenge their ideas. Christian fundamentalists also became involved with international issues in the 1980s as they channelled financial and military support to anti-communist groups in Latin America. Right-wing politicians exploited these fears, or perhaps shared them. Former US president Ronald Reagan claimed the country was engaged in a life-and-death struggle with the Soviet Union, the "Evil Empire" as he called it, and seemed to interpret world events as part of biblical prophecy.[3]

---

3. In 2002, President George W. Bush, who had also courted Christian fundamentalist support, suggested a similar elemental struggle between the US's "Infinite Justice" and an "Axis of Evil" comprising Iran, Iraq, and North Korea.

In general, fundamentalists are obsessed with sexual matters and gender relations. For example, under the fundamentalist Islamic regime established by the Ayatollah Khomeini in Iran, the sexes were strictly segregated, adulterers were stoned to death, and homosexuals were shot. Fundamentalists regard feminism and women's liberation movements as dangerous threats to moral order and what they call "family values" (as if to suggest that those who do not share their narrow, authoritarian attitudes do not value their own families). Fundamentalists believe women are inferior to men and must be subject to their command. Some oppose education for women while others focus on control over reproduction and opposition to abortion.

A recently discussed example of Islamic fundamentalist opposition to women's emancipation comes from Afghanistan. Afghan society was formed on patrilineal lines and based on traditions associated with nomadic pastoralism. Gender roles have traditionally been associated with property relations, with close kinship ties encouraging group cohesion. Men have had control over women and regarded them as property; women have been secluded and veiled and their virginity enforced as a mark of family honour. However, a 1978 socialist revolution in Afghanistan sought to transform women's status. Changes were introduced in marriage, family and property law, and literacy and education were available for girls. This was opposed by traditionalists, who responded violently, but women did gain, especially in urban centres, in terms of education, employment, and participation in public life. After the Soviet invasion, traditionalists sought control over the refugees who had fled the war and who sought shelter in Pakistan. Islamic fundamentalists supported by the Pakistani government, Saudi Arabia, and the United States wanted to use the refugees to achieve their political program, including restoring former conditions of patriarchal control.

Fundamentalist opposition to women's emancipation was very extreme. The Afghan *mujahideen* differed from other resistance and guerrilla movements because they did not recruit women as fighters and did not include women's emancipation in their program. After deadly conflict among rival *mujahideen* groups, the most extreme fundamentalist faction, the Taliban, took over Afghanistan and imposed a strict religious ideology, in which women had to be covered during the limited conditions under which they are allowed outside the home, girls were not to be educated, no music was allowed, and adulterers were stoned to death. After the US government decided to bomb Afghanistan in retaliation for the September 11, 2001, terrorist attacks, corporate media exhibited a new-found concern for the plight of Afghan women and suggested that the bombing would liberate them. However, as thousands of Afghan civilians were killed as "collateral damage" in the "war on terror," the Revolutionary Association of the Women of Afghanistan (RAWA) warned that this would empower fundamentalist forces in the region and elsewhere.[4] As the US positioned the Northern Alliance forces to take over from the Taliban, the RAWA protested that

---

4. Revolutionary Association of Afghan Women, Press Release 15 Nov. 2001 <http://www.accuracy.org>.

this was unlikely to improve conditions for the civilian population since the Taliban had been welcomed into Kabul in 1996 as liberators from the brutality of the Northern Alliance. The RAWA pointed out that the two groups shared a similar ideology and denounced them both as "religio-fascists."[5]

The case of Afghanistan shows that fundamentalism is not a matter of beliefs but of action. Fundamentalists want their sacred texts to be put into practice. Interpreting these texts in the most literal reading, they want their message to be applied to contemporary life. In order to create the societies they want, fundamentalists seek political power, and some movements even want to form their own states. Where such states have been established, repression is the rule. In Afghanistan, for example, the Taliban tried to force the tiny Hindu minority to wear an identifying saffron-coloured patch, evoking memories of the yellow star that the Nazis forced European Jews to wear. In Iran, the Khomeini regime considered members of the Baha'i religion as apostates from Islam and imprisoned and executed many of them. Fundamentalists may claim to act out of love, but their most striking characteristic is their rigid intolerance of those who do not share their beliefs.

Two days after the terrorist attacks on the US, two of the most prominent leaders of the "born-again" Christian right appeared on a popular religious television program. With his host Pat Robertson's nodding assent and final statement of complete agreement, Jerry Falwell made the following statement, among others, on the events of September 11th:

> God continues to lift the curtain and allow the enemies of America to give us probably what we deserve.
>
> The abortionists have got to bear some burden for this because God will not be mocked. And when we destroy 40 million little innocent babies, we make God mad.
>
> I really believe that the pagans and the abortionists and the feminists and the gays and the lesbians who are actively trying to make that an alternative lifestyle, and the ACLU (American Civil Liberties Union), People for the American way (an organization opposed to right wing extremism)—all of them who have tried to secularize America.
>
> I point the finger in their face and say: 'You helped this happen.'[6]

Families of victims who might have been viewing this TV show, one assumes, would be forced to the conclusion that God certainly was not on the side of their loved ones. Clearly, this is not an instance of religion bringing comfort to the bereaved.

---

5. <http://rawa.fancymarketing.net>, 11 Sept. 2002.

6. *The Globe and Mail*, 15 Sept. 2001: A2.

These few examples indicate the ease with which repressive groups use religion to claim authority for their activities. Indeed, within cultures of prejudice it is virtually standard practice for such groups to appeal to some timeless truth as a means of consolidating their power. Just as racists appeal to essential biological differences to claim that their acts of discrimination are justified, fundamentalists invoke supernatural sanctions for their particular prejudices and use this as a rationale for imposing their beliefs on others. Religion serves as one of the most effective institutions in cultures of prejudice because fundamentalists can assert that their actions in society are legitimized by sacred texts and a divine, omniscient being whose authority cannot be challenged.

John S. Sorenson

CHAPTER 6

"Either you are with us or you are with the terrorists"

A mind-numbingly ridiculous Hobson's choice offered up by US President G.W. Bush, September 20, 2001

Cultures of prejudice are characterized by a lack of introspection and aversion to self-criticism. They divide the world into good (us) and evil (them). The terms of this stark binary are often reinforced by appeals to supernatural sanctions; within this fundamentalist logic our own actions are good by definition, and any opposition to them is satanic. This is the logic behind the terrorist attacks on the United States on September, 2001. The attacks were a major atrocity; however, the reaction to that atrocity has followed the same fundamentalistic logic, and the result has been to compound the suffering of millions of people with a frenzied mixture of revenge and imperial arrogance.

Corporate media constructed a narrative of an innocent America betrayed, raising analogies with the 1941 raid on Pearl Harbor, overlooking the fact that the Japanese had attacked a military base in a colony that the US had acquired by force. Because of the intention to maim and kill civilians, a more appropriate analogy would have been with the US atomic bombing of Hiroshima and Nagasaki. The September 11th attacks were presented as the product of inexplicable hatred. Those who suggested that the attacks should be seen in political context were shouted down as unfeeling, anti-American brutes. Americans interviewed on television asked, "Why do they hate us?", as if US foreign policy had not created enemies everywhere through its ruthless pursuit of undisputed US hegemony, imposed by violent means often directed at civilian populations. The use of violence to achieve political ends—a standard definition of terrorism—has been characteristic of US foreign policy. Media, government, and much of public opinion were determined not to understand this. For example, video footage of Palestinians celebrating the attacks was received as more proof of Arab depravity. The fact that the US has been Israel's main supporter, providing the weapons to maintain the occupation and kill large numbers of Palestinians, was disregarded; not surprisingly, Palestinians who had been pushed to the limits of desperation by Israeli state terrorism found some grim satisfaction in seeing the US receive a taste of the bitter fate they had been forced to endure for decades. Outrage at the Palestinians' behaviour conveniently overlooked the fact that Americans had once danced in the streets to celebrate the dropping of atomic bombs on Japanese cities. Any attempts to raise considerations of why the US is widely resented were simply dismissed. For example, New York's mayor rejected an offer of $10 million in relief aid from a Saudi prince, because it was accompanied by a critique of US Middle East policy.

One consequence of the bombing was that a vast surge of racism swept through North America as the culture of prejudice was given free expression. When white supremacist Timothy McVeigh carried out the bombing of a federal building in Oklahoma City, Middle Eastern terrorists were immediately blamed. On September 11, 2001, many jumped to the same conclusion before any evidence had appeared. Americans interviewed in the immediate aftermath suggested that it would be necessary to go "over there" to punish the perpetrators; at this point, no evidence existed of who the bombers were, so "over there" was just a vague expression of xenophobic rage. In any case, many believed it would be more expeditious simply to attack suspicious characters at home. Therefore, across North America, Muslims became targets; mosques were threatened or damaged and people were physically assaulted. Apparently, for some, any "foreigner" would do: inspired by a series of attacks on mosques throughout southern Ontario, racists in Hamilton burned down a Hindu temple. Sikhs were insulted and beaten and, in Arizona, shot to death, presumably because they "looked like Muslims."[1]

While the September 11th attacks provided racists with an incentive to attack some of their fellow citizens, they also offered opportunities to those who advocated a right-wing agenda. While some white supremacists seized the incidents as a reason to attack Muslims, the US-based neo-Nazi group National Alliance cheered the destruction of the World Trade Center because the group believed that many Jewish people had been killed.[2] Before he was forced to revise his statements because of their "insensitivity," Christian fundamentalist Reverend Jerry Falwell opined that the attack was allowed to happen because a supernatural being was mad at the US because of all of America's "non-believers and secular institutions, its feminists, homosexuals and civil-rights groups."[3] No such revisions were required from those who had sought bigger military budgets and who now claimed justification. Whereas the already-existing, formidable array of security devices and high-technology weapons had failed to stop a few hijackers armed with box-cutters, in the US support was now announced

1. *The Globe and Mail*, 21 Sept., 2001. Again, we may compare these reactions to those that followed the discovery that a home-grown terrorist had carried out the bombing in Oklahoma: there were no attacks on white men with crew-cuts.

2. Tim Wise, "Holding Terrorists Accountable? It Depends on the Color and the Cause," <http://wwwzmag.org/wiseterror.htm> 4 Nov., 2001.

3. Doug Saunders, "US got what it deserves, Falwell says," *The Globe and Mail*, 15 Sept. 2001: A2.

for the proposed militarization of outer space. The war on terrorism boosted the right-wing agenda in virtually every department: as increased "defense" spending was promoted as an urgent necessity, and as opposition to corporate globalization or oil-drilling in Alaska's National Wildlife Refuge was depicted as anti-American. Environmental groups like the Sierra Club dropped all challenges to the Bush government's environmental policies, while Greenpeace and the World Wildlife Fund scaled back their activities.[4]

The US was presented as the innocent victim of terrorism. While a few journalists did note that those whom some considered "terrorists" were seen by others as "freedom fighters," corporate media ignored the US as the main source of global terrorism. Within "mainstream" discussions, such a suggestion is literally unthinkable, despite the extensive historical record. After World War II, the US provided a haven for Nazis fleeing Europe. Those terrorists were followed by others from Vietnam, Cuba, Haiti, and elsewhere, and the US sponsored terrorist states in Indonesia, Israel, and Turkey. The US provided training in techniques of torture, repression, and terror for tens of thousands of Latin American police and military officers in its School of the Americas (popularly known as the "School for Assassins," but more diplomatically renamed in 2000 as the "Western Hemisphere Institute for Security Cooperation") at Fort Benning, Georgia; many of the graduates went on to lead death squads in places such as El Salvador and Honduras and to distinguish themselves through the indiscriminate slaughter of thousands of Guatemalan peasants. Little of this information was considered relevant in "mainstream" media. For example, when the School of the Americas was mentioned by an audience member during a televised Canadian Broadcasting Corporation "town hall" meeting, news anchor Peter Mansbridge demonstrated his grasp of contemporary political reality by stating he was "not aware" of the institution and showed no interest in following up on its relevance.

The US record of support for terrorist activities in Latin America is a long and extremely bloody one. In the early 1980s the US funded training camps for Nicaraguan counter-revolutionists (the Contras), many of them remnants of the National Guard that had brutally repressed the population under the Somoza dictatorship. While the Contras carried out terrorist attacks on the civillian population, the US intensified its joint military exercises with Central American armies and in 1983 invaded Grenada. Many Nicaraguans believed their country was next. In addition to its trade embargo, the US blocked international loans to Nicaragua from the InterAmerican Development Bank, the International Monetary Fund and the World Bank. In 1984 the US mined Nicaragua's only shipping harbour, damaging international vessels as well as local fishing boats and killing a number of Nicaraguans. When the International Court of Justice condemned the US for the unlawful use of force, ordered it to stop its international terrorist actions, and pay reparations to

---

4. *The Globe and Mail*, 21 Sept. 2001: A10.

Nicaragua, the US simply dismissed the verdict. Plainly, within the terms imposed by the culture of prejudice, violent actions carried out to achieve political ends are recognized as "terrorism" only when conducted by others.

The US education and sponsorship of terrorists was not limited to Latin America. The US also created the Taliban and Osama bin Laden's network. After the Soviet Union's invasion of Afghanistan, the US deliberately fostered a network of "freedom fighters" drawn from the most fanatical Islamic circles to create a *jihad* against the Soviet Union. Secretly funded by the Central Intelligence Agency (CIA), working closely with Pakistan's intelligence agency, recruits from many Islamic countries were indoctrinated in Pakistan's religious schools and then sent to Afghanistan. Although the Soviet Union withdrew from Afghanistan in 1989, civil war continued between Afghan "freedom fighters" who had turned the Afghanistan-Pakistan border areas into the world's largest producer of opium and heroin. Profits from drug sales were ploughed back into the civil war and also to help spread the idea of *jihad* to Muslim fighters in Chechnya and Bosnia. After the US established military bases in Saudi Arabia in 1990, this fundamentalist network turned against those who created it.

In his September 20th address to a joint session of Congress, US President George W. Bush delivered an ultimatum to other nations: "Either you are with us or you are with the terrorists." Despite a great international outpouring of sympathy for the victims of the attack, such ultimatums reinforce the image of the US as global bully and mask the fact that the US itself is a major perpetrator and sponsor of international terrorism. The fact that the CIA had created the Taliban as part of a network of radical Islamic fundamentalists organized to serve US foreign policy during the battle against communism was conveniently overlooked in what was constructed as a battle between a completely innocent and good America and the forces of darkness. The legitimacy of bombing Afghanistan was scarcely questioned. Yet it is unlikely that those who applauded the US bombings would have found it acceptable for the Sandanista air force to have carpet-bombed Washington, D.C., in retaliation for US support for the Contra army that was conducting terrorist attacks to depose the Nicaraguan government in the 1980s.[5]

Bush announced that the US would respond to the September 11th attacks through "Operation Infinite Justice," quickly renamed "Enduring Freedom" after it was pointed out that the original name, along with Bush's call for a "crusade," would be interpreted as an insult to Muslims. The campaign was to include not only aerial bombardment and ground troops, but also a revival of the covert actions (such as the 1973 Chilean coup, the Phoenix program that killed 20,000 suspected communists in Vietnam, and attempts to assassinate Fidel Castro) that led to scandals in the 1970s and 1980s. US Secretary of State Colin Powell announced that the ban on assassination was "under review," and intelligence experts endorsed the plan. Michael

---

5. Noam Chomsky, "Crucial Questions in the 'Age of Terror,'" <http://monkeyfist.com/Chomsky Archive/essays/mirror_html> September 25, 2002.

Richardson, a former counter-terrorism officer in Canada's foreign affairs department, said, "The problem with [capturing suspects] is you need evidence to convict them in a court of law. It's much tidier all around if you just do away with them."[6]

Opinion polls claimed to show that the public supported bombing Afghanistan because they believed it would stop terrorism. In fact, the likely result would be the opposite as the bombings killed innocent people and created more hatred. As no doubt intended by the bombers, Muslims around the world quickly came to regard the retaliatory bombing of Afghanistan as an assault on their co-religionists. It was not only Bush's clumsy rhetoric that suggested this but also the prevailing intellectual culture of North America, where an astonishingly oversimplified book such as Samuel Huntington's *The Clash of Civilizations* could be heralded as insightful scholarship and become the ur-text for journalists seeking easy explanations for complex historical and political issues.[7] For example, in the *Globe and Mail*, William Johnson's absurd "Pit Bill" column used Huntington's book as the basis for his claim that Muslims were essentially war-like.[8] *Globe* columnist Margaret Wente took the same approach to argue that it was simply a fanatical hatred of modernity that led to the attacks: "The poison that flows through the veins of the suicide bombers does not come from America. It comes from their culture, not ours. The root causes are in their history, not ours."[9] In the *National Post*, Mark Steyn actually advised the West to take up the "White Man's Burden" and colonize Afghanistan in order to bring civilization to the benighted natives, as imperial powers had done so unselfishly elsewhere.[10] Corporate media rejected any suggestion that US foreign policy might be a relevant consideration in understanding the terrorist attacks. *Globe and Mail* correspondent Marcus Gee wrote that any attempt to examine root causes was simply "making excuses for terrorism."[11] The paper's editorial for September 19th demanded, "Have these people no decency?"[12] and asserted that "there is no parallel" between the attack and "what the United States may have done in the past" because during the Cold War "the United States wore the white hat." This surely was consoling news for the millions who suffered either directly from US violence or under the brutal dictatorships it sponsored around the world. The *Globe*'s anonymous editorial writer deliberately misrepresents the arguments of those who, reasonably, seek to under-

---

6. Alex Roslin, "Return of the Hit Men," *Now* 18-24 Oct. 2001: 19.

7. Samuel P. Huntington, *The Clash of Civilizations and the Remaking of World Order* (New York: Simon and Schuster, 1996).

8. *The Globe and Mail*, 11 Oct. 2001: A19.

9. *The Globe and Mail*, 22 Sept. 2001: A13.

10. *National Post*, 9 Oct. 2001: A1.

11. *The Globe and Mail*, 22 Sept. 2001: A13.

12. *The Globe and Mail*, 19 Sept. 2001: A14.

stand the context of September 11th, suggesting that they are attempting to excuse or justify terrorism and that they lack sympathy for the victims. The *National Post* kept up a constant flow of moronic ideological ranting, often crossing the line into overt racism and deliberately misrepresenting the views of anyone who dissented from the prevailing jingoistic mood it was helping to create. For example, Jonathan Kay claimed that the critics of US imperialism considered radical Islam "as a sort of liberation movement," despite the virtually universal condemnation of its fanatical and repressive ideology among those critics.[13] None of the rational critics of US imperialism suggested that Osama Bin Laden was a noble defender of the rights of Palestinians or Iraqis, but many pointed out that he was able to exploit the widespread feelings of bitterness created by US actions in the past. Bombing Afghanistan intensified those resentments and allowed fundamentalist organizers to depict it as a war against all Muslims.

While we should rightly express our sorrow for the thousands killed and our sympathy for their friends and families, we should also be aware that those who have paid the highest price for the terrorist attacks on the US are the innocent, impoverished, and oppressed people of Afghanistan. After their country was smashed into rubble by the Soviet Union's invasion and internecine warfare between rival Afghan gangs, they came under the control of the fundamentalist Taliban forces, who imposed a repressive theocratic regime. Having been the Taliban's main victims for years, the people of Afghanistan were then forced to suffer in their stead as they became collateral damage in the US-led "war on terrorism." Even before the bombing began, Afghanistan was devastated by decades of war. Millions of Afghans were surviving on international food aid, itself abruptly eliminated by the evacuation of international agencies, the sealing of the Pakistan border, and the beginning of bombing raids. With winter approaching and remote areas becoming inaccessible, international agencies appealed for an end to the bombing to prevent the starvation of four million people, but the US instead intensified its attacks. In the face of such massive need, sporadic US airdrops of food rations stood revealed as mere propaganda instruments. Thus, the immediate effect of US policy was to increase the suffering of those who were the Taliban's chief victims and who had no connection to terrorism.

The longer-term goals of the bombing campaign seemed hardly to have been considered in the drive for revenge. Replacing the Taliban with their opponents, the Northern Alliance, seems unlikely to improve conditions in Afghanistan. Although most Afghans despised the Taliban, the Northern Alliance was hardly a popular choice. During their previous power struggles with the Taliban, neither side had shown much concern for the welfare of the population as they blasted Kabul into dust. For many, ideological differences were probably less significant than ethnic ties and assessment

---

13. *National Post*, 9 Oct. 2001: A6.

of individual opportunities: as the US bombing continued in November, Taliban soldiers had begun to defect to Northern Alliance positions.

By immediately resorting to a retaliatory military strike, the US reduced the chances of achieving the goal of bringing the perpetrators to justice. Military force may have satisfied a thirst for revenge and appealed to the same sensibilities that led to Bush's bizarre musings about Old West "wanted dead or alive" posters, but it is unlikely to stop terrorism. Indeed, the spectacle of innocent civilians being killed in Afghanistan is more likely to increase bin Laden's popularity and support for a holy war. Although the Taliban stated that they would hand over bin Laden for trial if the US could supply evidence of his involvement, the option of using international law, which would have created far fewer new recruits for *jihad*, was never seriously considered.

The reaction to the September 11th attacks demonstrates some of the fundamental features of the culture of prejudice. Government and corporate media determined the dominant discourse and presented the US as an innocent victim. Rather than analyzing the historical and political context that had created such resentment, commentary focused solely on the repressive views of Islamic fundamentalists, arguing that the attacks had been motivated by their hatred of western freedoms. Certainly the terrorists' vision is fanatically narrow and any society they would create would be bleak and oppressive. However, their expressed grievances did not refer to issues of individual morality and democratic freedoms but to US policy in the Middle East: sanctions on Iraq, support for Israel's military occupation of Palestine, and the US bases in Saudi Arabia and support to corrupt regimes in the region. Certainly, these are serious issues worthy of attention and ones that, if addressed, could greatly reduce the suffering of many. Yet rather than attending to these matters and pursuing the September 11th terrorists through a police investigation and trial in a criminal court, the US immediately resorted to warfare. The stated aim of the US attack on Afghanistan, and in subsequent calls for war against Iraq, was to eliminate terror. Killing thousands of impoverished and oppressed Afghans (and placing millions at risk of starvation) and intensifying the suffering of the civilian population of Iraq seems an unlikely means to achieve such ends. The wisest way to protect against terrorists would be to rethink the policies that stem from a culture of prejudice and that have helped to create them.

John S. Sorenson

suggested readings

Adachi, Ken. *The Enemy That Never Was: A History of the Japanese Canadians.* Toronto: McClelland and Stewart, 1976.

Anderson, Benedict. *Imagined Communities: Reflections on the Origin and Spread of Nationalism.* London: Verso 1983.

Barkan, Elazar. *The Retreat of Scientific Racism: Changing Concepts of Race in Britain and the United States between the World Wars.* Cambridge: Cambridge University Press, 1992.

Cannon, Margaret. *The Invisible Empire: Racism in Canada.* Toronto: Random House of Canada, 1995.

Chomsky, Noam. *The Fateful Triangle: the United States, Israel and the Palestinians.* Boston: South End, 1983.

Delgado, Richard, and Jean Stefancic, eds. *Critical White Studies.* Philadelphia: Temple University, 1997.

Diamond, Sara. *Spiritual Warfare: The Theo-Politics of the Christian Right.* Montreal: Black Rose, 1990.

Eller, Jack David. *From Culture to Ethnicity to Conflict: An Anthropological Perspective on International Ethnic Conflict.* Ann Arbor: University of Michigan, 1999.

Hill, Mike, ed. *Whiteness: A Critical Reader.* New York: New York University, 1997.

Hockenos, Paul. *Free to Hate: The Rise of the Right in Post-Communist Eastern Europe.* New York: Routledge, 1993.

Kincheloe, Joe L, Shirley R. Steinberg, Nelson M. Rodriguez, and Ronald E. Chennault, eds. *White Reign: Deploying Whiteness in America.* New York: St. Martin's, 2000.

Lee, Martin A. *The Beast Reawakens.* Boston: Little, Brown and Co., 1997.

Marshall, Peter. *Demanding the Impossible: A History of Anarchism.* London: Fontana, 1993.

Matsuoka, Atsuko, and John Sorenson. *Ghosts and Shadows: Construction of Identity and Community in an African Diaspora.* Toronto: University of Toronto, 2001.

Said, Edward W. *The Question of Palestine*. New York: Vintage, 1979.

—. *The Politics of Dispossession: The Struggle for Palestinian Self-Determination, 1969-1994*. New York: Pantheon, 1994.

Scharfe, Sharon. *Complicity: Human Rights and Canadian Foreign Policy: The Case of East Timor*. Montreal: Black Rose, 1996.

Sorenson, John. *Imagining Ethiopia: Struggles for History and Identity in the Horn of Africa*. New Brunswick, NJ: Rutgers University, 1993.

colonialism & globalization

CHAPTER 7

"Third world poverty is the result of traditional values"

First world conceits about "backward" societies

Cultures of prejudice interpret Third World poverty as the result of internal factors such as absence of a work ethic or lack of morals: people are poor because they are "undeveloped," indicating technological retardation linked to cultural flaws. It is suggested that something in their culture holds them back from being as modern as we are. They are prisoners of "outdated traditional values." These "traditional values" are vaguely defined but they seem to include such things as local orientation, more emphasis on kinship and family than on individual success, less-sophisticated technology and, in some cases, less emphasis on acquisition of material wealth (although we should also be careful not to romanticize other societies in this respect). Western influence is offered as a remedy: if "traditional" values, customs, and social organization prevent Third World societies from developing, they must overcome these values and start taking risks, becoming innovative and entrepreneurial. The usual advice is to let the free market help these benighted folks. This argument completely inverts reality. It constructs those in the Third World as "people without history,"[1] stuck in the same unchanging culture they have had since time began. It obscures the historical creation of poverty and underdevelopment.

Understanding European colonialism is fundamental to understanding the dynamics of global history and contemporary power relations. The idea that people in the Third World live in traditional cultures untouched by the modern world is completely mistaken. What are taken for traditional societies should be more properly seen as the wreckage of such societies, products of centuries of violent interventions and transformations. In contrast to claims of the modernization theorists, poverty is not a product of "tradition" but was created by colonialism and a global system of stratification that emerged with European industrialization. European imperialism had an immense impact on the world, transforming whole societies, forms of production, cultures, and values. By coming to dominate the world, Europe created

---

1. Eric R. Wolf, *Europe and the People Without History* (Berkeley: University of California Press, 1982).

an international economy that fostered underdevelopment. European development was based on exploitation of people in its colonies, the blood and sweat of the Third World. The entire planet was pushed into a common culture of capitalism, but not all were integrated at the same level. Colonialism divided the world into developed and underdeveloped sectors through genocide, slavery, destruction of cultures, and disruption of ecological systems. Understanding the colonial impact allows us to reject assertions that the Third World can develop by emulating a Western model. No Western countries experienced anything remotely like what happened to the colonial regions: the complete transformation of social, political, and cultural life under foreign domination. The Third World was underdeveloped through colonization, and contemporary conditions in the Third World are directly linked to Europe's imperialist expansion.

"Colonialism" denotes the establishment of state control over another country while "colonization" refers to the creation of permanent foreign communities in another country; these two processes do not always accompany one another. Much of the colonialism in Africa and Asia did not involve establishment of large colonial settlements but instead involved rule through native staff, supervised by a few European administrators. "Imperialism" refers to theories, attitudes, and actions of an empire: the process of extending political control over another territory to protect trade or establish military bases. Marxists use the term "imperialism" to signify a specific economic process: capitalist accumulation on a world scale in an age of monopoly capitalism and the creation of a world market. J.A. Hobson's 1902 book *Imperialism*[2] argued that as a nation is industrialized, it becomes more difficult for merchants and financiers to make profits from their capital because production exceeds consumption: more goods are produced than can be sold for profit. An excess of capital exists so they pressure government to acquire overseas colonies that will provide markets and profitable investments. Others argue that seeing imperialism in purely economic terms is too limited and overlooks other factors, such as religious ideologies that urge missionary activities and doctrines of racial domination and cultural superiority. In general usage, imperialism indicates the oppression and exploitation of weaker countries by stronger ones and is associated with overseas expansion of Europe through conquest. It is used almost interchangeably with "colonialism."

In the mid-sixteenth century, various social forms existed outside Europe: preindustrial states, kingdoms, and chiefdoms, but much of the world was occupied by the self-sufficient, small-scale cultures often described as tribal societies. At that time Spain, Portugal, England, and France began to exert control over some areas of the "New World"; by 1914, European powers controlled 85 per cent of the world. Other social forms were swept aside by industrialized states. By the mid-twentieth century almost all tribal territory had been conquered. Although Portugal and Spain estab-

---

2. John A. Hobson, *Imperialism*, 3rd ed. (London: Allen and Unwin, 1938).

lished the first colonies in the sixteenth century, essentially as overseas feudal estates, many had become independent by the early nineteenth century. The main period of colonial expansion began in the mid-nineteenth century as a means to control overseas territory, to develop European capitalism by dominating resources and overseas markets. European rivals scrambled to establish control over land, people, and raw materials. By 1878 Britain, Russia, China, and the US controlled about half the world. Britain was the major colonial power from 1800 to 1945 and at its peak controlled a quarter of the world.

In most colonies a few Europeans dominated vast native populations, aided by local collaborators who got a share of the spoils. Military power supported capitalist development of resources, markets, and trade. A huge variety of pre-colonial cultures, including kingdoms, chiefdoms, pre-industrial states, and tribal groups, were drawn into this system in subordinate roles. Local modes of production were destroyed and replaced by forms that suited interests of European powers, who developed their economies by exploiting the resources, labour power, and markets of their colonies. American and European economic development was largely based on the enslavement of uncounted millions of Africans, who were often worked to death to produce cotton, sugar, and other raw materials. This flow of raw materials allowed the rise of European industry and development of new technology, in turn leading to new gains in the colonial scramble. While European economies developed, the colonies were underdeveloped, although the local bourgeoisie also profited from these relationships while the bulk of the population was impoverished.

Colonialism's most direct impact on the colonized world was expressed through violence. Millions of indigenous people were killed, some in direct military attacks, others enslaved and worked to death in gold and silver mines. Spain's conquest of South America wiped out all but a small percentage of the population within a few decades. Under Belgian control, perhaps as many as ten million people died in the Congo region. Some governments had deliberate genocidal policies to eliminate native populations, while others simply allowed settlers to kill natives with impunity. Defined as sub-human, indigenous people were killed for sport; the killers often put their heads on display just as hunters mount animal heads in grisly celebration.

Depopulation was also effected by diseases spread both accidentally and deliberately among indigenous populations who had no resistance to them. For example, European settlement of Australia began in 1788, but by 1798 smallpox epidemics were raging throughout the interior long before any direct contact with Europeans. Although Europeans slaughtered many Aborigines, most died from epidemics of tuberculosis, measles, leprosy, influenza, and venereal disease. Whole societies were decimated. For example, in North America at the beginning of the fur trade, Mandan society (in the upper Missouri River area) was rich and powerful, with thousands of people living in permanent towns. Smallpox epidemics began in 1764 and by the nineteenth century only a few dozen Mandan people were left alive. In general, the indigenous populations of the "New World" declined by 90 per cent under colonialism's genocidal impact. The most devastating consequence of colonial conquest was the extermination of millions of people and the destruction of entire societies. Some cultures were completely lost and others survive only in fragmented form. It was not only direct physical violence and disease that struck at indigenous cultures. Europeans considered indigenous societies inferior and set out to systematically destroy them, demanding that they accept European values and norms. Indigenous religions, languages, and customs were banned, as in the case of the Potlatch in British Columbia. Across Canada, Native children were forced into residential schools, indoctrination centres where their cultures were degraded and the children themselves were beaten and sexually abused.

The scale of European imperialism was unparalleled in history. Conflict and invasions were not new, but European colonialism differed in scale and technological advances guaranteed vast advantages in power. The basic aim was to exploit the raw materials, land, and labour of indigenous peoples. As land was confiscated and people were conscripted as labourers, they lost economic autonomy; European states took control of resources, undermined existing economies, and replaced them with profitable cash crops for export. Colonized groups lost autonomy as they were incorporated into state systems. Colonial powers often set up compliant chiefs as authorities, using them in their own interests. Colonialism created new countries as Europeans carved out zones of control, erecting borders where none had existed previously, creating cultural discontinuities by putting different groups under one administrative system or dividing one group on opposite sides of a border. Labour needs also created new ethnic confrontations, as when, for example, Tamils were imported to work on tea plantations in Sri Lanka.

The colonial system broke down after World War II when weakened European powers were less able to resist independence movements. Nevertheless, independence came only after long struggles, such as anti-colonial wars against the French in Algeria and Vietnam and against the Portuguese in Angola and Mozambique. In the aftermath of colonialism, new states were created as independent nations, but in some cases decolonization was protracted and created enduring conflicts. For example, in the 1950s Eritrea, a former Italian colony, was federated with Ethiopia instead of becoming independent, leading to decades of war that devastated the entire region. Although most colonies became independent in the 1960s, an international system of control still existed. National independence did not guarantee political freedom. Corrupt and repressive regimes took power; ethnic conflicts erupted in many former colonies. Economic structures of colonialism persisted: former colonies still provided raw materials while rich countries controlled prices, banking and currency systems, and markets for sale of goods. Formally independent former colonies found themselves inserted into a world economy, forced to trade in a capitalist market while occupying subordinate positions and with little control over prices for imports or exports. With limited scope for action, governments had to meet demands of more powerful nations in order to get loans, aid, foreign investment, and military aid. The most impoverished countries fell farther behind with little chance they would develop along the same path of modernization that the West had taken.

Colonialism created economies geared to external interests, often based on single-crop production for export and immediate profits while discouraging other crops, rapidly transforming local economies and weakening the subsistence base, with infrastructure developed for resource extraction rather than local needs. Post-independence governments inherited this structural imbalance and continued to concentrate on export crops while peasant agriculture received little support. Postcolonial economies remained narrow and undiversified. Dependency and disarticulated economies limited opportunities for change, maintaining the Third World as a source of primary products within an international division of labour. This had devastating consequences for Africa in particular, where food production has declined since the 1950s. This was not a general agricultural failure. Production of export crops intensified while food production shrunk. Franke and Chasin[3] describe how African governments were encouraged to neglect food production in favour of cash crops: cotton production rose in Burkina Faso while sorghum and millet cultivation declined; in Mali while thousands starved in the Sahel, cotton production soared. In Tanzania tobacco production increased as maize declined. African governments were encouraged to specialize in exporting certain raw materials. Many former colonies, all producing the same monocrops, were completely at the mercy of market fluctuations. Colonial powers had transformed local economies to serve their own needs. A key example is contemporary cattle culture, based on the taste for animal flesh, part of a global system with wide-ranging dysfunctional and destructive effects. In Africa, many societies used animals for subsistence, and for centuries herding was an effective subsistence strategy. Through migration and other techniques to maintain ecological balance, Africans ensured that their herds did not deplete the land base. However, the situation is different today. Much of Africa is used for cattle and overgrazing is a major problem, turning millions of acres into desert and threatening the environment and human survival.

What happened? Colonial rule forced fundamental changes by arbitrarily carving Africa into states with borders, preventing free movement of herds and forcing herders to concentrate animals in limited areas, causing overgrazing, soil erosion, and desertification. Rangeland was further restricted as colonial powers enclosed large areas to grow cash crops such as peanuts and cotton which rapidly deplete soil, and herders were pushed to more fragile, marginal areas. All states dislike nomads: they are hard to manage. Decolonization did not change this: African governments also wanted to

---

3.   Richard W. Franke and Barbara H. Chasin, *Seeds of Famine* (Totowa, NJ: Rowman and Allanheld, 1980).

control populations and encouraged nomads to settle. One tactic was to drill wells to encourage sedentarism through a constant water supply. When nomads did establish semi-permanent settlements around these wells, surrounding areas were soon stripped of vegetation because too many cattle were restricted in limited areas.

Many African states turned to ranching to get a share of profits from Western markets for flesh. To protect commercial herds, vast areas were fenced in, disrupting migration of wild animals, many of which disappeared. International organizations encouraged larger cattle herds, overlooking the environmental impact. Commercial ranches pushed herders into more marginal areas, degrading the soil and turning fertile land into desert, exacerbating drought and creating famine: hundreds of thousands died in 1968-73 and 1982-84. Survivors became environmental refugees, deserting their communities for emergency relief centres or to eke out a squalid existence in bulging urban centres. The modern cattle complex is destroying Africa. Areas that were once lush and forested have been stripped of vegetation, eroded, and transformed into deserts. Millions of people are trapped on the verge of ecological collapse.

Cattle ranching also devastated Central America. Since 1960 over a quarter of Central America's forests have been cut to create pasture. Two-thirds of agricultural land is taken up by livestock, much of it sold to North America. Cheap hamburgers mean ecological disaster, social inequality, and violence in Central America. Half the peasants in Central America are landless, while elite families and transnational corporations own most of the land. Cattle ranching has boomed in Central America as US corporations invest heavily, providing equipment and technological support as well as money, weapons, and military training to repressive governments that protect corporate interests through horrifying violence directed against peasants and labour unions.

The same pattern exists throughout Latin America: a few families own everything while the majority of peasants are impoverished and displaced. Forests are cleared and the indigenous population is slaughtered. For example, in Brazil a few people own 80 per cent of the land and the vast majority of rural households are landless. In the 1960s the Brazilian government launched a plan to turn the Amazon forest into commercially productive land, giving huge tax breaks to ranchers and multinational corporations. Thousands of acres were deforested for millions of cattle. However, ranching is extremely inefficient since the land is unsuited for grazing; the thin soil is soon depleted and new areas are cleared so much of the forest is burned. Ranching on a colossal scale, covering millions of acres, constitutes a major environmental threat: the Amazon forests harbour over half of all living species on Earth and much of the planet's genetic diversity is being burned and bulldozed out of existence. There are also human costs to clearing the forest: Native people in the Americas have been under assault for the last 500 years, and in the Amazon pressure has increased tremendously since the 1960s as ranchers have sought land for cattle. Native people are under extreme pressure from direct occupation of land by ranchers and for road construction. Many indigenous peoples were massacred, but others were also affected by disease, malnutrition, and mercury poisoning from mining operations.

Given these massive transformations of environment and society, it is unconvincing to argue that problems of underdevelopment are a result of traditional attitudes. Third World impoverishment is due not to lack of a work ethic (and, in fact, most of the world's poor work constantly simply to feed themselves) but rather to the fact that the Third World has been working for the benefit of others for many centuries.

John S. Sorenson

CHAPTER 8

"The USA promotes freedom throughout the world"

America as saviour of the global community

Among the after-effects of the September 11th terrorist attacks on the World Trade Center and the Pentagon was the constraint on dissent and the characterization of opposition to the bombing of innocent civilians in Afghanistan as "anti-Americanism." A prime example is the reaction to an October 2001 speech by University of British Columbia professor Sunera Thobani at a conference in Ottawa.[1] Corporate media seized on her characterization of US policy as "soaked in blood" and presented her as a heartless ideologue and hate-monger. A *Globe and Mail* editorial denounced her "poisonous diatribe" as "just another chance to berate the Americans,"[2] while *Globe* columnist Margaret Wente described Thobani as "an idiot."[3] Just as charges of "anti-Semitism" are often used in an opportunistic and cynical way to undermine valid criticisms of Israeli policies, so does the term "anti-Americanism" serve to discredit critical thinking about the role of the US in a global culture of prejudice.

Understanding the steady decline of social and political conditions in the Third World since the end of World War II requires discussion of US imperialism. The US is often presented as a guardian of freedom and democracy. This ignores a long history of terrorism that begins with efforts to exterminate the indigenous population, includes the enslavement of millions of Africans, and continues through international military intervention and subversion. Since 1945, the US has pursued a program for global control, not freedom. Global domination was presented as a fight against communism, a struggle between forces of good and evil, and the US military was built up on the basis of deliberately exaggerated estimates of Soviet strength. Despite its rhetoric, the Soviet Union was anti-socialist and extremely repressive, as amply demonstrated by executions, deportations, concentration camps, starvation,

---

1. See the Epilogue to this book.

2. *The Globe and Mail*, 3 Oct. 2001: A16.

3. *The Globe and Mail*, 4 Oct. 2001: A19.

persecution, military interventions in East Europe, invasion of Afghanistan, and support for Third World dictatorships such as the Mengistu regime in Ethiopia. Before its eventual collapse in the 1980s, the Soviet Union's interventions were more limited in scope than those of the US.

From 1945 to the mid-1990s, the US military was deployed beyond its borders over 200 times. This included large-scale wars in Korea and Indochina along with various small wars and counter-insurgency operations in Central America, Africa, Asia, and the Middle East. US plans for post-war world order were laid out in 1950s *National Security Council Memorandum 68*, which Noam Chomsky describes as a key planning document of the US government, outlining two major post-war policies: to destroy the Soviet system and to create a global environment in which the US would preserve its wealth and power. In 1948 George Kennan, State Department Director of Policy Planning, noted,

> We have 50% of the world's wealth but only 6.3% of its population. In this situation we cannot fail to be the object of envy and resentment. Our real task in the coming period is to devise a pattern of relationships which will allow us to maintain this position of disparity.... We should cease to talk about the raising of the living standards, human rights and democratization. The day is not far off when we are going to have to deal in straight power concepts. The less we are then hampered by idealistic slogans, the better."[4]

To a large extent, the US has been able to maintain this division of wealth. In 1992, the United Nations found 83 per cent of the world's wealth concentrated in the North, benefitting 20 per cent of the world's population. The gap between rich and poor is growing: in 1960, the wealthiest nations were 30 times richer than the poorest; in 1990 they were 60 times richer. Distribution of wealth within countries shows the richest 20 per cent of the world's people are 150 times richer than the poorest 20 per cent.[5]

US planners exaggerated Soviet threats as a means to mobilize support for intervention in the Third World and to justify murder, torture, and repression. They warned that communism would find a receptive audience in the Third World so the US had to intervene aggressively. While claiming to act in the interests of freedom and democracy, the US tried to *prevent* democracy in the Third World, as well as at home.

Military spending was considered the key to US economic development, but it was necessary to convince the population to support military budgets and cut social spending. A standard propaganda device to mobilize reluctant populations is the threat of an evil enemy. The Soviet threat was used to gain support for unpopular policies

4. Quoted in Noam Chomsky, *Turning the Tide* (Montreal: Black Rose, 1986) 48.

5. United Nations Development Program *Human Development Report* (New York, 1992).

of increased military spending and to justify internal repression in the US. Corporate-funded anti-communist propaganda helped to weaken the labour movement and strengthen the power of business. The Soviet threat also was used to build an industrial system based on military production, which helped to secure corporate power and establish a world order in the interests of US corporations.

The real Soviet threat was not its inferior military capacity, but its ideological challenge to US domination. For its own purposes, the Soviet Union supported states like Cuba and Nicaragua that tried to avoid total US domination and blocked full exploitation of areas intended to provide raw materials, markets, and cheap labour. To crush such threats, the US supported military regimes in the Third World, training tens of thousands of Third World military and police officers in its School of the Americas, where they were indoctrinated in capitalist ideology and trained to use torture and terrorize civilian populations.

Major human-rights violators received consistent US aid. Before World War II, strong support existed for fascism in Italy, Germany, and Spain because fascism was regarded as legitimate self-defence of the rich and the middle classes against redistribution of wealth or "communism." US government and business leaders praised German and Italian fascist leaders as "moderates," just as similar appraisals were later made of various gangsters and killers who served US business interests in the Third World. Many US capitalists invested in Nazi war production, and major US corporations had Nazi connections. Along with their financial links, US business elites shared Nazi racist ideologies.

Although support for fascism waned when it threatened Western interests, it soon resumed. After World War II, fascist leaders were restored in North Africa, Italy, and Greece and democracy was subverted. US and British business interests worried about post-war conditions in Europe. Many elites had been fascist, while socialist and communist resistance and anti-fascist movements had gained prestige and were aligned with the working class and the poor. Western elites feared "disorder" (i.e., threats to their interests) and sought to destroy popular forces, block union movements, avert democracy, and rebuild the old political order. To achieve these goals, US intelligence recruited Nazis to help destroy anti-fascist resistance. For example, Klaus Barbie, the "Butcher of Lyon," was employed by US military intelligence and was later sent to Bolivia, where he worked with the CIA, became involved in the drug trade, and in 1980 helped engineer a military coup. The US also paid Walter Rauff (inventor of the portable gas chamber) to block communist influence in Italy; he was later sent to Chile, where he worked with military intelligence and established a base for neo-fascist groups. Walter Schreiber, Nazi chief of medical science who experimented on concentration camp inmates, went to Texas as a consultant for the US Air Force; he was sent to Argentina in 1952. Throughout Latin America, the US employed German Nazis to help repress leftist groups, to establish links with fascist elements of the military, and to support neo-Nazi regimes.

The US emerged from World War II with unprecedented economic and military power and set about designing a global system to suit US interests, that is, those of business elites. This called for reconstruction of European and Japanese capitalism. In 1947, the Marshall Plan instituted large-scale initiatives to reconstruct Europe, prevent communism, avert the collapse of the US export trade, preserve private enterprise, and restore business allies who had been discredited by fascist involvement. Japanese ruling classes were also re-established through US intervention, while working-class and communist movements were crushed.

The US intervened in various countries to achieve its goals. In Greece, the US supported right-wing forces against the Democratic Army of Greece (the popular communist-led resistance that fought the Nazis). In 1947, the US announced that all Greek political and economic matters would become its responsibility and launched counter-insurgency operations to prevent independent nationalism in Greece, which it saw as a threat to US control of Middle East oil. Thousands were killed, tortured, arrested, and placed in concentration camps. Although left-wing forces were defeated in 1949, the US continued to control Greek affairs, and from 1967 to 1974 Greece was ruled by a CIA-sponsored dictatorship.

Similarly, the US helped to overthrow Iran's parliamentary system in 1953 and re-established dictatorship under the Shah, hoping to gain control of vast oil reserves. After the CIA backed the Shah's coup, US companies obtained 40 per cent of oil concessions (previously controlled by Britain). Extremely corrupt, the Shah used US power to obtain his goals, and ruled through repression. SAVAK, the secret police created and trained by the CIA and Israel's MOSSAD covert operations unit, used torture regularly. Repression under the Shah and US support for torture and murder encouraged Iranians to regard Western lifestyles as corrupt and contributed to the eventual rise of Islamic fundamentalism.

Intervention in the Philippines is rooted in US colonization in the nineteenth century. Thousands were slaughtered in a brutal war directed against the civilian population by the same US troops that had recently been used to exterminate much of the indigenous population of North America; the same racist ideology fuelled both genocidal efforts. US colonization lasted until 1946, despite a brief Japanese occupation, and the economy was dominated by the US and a small, local land-owning elite. When the Philippines received nominal independence, the Communist Party, which had led anti-Japanese forces during World War II, was suppressed with US assistance. Ferdinand Marcos, who became president in 1965, was one of the Third World's most corrupt leaders, transferring huge amounts of public funds into his own accounts and those of family and friends, while transforming the military into his personal army. While Marcos and his friends enjoyed fabulous wealth, most of the population were desperately poor, without health care, education or housing. Cheap labour and generous tax breaks for foreign investment allowed US corporations to operate with extremely low costs. Expansion of export-oriented agriculture dispossessed the peasants, rendering the majority landless, created deforestation, reduced food production for local consumption, and resulted in widespread disease and malnutrition. Opposition was repressed through extensive human rights violations, including torture and assassination by the US trained police and military. Although an earlier peasant-based guerrilla insurgency in the 1950s was smashed with US military aid, advisors, and counter-insurgency operations, the New People's Army launched a guerrilla war. Again the US helped the military to crush the opposition that had spread through most levels of society; this opposition had taken an anti-US character because the US had supported Marcos' depredations to achieve its own interests (just as backing the Shah created anti-West opposition in Iran). The US wanted to use Marcos as a puppet but found it hard to control his greed. This avarice created strong opposition, and eventually the US tried to distance itself from him. Although Marcos was eventually deposed in 1986, guerrilla war did not end and US military aid continued under Corazon Aquino. CIA involvement in counter-insurgency increased, helped by fanatical right-wing Christian fundamentalist groups who encourage vigilante death squads to kill communists, union activists, and more liberal religious leaders. Opposition continues because the conditions that created it, the desperately poor situation of the majority of the population, have not changed.

In Latin America, the US has substantial economic interests that it does not want threatened by nationalism or calls for social justice. US planners saw the military as an ally and removed other leaders who interfered with US business interests. For example, in Guatemala the CIA organized a 1954 coup to depose the government of Jacobo Arbenz, who had been reluctant to grant oil concessions to US companies and introduced land reform that affected the giant United Fruit Corporation. Arbenz wanted United Fruit to improve conditions by paying a minimum wage that would allow workers to avoid malnutrition and starvation. The government also expropriated unused land of United Fruit and gave it to peasants so they could feed themselves, and offered to pay compensation to the corporation. United Fruit, with close links to the US government, lobbied for the overthrow of Arbenz, pointing out that agrarian reform was a dangerous threat that might appeal to workers and peasants elsewhere who were similarly oppressed by local ruling classes and US corporations and who might aspire to a minimum standard of living. The US government and United Fruit cooperated in a massive propaganda campaign, warning that Guatemala had been taken over by communists and that a serious threat from the Soviet Union existed. The US supported military officers connected to Guatemala's oligarchy who were unhappy about land reform. The coup restored United Fruit's land and reversed social reform, dismantling co-ops and literacy programs. Thousands of Guatemalans—teachers, unionists, students, and peasants—disappeared or were arrested or murdered. The pattern continued: death squads, massacres, and torture designed to terrorize the population and keep them in squalor while large land-owners and US corporations profited. For decades, the US continued to support a series of brutal dictators in Guatemala.

The development model imposed on Guatemala was much the same as else-where in Latin America: a focus on cattle and agricultural products for export. The results of development included extensive deforestation, destruction of subsistence agriculture, impoverishment of most of the population, hunger, malnutrition, gen-eralized misery and fear, pesticide poisoning, genocidal attacks on villages that might provide assistance to anti-government guerrillas (themselves created by these conditions) with over 100,000 killed, thousands missing, forced relocation, mass refugee move-ments, slavery, and child prostitution. Such conditions offered US corporations a good climate for business: workers earned a few dollars for a sixteen hour day in appalling conditions and union organizers were murdered. Eventually, global recession, falling prices, rising inflation and unemployment, and high military spending created eco-nomic disaster and convinced the junta to allow a civilian government to take over, although they would still control it and block investigation of human rights violations.

These few examples are part of a much longer record of US brutality. Seeking hege-mony in Asia in the 1960s, the US destroyed Vietnam, Laos, and Cambodia through saturation bombing. In Chile, a CIA-directed coup deposed the elected Allende gov-ernment and resulted in the deaths of thousands. The US provided lists of "com-munists" (a conveniently all-inclusive term) for the Indonesian military junta, who killed up to a million people in 1965, and supported the same murderers in their geno-cidal attack on East Timor. The US supported death squads in El Salvador and sup-plied the terrorist Contra guerrillas in their efforts to overthrow the Sandinista government of Nicaragua. The US has supported fascist regimes around the world, backed the apartheid state in South Africa, supported Israel's invasion of Lebanon and its ongoing occupation of Palestine, and maintained its long and destructive embargo on Cuba. The US has invaded or bombed countries such as Grenada, Haiti, Libya, Panama and Sudan. The bombing of Iraq and sanctions against that country have killed up to a million people. The US provides major support to the governments of Colombia and Turkey, both of which have terrorized and attacked their own populations. These cases demonstrate how the US government has used violence and terrorism to maintain the structural inequalities of global capitalism.

Rather than promoting freedom throughout the world, the US has carried out a comprehensive program of state terrorism through officially declared wars and through counter-insurgency operations. It has attacked civilian populations, deposed governments, and created and maintained some of the world's most vicious dictatorships. These activities have helped to create a globalized culture of prejudice in which the bulk of the world's population is denied even their most basic needs while a small elite enjoys fantastic wealth and power. Those who applaud the USA as a defender of global freedom should bear in mind these historical realities. To point them out is neither to engage in "anti-Americanism" nor to ignore the brutality of other states, but merely to recognize that all states serve the interests of the rich and the powerful and that the US is dedicated to serving these interests on a global scale.

The campaign to dismiss critical analysis as "anti-Americanism" demonstrates the ubiquity of hegemonic power in the culture of prejudice and the ability to redefine historical and political realities. The actual record of violence and terrorism conducted in the service of US business interests and strategic goals is seldom allowed to intrude upon the picture of altruism and saintly beneficence that is constructed in corporate media and in the statements of business and political leaders. Since September 11, 2001, the US has been portrayed as the innocent victim of international terrorism rather than as its main perpetrator and sponsor. The atrocities of US imperialism are ignored and even the term "imperialism" itself rarely figures. When it does, it is immediately rejected. For example, columnist Margaret Wente dismisses charges of imperialism as a mistaken notion of a foolish intelligentsia as she praises President George W. Bush (and by extension the US): "Actually he's not an imperialist. He's a genuine idealist, who wants to spread democracy and freedom because he thinks those things will make people happier and better off and the US more secure."[6] While dissident voices are not completely banned, the corporate control of mass media ensures that they are marginalized. The power of corporate media ensures the dissemination of propaganda that portrays the US as the sentinel of freedom. It is the role of critical scholars to challenge these hegemonic depictions and the apologists for imperialism and international terrorism.

John S. Sorenson

---

6. *The Globe and Mail*, 7 Nov. 2002: A25.

CHAPTER 9

"Free markets pave the way for social development"

The World Trade Organization as benign force for social good

Advocates of "free markets" (or what used to be called capitalism) insist that these will benefit social development and increase everyone's happiness. This seems highly unlikely, given that in fact free markets do not exist and that all of the so-called "developed" nations have attained their prosperity through vigorous intervention from powerful states. What the advocates of "free markets" are actually demanding is that they should be freed from any intervention from the state that might interfere with their profits. Of course, intervention by the state and the provision of subsidies from public funds will still be welcomed in the form of tax benefits, training, and start-up programs, or if profits take a downturn and a bail-out is needed to avoid market discipline.

The so-called "free market" system is actually a plan to establish the global domination of wealthy corporations. The corporations promoting the "free market" agenda are among the strongest economic powers in the world. Over half the world's largest economies are corporations, not countries, and many corporations have larger revenues than that of many nations combined. Although there are tens of thousands of transnational corporations, most of them are based in Europe, Japan, and North America. The size and power of these corporations mean that they have been able to exert a strong influence over national governments, which are themselves largely composed of individuals with direct links to major corporations and who share the same goals and values. Over the last several decades, the transnationals have succeeded in substantially driving down the corporate tax rate in virtually all industrialized countries. Through their powerful lobby groups and influence over mass media, they have been able to shape the analysis of public affairs.

The government of Canada, under the influence of lobby groups such as the Business Roundtable and think-tanks such as the Fraser Institute, has been a vigorous supporter of the corporate free-trade agenda. Canada was a proponent of the *North American Free Trade Agreement* (NAFTA), the regional pact that was instrumental in establishing corporate domination. While advocates of the NAFTA argued that jobs would be created, groups such as the Council of Canadians have pointed out that these have been mainly low-waged, non-union, service-sector positions and the overall result has been a net loss of jobs. The NAFTA was to be followed by the *Multilateral Agreement on Investments* (MAI), and Canada again was a major cheerleader for this agreement, which would have established a system of complete freedom for corporations. Negotiations for the MAI were done in secret and were only exposed when Canadian activists used the Internet to circulate the secret documents. The MAI would have given even greater power to corporations by according them the same legal status as nations. Under the MAI, corporations would have had the right to enforce their interests through their power to sue governments over any laws that might affect their profit or even their potential to profit. Corporations would have received the power to challenge public funding of essential services and social programs as unfair subsidies that would interfere with the free market. Any public services that could still exist in such a context would have been legally required to operate with the same criteria as for-profit businesses. Foreign investors would not have been required to demonstrate any local benefits. Essentially, the MAI would have allowed corporations the right to determine how they would operate globally while reducing the power of governments and their citizens. Fortunately, the MAI was overturned by the massive public protests that followed the exposure of the secret plans.

However, having failed to impose the MAI, advocates of free markets have sought to introduce its provisions through other treaties such as the *Free Trade Agreement of the Americas* and through organizations such as the World Trade Organization (WTO). The WTO was established in 1995 through the Uruguay Round of the *General Agreement on Trade and Tariffs* (GATT). The focus of GATT was to promote trade by the elimination of tariffs, but the WTO has gone beyond this and is dedicated to eliminating non-tariff barriers to trade. Essentially, this means the elimination of all national legislation that seeks to protect the environment, support public health, and secure the rights of workers and consumers. All other values are subordinated to "trade," which essentially means ensuring profits to corporations. The creation of the WTO meant that corporations would now be served by a global organization with the power to make and unmake laws in their own interest against those of national governments.

The WTO is based in Geneva, Switzerland, and is staffed by squads of bureaucrats. Although all 137 member countries supposedly have equal input into the WTO, in reality it is dominated by what is known as the Quad: Canada, the European Union, Japan, and the US. These states have many negotiators who exert a key influence over the organization and they work in the interests of their own nationally based corporations. Corporations also exert their interest over the WTO through the work of lobbyists, consultants, and advisory committees, which are composed almost entirely of representatives from major industries. Unions, environmentalists, human rights groups, non-governmental organizations, and consumer associations are excluded. Essentially, the WTO is a mechanism designed to ensure the supremacy of corporate interests over those of people. The WTO was created in order to shift decision-making powers away from national governments (which are, of course, reflective of internal structures of class and power but where there is at least the potential for people to advocate for their rights and interests) and deliver these powers into the hands of secretive panels of unaccountable bureaucrats. The WTO's charter specifies that member states must ensure that their laws conform to the international standards developed through various multilateral agreements. Member states, acting at corporate behest, are then able to challenge the laws of any other state if they believe such laws may interfere with their ability to profit. Any law designed to improve the well-being of citizens, to promote public health or protect the environment can be challenged if it interferes with a corporation's ability to make money. In this context, European corporations have opposed environmental laws in North America while North American corporations have beaten down such regulations in Europe. Through such harmonization of standards, corporations can ensure that advanced standards of environmental and labour legislation can be rolled back to minimum levels. States that do not change their laws to conform to WTO standards are to be punished by severe trade sanctions.

The WTO's deliberations on trade disputes are held in closed sessions. The panelists who judge the disputes are selected on the basis of past experience in GATT, membership on national trade delegations or as lawyers who have advocated in a previous trade dispute, ensuring a uniform perspective. No conflict-of-interest guidelines exist and there is no requirement to consult independent experts. All data are confidential; no documents or transcripts are released and there is no review of the proceedings. Ordinary citizens and organizations formed to serve public interest are not only barred from attending WTO meetings but are also unable to obtain details of the proceedings or to launch appeals against any WTO decisions. By shifting power away from national governments and placing it in the hands of these unelected bureaucrats, the WTO is fundamentally anti-democratic. The WTO's guiding principle, taken from the culture of corporate capitalism it serves, is that of trusteeship or fiduciary duty: profits must be maximized and all expenditures must be minimized, even if this means eliminating protection for the environment or workers or any social benefits.

The WTO requires all countries to adopt legislation that is least restrictive to trade. It is dedicated to eliminating any differential treatment related to how products are produced. Thus, countries will not be allowed to place any restrictions on products that damage the environment, that are produced through the use of child or slave labour, or that involve the suffering of animals. Concern for trade always predominates over any concern for the environment, health or safety, and the WTO has consistently opposed any regulations that seek to offer protection in these areas. The WTO wants to privatize all public services in education and health; corporations eagerly anticipate the profits that will flow to them after the dismantling of public health care. Without restrictions on corporate activity, every country faces pressure to lower wages, reduce taxes, and eliminate any environmental protection that may constitute an obstacle to corporate profit. The effect is to create a race to the bottom.

Many of the WTO's rulings have been directed toward the elimination of food-safety standards. Rather than creating rules that would guard people from dangerous products, the WTO has insisted that before any product can be banned, it must be proven to be unsafe. This inverts the logic of the Precautionary Principle, which advises that scientific evidence of risk is a sufficient reason to prevent the sale of a product. Apart from the obvious ethical imperative to prevent harm, the Precautionary Principle also makes sense in terms of cost-effectiveness, since the expense of dealing with the consequences of exposure to toxic material can far outweigh any costs of prevention. The WTO ignores these rational measures and places the burden on states to furnish irrefutable scientific evidence that a product is harmful or dangerous rather than requiring corporations to demonstrate that their products are safe. For example, when Australia tried to ban imports of live salmon, fearing contamination of local stocks, the WTO ruled that Australia would first have to conclusively demonstrate the harmful effect. Needless to say, corporate-funded lawyers are always on hand to question the matter of what constitutes conclusive proof. Whereas common sense would suggest that conclusive proof of a product's safety should exist before it is marketed, the WTO reverses this logic and forces people and governments to prove the danger. Clearly, the WTO puts profits before people.

The WTO promotes a downward harmonization of standards on safety and environmental protection. These standards are already set far too low due to extensive corporate influence. However, the WTO seeks to drive them down even further. Any country that seeks to adopt or maintain laws that are more protective of public health and safety or of the environment must face a long and expensive struggle to prove their case. For example, the WTO's *Sanitary and Phytosanitary Standards Agreement* (SPSA) states that food safety must be based on the standards set by the Codex Alimentarius, an organization heavily influenced by corporate interests. The SPSA rejects the Precautionary Principle by demanding not simply a scientific demonstration of risk but requiring conclusive proof of harm and proof that the chosen response is appropriate.

In 1997, North American meat companies and biotechnology interests were behind the WTO's ruling against the European Union's ban on beef laced with hormones shown to be carcinogenic. The WTO ruled that the European Union would have to import the hormone-infected beef from the US because no conclusive long-term data existed to prove that ingesting the hormones in beef was harmful, even though the hormones themselves had been proven to cause cancer. When the EU decided to continue with its ban on the tainted beef, the US imposed retaliatory tariffs on imports that have cost millions.

The WTO has already had a negative impact in environmental terms. It has undermined legislation that was created through years of determined effort and was intended to protect endangered species and the environment. For example, following the shameful precedent of the 1991 GATT panel that ruled against the US government's *Marine Mammal Protection Act* (which had prohibited use of purse seine nets that were killing millions of dolphins along with the intended tuna catch), in 1998 a WTO panel rejected the US *Endangered Species Act*, which had sought to protect sea turtles from shrimp nets. Canada and the US used the WTO to oppose the European Union's prohibition against the use of vicious leg-hold traps against fur-bearing animals.

The WTO has also given a green light to corporations that pollute the environment. For example, in its very first ruling the WTO demonstrated that it put corporate profits above environmental safety: in 1996, a WTO panel ruled that the US *Clean Air Act*, which was intended to reduce gasoline emissions, violated trade rules. This attack on environmental protection laws set the pace for successive rulings. The US and the European Union used the WTO to oppose a Japanese law that would lower polluting emissions levels from cars, while US electronics corporations used the WTO to reject European Union proposals to limit industrial pollution. In 1996, a US corporate lobby group pushed the WTO to end eco-labelling of various products to evade the EU's policies in favour of recycled paper. In 1998, Canada used the WTO to challenge a French ban on asbestos, a proven carcinogen; as the world's second-largest exporter of asbestos, Canada argued that safety of this material could be ensured through proper use.

The record of WTO rulings constitutes a determined assault on environmental protection legislation in the interests of corporate profits. With remarkable consistency, the WTO has ruled against every single environmental protection policy it has reviewed. There has been a similar consistency in WTO decisions about the health and safety legislation it has reviewed.

The WTO undermines the power of governments to enact any legislation that might serve non-commercial objectives, and indeed demands that governments act only with commercial objectives. For example, when some US municipal and state governments used selective purchasing to avoid support to the military dictatorship of Burma, corporate groups rushed to quash this threat to their profits. The European Union and Japan argued that this violated the WTO ruling that government purchasing should be based on economic criteria alone.

Through measures such as the *Trade Related Aspects of Intellectual Property* (TRIPS) agreement, the WTO ensures that vital food and medicine resources are appropriated by corporations. Under TRIPS, all countries must adopt US-style patent rights; this allows corporations to acquire and patent local knowledge and genetic and biological resources, even if these have been developed over many generations by indigenous communities. Pharmaceutical and agricultural corporations can simply appropriate the knowledge developed by local communities and claim exclusive control over that knowledge. A well-known case is that of the neem tree, used for centuries by indigenous people in India for a wide variety of medicinal purposes as well as for fuel and building material; Indian scientific research in the twentieth-century encouraged further development. Ignoring this collective form of "ownership," the US-based corporations W.R. Grace and the Native Plant Institute and Japan's Terumo corporation have now claimed patents on neem products. Profits from its monopoly on these products will flow to the corporation, not to the local communities who developed the use of the neem tree. Similarly, corporations are claiming ownership of seed varieties developed by indigenous farmers in India.

Although public protest prevented implementation of the MAI, the WTO is determined to achieve the same ends through other means. The *General Agreement on Trade in Services* (GATS) is essentially the MAI in a new guise. Article VI.4 of the GATS provides a means by which the WTO establishes its own power over that of governments by giving the GATS Disputes Panels final veto over government decisions. The Panel will determine if any law or regulation is "more burdensome than necessary" to the interests of trade. This means that rather than an elected government being the body that acts to balance the rights of citizens and the environment against those of corporations, this power will be ceded to the GATS Panel. Governments will become, at best, consultants to the process, but their main role will be to implement the GATS Panel's decisions. Whereas NAFTA's Necessity Test requires that states must adopt the measures that are least restrictive to trade, GATS ensures that government laws and regulations will be eliminated if they interfere with trade. This provides corporations with a means to eliminate any laws that stand in the way of their profits. The goal of protecting the public's interest would not be an acceptable defence of national laws against corporate interests.

Unlike governments, which are at least sometimes required to hold public hearings with debates and evidence, the GATS decisions are to be made in secret meetings. Not only would the meetings exclude the public, unions, non-governmental organizations, human rights groups, media, and so on, but no records of the meetings would be made available. In other words, the WTO intends to use GATS as a means to override democracy and implement corporate rule. The WTO serves the interests of powerful corporations at the expense of the global public and the environment. Tens of thousands of people have realized this and taken to the streets to protest WTO meetings. The response has come in the form of tear gas and clubs, as police forces are deployed to impose the corporate "free trade" agenda on citizens who do not want it.

Under this system, all other values are to be subordinated to those of trade and profit. All laws relating to health, safety, the environment, animal protection, and consumer welfare are to be scrapped if they interfere with trade, as they necessarily will. None of these vital concerns are to be considered on a par with profits. Trade is to be promoted even if this undermines the quality of life for masses of people, devastates the environment, and leads to species extinction. Through its sanctions, the WTO is dedicated to weakening the ability of governments to act in the interests of their citizens. Instead, governments will be forced to become the servants of corporations. Governments will be prevented from adopting any new legislation that can protect them from the ravages of corporate predators. The WTO will have the power to rule on the legitimacy of national laws and to strike them down if they interfere with corporate profits.

While the rhetoric of "free trade" suggests that eliminating government red tape and allowing the market to operate without interference will create a better world for all, the results so far indicate a disaster for the environment, workers, and the poor, while a small corporate elite skims off massive profits. Rather than eliminating restrictions on trade, what is required are *more* regulations. These regulations should ensure the primacy of environmental protection, the promotion of human rights, and improvement in the conditions of life for oppressed and exploited groups. Abolishing the WTO is a necessary first step in achieving these goals.

John S. Sorenson

suggested readings

Ali, Tariq. *The Clash of Fundamentalisms: Crusades, Jihads and Modernity*. London: Verso, 2002.

Bukharin, Nikolai. *Imperialism and World* Economy. New York: Monthly Review Press, 1973.

Chomsky, Noam. *Turning the Tide: U.S. Intervention in Central America and the Struggle for Peace*. Montreal: Black Rose, 1986.

——. *Profit Over People: Neoliberalism and Global Order*. New York: Seven Stories, 1999.

Clarke, Tony, and Maude Barlow. *MAI: The Multinational Agreement on Investment and the Threat to American Freedom*. Toronto: Stoddart, 1997.

Dobbin, Murray. *The Myth of the Good Corporate Citizen*. Toronto: Stoddart, 1998.

Ellwood, Wayne. *The No-Nonsense Guide to Globalization*. Toronto: Between the Lines, 2001.

Fanon, Frantz. *The Wretched of the Earth*. New York: Grove, 1968.

Kiernan, V.G. *Imperialism and Its Contradictions*. New York and London: Routledge, 1995.

Kolko, Gabriel. *Confronting the Third World*. New York: Pantheon, 1988.

Korten, David C. *When Corporations Rule the World*. West Hartford: Kumarian, 1995.

Lenin, V.I. *Imperialism, the Highest Stage of Capitalism*. Peking: Foreign Languages Press, 1970.

Magdoff, Harry. *Imperialism: From the Colonial Age to the Present*. New York: Monthly Review Press, 1978.

Mander, Jerry, and Edward Goldsmith, eds. *The Case Against the Global Economy*. San Francisco: Sierra Club, 1996.

Rodney, Walter. *How Europe Underdeveloped Africa*. London: Bogle-L-Ouverture, 1972.

Schlesinger, Stephen, and Stephen Kinzer. *Bitter Fruit: The Untold Story of the American Coup in Guatemala.* New York: Anchor Press, 1990.

Shrybman, Steven. *The World Trade Organization: A Citizen's Guide.* 2nd ed. Toronto: James Lorimer and the Canadian Centre for Policy Alternatives, 2001.

Todorov, Tzvetan. *The Conquest of America: The Question of the Other.* Trans. R. Howard. New York: HarperPerennial, 1992.

Veltmeyer, Henry, and James F. Petras. *Globalization Unmasked: Imperialism in the 21st Century.* London: Zed Books, 2001.

Wallach, Lori, and Michelle Sforza. *The WTO: Five Years of Reasons to Resist Corporate Globalization.* New York: Seven Stories, 1999.

Wolf, Eric. *Europe and the People Without History.* Berkeley: University of California, 1982.

PART FOUR

poverty & social dispossession

CHAPTER 10

"The welfare state Rewards Laziness"
The poor are different from "the rest of us" prejudice

One of the most terrible pillars of the culture of prejudice is the one that is supported by attitudes, ideologies, social policies, and social constructions which lead ordinary people to believe that the economically disadvantaged are inferior, and that their misery is all a fault of their own. Animosity and suspicion are especially aimed at the recipients of social assistance, who are said to be lazy "freeloaders" with their hands in the public purse, whether they need it or not. In any group, there always seems to be at least one person willing to expound at length about "welfare queens" or someone who has an anecdote about a person who has "cheated the system," as if no one ever cheats systems by taking advantage of tax fraud opportunities or taking crib notes into academic examinations. Here is a case study of a welfare recipient who did precisely that: "cheated the system."[1]

After a record-breaking six-day heatwave, the body of Kimberly Rogers was discovered in her attic apartment in Sudbury, Ontario, probably about two days after her death. When she died, she was single, 40 years old, and eight months pregnant. She had been convicted of defrauding the welfare system. No question. She admitted her guilt for this crime three months before her death.

Let us examine whether or not laziness was her motivation to defraud the system. Her crime was to accept student loans and not report them to the social assistance authorities. She would have been unable to gain her college degree on either her welfare cheques or the loans alone. The latter were used for tuition fees, textbooks, and transportation to the college and to the agencies where she had work placements. Her former teachers spoke highly of her academic performance and of the support she provided to her classmates. She graduated at the top of her class from a program in social work. It would be hard to make a case that this woman, even though she

---

1. The information for this case study is derived from two articles in *The Globe and Mail* ("Ontario MPs demand inquest," 16 Aug. 2001: A6) and ("Bleak House," 18 Aug. 2001: F1 and F8). The former was written by Richard Mackie of Toronto and Keith Lacey of Sudbury. The latter was written by Lacey and Mark MacKinnon, also of Sudbury.

broke the rules, was just trying to get a free ride on the social assistance system. Indeed, it could be argued that, by improving her education, she was doing her best to get herself off the welfare rolls.[2]

So what was the result of the criminal justice response to Kimberly Rogers' welfare fraud? Did the punishment fit the crime? She and the child she was expecting were condemned to six months of house arrest. She was ordered to pay back $62,000, a figure representing all the student loans and all the social assistance payments she received when she was trying to drag herself out of poverty. Welfare payments were terminated, and she had no support from either her family or the man who impregnated her, although he did give her a few hundred dollars on the condition that she never ask for more.

It is difficult to comprehend how Ms. Rogers could be expected to find a source of income, since she was allowed out of her apartment for only three hours a week, on Wednesday mornings so she could "shop." In addition, the judge who imposed this sentence apparently did not ask himself how she would be able to deliver a healthy baby under the conditions he imposed. The month following her sentencing, welfare cheques were reinstated, pending her lawyer's appeal that the sentence constituted cruel and unusual punishment. Because of Ms. Rogers' fraud conviction, however, she was paid less than the amount to which she normally would have been entitled. As a result, rather than having $70 per month to spend after paying her rent, she had only $18.

If Kimberly Rogers had been imprisoned in a correctional facility, she would have been fed regularly. She would not have had to worry about paying her rent every month, or about her local food bank not being open on Wednesday mornings. Presumably, her health would have been monitored by medical personnel during her last months of pregnancy, and she would not have had to pay for prescription medications, including her antidepressants.[3] Women's prisons are far from desirable places to live, but a custodial sentence would have been a far better alternative than the conditions imposed on this particular woman.

This case reminds us that, although debtors' prisons and workhouses have been consigned to history, Kimberly Rogers was sentenced to the equivalent of a debtors' prison in twenty-first century North America, with the sole difference being that no prison staff or other prisoners were on hand to watch her die. Enduring negative attitudes about, and social responses to, the poor are alive and well. An historical perspective on one line of social thought about the poor can help us understand how the past haunts us still.

---

2. Only a few years earlier, welfare recipients were legally entitled to obtain student loans.

3. At time of writing, it appears that her death may have been self-inflicted, with an overdose of these antidepressants. Should we be surprised that Kimberly Rogers received medication for depression? Put yourself in her shoes, and consider what your state of mind might have been.

THE LEGACY OF SOCIAL DARWINISM

Charles Darwin is one of the most notable names in Western thought because his ideas so strikingly changed how human beings saw themselves and their world. He proposed that life forms adapted to the changing environments around them through reproductive success. People were already familiar with the idea of selectively breeding horses, dogs, and farm animals, with the understanding that offspring often display characteristics of their parents. After Darwin, birds, butterflies, and the fish of the sea could now be seen, not as God-given finished products, but rather as creatures who survived in whatever form they happen to have because their ancestors had features that permitted them to survive long enough to produce offspring capable of producing yet another generation. Darwin called this "natural selection," in contradistinction to the deliberate selections made in domestic breeding.

An important thing to remember about evolution is that Darwin was not suggesting that species become "better" as they evolve. Species simply evolve because they inherit characteristics advantageous to survival within a given ecological environment. Arctic hares whose fur turns white before the snow flies are not "better bunnies"; their natural ability to change for the season is simply something their ancestors passed down to them as a result of their own success at surviving and breeding. If local weather patterns were to change, changing fur colour would invoke no advantage. Species are mutable: end of argument.

The danger of the idea that evolution leads to "higher" life forms arises because of the way humanity was integrated into evolutionary theorizing. In the *Origin of Species* (1859), Darwin hinted that humans might be the outcome of natural selection. In his *Descent of Man and Selection in Relation to Sex* (1871), he became more serious about this topic. Some people were shocked by the idea that humans were not delivered to the Garden of Eden fully formed, like the depictions of Adam and Eve in Renaissance paintings. Some people found the idea that we might be descended from "the apes" to be hilarious. Nevertheless, a frightening aspect of the societal reaction to Darwin's thought is how swiftly the culture of prejudice turned it into an "explanation" for why other peoples, including "barbarian races," could be reasonably considered as inferior. Of particular concern is how it was used to justify the poverty and dispossession of people living in the capitalist economies of Europe and North America.

In the late 1800s, there was a great deal of concern expressed over squalid urban slums in London and New York, for example. This concern was not misplaced, as the urban poor of industrialized nations lived in appalling conditions of malnutrition, filth, disease, insanity, and social disorder. What was to be done? The "welfare state" was many decades in the future, and what little was done to ameliorate the miseries of poverty were charitable interventions. Looking for a solution to the problem of poverty, considerable numbers of influential people turned to "Social Darwinism" for an answer.

Herbert Spencer, considered to be one of the "fathers" of Sociology, was writing at the same time as Darwin and was a social theorist whose name has become synonymous with "Social Darwinism." He argued that social progress was accomplished as a result of competition between races, as well as among individuals. Over time, societies become more and more complex and differentiated, and higher or more sophisticated social forms emerged. This history of struggles and triumphs was governed by the law of the "survival of the fittest," a phrase coined by Spencer and not used by Darwin until he borrowed it for the fifth edition of his *Origin of Species*. According to Spencer, superior humans and social institutions prevail, and inferior forms fail.

The denizens of the slums, workhouses, and prisons, according to this worldview, are self-evidently inferior varieties. Their rates of morbidity and mortality are high due to the wretched conditions in which they live, and this is probably all for the best. Any attempts to raise them out of their poverty is counterproductive, as they would simply be given a better chance of reproducing more of their ilk. So they are best left to their own devices and to early deaths from starvation and disease. Although Spencer was responsible for promoting this line of thought, he apparently thought that a limited amount of charitable work was permissible, because it promoted the moral character of the benefactors who provided it.

The modern mind can be forgiven for reeling at the abject cold-bloodedness of this policy approach to the problem of poverty. Its underlying logic, however, can be understood by considering the perspective of the privileged classes of the time. As Pat Shipman has written,

> Worldly success had been accepted (in the Protestant tradition) as *prima facie* evidence of goodness or divine approval; now that a scientific rather than a religious standard was to be met, worldly success was obviously an indicator of Darwinian fitness and genetic superiority. The poor and the working classes, who lived in squalor and misery, suffered because they were made of inferior stuff; their struggles were simply the manifestation of Nature's plan, of natural selection, and to interfere was to doom the society, the race, or even the species as a whole. Society and the economy would be led by those most fit to lead—those who had been selected over long generations of superior performance—and it was folly to contemplate any rapid or profound changes.[4]

---

4. Pat Shipman, *The Evolution of Racism: Human Differences and the Use and Abuse of Science* (New York: Simon & Schuster, 1994) 108.

This is a nice, neat solution, as long as one can put aside the lingering suspicion that at least some of these poor souls deserve humanitarian consideration.

But humanitarian concerns aside, Social Darwinism simply does not make sense. As world population statistics reveal, the best way to lower the birth rate of a population is to raise its economic security. Providing education for people, especially women, and opening opportunities for them to provide for themselves and their families is an excellent form of birth control. Furthermore, Darwin focused on reproductive success *between* species (for example, why little mammals survived and dinosaurs did not), not about success or failure *within* species (for example, between the rich and the poor). Besides this, nineteenth-century observers should have realized that Social Darwinism was a preposterous idea because, although the poor died younger than the more well-off, they did not die before they had a chance to produce babies.

The reason we should consider such a cruel and scientifically suspect social theory in the context of this book is because, often in carefully couched words, it still lives and is promulgated in modern times. Psychologists, historians, botanists, economists, and theorists from a variety of disciplines are happily pursuing Social Darwinist studies.[5] Some discredited ideas die hard, and they are often the most dangerous ones. The notion that the poor are somehow inherently different from the economically successful is one of them.

Let us take a different viewpoint. Ask yourself whether or not it seems fair and reasonable that 20 per cent of Canada's children are being raised in poverty, the second highest rate of child poverty in the industrialized world?[6] Then ask whether you believe that Canadians have somehow managed to keep alive an inferior gene pool of lazy people destined to be poor? Then ask how Sweden or the Netherlands managed to reduce this genetic malfunction in their populations? The inevitable conclusion has to be that social policies and economic relationships propel people into poverty, not their genetic makeup. In 1976, the Canadian government signed the *International Covenant on Economic, Social and Cultural Rights*,[7] agreeing to ensure its citizens "an adequate standard of living" for their families, "including adequate food, clothing and housing," and committing itself to the "continuous improvement of living conditions." Since then, we have seen only an increase in the number of food banks, homeless people in our urban landscapes, breakfast programs for children, and soup kitchens to feed those who cannot feed themselves and their families. Adequate standards of living have not been incorporated into the *Charter of Rights and Freedoms*.[8] One provincial

---

5. John Horgan, "The New Social Darwinists," *Scientific American* (Oct. 1995): 174-81.

6. The UN Special Session on Children, *Putting Promises into Action: A Report on a Decade of Child and Family Poverty in Canada*, <http://www.campaign2000.ca/re/unsscMAY02/unintro.html>, May 2002.

7. Office of the High Commissioner for Human Rights, *International Covenant on Economic, Social and Cultural Rights*, <http://www.unhchr.ch/html/menu3/b/a_cescr.htm>, October, 2001.

8. Erminie J. Cohen, *Sounding the Alarm: Poverty in Canada*, <http://www.stthomasu.ca/research/AHRC/ERMINIE.HTM>, October, 2001.

premier cut the food allowance for pregnant welfare recipients on the basis that "they might spend the money on beer."[9]

Does it make sense to tolerate one in five children being raised in poverty and deprivation? Is it not in Canada's best interests to see to it that all citizens are adequately housed, clothed, fed, and educated? What possible benefit can high rates of poverty provide to a twenty-first-century "modern" society, and what possible harms can result? Critical social scientists will ask you to balance this equation and come to your own conclusions. Most certainly, they will urge you not to blame the poor for any presumed innate lack of ability to succeed. "Poor bashing" is as much a cheap trick as blaming people for their sexual orientation or assuming that whites are superior to people of colour.

Judith C. Blackwell

---

9. John Ibbitson, "Foes froth over Harris beer gaffe: Premier issues apology," *The St. Catharines Standard*, 17 April 1998: A1.

CHAPTER 11

"Idle hands are the Devil's workshop"
More myths about poverty

Cultures of prejudice are characterized by class bigotry and hatred. In societies where the acquisition of money and material goods is extolled as the very pinnacle of human achievement, those who fail to amass money or do not display suitable single-mindedness toward its acquisition are not only reviled as lazy losers but are considered a threat to the entire value system. Unsurprisingly, the poor are often considered less than human, as this makes it easier to exploit them. In Canada, a moral panic was created around the issue of workfare, based on hatred of the undeserving poor.

Hatred of the poor exists in many societies. For example, ruling castes in India considered lower castes lesser beings. They believed members of lower castes were working out karma from past sins. Thus, no obligation to help them existed and it was said that doing so would actually harm them, as it would interfere with their reincarnation. In Western societies, there is a long history of speculation about the nature of poor people. Many argue that rich people and poor people have different characters, that rich people are better motivated and possess a more developed moral character. Sociologists helped to promote such views. As discussed in Chapter 10, Social Darwinists such as Herbert Spencer endorsed theories proposing the "survival of the fittest." Functionalists suggested that a social system must reward the best and the brightest to encourage their rise to the top. In contrast, they believed that the poor would not work unless forced to do so. Because of their peculiar character, only deprivation would induce them to make an effort, so it would be necessary to remove all support by eliminating welfare.

Some academics sought to identify personality characteristics innate to different classes. For example, Edward Banfield found the poor to be impulsive, undisciplined, unreliable, and lacking the sense to save for the future, unlike the more orderly upper classes, who could delay gratification and control their impulses. He argued that the poor stay poor because their families or cultures fail to provide proper

ethical principles.[1] Banfield saw poverty as an act of will or a result of family structure and developed the notion of a "culture of poverty": cultural conditions among
the poor keep them this way. Consistently, such studies depict the poor as dysfunctional, pathological, and morally undeveloped. Essentially, they suggest that poverty
is caused by unwillingness to work. This is a particularly satisfying argument for those
who enjoy more privileges. Rather than being the result of an entrenched system of
inequality or imbalance of power, poverty can be seen to exist because the poor do
not want to work or improve themselves. They have limited needs and may even find
their impoverished condition suitable to their restricted tastes.

The belief that the poor create their own impoverishment and then go on to enjoy
it derives from an unwillingness to look at actual material conditions. The jobs
available are largely demeaning, poorly paid, and lacking opportunity and respect.
In addition, the poor face racism, substandard housing and education, overcrowding, poor nutrition, disease, and lack of community services and facilities. Often the
poor do not "save for the future" because they have no means to do so; many are unable
even to take care of the present. By stressing cultural factors and emphasizing individual responsibility, the privileged overlook structural conditions that create and maintain widespread poverty.

It is not only privileged elites who hold such images of the poor. The working
class also hate the poor; they imagine themselves to be the victims of the poor (and
their accomplices, bleeding-heart liberals who want to spend tax money on them).
Neo-liberal ideology plays on these fears, claiming that taxes from the working
class go mainly to social programs to aid the poor. These social programs are then
cited as the cause of budget deficits. On the other hand, organizations like the
National Council of Welfare Canada point out that it is more a question of prior-
ities: the amount needed to cover costs of daycare for those who need it is approximately equal to what corporations receive in tax write-offs for entertainment
expenses. Public debt is blamed mainly on the poor, elderly and welfare mothers rather
than on the rich who benefit from such tax breaks.

Myths about welfare abound. These myths depict throngs of able-bodied adults
lolling about, collecting welfare rather than accepting a job. In reality, most recipients of social assistance are children, old people, single mothers, and persons with
mental or physical disabilities. Many who are eligible for welfare actually refuse to
take it.[2] Rather than avoiding work, most people on welfare are eager to work and
have a strong belief in a work ethic.[3] Many ideas about the poor are based on anec-
dotes, emotion and speculation. In the late 1990s in Ontario, there was widespread

1. Edward Banfield, *The Unheavenly City* (Boston: Little, Brown, 1970).

2. Jonathan H. Turner and Charles E. Starnes, *Inequality: Privilege and Poverty in America* (Pacific Palisades, CA: Goodyear, 1976).

3. Leonard Goodwin, *Do the Poor Want to Work?* (Washington: Brookings Institution, 1971).

belief that welfare abuse was extensive. In Toronto a "hot line" was established for tips regarding welfare cheaters. However, half of those who were reported were not receiving welfare at all and only a tiny number of suspected cheaters were found guilty of abusing the system.

Apart from a few well-organized larger-scale frauds, the amount of money involved in welfare abuse is insignificant compared to the large amounts that the wealthy can amass by manipulating tax laws. Wealthy people can appropriate large portions of national wealth through inheritance and manipulation of tax laws, but few would characterize them as lazy, morally corrupt cheaters. In contrast, suspected welfare fraud provokes outrage.

A common misconception is that people on welfare are rolling in money and enjoy a luxurious lifestyle. However, Canada's level of support to families is one of the lowest in the industrialized world, with income from welfare payments far below poverty levels. A University of Toronto study found that welfare recipients in Ontario were unable to meet their basic nutritional needs, based on the guidelines of the province's Health Ministry.[4] Nevertheless, the idea persists that welfare recipients sit around enjoying life and taking advantage of public generosity while useful work could be performed. One must question how many people actually do find welfare attractive; how many *choose* to be on welfare because they do not want to work?

Life on welfare is certainly not luxurious; in fact, it tears families apart. For example, in 1996 in Barrie, Ontario, the Simcoe County Children's Aid Society reported that two families put their children up for adoption after large welfare cuts meant they could no longer afford to feed, clothe and shelter them; six families in the Waterloo area asked Family and Children's Services to take their children because they could not afford to feed them. Such cases vividly suggest the real quality of life on welfare: such abundant happiness and luxury that people must give their children away. And, contrary to a belief that people easily obtain welfare and then proceed to enjoy an indolent and unsupervised lifestyle, it is actually difficult to get welfare in the first place. Applicants are insulted and harassed, and those who do receive welfare are kept under surveillance and suffer the stigma of being considered social parasites.

At the heart of ideologies critical of policies to assist the socially disadvantaged is a fear that giving aid to the poor will cause moral corruption by reducing their incentives to work. The constant preoccupation is to enforce incentives for work by subjecting the poor to degradation as a condition for receiving (minimal) assistance. In England, the 1834 *Poor Law Report* claimed that Poor Laws instituted in Elizabethan times were themselves the cause of poverty: because relief was too generous, lazy people got too much and would no longer work. This fear of generosity has been a constant preoccupation of British social policy, and it also contributed to the notion of the *un*deserving poor. There were constant efforts to examine the hearts and minds of the poor,

---

4. *The Globe and Mail*, 13 March 2002: A8.

and to root out cheaters. The Poor Laws forced the poor to work if any job was offered. This was a bargain for capitalists who depended on cheap labour to generate high profits. In the nineteenth century the able-bodied poor could be forced to enter the workhouse to obtain relief. Separated from their families, uniformed inmates had to perform mindless, repetitive labour to earn minimum subsistence.

In *Anarcho-Syndicalism*, Rudolf Rocker describes the effects of the Poor Laws: whereas formerly, the law required society to aid those who had fallen into need, the Poor Law "branded poverty as a crime and laid the responsibility for personal misfortune upon alleged indolence." The Law was influenced by the doctrines of Malthus, who "announced in blunt words that the poor man forced his way into society as an uninvited guest, and could therefore lay no claim to special rights or to the pity of his fellow men. Such a view was, of course, grist to the mill of the industrial barons and gave the required moral support to their unlimited lust for exploitation." The new laws took responsibility for aid to the poor away from religious authorities and placed this in the hands of a central authority appointed by the state:

> He who, smitten by fate, was compelled to seek refuge in the workhouse, surrendered his status as a human being, for those houses were outright prisons, in which the individual was punished and humiliated for his personal misfortune.
>
> In the workhouses an iron discipline prevailed, which countered any opposition with strict punishment. The food was worse and more inadequate than in actual prisons, and the treatment so harsh and barbarous that children were often driven to suicide.
>
> Families were separated and their members permitted to see one another only at limited times and under the supervision of the officials. Every effort was directed to making residence in this place of terror so unendurable that only the utmost necessity would drive human beings to seek in it a last refuge.
>
> For that was the real purpose of the new poor law. Machine production had driven thousands out of their old means of living—in the textile industries alone more than 80,000 hand weavers had been made beggars by the modern big plants—and the new law saw to it that cheap labour was at the command of management, and with it the possibility of constantly forcing wages lower.[5]

The aim was to ensure that only truly desperate people would enter workhouses. To avoid the ghastly conditions there, most poor people sought any job on the market, meaning they would work cheaply.

---

5. Rudolf Rocker, *Anarcho-Syndicalism* (London: Secker and Warburg, 1938) 39-41.

In nineteenth-century Canada, industrialization made people dependent on wage labour and forced them to move to find jobs. A moral panic developed in Ontario concerning the vast numbers of jobless men seeking work and resulted in a campaign against the poor to ensure they would not be coddled. The Charities Movement required any single man seeking aid to chop wood or break stones for hours to receive a bowl of soup, a bit of bread and a place to sleep. When the Depression struck in the 1930s and one-third of workers lost their jobs, a major crisis was created around the need for public welfare. Again, many worried that the undeserving poor would take advantage of this situation. Fear of "communism" and widespread sympathy for socialist ideas among the population led the Department of National Defence to create work-camps in remote northern and western Canada. No able-bodied single man could get relief outside these camps. The camps were created with an explicit moral purpose: to combat a state of mind ostensibly diseased by idleness.[6]

In the 1990s these anxieties about the poor resurfaced as many argued that welfare should be replaced by "workfare," schemes requiring workforce participation as a condition for public assistance. Right-wing politicians seized on workfare because it allowed them to manipulate public emotions and provided vulnerable targets for the rage many working people felt as their own standards of living were threatened by neo-liberal programs and restructuring under international trade agreements. Workfare suggests that unemployment is the fault of lazy people. The argument does not consider structural conditions and recognize that many people are not working because there are no jobs for them; instead it argues that people are not working because they are lazy. (It also maintains a narrow definition of work. For example, single parents looking after children perform socially valuable work, but this is not recognized as such. The idea that working for wages is a form of slavery is, of course, not even considered.)

Workfare advocates misrepresent the nature of welfare. Welfare was intended to help people who need it. It was not created as something people should have to work for. Workfare advocates want to force people to work and demand that those who refuse to take any kind of work, no matter how meaningless or degrading, will lose benefits. This assumes that poor people should lose the right to choose.

It is not clear that workfare will foster the sense of individual responsibility that advocates champion. People on welfare share the problem of unemployment, but many are also victimized by violence, abuse, mental illness, disability, and emotional problems. Such people may feel defeated and crushed and, certainly, achieving some success in meaningful activity might help them. Yet it is difficult to see how forcing people to do meaningless jobs on workfare will help their self-esteem or produce a sense of social responsibility. People resent being forced to do meaningless jobs that will not help them but are merely intended to create the impression that they are not "getting something for nothing." It would be more useful to create real jobs that would

---

6. James Struthers, "Can Workfare Work? Reflections from History" <http://caledonist.org/struth.pdf> February, 1996.

allow people to earn a decent living and feel a sense of pride. Similarly, more useful than a fanciful story of the laziness of poor people are structural explanations that explain why jobs are scarce.

One proposed rationale for workfare is that it will save money. In fact, workfare is very expensive, largely because of administrative costs. Officials must monitor the program and supervise the workfare workers. The effect of workfare in terms of people getting permanent jobs is low, as is the effect on welfare caseloads and expenditures. The income gained by people on workfare is too low to lift them out of poverty.

The experience of workfare programs is uninspiring. Quebec's experience with workfare demonstrates some problems. In 1990 welfare recipients had their benefits cut but could "earn" them back by participating in a six-month work program. The rationale was that employers would hire the program's workers permanently after this six-month period. The plan failed as employers seized their fantastic opportunity: they fired their workfare workers after six months and hired new ones. Workfare actually served as a subsidy to corporations and businesses, providing them with cheap labour. After a six-year test, Quebec scrapped workfare. Similar lack of success has been reported from other provinces that adopted workfare schemes.[7]

Why is workfare such a popular idea? Many who support it misunderstand the situation: What they see as the causes of poverty—apathy, lethargy, lack of hope—are more often its effects. Workfare offers emotional appeal and easy answers to complex problems. Rather than analyzing the real situation, proponents can blame the victims while sparing themselves any rigorous thought. Affluent people usually see the system as one of unlimited opportunities and believe poverty is due to failure to take advantage of those opportunities. Having profited from the system, they believe in it and express a self-congratulatory view: "we worked hard and deserve our success"; the failure of others to achieve similar success must be the fault of those individuals themselves. The explanation always shifts the cause of unemployment away from structural factors to the moral character of the poor.

Essentially, workfare promotes a similar story and offers the poor as scapegoats and easy targets. The poor are depicted as being to blame for their own problems. Workfare remedies the situation by punishing the poor, shifting focus from structural factors to lazy people. For those who have jobs, joblessness typically is seen as a test of moral character. Many think welfare recipients should be forced to take any kind of job for low pay. The suspicion is that they are, somehow, secretly enjoying themselves on the meagre relief they receive. In reality, most people on welfare want to work and to be self-sufficient. When some of the poor are unwilling to take certain jobs, it may be because they see them for what they are: dangerous, unhealthy, degrading, psychologically stressful, poorly paid, lacking security, and offering no future.

---

7. Eric Shragge, ed., *Workfare* (Toronto: Garamond, 1997).

Corporations promote these attitudes toward the poor and welfare through their propaganda institutions such as the Business Council on National Issues, the Fraser Institute, and the National Citizens Coalition. They constantly extol ideas about competition, free enterprise, and the need for less-intrusive government. They not only push the government to adopt policies that are useful to business, but direct their propaganda towards the working class to exploit their fears and resentment about increasing tax burdens. In reality, corporations don't want to be "free" or competitive themselves (they are authoritarian organizations that avoid competition through collective efforts to manage markets). Corporate calls for "less government" are selective, because they want to benefit from government assistance but want no interference with profit-seeking behaviour (such as labour laws, environmental protection, etc.—these are dismissed as the illegitimate interference of "special interests," or "big unions," "tree-huggers," etc.).

While corporate propaganda churns out paeans to individual effort and anti-welfare screeds, corporations themselves are among the biggest beneficiaries of welfare in the form of tax concessions, credits, holidays, and remissions. Corporations mobilize armies of accountants and lawyers to find ways to avoid taxes. The largest, richest corporations frequently pay no tax at all while making huge profits. Extensive tax fraud among corporations involves billions of dollars. While assistance to poor individuals is always tightly regulated, accompanied with a hefty dose of moralism and often delivered in such a way as to degrade recipients, giveaways to corporations are extremely generous and virtually unsupervised. Corporations receive billions in annual loans, grants, and wage subsidies. Corporations also benefit from indirect assistance through government-funded infrastructure: roads, airports and railways, as well as through publicly funded education and research. By diverting working-class ire toward the "undeserving" poor, highlighting the depravity of the welfare recipient who squanders his or her pittance on a consoling six-pack of beer, the rich can enjoy their wealth undisturbed.

John S. Sorenson

CHAPTER 12

"Indians shouldn't have any special rights"

Belief that aboriginal peoples are "just another minority group"

Many Canadians seem to believe that, while some unfortunate events may have happened in the past, indigenous people in Canada should not receive any "special" treatment and should now adjust themselves to "mainstream" society. These arguments overlook the impact of history and decontextualize the situation of indigenous people.

For the last five hundred years, all across the globe indigenous societies have been under attack. The impact of colonialism on these societies was unparalleled in history. Millions of people died, some exterminated through direct attacks, others from imported diseases. Indigenous cultures were smashed. In Canada, the European conquerors pursued a deliberate policy to undermine existing values and practices and to transform the survivors of the cultural smash-up into replicas of themselves.

Although Europeans considered the indigenous population of Canada useful during the years of the fur trade, they soon came to be seen as obstacles. As colonists began to develop agriculture, new patterns of exploitation arose, and in 1876 Aboriginal peoples were placed under the total control of occupying forces by the *Indian Act*. The *Indian Act* determined every aspect of life for indigenous people. Native people were displaced from their lands and located on reservations that were only a fraction of their territory. Even these fragmented holdings were eroded and millions of acres of reservation lands were simply expropriated. Native people were forced to move to less valuable land at the wishes of the government. The *Indian Act* placed indigenous people under an apartheid-like system; indeed, Canada actually served as a model for the racist South African state. Native people could not leave the reservation without a pass issued by the government's Indian Agent. These bureaucrats had virtually unlimited power over the lives of Native people. They had the right to enter Native people's homes at will and if they did not approve of the conditions they saw they could remove children from their families; many of these children were placed with non-Native foster parents, contributing further to their alienation. A 1914 amendment to the *Indian Act* prohibited Native people from taking part in any cultural ceremony without the Indian Agent's approval. Native farmers were not allowed to sell their produce without the Agent's permission. Laws were developed to ensure that indigenous people could not develop a strong economy: in Manitoba, native farmers were forbidden to use agricultural machinery and had to make their tools by hand. Other laws ensured that Native people would be politically powerless. Assembly of more than two Native people was outlawed in 1884. Vagrancy laws ensured that Native people could be arrested or removed if they were found to be "loitering." Status Indians, those who were defined as such in law, could not vote until 1960 unless they gave up their claim to any of the limited benefits of the *Indian Act*. In defining who was to be identified as an Indian, the Act also discriminated on the basis of gender: any Native woman who married a non-Native man would automatically lose her status, although Native men did not face the same consequences if they married non-Native women.

The policy behind the *Indian Act* was one of assimilation. The Canadian government was determined to eradicate indigenous cultures and force Native people to adopt European language, customs, and values. Indigenous cultural practices, such as the Sun Dance on the Prairies and the Potlatch in British Columbia, were outlawed. Christian groups were given land and allowed to conduct their proselytization campaigns among the Native population; many of them focused their efforts on restructuring the "backward" traditions of matrilineal societies in order to make them conform to the norms of patriarchal Europeans.

From the nineteenth century until 1960, Native children were forced into residential schools run by European religious groups. In these schools, children were physically punished for speaking in their own language and indoctrinated with the superiority of European culture while their own traditions were dismissed as savage and backward. The intent was to destroy indigenous cultures. Even those who would reject the application of the term "genocide" to this process (because it did not involve direct slaughter) must recognize this as an exercise in ethnocide. The residential schools were also the site of rampant sexual abuse and severe physical discipline. These practices traumatized entire generations of Native people and the effects continue to be seen in disproportionately high levels of alcoholism, depression, suicide, and family violence. Native women, facing discrimination on the basis of class, gender, and "race", are particularly affected by violence. As a result of the dysfunctional family atmosphere created through these circumstances, Native people endure far higher levels of illiteracy, unemployment, welfare dependency, and incarceration. Conditions on most of Canada's reservations are nothing short of a national scandal, with the population trapped in conditions of poverty, despair, and violence. All of these can be seen to be the direct consequences of the discrimination that Native people have faced for centuries in Canadian society.

At the same time, Native people continue to be subjected to systemic racist violence. For example, in 1971 a number of white men gang-raped and then murdered a young Cree woman, Helen Betty Osborne, in The Pas, Manitoba; the RCMP and many of the respectable citizens of The Pas colluded to cover up the murder, and only after the case was reinvestigated in 1987 was one of the men sentenced. In Saskatchewan, police enlivened their winter evenings by driving intoxicated Native men to rural areas and leaving them to freeze to death. When Mohawks, exasperated after 200 years of trying to reclaim their land at Kanehsatake (Oka) near Montreal, blockaded a rural road to protest planned expansion of a golf course in 1990, local citizens lined the road to shout racist insults and hurl stones at them; this was followed by an assault by provincial police, who may have shot one of their own officers. And, after years of evasion, Ontario premier Mike Harris was finally forced to testify about his role in ordering police to evict Native protesters from Ipperwash Provincial Park, where Anthony "Dudley" George was killed in 1995 by a policeman who was eventually convicted of criminal negligence.[1]

Many indigenous people have seen their way of life destroyed or threatened by industrial development. For example, the Ojibwa of Grassy Narrows in northern Ontario were forced to relocate in 1964; the move constituted a major disruption of social life, followed by the discovery that they were being poisoned by uncontrolled mercury pollution spewed out from industries in the town of Dryden. Closure of polluted rivers destroyed the group's economic base and exacerbated the desperate conditions of alcoholism, violence, and suicide. Similarly, the Innu of Labrador are threatened by a multi-billion-dollar mining development at Voisey's Bay, the world's largest nickel deposit. Although the Innu were never consulted about the project, it will drastically affect their culture and also create a devastating environmental impact. Innu were also subjected to the disruption of deafeningly loud low-level flight training and bombing exercises carried out by NATO air forces at Goose Bay. The Innu never signed a treaty to give up their land and thus are still under colonial domination. This has deprived them of control over their own lives and subordinated them to the institutions of those who have invaded their land. In northern Quebec, the huge James Bay hydroelectric project was halted temporarily by Innu and Cree residents of the area who had never surrendered their rights to the land; unsure of a court ruling on the issue of Aboriginal title, they finally signed a 1975 settlement that would give them a share of the royalties and some control over the remaining land that would not be flooded. Residents of southern Quebec reacted as if the Innu and Cree had been treated to an undeserved bonanza; years later, however, the promised benefits had not improved the lives of many of these indigenous people. The same

---

1. Ontario taxpayers funded Harris' legal bills (which had reached $1 million by 2002) for what *The Globe and Mail* (12 March 2002: A7) called a "completely unnecessary" lawsuit to avoid a public inquiry into the shooting.

arrogance that led Quebec's political rulers to overlook the rights of indigenous peoples before the James Bay project still exists: Quebec nationalists have repeatedly asserted that they would have sovereignty over Native people if Quebec were to separate from Canada.

Another example comes from northern Alberta, where the tiny Lubicon Cree nation have been resisting the invasion of their land by major oil companies and transnational corporations. Like the Innu, the Lubicon never signed over their rights to the land and therefore retain those rights in the present. Nevertheless, oil companies moved into their area in 1979 and began drilling hundreds of wells, disrupting the Lubicon way of life. The Lubicon received no royalties although the oil companies made billions of dollars in profit from their land. When the Lubicon challenged the oil companies in court, the provincial government responded by retroactively changing laws and trying to dismiss their case, as oil extraction continued. Frustrated by government stalling, the Lubicon, like the Mohawks in Ontario, were forced to erect blockades, which were duly demolished by the RCMP. After the Lubicon rejected a 1989 offer from Brian Mulroney's federal government that would still leave them dependent on welfare, the federal government tried to undermine their resistance by funding rival band leaders and even went as far as creating a new band, the Woodland Cree, who were offered $1,000 per family to vote for the proposed agreement. While struggling against provincial and federal governments and the oil companies, the Lubicon also had to face a new threat from the Daishowa paper-manufacturing corporation, which obtained rights to clear-cut all the Lubicon forest territory, despite ongoing Lubicon legal claims. An international consumer boycott was organized, demanding that Daishowa not log the area until Lubicon claims had been settled and environmental agreements had been put in place. Daishowa responded by taking legal action against the tiny solidarity group Friends of the Lubicon; an Ontario court ruled in 1996 that Friends of the Lubicon could not ask the public to support the boycott, because it would cost the corporation money. Although an injunction against the boycott was lifted in 1998 and an out-of-court settlement with Friends of the Lubicon was reached in 2000, the Lubicon themselves still face intransigent governments that are determined not to recognize their rights.

The argument that indigenous peoples should not have special rights was put forward as policy under the Liberal government of Pierre Trudeau. His government maintained that Native people should be treated in the same way as other minority groups in Canada. This argument overlooks some key points. Unlike all other minority groups, who opted to move to Canada, Native peoples have lived here for thousands of years. When Europeans arrived, the indigenous people lived in self-governing societies. Many groups of indigenous people never signed treaties giving up their land. Instead their territory was occupied and stolen from them by an invading force. European colonists argued that Native people had no right to the land they lived on and that land was of no value to them, a convenient argument that allowed them to claim it for themselves. Although Canada's 1982 Constitution did recognize Aboriginal rights, many people still assert that Native people must "learn to live like the rest of us." These claims are based on ignorance and racism. To argue that Native people are just like other minorities in Canada is to turn a blind eye to the centuries of oppression they have endured and to the devastating long-term effects that have been caused by the unprecedented assault on their culture and the deliberate destruction of their economic bases. Most Native people do not dream of recreating a lost world that existed before Europeans took their land. Rather, they seek opportunities to preserve their autonomy and dignity in a society that has been imposed on them and to exercise the rights that are legally theirs. Unfortunately, they have had to appeal to international fora such as the United Nations in order to convince Canada to respect those rights, while for its part the Canadian government has worked consistently to oppose indigenous rights and self-determination in such fora. Unfortunately, the Canadian Human Rights Commission's 1990 assessment of the situation of Canada's indigenous people as a "national shame" still holds true today.

The situation of Native people is at the very core of Canada's culture of prejudice. Canada's identity and history have been presented in terms of a myth of "two founding peoples." This narrative has celebrated the "settlement" of Canada by brave European pioneers and excluded the existing indigenous people almost entirely, making them invisible or treating them as savages or children to be civilized. History begins when Europeans arrive. Even when the presence of Native peoples is acknowledged, this is often done in a cursory manner; for example, the recent CBC television series "Canada: A People's History" devotes part of the first episode to 15,000 years of indigenous societies and all of the following sixteen episodes to 500 years of European occupation. The national mythology of Canadian identity celebrates European colonialism as a process of development and modernization in which settlers occupy empty land or wilderness. It is simply accepted that Europeans had the right to claim this territory as their own because of their "advanced" civilization. Treaties that were negotiated with indigenous groups often involved deceit and manipulation. Those Canadians who are outraged by contemporary Native protests and land claims should recognize that these are the inevitable products of colonial occupation. Colonialism implemented a system of institutionalized racism to maintain the superiority of European colonizers and to denigrate and undermine the integrity of Native societies.

The claim that Native people should not have any special rights in Canada is an attempt to deny the reality of our culture of prejudice: the colonial occupation of the territory and the existence of a social, political, and economic system that has been created to serve the interests of the colonizers at the expense of indigenous people who originally inhabited the area and owned all of its land and resources. Canadians may sometimes feel that our colonial past is less troubling because, unlike the United States, the Caribbean, and Latin America, it was not founded on the genocide of indigenous populations (with the exception of the Beothuk in Newfoundland). However, the definition of genocide is not limited to mass murder. Raphael Lemkin, who coined the term "genocide" to describe what was happening to European Jews under the Nazis, specifies that it includes other techniques "aimed at the destruction of the essential foundations of the life of national groups."[2] Recognizing this, we should see our colonial history for what it is and understand the manipulation of treaties, institutionalized racism, and policies of assimilation as genocidal practices intended to eradicate indigenous cultures. We should not assume that Native people are asking for special privileges that others will not receive. To reject the culture of prejudice is to understand that Native people are not like various groups of immigrants who have arrived later, but they are indigenous nations who negotiated legal treaties with colonial authorities. Just as we have the obligation to uphold these treaties, these nations have the right to self-determination and to decide what relationship they wish to have with Canada.

John S. Sorenson

---

2. Ward Churchill, *A Little Matter of Genocide: Holocaust and Denial in the Americas, 1492 to the Present* (San Francisco: City Lights, 1997) 70.

CHAPTER 13

"If unemployed people can't find jobs, they should start their own businesses"

Anachronistic view concerning "individual responsibility," work, and the sanctity of small business enterprise

From an early age, most of us born in the capitalist West are encouraged to believe that one of the pillars of our way of life is the free enterprise system. "Free markets" are celebrated as the most rational means to organize economic activity, and few things are held more sacred than the right of individuals to start up businesses with the aim of enriching themselves. The mutual competition of tens of thousands of privately-owned and profit-oriented businesses is claimed to be the real engine of economic growth—and a guarantee that people's needs for a wide array of goods and services will be met efficiently and at the lowest possible cost to consumers. While Karl Marx's analysis of the capitalist mode of production is regularly said to be outdated (concerned as it allegedly was with nineteenth-century conditions), the ideas of the *eighteenth-century* economist Adam Smith are routinely celebrated as eternal truths that are as relevant today as they were when they were first enunciated over two centuries ago.

According to Smith, the wealth of society is maximized when people are free to produce for a market in a completely self-interested fashion, unimpeded by barriers to trade or other government interference. This *laissez-faire* doctrine is today presented as the solution to the economic malaise that has gripped much of the world economy since the early 1970s. The centrepiece of this neo-Smithian economic orthodoxy is the proposition that the backbone of the modern economy is small business and that small businesses flourish when labour markets are allowed to operate "freely" and "flexibly." This all sounds eminently reasonable—after all, who is going to come out against freedom and flexibility? The only problem is that free markets and human freedom are not at all the same thing. For when impersonal market forces are given free rein to allocate economic resources in accordance with "supply and demand" and the requirements of "profit maximization," this can only further empower those with abundant marketable assets while restricting the options of those who have little more to sell than their own ability to work. "Free markets"—and free labour markets in particular—have always been a boon to the already wealthy and powerful and a curse to those with little property or competitive advantage. And yet the experience of over two centuries of capitalist development has left the fundamental premises of "free market"/ "free enterprise" ideology seemingly undisturbed in the minds of those whose interests are served by it.

The reality of the so-called "free enterprise" system is very distant from the mythology. Free market competition, over time, leads to corporate concentration and to monopoly and oligopoly. Far from creating opportunities for large numbers of people to own their own businesses and to create a society of small-scale commodity producers and merchants (Adam Smith's vision of the ideal society), the operations of the capitalist market have driven the great majority of the population into dependence upon wage-labour. The traditional petty-bourgeoisie of small farmers, craftspeople, professionals, and merchants has been reduced from a large majority of the North American population in the nineteenth century to less than 10 per cent today. Yet we continue to be told that the problem of unemployment and underemployment that plagues the advanced capitalist world at the dawn of the new millennium can be solved only by the job-creating activity of small businesses. To evaluate this argument we need some perspective on the real place of small- and medium-sized businesses in today's economy and the nature and scope of the unemployment problem we face.

By 1988, 200 companies held more than 60 per cent of all manufacturing assets in the United States. This compares to 46 per cent in 1929 and 55 per cent in 1959. Furthermore, less than 1 per cent of all corporations controlled two-thirds of all corporate assets.[1] In 1969, 88 per cent of US companies held assets worth less than $500,000, and cumulatively these assets accounted for only 6 per cent of all corporate assets in the country. Studies have also shown that there is a direct connection between the size of a company's assets and its profitability. For the period 1931-61, and excluding the war years of 1940-47, Howard Sherman reported a long-term *rate of profit* of 10.4 per cent for companies valued at over $50,000,000, of 4.1 per cent for those valued between $50,000 and $100,000, and of *minus* 7.1 per cent for those valued under $50,000.[2] Corporate concentration is even more pronounced in Canada, where, by 1987, the top 1 per cent of all enterprises controlled 86 per cent of all assets and made 75 per cent of all profits. Indeed, in Canada, the top one-hundredth of 1 per cent of all enterprises (about 100 companies) controlled 56 per cent of all assets.[3]

With low or non-existent profit margins and few assets, small- to medium-sized businesses still create far more jobs than do the big transnational corporations operating in the US and Canada. The problem is that most of those jobs are of poor quality. As a rule, smaller companies provide low-wage employment with few if any

---

1. Michael Parenti, *Democracy for the Few* (New York: St. Martin's Press, 1988) 11.

2. Howard Sherman, *Profit Rates in the United States* (Ithaca, NY: Cornell University Press, 1968) 41.

3. Mel Hurtig, *The Betrayal of Canada* (Toronto: Stoddart, 1991) 181.

benefits. So where does that leave the growing "reserve army of unemployed"—the chief victims of the concentration of capital and the imperatives of contemporary capitalist production?

Global unemployment and underemployment is now estimated to be around 30 per cent for the world's workforce—and this figure is based on *official* unemployment statistics that usually understate the real level of unemployment. In the developed industrialized world, most countries saw official unemployment rates of 10 per cent or more for much of the 1990s. A conspicuous exception was the United States, which boasted a relatively low official rate of about 5 per cent. But how real was this US success story?

Like other countries, the US excludes so-called "discouraged workers" from its calculations. The unemployment rate is defined as the percentage of the total (employed and unemployed) workforce that is composed of unemployed workers actively seeking employment. Thus, for a jobless person to be considered officially unemployed, she or he must be collecting unemployment insurance or registered with a government agency charged with finding work for the unemployed. Since government employment agencies are typically not very helpful to unemployed individuals in times of high unemployment, many jobless individuals are simply dropped from the official workforce statistics once their unemployment insurance benefits expire. In the United States, this can happen within a year of a job loss, since the US system of unemployment insurance allows workers to collect benefits for no longer than six months (a very short period compared to that allowed in Canada and Western Europe). But there are two other "sleights-of-hand" involved in the calculation of the US unemployment rate that deserve attention. The first is that by not including the 1.5 million people in prison and the 8.1 million on parole in its labour-force survey, the US government reduces its official unemployment rate by more than 5 percentage points. (It is worth noting that over the same period that the US prison population swelled from half a million to 1.5 million, about one million jobs were lost in US manufacturing!) The second consideration is that the members of the US armed forces are lumped together with the civilian workforce in calculating the unemployment rate, a procedure that further reduces the official rate by about one per cent. Correcting for these significant survey distortions, the Council on International and Public Affairs (CIPA) has estimated that the *real* rate of unemployment in the United States was at least 11.4 per cent in the boom year of 1997—more than double the official rate.[4] Even that estimate does not take into account the problem of discouraged workers that skews official tabulations of the unemployed in the United States as elsewhere. Correcting for the problem of discouraged workers as this is reflected in labour-force participation rates, the Canadian Auto Workers

4. Cited by Ed Finn, "Lying with Statistics: US unemployment rate down to 5%? Don't believe it!" *CCPA Monitor* (November 1997): 4.

union has estimated that Canada's true unemployment rate exceeded 13 per cent throughout the period from 1992 to 1997, rather than fluctuating between 11 per cent and 9 per cent as reported by Statistics Canada.[5]

A global economy whose productive assets are overwhelmingly concentrated in the hands of several hundred large corporations that employ a tiny fraction of the world's workforce is an unprecedented development in human history. But the logic of capitalism is to treat those it cannot employ as simple "surplus population." During England's industrial revolution of the early nineteenth century, the Reverend Thomas Malthus (who never allowed the precepts of Christian charity to cloud his better economic judgment) enunciated the principle that economic progress and the betterment of society require the reduction of the surplus population—if need be through mass starvation. Malthus' premise was a simple one: in the context of a market economy, human labour should be treated as a commodity like any other. If demand existed for it, the worker could earn a livelihood; if not, then the worker could expect nothing at all from society. (Not surprisingly, Malthus and his fellow pro-business economists were the inspiration for the character of Scrooge in Charles Dickens' famous novel *A Christmas Carol*.)

Such cold-hearted capitalist logic seems unacceptably inhumane to most of us, but what is seldom considered is that it is also quite irrational. Why should *any* human being be rendered unproductive and designated as disposable surplus? What is the nature of an economic system that cannot find a way for over one billion unemployed and underemployed people worldwide to contribute productively to the satisfaction of human needs, beginning with their own? By what perverse logic have we come to believe that unemployment is a natural state of affairs?

Wasteful and irrational as it clearly is, unemployment has a definite function within an economic system based upon exploitation and class antagonism. The existence of a reserve army of labour has the effect of preventing workers from demanding "unreasonably" high wages and threatening profits. Fear of being fired and of not being able to find alternative employment disciplines the worker to embrace the ethic that s/he owes the boss the greatest possible work effort. The economic insecurity that mass unemployment breeds within the workforce also encourages rivalry, competition, and jealousy among workers, rendering it more difficult for labour to unite against capital. Furthermore, the existence of "a group of unemployed or underemployed individuals ... makes the workers who do have jobs feel that they have some vested interest in the system, because they are better off than the very poor."[6] Therefore, from the point of view of the capitalist owners of the economy, unemployment serves their interests in a perversely "rational" fashion.

---

5. "The Jobs Crisis Continues," *Economic and Social Action* 3:1 (September 1997): 2.

6. A. Szymanski and T.G. Goertzel, *Sociology: Class Consciousness and Contradictions* (New York: D. Van Nostrand Co., 1979) 134.

Mass unemployment also has destabilizing effects on society, however, as well as definite costs. Malthusian indifference to the plight of the unemployed and the working poor is not possible in every region of the world economy—though, tragically, it is all too prevalent in the Third World. The capitalist rulers learned long ago that to fail to provide a "social safety net" for displaced workers and the economically indigent in the most developed capitalist countries would be to invite social upheaval, up to and including Marxian social revolution. At the same time, a "too generous" system of social assistance must be avoided in order to safeguard the disciplinary rigours of the free labour market and minimize the adverse effects of high state expenditures on profitability.

Today, with the spectre of Marxian socialism seemingly exorcized and the prospect of social revolution remote in the advanced capitalist world, the attitude of society's power brokers and policy makers toward the unemployed has become much less indulgent than it used to be. As the problem of large-scale *structural* (as opposed to *voluntary*) unemployment has become increasingly intractable, and the costs associated with unemployment insurance and social assistance correspondingly greater, a hue and cry has been raised about the dangerous growth of government debt and deficits, and the climate has been created for a new conventional wisdom according to which the only long-term solution to high unemployment levels is the removal of "disincentives to work." What this means in the concrete is that those who are jobless should be *forced* to work—whether in government "workfare" schemes that often displace unionized labour, in "training programs" that are often a disguised subsidy to businesses, or in "self-employed" activities that reinforce the ethos of "free enterprise" while providing wretched incomes for a growing number of reluctant, but desperate, would-be "entrepreneurs." As we hear reports of the growing number of small businesses that have been created in recent years, we should bear in mind that many of them have been started by people whose only alternative was dependence upon a shrinking, and in some jurisdictions disappearing, welfare cheque. Yet even in the mid-1980s, during a period of relative economic buoyancy, it has been estimated that the average small business in Canada had a life expectancy of only 18 months, with two-thirds of new businesses going bankrupt.[7] At the same time, about two-thirds of self-employed workers in 1986 had an annual income that was below the median income for all wage and salary earners in Canada. This general pattern characterizes the United States as well.

Not only do most self-employed small-business owners subsist on below-average incomes, they also tend to put in longer than average hours of work. Their activity is often essential to the profitability of the big corporations, and yet small-business owners, influenced by anachronistic ideologies and corporate propaganda, are likely to blame their plight on "unions" and "tax-and-spend governments." The

---

7. Sylvia Hale, *Controversies in Sociology: A Canadian Introduction* (Toronto: Copp Clark, 1990) 257.

minority of small-business owners who enjoy some success after many years of hard work are likely to be among the most intransigent defenders of private enterprise—ideological bulwarks of a system that has not only taken advantage of them, but forced them to exploit *themselves* and often other family members as well.

Historical experience shows that self-employment and small-business enterprise are not solutions to the problem of mass unemployment. To find a real solution to the problem we must first be clear on the underlying causes. Fundamentally, these causes are to be found in the labour-saving and labour-displacing bias of technological change under capitalism, and in the slower rates of economic growth associated with a declining rate of profit.[8] Under such conditions, progressive measures to alleviate unemployment—such as a shorter work week with no loss in pay—are not likely to be considered by the capitalist owners or the governments that serve them. Instead, amid high levels of unemployment, the big corporations are actually increasing compulsory over-time work for their shrinking labour forces, preferring to pay time-and-a-half wage rates than to incur the expense of hiring new full-time workers who would be entitled to an array of costly benefits. With their eyes fixed firmly on the "bottom line," corporate executives are not only indifferent to new job creation; they are intent on lengthening the average work day, thereby destroying a hard-won gain of the labour movement: the forty-hour work-week.

A progressive solution to the worsening global problem of unemployment and underemployment will not be found within the framework of the existing world capitalist economy. It will be found only by creating an economic and social order that obeys a very different logic than that of profit maximization—an order in which it is working people who reap the benefits of labour-saving technology rather than capitalist owners who reserve those benefits exclusively for themselves.

Murray E. G. Smith

---

8. See Murray E.G. Smith and K.W. Taylor, "Profitability Crisis and the Erosion of Popular Prosperity: The Canadian Economy, 1947-1991," *Studies in Political Economy* 49 (Spring 1996); Fred Moseley, "The Rate of Profit and the Future of Capitalism," *Review of Radical Political Economics* 29:4 (Fall 1997); Fikret Ceyhun, "Multinational Corporations and the US Economic Crisis," *Review of Radical Political Economics* 29:4 (Fall 1997).

CHAPTER 14

"Recent trends toward falling living standards show that there are 'natural limits' to the expansion of human prosperity"

Naturalistic explanation for why the rich get richer and the poor get poorer

Productivity levels throughout the world are higher today than they have ever been in history. Human beings can produce more material goods and services with the performance of a given amount of labour than at any point in the past. Our scientific knowledge and advanced techniques of production mean that we are able to produce a volume of material wealth unimaginable even a century ago. Why then are living standards for the great majority of humankind either stagnating or falling? There are really only two possible broad explanations for this phenomenon. Either improvements in human prosperity are running up against a barrier of "natural limits" (that is, a scarcity of vital natural resources which is driving up the costs of production), or else the social relations and institutional conditions in which the production and distribution of material wealth occurs are somehow preventing the great mass of humanity from benefitting from higher levels of productivity.

Poor management and waste of non-renewable natural resources (such as oil) are clearly problems with which humanity must contend. Nevertheless, in a global economy where gross output *per capita* has risen over the same time-span that the living standards of the majority of people have fallen, it seems clear that an increasingly unequal distribution of wealth is responsible for the declining fortunes of the majority. The gap between the rich and the poor widens each year, both between countries and between different classes within countries, and this trend cannot be explained by pointing to raw material or energy shortages that might episodically drive up the costs of production. Indeed, the real growth of a broad range of primary commodity prices has been *negative* since World War II, indicating that the costs of many material inputs to production have actually declined. Writing in 1988, Susan George noted,

> Today commodity prices are going, going, gone. The IMF, which does keep good track of these matters, measures the purchasing power of a

basket of thirty primary commodities, excluding gold and oil, in terms of the manufactured goods that they can buy. Starting from 100 in 1957, the IMF index has risen above that index only twice, in 1973 and 1974. Ever since, though there have been peaks and valleys, the trend has been downwards. By 1985 the index had plummeted to the lowest level ever recorded—a dismal 66.[1]

How then do we account for the fact that rising productivity levels are accompanied both by an increasing disparity in the distribution of wealth and by declining or stagnating living standards for a majority of humankind? The answer is that the social relations that underpin the world capitalist economy confer a *contradictory* dynamic upon it. The scientific rationality that makes possible the production of more material wealth with the application of less living labour works against the social imperative of the capitalist economy to measure this wealth in terms of labour time expended. The social imperative to measure material output in terms of what Marx called "abstract social labour"—the phenomenal form of which is money—is in turn linked to the fact that the capitalist mode of production is based upon the exploitation of one social class by another. Moreover, the capitalist economy is geared toward reproducing capitalist class domination under conditions where capitalists also confront each other as market competitors and where a purely *formal equality* exists between all economic agents in the sphere of commodity exchange.

Thus, the capitalist mode of production encompasses a complex of social relations that are at once exploitative, competitive, and egalitarian. However, the supreme imperative of the capitalist system is the appropriation of the surplus labour performed by wage-earners by the capitalist owners of the productive assets of society. Under conditions of generalized commodity production, where labour power is itself a commodity and most production is geared toward the market, the domination of capital over labour can only be reproduced if social labour remains both the "social substance" and the "measure" of the value of everything that is produced for sale on the market.

Very simply, "capital in general" must appropriate and realize the surplus value produced by living labourers in order to maintain its class domination. But individual capitalists are compelled under the pressure of competition to do things that reduce the costs of production through labour-saving innovation. Indeed, individual capitalists can increase profits at the expense of their capitalist competitors by adopting labour-saving and labour-displacing techniques of production which lower unit costs. At the "micro" level this strategy for maximizing profits seems eminently rational; but at the "macro" level it leads to a proportional decline in the total cap-

---

1. Susan George, *A Fate Worse than Debt* (Harmondsworth, Middlesex: Penguin Books, 1988) 62. For more recent data, see <http://www.info.org/external/np/res/commod/table12.pdf>.

ital investment in living labour and an increase in the investment in such "objective elements" of the production and reproduction process as machinery and energy. The result is that the average rate of profit for the social capital as a whole tends to fall over time. The displacement of living labour from production, motivated by inter-capitalist competition and by the drive of capital to make itself as independent as possible of potentially recalcitrant living labourers, has the unintended consequence of reducing the magnitude of surplus-value produced relative to the overall capital investment. Other things being equal, this process produces a downward pressure on the average rate of profit, setting the stage for recurrent capitalist economic crises. A growing body of theoretical and empirical work in Marxist political econ-omy over the past few decades demonstrates the continuing vitality and explanatory power of these ideas, despite the efforts of more conventional economists and social scientists to dismiss them out of hand.[2]

This Marxist account of capitalism's crisis tendencies is based ultimately on the notion that what is rational from the point of view of enhancing productivity and increas-ing the volume of material wealth becomes more and more incompatible with the cap-italist imperative to appropriate surplus value from living wage-labourers. As the capitalist mode of production develops, the contradiction between the "natural" and the "social" dimensions of production intensifies, producing substantively irrational results. Thus, this account challenges the dominant "common sense" view of the rationality and effi-ciency of the capitalist "free market" economy—a view that is rooted in the *prejudice* that rationality is defined by whatever serves the specific interests of the dominant capitalist class. It also explains in a way that no other theory can why an increasingly productive capitalist economy can also "produce" declining living standards and increasing misery for the majority of humanity.

Murray E. G. Smith

---

2   For a review of the relevant literature, see Murray E.G. Smith, *Invisible Leviathan: The Marxist Critique of Market Despotism beyond Postmodernism* (Toronto: University of Toronto Press, 1994).

CHAPTER 15

"The real culprit for the poverty gap (between rich and poor countries) is not uneven trade, but excessive population growth"[1]

Neo-Malthusian prejudice

The corollary to the idea that the world's most pressing social and economic problems are the result of natural limits on the production of material wealth is the widespread view that the specific problems facing the impoverished regions of Asia, Africa, and Latin America are due largely to excessively high rates of population growth. While the notion of natural limits to growth deflects attention away from the failures of capitalism and the "free market" in meeting human needs, the "population explosion" thesis blames the plight of the Third World on the reproductive behaviour of its inhabitants. Overlaying the theme of natural limits, therefore, is the theme of blaming the victim.

The idea that famine and pestilence are attributable to excessive population growth is hardly a new one. It has been a familiar argument of those seeking to absolve existing social institutions of responsibility for human misery for at least two centuries. Its most influential and famous champion was the Reverend Thomas Robert Malthus, who argued that England had reached its maximum desirable population in 1798 and that agricultural production could not keep up with the prevailing rate of population growth of the early 1800s. Malthus posited a "natural law" of population according to which population tends to grow geometrically (2, 4, 8, 16, 32 ...) as agricultural output grows only arithmetically (1, 2, 3, 4, 5 ...). Even though it is now universally recognized that Malthus failed to anticipate the capacity of new technologies and farming methods to dramatically increase production and thus support an expanding population, his basic propositions are still thought by many to be relevant to present-day global issues. Population growth, argue the neo-Malthusians, is not only the chief cause of poverty in the so-called developing world; it is, according to the Science Summit of 1993, also a major cause of severe environmental stress, including "the growing loss of biodiversity, increasing greenhouse gas emissions, increasing deforestation worldwide, stratospheric ozone deple-

---

1. Diane Francis, *The Financial Post*, 2 June, 2001.

tion, acid rain, loss of top-soil, and shortages of water, food, and fuel-wood in many parts of the world."[2]

Interestingly, this neo-Malthusian perspective is disputed by the African Academy of Sciences. In a 1993 statement, the Academy wrote that "whether or not the Earth is finite will depend on the extent to which science and technology is able to transform the resources available for humanity. There is only one Earth—yes; but the potential for transforming it is not necessarily finite." Even with existing technology most experts agree that the Third World could feed as many as 32 billion people. The fact that millions starve to death each year around the world is not due to an overall global shortage of food, but rather to an inequitable distribution of global agricultural output, not to mention the waste of a good portion of that output and the underutilization of land that could increase it still more. Moreover, poverty-stricken Third World countries are often less densely populated than "developed" European nations. If the five billion inhabitants of the Third World were relocated to the United States, the latter would still be less densely populated than present-day Belgium. As Susan George has put it, "The first thing to realize when trying to think straight about population/food is that hunger is not *caused* by population pressure. Both hunger and rapid population growth reflect the same failure of a political and economic system."[3]

The capitalist world system, despite pious expressions of concern by its power brokers over the deplorable poverty facing much of humanity, has shown itself to be incapable of either promoting the development of a system of food production and distribution adequate to the task of eradicating world hunger, or of allowing the kind of economic development in the Third World that would encourage lower birth rates. Even if we accept the notion that a lower rate of global population growth would be desirable for ecological reasons, the dominant ways of thinking about the issue in the West remain misguided at best and cold-blooded at worst: misguided when the emphasis is placed on the need to "educate" people in the Third World about the methods they can use to reduce the size of their families, and cold-blooded when the emphasis is placed on simply "letting nature run its course." Replicating the mindset of the misanthropic and puritanical Malthus, cold-blooded would-be "realists" even insist that if the poor of the Third World are not prepared to limit their copulation and reduce the number of their babies, then they should expect no "handouts" from the affluent West, and should be left to die from the hunger and pestilence that result from their "irresponsible" reproductive behaviour. "If they would rather die," as Ebenezer Scrooge observed so delicately about the wretchedly poor of nineteenth-century England, "they had better do it, and decrease the surplus population."[4]

---

2. Quoted in John Gillott, "Too many people?" *Living Marxism* 71 (September 1994): 34.

3. Susan George, *How the Other Half Dies: The Real Reasons for World Hunger* (Harmondsworth, Middlesex: Penguin Books, 1981) 59.

4. Charles Dickens, *A Christmas Carol* (New York: Simon and Schuster, 1983) 16.

Such thinking has no scientific basis whatsoever. Its real basis is xenophobia, racism, and a guilty loathing of the "wretched of the earth." Indeed, whether it is dressed up in the humanitarian garb of promoting population control through contraception and family planning or in the harsh pseudo-realism of "letting nature take its course," the common denominator of this way of approaching the issue is the mistaken assumption that, for Third World families, children are an economic liability rather than an asset. Transnational Institute scholar Susan George has commented incisively on this question:

> Another baby for a poor family means an extra mouth to feed—a very marginal difference. But by the time that child is four or five years old, it will make important contributions to the whole family—fetching water from the distant well, taking meals to father and brothers in the field, feeding animals. Later the child will help with more complicated tasks which would devolve upon the mother of the household if she could not count on her children.... Most Third World mothers have only a 50/50 chance of seeing their children live beyond the age of five. Once we realize that children are an economic *necessity* for the poor, then we can understand that poor families will have to plan their births every bit as carefully as couples in Westchester or West Harrow—and allow for the predictable mortality rate.... If we stopped looking just for a moment at what *we* consider to be the problems of the poorest people ("too many children") and tried to look at life from their point of view ("my children are my only wealth"), then we might realize that "appropriate technologies" to lessen population growth without social changes making children less *necessary* cannot possibly have any effect.[5]

George's observation is fully in accord with a well-established demographic principle: the rate of population growth tends at first to increase and then to decline dramatically with advances in industrialization and modernization. The experience of Europe, North America, and Japan confirms that the "demographic transition" to lower birth and death rates, resulting eventually in a low or even negative overall rate of population growth, occurs when people are liberated from the burdens of subsistence or low-productivity agriculture and are able to enjoy the benefits and elevated living standards associated with a diversified modern economy. Poverty is not caused by overpopulation; rather, high rates of population growth result from the inability of poorer regions of the world to make a full transition to modern industrialism. Furthermore, the sources of this blocked transition are to be found precisely in the dynamics of a world political-economic system that transfers enormous

---

5. George 59-61.

wealth from the poorer to the wealthier regions of the planet, while treating the Third World as a "shock absorber" for the economic crisis tendencies recurrently generated in the advanced capitalist world.

Diane Francis and others like her in the business press sneer at the notion that global poverty results from "uneven trade," but the evidence is overwhelming that patterns of unequal exchange in global markets have been a major factor in creating the enormous and widening gap between the developed capitalist "North" and the impoverished regions of the global "South." Yet this "imperialism of trade" is merely the tip of the iceberg, for unequal exchange is fundamentally the result of the uneven development of capitalist production on a world scale. The first-born nations of capitalist civilization enjoy an enormous head start in navigating the waters of a ruthlessly competitive world economy. They achieved this head start not only by pioneering the wage-labour system and capitalist industry, but also through a "primitive accumulation of capital" made possible by the dispossession of Aboriginal populations from their ancestral homelands, the establishment of chattel slavery in the Americas, the colonial and neo-colonial subjugation of millions in Asia, Africa, and Latin America, and the ruthless plunder of the natural resources of what is now referred to euphemistically as the "developing world."

The masters of the developed capitalist countries wish to deny the culpability of their "world order" for the misery that prevails in the South, and they pretend that the disadvantaged of the world can improve their lot by playing by the rules laid down by the chief beneficiaries of that order. Yet the historical record shows that uneven development is an inescapable feature of world capitalism and that its fundamentally antagonistic social and economic relations must produce fabulous wealth at one pole and the most profound misery at the other. The overpopulation theory is a convenient way to distract well-meaning people from recognizing that reality—and to further victimize the world system's most vulnerable populations. In the last analysis, it reinforces the prejudice that the problems of Third World poverty and underdevelopment stem from the shortcomings, ignorance, and irresponsible behaviour of poor people rather than from the diabolical workings of an unjust and irrational world system.

Murray E. G. Smith

suggested readings

Berger, Thomas. *A Long and Terrible Shadow: White Values, Native Rights in the Americas, 1492-1992*. Vancouver: Douglas and McIntyre, 1991.

Churchill, Ward. *A Little Matter of Genocide: Holocaust and Denial in the Americas, 1492 to the Present*. San Francisco: City Lights, 1997.

Chomsky, Noam. *Year 501—The Conquest Continues*. Montreal: Black Rose Books, 1993.

Ehrenreich, Barbara. *Nickel and Dimed: On (not) Getting by in America*. New York: Henry Holt & Co., 2001.

George, Susan. *The Debt Boomerang: How Third World Debt Harms Us All*. Boulder, CO: Westview Press, 1992.

Goldberg, Gurtrude Schallner, and Eleanor Kremen, eds. *The Feminization of Poverty: Only in America?* New York: Praeger, 1990.

Jaimes, M. Annette, ed. *The State of Native America: Genocide, Colonization, and Resistance*. Boston: South End, 1992.

Monture-Angus, Patricia. *Journeying Forward: Dreaming First Nations' Independence*. Halifax: Fernwood, 1999.

Piven, Frances Fox, and Richard A. Cloward. *Regulating the Poor: The Functions of Public Welfare*. New York: Vintage, 1972.

Ryan, William. *Blaming the Victim*. New York: Vintage Books, 1972.

Shkilnyk, Anastasia M. *A Poison Stronger Than Love: The Destruction of an Ojibwa Community*. New Haven, CT: Yale University, 1995.

Shragge, Eric, ed. *Workfare: Ideology for a New Under-Class*. Toronto: Garamond, 1997.

Stannard, David E. *American Holocaust: The Conquest of the New World*. Oxford: Oxford University Press, 1992.

Tabb, William K. *The Amoral Elephant: Globalization and the Struggle for Social Justice in the Twenty-First Century*. New York: Monthly Review Press, 2001.

PART FIVE

social class

"class inequality is an inevitable feature of the human condition"

Misanthropic belief that "There will always be a ruling class"

Confronted with the facts about the extent and nature of the class inequalities existing in contemporary capitalist societies, most people will agree that they are outrageous and unjustifiable. At perhaps no point in modern history, however, has the will to do something about it been so weak as it is today.[1] This state of affairs is due not so much to the success of world capitalism in "delivering the goods" as to the historic discrediting of the socialist/communist alternative in the wake of the collapse of the Soviet bloc. Indeed, for many, the whole experience of Soviet-style socialism seems to confirm what is surely one of the hoariest of arguments against "socialist utopianism"—the claim that "class inequality is an inevitable feature of human existence," and that consequently "there will always be a ruling class." Yet, of all the arguments invoked against Marxism and other socialist doctrines, this is surely one of the easiest to refute.

One of America's leading anthropologists, Marvin Harris, has written eloquently against the notion that human nature lends itself irrevocably to hierarchical forms of social organization:

> … [L]et me hear no more of our kind's natural necessity to form hierarchical groups. An observer viewing human life shortly after cultural take-off would easily have concluded that our species was destined to be irredeemably egalitarian except for distinctions of sex and age. That someday the world would be divided into aristocrats and commoners, masters and slaves, billionaires and homeless beggars, would have seemed wholly contrary to human nature as evidenced in the affairs of every human society then on earth.[2]

---

1. This is notwithstanding the recent burgeoning of an "anti-globalization movement" with strongly anti-capitalist overtones.

2. Marvin Harris, *Our Kind* (New York: HarperPerennial, 1990) 351.

The anthropological evidence to which Harris appeals is quite unequivocal on one point. For most of the time that human beings have existed on this planet we have lived under "a form of communism"—that is to say, in the "absence of private possession in land and other vital resources."[3] Even so ardent a champion of modern "free-market" capitalism as Friedrich von Hayek concedes this point, noting with considerable regret that this heritage suggests that the "natural" predisposition of the human species is toward social equality and economic collectivism.

Still, it might be objected, is it not the case that even in the simplest and most egalitarian societies—the hunting and gathering communities that prevailed for tens of thousands of years prior to the appearance of settled agriculture—some "social ranking" occurred? Yes, of course. But this point can be easily acknowledged without accepting the larger claim that "class inequality" is inevitable—for social ranking can take many forms, including non-antagonistic ones, while class division is necessarily antagonistic. In other words, class division presupposes social ranking, but social ranking is by no means synonymous with class division. Indeed, class division is an antagonistic and exploitative form of social ranking that develops only under specific historical conditions. It is not only different in degree but also in kind from what the Canadian sociologist Dennis Forcese has called "minimal stratification"—the first form of hierarchical differentiation that is inherited across generations.[4]

In the earliest human societies, survival depended on the ability of group members to rely upon one another to provide for the collective needs of the group. Hunters would share their catch with the rest of the group, with equitable shares of the meat being consumed by all. In such a system of "reciprocal exchange," providers do not specify "how much or exactly what they expect to get back or when they expect to get it.... To call attention to one's generosity is to indicate that others are in debt to you and that you expect them to repay you. It is repugnant to egalitarian peoples even to suggest that they have been treated generously."[5] Surviving examples of band and village egalitarian communities are, moreover, conspicuously free of "paramount chiefs," let alone aristocratic landholders or all-powerful monarchs. Harris points to traditional Inuit and !Kung bands in which "leaders"—often outstanding hunters—lack all formal authority and "can only persuade, never command."

The skeptic might reply by arguing that resistance to structured hierarchies may be a feature of very simple societies lacking much in the way of technology or economic surplus, but that such hierarchies seem endemic to settled societies that have the ability to accumulate wealth which is not immediately consumed. Is there not a human propensity to divide up into antagonistic social classes once it becomes pos-

---

3. Harris 354.

4. Dennis Forcese, *The Canadian Class Structure* (Toronto: McGraw-Hill Ryerson, 1997) 10-11.

5. Harris 345.

sible for some people to specialize in activities of a strictly non-productive nature? There is some truth to this argument, inasmuch as the appearance of a social surplus is an indispensable condition for the "liberation" of certain individuals from production and their exclusive involvement in military, religious or administrative affairs. Indeed, the first ruling classes in history were composed of warriors and priests whose relatively comfortable lifestyles were predicated on their appropriation of the fruits of "commoners'" labour. But it can also be hypothesized that class division was historically the result of the existence of a *too-limited* surplus. If there is a tendency for human communities with growing but still-limited surpluses to divide up into antagonistic classes, perhaps this tendency can be overcome with the advent of human capacities that make possible an *abundance* of material wealth for all human beings. Perhaps under such "post-scarcity" conditions, the original human tendency to resist not only class division but also invidious social ranking of any kind will reassert itself. This, at any rate, is the hypothesis entertained by those who follow the Marxian socialist tradition, and it is, from an anthropological standpoint, a not unreasonable one.

The transition from egalitarian tribal communism to a class-divided society was a long and protracted one. Reciprocal exchange gave way to systems of "redistribution" in which "people turn over food and other valuables to a prestigious figure such as a headman, to be pooled, divided into separate portions, and given out again."[6] Initially, redistributors were rewarded solely with admiration and prestige. The more surplus they were able to procure for redistribution—typically at big feasts like the "potlatches" of the Amerindian tribes of the Pacific North West—the greater their honorific reward. With the emergence of competition between redistributors, we see the appearance of the phenomenon of the "big man"—what Harris calls "mumihood" (after the name accorded the chief redistributor by the Siuai of the Solomon Islands). The success of a "big man" redistributor depended in large measure on his ability to increase production so as to generate larger and larger surpluses available for consumption at tribal feasts. Eventually, redistributive exchange involved a rupture with the "modesty" associated with reciprocal exchange, in favour of flagrant boastfulness—loud proclamations by the big man and his coterie that he is a great and generous provider. Harris hypothesizes that "headmen and mumis are individuals who have an especially strong desire for approval (presumably as a result of a mix of childhood experience and heredity)."[7]

The transition toward structured social (and eventually class) inequality "gained momentum wherever extra food produced by the inspired diligence of redistributors could be stored while awaiting *muminai* feasts, potlatches, and other occasions of redistribution. The more concentrated and abundant the harvest and the less perishable

---

6. Harris 358.

7. Harris 366.

the crop, the greater its potential for endowing big men with power over people."[8] Yet for this potential to be realized a further ingredient was necessary: warfare. As Harris notes, "the opportunity to break away from the traditional restraints on power would increase as chiefdoms expanded their territories and grew more populous, and as stores of food and other valuables available for redistribution increased proportionately. By allocating different shares to those who were most co-operative, loyal, and effective on the battlefield, chiefs could begin to build the nucleus of a noble class backed up by a police force and a standing army."[9] Yet, while a storable agricultural surplus and warfare were necessary ingredients in the emergence of class-divided "kingdoms," they were by no means always sufficient conditions. Many chiefdoms were blocked from transforming themselves into kingdoms as a result of successful rebellions by disaffected commoners—and sometimes by the latter's mass exodus.

The obstacles to the break-up of human society into antagonistic social classes were so strong—and the egalitarian impulse so powerful—that it took tens of thousands of years before human beings in some parts of the world made the "ascent" to class-divided "civilization." Harris notes that "redistributors who reward themselves first and in greater measure have always needed ideologies and rituals that legitimize their appropriation of social wealth."[10] The ascription of divine religious status to rulers, as well as the awe-inducing "conspicuous consumption" of their life styles, have played a major role in entrenching their power and privilege on the basis of the idea that they are innately "superior" to commoners. One of the contradictions facing the ruling class of a capitalist society is that its basic social relations undermine the idea of the "divine right of kings"—that is, the notion of human inequality based upon inherited privilege—even as it enormously expands the material inequality dividing the capitalist property owner from the ordinary wage-labourer. Indeed, capitalist society necessarily promotes the idea that there is "room at the top" for all those talented, industrious or lucky enough to get there. The problem is that this encourages an ideology of "equal rights" that is profoundly subversive to a social system that remains wedded to the principles of class exploitation, inheritable wealth, and differential access to opportunities for "success."

Ironically, the egalitarian ethos that permeated tribal-communist societies for tens of thousands of years has been revived within a socio-economic system that has produced not only more social inequality than any other in human history but also a development of human capacities that promises an end to human scarcity and with it the deepest mainsprings of warfare. Is it unreasonable to speculate that such capacities, liberated from the antagonistic social relations in which they have developed, might

---

8. Harris 378.

9. Harris 383.

10. Harris 370.

yet help humankind usher in a new age of human equality—a classless society founded on the recognition that the very survival of the human species (and not simply this or that "tribe") depends upon the co-operative and democratic management of a collectively-owned economic base? If "primitives" could come to an understanding that reciprocal exchange was vital to their physical survival, and develop norms of behaviour and conventions reflecting that reality, surely humankind, at the dawn of the third millennium, may yet be able to cast off the ideological baggage of class-divided society and forge a non-antagonistic global community that can both take full advantage of the fruits of modern science and address our collective problems unfettered by the claims of a tiny minority that the productive resources of the planet belong to them "by right"—whether divine or otherwise.

Murray E. G. Smith

CHAPTER 17

"As a rule, the rich deserve their wealth"

corollary to the absurd notion that the poor deserve to be poor

"In general, the rich deserve their wealth. You're not being fair or a good sport to think otherwise." (A Brock University sociology student criticizing Marx and admiring Bill Gates in 1998.)

In 2000, Bill Gates, Chairman of Microsoft Corporation, was the owner of corporate and personal assets valued at over $70 billion. He had amassed this fortune in less than twenty years, making him the greatest entrepreneurial success story of the late twentieth century. Gates' personal wealth exceeded the value of the Gross National Product of dozens of countries around the world, including that of Ireland, a nation of 3.56 million people. Did he "deserve" to be this wealthy?

Many people think that Gates deserves every penny he has acquired, so long as he did so legally. Many others feel quite viscerally that so great a concentration of wealth in the hands of a single individual is morally repugnant, regardless of how he made his fortune. A wide gulf would seem to exist between two irreconcilable sets of "values"—one that upholds the freedom of the individual to acquire unlimited wealth, and another that insists that at least some limits should be placed on the wealth that a single individual can accumulate.

What conceptual resources can social science bring to bear in sorting out such a dispute? Very little, some social scientists would answer. In their opinion, the task of the social scientist is to describe and analyze as objectively as possible "what is," while the question of "what ought to be" is an entirely separate matter that social science has no special capacity to illuminate. Other social scientists share the assumption that "facts" and "values" are logically distinct, but they still insist that no social scientist can ever be "value free" in his or her scientific endeavours. This latter group might argue that moral revulsion toward the gross social inequality exemplified by Gates' fortune is a perfectly legitimate inspiration for a social scientific practice that not only describes and analyzes concentrated wealth, but seeks also to expose its socially destructive consequences.

Karl Marx, the founder of "scientific socialism," may be seen as the leading representative of a third group of social scientists who believe that values, morals, and ethics (together with other products of human consciousness) can never exist "independently" of the material-social conditions of human existence. From this perspective, all notions of what is "fair" or "right" must be seen as heavily conditioned by historical and social context. As Marx observed, "Right can never be higher than the economic structure of society and its cultural development conditioned thereby."[1] It follows from this insight that propositions like "the rich are generally deserving of their wealth" must be understood in relation to the historically specific features of an economic structure that allows for the kind of concentrated economic wealth exemplified by Gates' fortune.

Let us begin with a simple but telling observation: the great majority of people in the world need to perform labour in order to obtain an income. For wage labourers in particular, access to the necessities of life depends on their performance of labour in both the household and market economies. Wages (and even most salaries) are based on contracts between employers and employees in which the latter agree to sell their "capacity to work" in exchange for a definite amount of remuneration. Those who employ wage-labour are so concerned with the precise measurement of the time worked and with ensuring that this time is well spent that they resort to everything from punch clocks to time-and-motion studies to ensure that the remuneration is "deserved." And yet these same employers enjoy incomes that are in no sense related to the "work" they perform. Rather, the "employer class"—also known as capitalists or bourgeoisie—derive their income (whether in the form of direct profits, stock dividends or executive salaries) overwhelmingly from their *ownership* of business assets and from their consequent ability to lay claim to a huge share of the wealth produced by the working class.

From Marx's perspective, Bill Gates possesses a huge fortune not because he "earned" it but rather because the "rules of the game" under capitalism permit a few to accumulate vast personal wealth at the expense of the larger population. Gates has proven to be a particularly lucky—and, no doubt, very adept—player in that game. Undeniably, his own activity has had some considerable bearing on the fact that he was "selected" to be one of those fortunate few—after all, personal ambition and talent are almost always significant factors in the success of individual capitalists. Even so, Gates' personal attributes and good fortune should not obscure this simple fact: outside of a social and economic order based on private ownership of the productive assets of society and the pursuit of private profit through the exploita-

---

1. Karl Marx, "Critique of the Gotha Programme," in Karl Marx and Friedrich Engels, *Selected Works*, Volume 3 (Moscow: Progress Publishers, 1970) 19.

tion of wage-labour, a "success" of Gates' type and magnitude is simply impossible to conceive.

The question that Marx and his followers pose about the concentration of society's wealth in the hands of a small minority is *not* whether individual capitalists "deserve" their wealth—for, judged by the rules and standards of the existing social order, they usually do. Rather, Marx's fundamental question concerns whether or not the "capitalist rules of the game" are promoting social progress and human well-being. Are the historically specific social relations that define and constitute capitalism making a positive contribution to the human condition? To understand the way that Marx answered this question we must consider his views on "human progress" as well as his analysis of capitalism's defining social relations.

Marx's fundamental criterion of human progress is the expansion of human freedom, by which he understood the freedom of each and every human individual to realize his or her capacities to the fullest—the freedom of individuals to develop themselves in an "all-round" fashion. In the words of *The Communist Manifesto*, Marx looked forward to a society "in which the free development of each is the condition for the free development of all."[2] But to realize such a society, humanity must liberate itself from a host of persistent fetters on its collective capacities, and this requires a struggle to alter the human relationship to nature as well as relationships among human beings. Marx believed that human history, at least since the advent of the first class-divided societies, has been marked by a struggle to subdue the forces of nature and by struggles between subordinate and dominant classes. Yet Marx also acknowledged that class division—the exploitation of the many by the few—has been an important and even necessary spur to the development of labour productivity and to such "forces of production" as tools, technology, science, and productive technique. Without this development, he believed, humanity could not free itself from the harsher burdens imposed by nature or from the ignorance and superstition that bind people to "traditional" (oppressive) institutions and ways of life. Hence, while struggles between classes have persistently involved ideals of human equality and social justice, such aspirations require for their fullest realization a maturation of human capacities permitting both intellectual growth and the creation of an abundance of material wealth. Without material abundance, the struggle for necessities between human individuals, groups, and communities will continue to perpetuate the social structures of inequality between classes and peoples that we have seen throughout recorded history.

This general conception of human history informed Marx's specific analysis of modern capitalism: its constitutive social relations, its "laws of motion," and the fundamental "rules" governing people's behaviour under capitalism. In brief, Marx thought that capitalism fulfills an historically progressive role in dramatically expand-

---

2. Karl Marx and Friedrich Engels, *The Communist Manifesto* (New York: Monthly Review Press, 1998) 41.

ing the forces of production and advancing labour productivity; but he also believed that, at a certain stage of capitalism's development, the social relations of production that define the capitalist profit system must begin to impede the growth of human capacities and eventually thwart the potential development of the productive forces, thereby also impeding progress toward a qualitatively freer and more harmonious society. Accordingly, for Marx, the capitalist relations of production—the rules of the game under capitalism—are subject to an historical evaluation. There are no eternal and fixed "ethical norms" or "moral imperatives" that can tell us whether this mode of production—one that has permitted Bill Gates to become so fabulously rich—has finally outlived its ability to promote human progress; rather, this question requires a careful scientific assessment.

Capitalism involves the production of goods and services that are destined to be sold on the market for a profit. Such goods and services, insofar as they are products of human labour and capable of reproduction by human labour, are called commodities. Commodities have a dual character: on the one hand they have "use-value" (they fulfill some need or want of a consumer); on the other hand, they have "exchange-value" (the capacity to command remuneration, usually in money, through market exchange). In a capitalist society, where commodity production and exchange are increasingly generalized and where the capacity to work has itself been made into a commodity on a very wide scale, material production thus assumes the "social form" of the production of goods and services for the market with the aim of realizing a *profit*.

As important as formal equality and competition are to defining capitalist social relations, they tend to conceal what Marx regarded as the most fundamental of these relations: the exploitation of wage-labour by the owners of capital. By its very nature, capital is value seeking to enlarge itself. Capital's "inner need" is to continuously appropriate ("vampire-like," says Marx) the surplus labour that produces its lifeblood, the surplus value that allows for its continuous expansion. The appropriation of surplus labour occurs within the sphere of material production, and is the result of the inequality that exists between capital and wage-labour within that sphere. Marx shows that it is only through capital's exploitation of wage-labour in the factories, mills, mines, and other workplaces that are the sites of surplus-value production that it is able to lay its "golden eggs"—to generate profit.

Surplus value is the "social substance" of private profit, but value is itself simply an expression of definite and historically conditioned social relationships. It is a social relation arising from a society-wide division of labour in a historical context where labour power itself has become a commodity.

Marx's "labour theory of value" does not suggest, as many of its critics mistakenly assert, that the prices of individual commodities are directly determined by their labour-value content. Marx recognizes that many factors bear on the formation of individual prices, among them the variable relationship between supply and demand, the tendency of rates of profit to equalize, and international monetary exchange rates. But he does insist that labour-values are the "centres of gravity" of commodity prices and that they establish certain parameters or limits at the level of the capitalist economy as a whole. Marx's theory of labour-value, then, is not so much a theory of price formation as a theory of *why* social labour assumes the form of value under capitalism and of *how* a social division of labour is articulated in an economy characterized by private production for the market. This is the necessary starting point for his analysis of the contradictions and laws of motion of the capitalist mode of production.

The three key tenets of Marx's theory of labour-value are the following: a) living labour is the sole source of new (as distinct from previously existing) value; b) value exists as a definite quantitative magnitude at the level of the capitalist economy as a whole (one that sets limits on aggregate prices, profits, and wages); and c) in a capitalist economy, material wealth is measured in terms of abstract socially necessary labour time (value), the necessary form of appearance of which is money. Marx's whole analysis in his major work *Capital* is concerned with exploring the far-reaching implications of these three propositions.

Proceeding from this understanding of the law of labour-value under capitalism, Marx was able to expose the specific mechanism whereby class exploitation occurs within capitalist society. The key to his theory of surplus-value—of how value is appropriated by the capitalist owners from those who produce it through their productive activity—is the distinction he draws between the value of labour power (the wages received by productive workers) and the total new value created by living labour. What the capitalist purchases from the wage-labourer is not the latter's "labour"—the actual amount of "labour performed"—but rather the worker's capacity to labour. This capacity to labour enters the production process as a very special input commodity, for it is the sole input to production that is capable of transferring more value to the new commodity product than it is worth. All other inputs to production, regardless of how technologically sophisticated they may be, are mere "things" representing a definite amount of past labour. These things can impart to the new product only a definite amount of previously existing value. Thus raw materials and fuel give up their value as they are consumed in production, while tools, machinery, and building structures undergo a process of depreciation in which a fraction of their value is transferred to the output commodity. Labour-power, on the other hand, as a capacity of living human beings, is inherently variable in its contribution of value to the new commodity product. Depending on how efficiently and intensively labour power is consumed (which depends in large measure on the quality of the tools and equipment in use, as well as on how well the labour process is organized and managed), a larger or smaller amount of surplus-value will be produced. This surplus-value is precisely the difference between the value of the workers' wages (defined largely by the cost of reproducing labour power) and the total amount of new value that has been added to the new ("output") commodity by the activity of living labour.[3]

Thus, it is only by examining what transpires in the sphere of production that the capitalist exploitation of wage-labour is rendered visible. So long as we look only at what is happening in the market—in the sphere of circulation, where the principle of the "exchange of equivalents" prevails —the fundamentally exploitative character of the capitalist mode of production remains concealed. As Marx puts it in a scathing critique of the fixation of conventional economics on market phenomena, once we move beyond the sphere of circulation to the sphere of production we also move from a realm of (purely formal) "freedom and equality" to a realm of tyranny in which capital unmistakably dominates wage-labour:

> When we leave this sphere of simple circulation or the exchange of commodities, which provides the "free-trader *vulgaris*" with his views, his concepts and the standard by which he judges the society of capital and wage-labour, a certain change takes place, or so it appears, in the physiognomy of our *dramatis personae*. He who was previously the money-owner now strides out in front as a capitalist; the possessor of labour-power follows as his worker. The one smirks self-importantly and is intent on business; the other is timid and holds back, like someone who has brought his own hide to market and now has nothing to expect but—a tanning.[4]

Marx's theories of value and surplus value are certainly controversial and hardly immune to theoretical criticism. Yet it should be clear that they seek to ground an evaluation of class inequality under capitalism in an objective analysis of real social processes. In drawing the conclusion that capitalism is an historically limited system, one that must eventually give way to a higher (socialist and eventually communist) form of social organization, Marx argues that capitalism brings the social phenomenon of exploitation to its highest point while also creating conditions in which it is increasingly irrational to measure human wealth in terms of labour time. By sponsoring an ongoing technological revolution, capitalism lays the basis for an increasingly automated economy that requires the input of less and less human labour. But this process proceeds exceedingly unevenly and with more and more fits and starts due to capital's "need" to measure wealth in terms of money—which is fundamentally the necessary form of appearance of abstract social labour. There is a "need" to measure wealth in this fashion, however, only in a society organized around the principle of the exploitation of one class by another. The conflict or "structural

---

3. For a discussion of Marx's theory of surplus value, see Murray E.G. Smith, "Alienation, Exploitation and Abstract Labor: A Humanist Defense of Marx's Theory of Value," *Review of Radical Political Economics* 26:1 (March 1994).

4. Karl Marx, *Capital Volume One* (New York: Vintage, 1977) 280.

contradiction" between capitalism's dynamic toward labour-saving and labour-displacing technological innovation, on the one hand, and its imperative to exploit living labour, on the other, sets the stage for periodic crises of the capitalist economy and for a protracted historical-structural crisis of the capitalist mode of production signifying the exhaustion of its once-progressive role in extending human capacities.

In Marx's view, the resolution of this conflict requires that the working class—the great majority of the population under conditions of mature capitalism—must wrest political and economic power away from the capitalist class through a revolutionary struggle, and then proceed to the construction of a new social order. In this process of struggle and social transformation, the socialist workers' movement will undoubtedly be influenced by considerations of morality and social justice; but it will also base its program on the firm conviction that capitalism not only "ought" to be consigned to the scrap heap of history, but that it must *be* to secure real social progress and to safeguard the very future of humanity. Sooner or later, Marx believed, the morality, ethical norms, and notions of social justice that are part and parcel of the capitalist order, and that serve to conceal and justify its enormous inequities, will be seen by the working-class majority for what they are: the anachronistic and self-interested prejudices of a capitalist ruling class that has long since exhausted its historically progressive role.

Murray E. G. Smith

CHAPTER 18

"A classless society in a complex and economically developed society is impossible; it is an unrealistic utopia"

Excuse for gross social inequality amidst tremendous wealth and productive capacity

Every ruling class in human history has sought to convince those over whom it rules of the naturalness and the inevitability of the prevailing social order. The ancients believed that the institution of chattel slavery had always existed and always would. The feudal aristocracy of medieval Europe upheld, with the indispensable assistance of the Roman Catholic Church, the idea that the rigid hierarchy of the feudal social order was divinely sanctioned—that a privileged few were "born to rule" while others (the great majority) were destined only to toil.

Today we know better. Today the dominant ideology (or conventional wisdom) of our society maintains that the physical person of a human being should never be the personal property of another and that all human beings ought to enjoy the benefits of equal rights and democratic forms of government. A humane and truly civilized society, we are told, must strive toward the goal of equal opportunity and a meritocratic system of rewards. Yet as much as the idea of "equality of opportunity" is rhetorically upheld, the idea of "equality of condition" is reviled—and not just the austere "absolute" equality of condition that exists only in ascetic monastic orders or millenarian religious communities, but even the approximate equality of condition that is the goal of Marxian socialism. The outcome of the "free competition" for economic rewards, social honour or political power must continue to be not just a minimal degree of inequality, but the kind of massive inequality that characterizes the contemporary world capitalist order. To speak of a move beyond capitalism—to a society that would replace class division by egalitarian and democratic principles of social and economic organization—is to indulge in utopian fantasizing. That, at any rate, is what we are encouraged to believe by those who would have much to lose if the idea of a "classless society" were to seize the imaginations of the majority of humankind.

Can the human majority expect to do better under an economic and social order that takes the productive assets of society into collective ownership and subjects them to a rational plan? The capitalists and their immediate hangers-on respond unhesitatingly in the negative. Prior to the Russian Revolution of 1917, the capitalist rulers disseminated the idea that a large and complex industrial society could never be subjected to a plan—that "free markets" and "private enterprise" were absolutely indispensable to economic growth and development. They also insisted that only "free enterprise"—the pursuit of profit on the basis of private ownership of the means of production—could provide people with the psychological incentives required to be innovative and to work hard. These ideas were shattered by the actual experience of "socialist construction" in the Soviet Union and other countries. For whatever else may be said about the shortcomings of these "experiments" in building an alternative, non-capitalist form of industrial society (and much can be said on this score no doubt), the fact of the matter is that Soviet-style "actually existing socialism" demonstrated that neither "private enterprise" nor the market allocation of economic resources is necessary for rapid economic development, industrialization, or scientific inventiveness. In spite of civil war, economic embargoes, repeated foreign invasions, and horrific bureaucratic mismanagement and terror, the USSR rose within the space of just forty years from being one of the most backward countries in the world to being one of its greatest industrial and military powers. Indeed, on the fortieth anniversary of the Russian Revolution in 1957, the USSR became the first country to launch an earth-orbiting satellite, refuting the notion that only the capitalist profit motive can stimulate scientific creativity.

If the strengths of the Soviet achievement undercut some of the traditional capitalist arguments against Marx's vision of a classless, socialist society, the flaws and undoubted horrors of "Soviet socialism" reinforced another: the argument that all human societies are necessarily divided into rulers and ruled, and that the socialization of the economy could only create conditions favourable to the emergence of a state bureaucratic elite that would be as self-serving and ruthless a "ruling class" as any that had ever existed.

Where the economists' arguments against socialism had failed, the arguments of such sociologists as Max Weber, Robert Michels, and Vilfredo Pareto seemed vindicated in light of the experience of Stalinist "state socialism." Weber's theory of bureaucratic domination, Michels' "iron law of oligarchy," and Pareto's theory of "ruling elites" all supported the idea that class domination—the rule of the few over the many—is an endemic feature of the human condition.[1] Just after the Bolshevik Revolution of 1917, Weber announced that for the foreseeable future it was the dictatorship of the official, and not the revolutionary rule of the working class, that was on the march.

1. For Max Weber's views on bureaucracy and the "legitimate" forms of domination see his *Economy and Society: An Outline of Interpretive Sociology* (Los Angeles: University of California Press, 1978). For an excellent overview of the elite theories of Pareto and Michels, among others, see Tom Bottomore, *Elites and Society* (New York: Basic Books, 1964).

In his classic study of the German Social Democratic Party, Robert Michels argued that the egalitarian and democratic ideals of German socialism were powerless to prevent the bureaucratic centralization of its most important organizational instrument. He who says organization, he declared, necessarily says oligarchy.[2]

These and subsequent sociological arguments against socialism took their ground not on the discredited ideas of "social Darwinism" ("those on top are there because they are stronger and smarter—in a word because they are more *fit*"), but on the seemingly reasonable proposition that the only effective way to organize large numbers of people is bureaucratically and that, consequently, power must devolve to those at the pinnacle of the bureaucratic hierarchy. Since those with power have a natural desire to hold onto it, it is highly desirable for a modern complex society to possess a plurality of bureaucratic elites. The problem with socialism, according to this argument, is that it allows for a centralization of power in the hands of a single bureaucratic oligarchy—that which exercises state power. By contrast, capitalism involves an array of mutually contending and competing bureaucracies. The political power of the state bureaucracy is checked by the economic clout of privately owned businesses, each of which generates its own bureaucratic structures. Moreover, other institutions of "civil society"—trade unions, churches, universities, and so on—also become loci of bureaucratic power. It is only in the context of such a diffusion of bureaucratic power—made possible by the separation of the economic and the political under market capitalism—that a limited, but nevertheless precious form of representative democracy can flourish. Thus, despite its tendency to promote extreme forms of social inequality, capitalism stands as an obstacle to "totalitarian" forms of political rule. From the standpoint of the ideals of democracy and individual liberty, then, capitalism is the best of all possible worlds. Socialism may promise a truer form of democracy and a greater degree of equality; but the road to a totalitarian hell is paved with the socialists' "good intentions," and this is amply confirmed by the historical experience of Stalinism.

We will consider the Weberian argument that bureaucracy is indispensable to organizational efficiency in Chapter 36. What needs to be addressed here is the tacit assumption—made by so many who are anxious to write off Marxian socialism—that *all* of the conditions specified by Marxists for the creation of a "classless society" were present in Soviet society after the revolution and that, despite this, a bureaucratic oligarchy was able to usurp power and arrogate to itself many of the material privileges associated with the ruling classes of the capitalist West. This assumption cannot withstand the slightest scrutiny. Its plausibility, however, was reinforced from an unexpected quarter: the Soviet bureaucracy itself. The Stalinist bureaucratic oligarchy was ideologically committed to the notion that all of the conditions for the "construction of socialism" were present within the geographical confines of the Soviet Union, and Soviet leader Nikita Khrushchev even boasted that what Marx called the

---

2. See Chapter 36 of this book.

highest stage of socialism—a classless communist society—would be achieved by 1970! Surely, the Soviet Communist leadership—good Marxists that they all claimed to be—could be taken at their word when they said that "socialism" had already been achieved in the Soviet Union as early as 1936. Or could they?

The ideological convergence between the Stalinists of the East and the anti-communists of the West consisted in this: both sides accepted the idea that Marxian socialism was consistent with the idea of building socialism in one country, even one so comparatively backward as the Soviet Union. Yet Marx and Engels had rejected this idea as early as 1846, writing in *The German Ideology* that, "[e]mpirically, communism is only possible as the act of the dominant peoples 'all at once' and simultaneously, which presupposes the universal development of productive forces and the world intercourse bound up with communism."[3]

Marx's optimism concerning the ability of the working class to build an egalitarian socialist order on the road to achieving a classless society may *appear* to have been misplaced in light of the actual experiences of "socialist construction" in this century; but an historically concrete assessment of these experiences reveals that the theoretical presuppositions underlying Marx's optimistic expectations have been more than amply confirmed. For Marx always insisted that the material preconditions for a genuinely socialist transcendence of capitalism would have to include the "forces of production" brought into being by capitalism itself. Such productive forces would include a fully global division of labour, a technologically advanced economic infrastructure and productive apparatus, and a well-educated and politically conscious working class capable of assuming the tasks of self-administration and therefore of "self-emancipation." It is only too obvious that the conditions under which Soviet-style "socialism" was constructed in this century were marked instead by a comparatively low level of development of the productive forces so defined.

Basing himself upon this classical Marxist understanding, one of the central leaders of the Bolshevik Revolution, Leon Trotsky, developed an incisive analysis of the Stalinist degeneration of the revolution as early as 1936. In *The Revolution Betrayed,* Trotsky argued that Stalinism—the social phenomenon of bureaucratic rule on the basis of socialized property forms—was a nationalist and fundamentally anti-working-class departure from Marxism that was paving the way for the restoration of capitalism. Trotsky's analysis was unique in accurately predicting the ultimate fragmentation of the Soviet bureaucratic oligarchy that occurred in the 1980s, and the attempt of a significant section of the so-called *nomenclatura* to transform itself into a nascent capitalist class that occurred in the 1990s.

Arguably, the demise of the Stalinist project of building a bureaucratized caricature of "socialism in one country" fully confirms Marx's prognostication that the

---

3. Karl Marx and Friedrich Engels, *The German Ideology,* excerpted in K. Marx and F. Engels, *Selected Works* Vol. 1 (Moscow: Progress Publishers, 1969) 37.

practical premise for the development of fully socialist institutions, relations, and practices is the abolition of capitalism on a world scale, and the incorporation of the productive forces created under capitalism into a socialist international division of labour. Without this, Marx and Engels observed, "*want* is merely made general, and with destitution the struggle for necessities and all the old filthy business would necessarily be reproduced."[4] It was precisely extreme economic scarcity—the product of the uneven development of capitalism on a world scale, the peculiarities of Russian social development, and the siege conditions in which the isolated revolution repeatedly found itself—that clearly paved the way for the new form of social differentiation represented by Stalinist rule, a parasitic bureaucratism that fell short of a new type of "class domination," but which did, as Trotsky predicted, prepare the ground for the re-establishment of capitalist class rule.

All of this should establish why it is inappropriate to see the Soviet experience as an adequate "test" for Marx's proposition that an egalitarian and democratic socialist order, with an increasingly "classless" character, is an historically possible and desirable goal. Needless to say, however, it does not provide positive confirmation of the proposition. Such a confirmation could only be provided in the event that "socialist construction" were to be attempted under the conditions that Marx specified as necessary. However, such an eventuality will depend on the capacity of human beings to continue to "imagine" a better future in a significantly different social order, and to act to achieve it. The Marxist scholar Ernest Mandel has noted that "Lenin of all people ... actually drew attention to the 'right to dream', nay the 'need to dream', provided that the dream is about what does not yet exist but could come about under a certain set of circumstances. To make such dreams 'come true' implies both the existence of the material preconditions, and human endeavor, projects, the will to act, and the capacity for effective action."[5] It is precisely the capacity to dream and to act decisively to bring about a better world that is paralysed by the pernicious yet influential argument that the experience of Stalinism proves that Marxian socialism is an unrealistic and dangerous "utopia." It is a sure sign that a social system has become moribund when its defenders must resort to such dishonest arguments in order to stifle the natural human impulse to "dream."

The question of whether a classless society is possible should be seen as an open question requiring rational analysis and debate, and above all the test of practice. Yet it is precisely a practice directed toward the realization of such a society that the powers-that-be within our society seek to thwart by insisting that the ideals of Marxian socialism are a "utopia" that can lead in the real world only to a Stalinist dystopia. Before we relinquish our "right to dream," however, we should remember just how much past human progress depended upon the willingness of far-sighted

---

4. Marx and Engels 37, emphasis in original.

5. Ernest Mandel, *Power and Money: A Marxist Theory of Bureaucracy* (London: Verso, 1992) 233.

people to act, often at great self-sacrifice, on behalf of their "unrealistic dreams." As Mandel reminds us:

> The platitude that 'Marxian socialism' does not exist anywhere in the world today is tirelessly repeated as, in effect, an argument against all human progress. But was it utopian to fight for the abolition of slavery, which existed on a large scale for more than a thousand years? Was it utopian to seek an end to serfdom? Religious oppression, including the burning of heretics at the stake, was a 'fact of life' for at least five centuries. Was it then utopian to try to establish freedom of conscience and freedom of thought? Parliaments existed for many hundreds of years on the basis of an extremely narrow franchise. Was it therefore utopian to fight for universal suffrage? Why should it be utopian to try to do away with wage-labour and gigantic state bureaucracies, which after all have been central structures of society for no more than two hundred years.... Utopia, in the broad sense of the word, has been one of the great motors of the eventual achievement of historical progress. In the case of slavery, for example, its abolition would not have happened when and as it did if revolutionary or 'utopian' abolitionists had limited themselves to a struggle to better the conditions of slaves within the 'peculiar institution.'[6]

With its battle cry against the supposedly "utopian" idea of a classless society, the culture of prejudice reveals itself to be the enemy of continuing progress toward human emancipation.

Murray E. G. Smith

---

6. Mandel 233.

CHAPTER 19

"Most people belong to the middle class"
Myth of the "middle-class society"

If asked how they would locate themselves within a class structure divided into upper, middle, and lower classes, most people living in the advanced capitalist world would probably answer that they are members of the middle class.[1] According to the popular view, the upper class is composed of the rich, while the lower class consists of economically disadvantaged to very poor people. The middle class is typically conceived as the societal majority, encompassing its own upper, middle, and lower sub-categories. This conventional understanding of class structure is closely connected to the notion of a "middle-class society"—a society in which the prevailing institutions are presumed to support the values and interests of the "middle-class majority," and in which the political clout of this majority is considered decisive in the democratic policy-making process.

Little wonder, then, that respectful references to the middle class and to "middle-class interests," "middle-class values," and "middle-class aspirations" are commonplace features of the political cultures and discourses of most liberal-democratic, capitalist societies. In the algebra of conventional politics, the middle class is a veritable "x" whose content or value is both ineffable and subject to continual redefinition at the level of individual subjectivity. In view of this indeterminacy, winning political strategies are widely understood to depend on an accurate definition of the views and subjectively perceived interests of the large majority within society who, at any particular time, regard themselves as members of the middle class.

Mainstream politicians accept and abet the idea of the "middle-class society" in good measure because winning electoral formulas almost always take it for granted. Beyond such pragmatic considerations, however, this notion is widely understood to be key to the political stability of liberal-democratic capitalism, in large part because it strengthens the myth of "democratic majority rule" that is otherwise

---

1. Adapted from Murray E.G. Smith, "Rethinking 'the Middle Class': Ideological Constructions and Contradictory Structural Locations." *Brock Review* 6: 1/2 (1997): 56-73.

belied by the enormous concentrated economic power of huge corporations. This is not to say that the idea of the "middle-class society" is a mere illusion, deliberately perpetrated by political, economic or media elites in an effort to dupe the masses. On the contrary, the notion has real and substantial social-psychological foundations in the lived experiences of most members of advanced capitalist, liberal-democratic societies. Yet it is no less an *ideological* notion on this account if by "ideology" we understand a way of thinking and of seeing things that is partial and one-sided, that treats prevailing social inequities as "natural" and "eternal," and that serves dominant class interests.

To say that the idea of a "middle-class majority" serves an ideological function is to suggest that it conceals fundamental aspects of capitalist social reality and its attendant class structure. Even so, all too many social scientists, including many otherwise critical ones, are prepared to lend their scholarly authority to it. A case in point is the Canadian sociologist Dennis Forcese, who criticizes the notion that Canadian society is "classless" in the following terms:

> What classlessness has meant is peculiar to the middle class. Middle-class Canadians tell researchers that they perceive themselves as living in a homogeneous middle-class society. We are taught to think in such a fashion by our parents, peers, the media, and the schools…. The myth of a middle-class society of equal opportunity is thereby perpetuated. As one author sums it up, 'Canadians see their society as "classless" because the vast majority of persons with whom they interact are, just as they themselves are, members of the middle class. It is precisely because we perceive our structure in this way that we ignore both the extremes, that is, the poor and the rich. The larger the middle class the less visible the extremes' (John Hofley, 1971).[2]

Notwithstanding his well-intentioned concern with making poverty and concentrated wealth "visible" to average Canadians, Forcese (following Hofley) effectively replaces the myth of "classlessness" with the similar and no less pernicious myth of a "middle-class majority." Moreover, Forcese fails to recognize that it is altogether arbitrary to define the rich and the poor as the "extremes" of the class structure and that this way of seeing social reality obscures the antagonistic capital/labour relation that is central to the dynamic and developmental logic of a capitalist class society. How is it possible for so well informed an observer of class structure as Forcese to miss these points? The answer is that the theoretical framework of his class analysis is one that begins with the premise of a "middle-class majority"—a premise with deep roots in the dominant ideology and social psychology of advanced capitalist societies.

---

2. Dennis Forcese, *The Canadian Class Structure* (Toronto: McGraw-Hill Ryerson, 1986) 24.

The habit of identifying the middle class with middle-income groups comprising the majority of the population is one that has many sponsors, including the institutional agencies that Forcese cites as perpetrators of the myths of classlessness and equal opportunity. Families, schools, churches, mainstream political parties, governments, and mass media are faithful disseminators of ideas and images of society that emphasize social harmony, a symmetry of merit and reward within the "free enterprise" system, and the naturalness of "class peace." During normal times, such "harmonist ideology" resonates well with most members of society, in good part because it seems to discourage "unnecessary" conflict and disruptions to social order and community life. Those who benefit most from the existing social arrangements and inequalities do their utmost to disseminate this ideology through established institutions, while those most resistant to it are unlikely to find a large audience for their arguments except during periods of acute social, economic, and political crisis.

While recognizing the importance of harmonist ideology in promoting the notion of a "middle-class society," we must also give due consideration to a number of social-psychological factors rooted in "reference group dynamics." As Kelley and Evans point out,

> People's subjective images of class and class conflict reflect a mixture of both materialist forces and the vivid subjective images of equality and consensus among family, friends, and coworkers. These reference group processes distort perceptions of class: They make most people think they are middle class, thereby weakening the link between objective class and subjective perceptions of class and class conflict, fostering consensual rather than conflictual views of class relations, and attenuating the links between class and politics....[3]

By materialist forces, Kelley and Evans understand those "objective" aspects of class position that are defined by ownership and control of the means of production (traditional Marxist criteria) as well as by educational attainment, occupational status, and income level (criteria associated with functionalist stratification theory). While it is perhaps problematic to treat perceptions of occupational status as an objective or materialist indicator of class, Kelley and Evans argue, with some justification, that reference group dynamics can have a more powerful impact on people's perceptions of their class position than "materialist forces." One might quibble with the assumption that reference group processes are not themselves "materialist forces," but, leaving this question aside, Kelley and Evans are right to observe that

---

3. Jonathan Kelley and M.D.R. Evans, "Class and Class Conflict in Six Western Nations," *American Sociological Review* 60 (April, 1995): 157.

people often "perceive the world as an enlarged version of their reference group."[4] For this reason,

> [People] assess their class locations in light of the educational levels, occupations, and incomes of the people around them. Because family, friends and coworkers are usually similar...most people see themselves as average and unexceptional. Moreover, even very high-status people place many others above themselves, and very low-status people see others even lower.... Hence, most people locate themselves near the middle of the class hierarchy.[5]

Surveys of popular perceptions of class in six western countries confirm that subjective class identification is overwhelmingly with the "middle classes" in a standardized ten-class schema. In Australia, Austria, Germany, Switzerland, the United States, and Great Britain, "the modal class position is near the middle of the 10-class scheme, with a majority perceiving themselves to be in class 4, 5, or 6."[6] This leads Kelley and Evans to conclude that "There is no evidence of a numerically dominant lower class, as traditional materialist theories posit. Instead, reference group forces restrict the subjective arena to a narrow range in the middle of the class hierarchy."[7]

Kelley and Evans are undoubtedly correct to point to reference group dynamics as a powerful factor inhibiting the development of a class-conscious workers' movement and encouraging the notion among working-class people that they are rather typical members of a middle-class society. Indeed, the existence of powerful forces deflecting the development of "proletarian class consciousness" would hardly be a revelation to Karl Marx and his successors. Furthermore, Kelley and Evans are unable to cite any evidence that Marxist or other "materialist" class theorists have ever maintained that the so-called "lower class" is "numerically dominant." Marx's actual view was that the development of capitalist society would bring about a long-term proletarianization of most of its population by rendering the majority dependent on the sale of labour power for a wage. Accordingly, it was a working-class majority that Marx anticipated, not a "lower-class majority." Moreover, the key political and pedagogical task from Marx's perspective was hardly to combat workers' perceptions of themselves as average members of the "middle strata" of society, and still less to convince the working-class majority that they belong to a "lower class," but to impart to them an understanding that (a) capitalism operates primarily in the interests of the capitalist class and at the expense of those who must work for a living,

---

4. Kelley and Evans 158.

5. Kelley and Evans 158.

6. Kelley and Evans 166.

7. Kelley and Evans 166.

and (b) capitalism can and should be replaced by a new socialist order that can serve the interests of the working-class majority. Such an understanding is the essence, for Marx, of proletarian class consciousness. At the same time, contrary to what Kelley and Evans imply, Marx never held that such a political class consciousness could arise spontaneously among working-class individuals under the impact of "materialist forces." If it could, there would be no need for political organization, agitation, and education to help the working class to overcome all the subjective and ideological obstacles that impede an objective and scientific understanding of capitalist social reality—obstacles to class consciousness that have engaged the theoretical and practical interest of Marxists for well over a century.

The strength of Marxist class theory is its commitment to a conception of class that is both "relational" and based on objective criteria (primarily structural position within a particular mode of production) rather than on subjective and arbitrary notions. But Marxist class theory is by no means homogeneous. Significant differences exist between such theorists as Erik Olin Wright, Guglielmo Carchedi, and Robert Weil. Wright dispenses with the concept of the middle class entirely, deconstructing this commonsense notion into a traditional petty-bourgeoisie of self-employed, property-holding labourers and a series of "contradictory class locations."[8] He regards the petty-bourgeoisie as a remnant of non-capitalist, independent (or simple) forms of commodity production: a distinct class unto itself whose members are characterized by ownership of means of production, self-employment, and non-reliance on the exploitation of wage-labour. For Wright, objectively "contradictory class locations" exist between this traditional petty-bourgeoisie and the capitalist class (small employers who command the labour of others); between this petty-bourgeoisie and the working class (salaried employees who direct their own labour, but not the labour of others); and between the bourgeoisie and the working class (managers, supervisors, and foremen, who embody some of the characteristics of both capital and labour). Taken together, Wright's contradictory class locations encompass most of the elements that Carchedi refers to as "the new middle class"—a class whose "structural interests are contradictory since this class partly performs the function of labour (i.e., it carries out the labour process) and partly performs the function of capital (i.e., it carries out the work of control and surveillance within the production process)."[9]

Weil provides a compelling argument for the proposition that the traditional petty-bourgeoisie, together with Wright's "contradictory class locations," should be regarded as elements straddling the capital-labour divide, and that the petty-bourgeoisie is thus itself in a contradictory structural location. On this view, the petty-bourgeoisie is not a surviving remnant of a commodity-producing mode of production that existed prior to capitalism, but an integral component of the capitalist mode of

8. Erik Olin Wright, *Class, Crisis and the State* (London: Verso, 1978).

9. Guglielmo Carchedi, "Class Politics, Class Consciousness, and the New Middle Class," *Insurgent Sociologist* (1988): 119.

production. Although it has roots in pre-capitalist forms of commodity production, the petty-bourgeoisie has long been "capitalistic" in character. It combines within itself the role of capital (ownership of means of production/the imperative to exploit labour) and the role of wage-labour (the performance of labour/the imperative to work for a living). As Weil notes, "for Marx the idea of 'self-employment' involves both being a 'wage-earner' for oneself and gaining a 'rentier' profit from capital as well. It arises precisely because even 'self-employed' small owners, the 'pure' petty-bourgeoisie, are capitalistic."[10]

Weil makes the important point that what is fundamental to a proper Marxist understanding of "classes" in general, and the "middle class" in particular, is Marx's law of labour value, which maintains that the sole source of all new value, including the surplus-value realized as profit, is living labour.[11] He argues,

> For [Marx], commodity and labor value are both aspects of a single "unity," bearing the nature of each other even when "formally" apart. It was this that enabled him to see that even the "pure" petty bourgeoisie simultaneously realize the full value of their labor and at the same time treat it capitalistically as wages and profit....[12]

Weil rejects Wright's conception of the traditional, self-employed petty-bourgeoisie as "neither exploiter nor exploited." This notion is one-sided and at odds with Marx's insight that the petty-bourgeoisie is, in fact, "neither exploiter nor exploited" *and* "both exploiter and exploited." Under capitalist economic conditions, the "pure" petty-bourgeois, no less than the capitalist, is obliged to appropriate surplus labour; and where the petty-bourgeois producer is not in a position to appropriate the surplus labour of others (typically family members), he is compelled to appropriate his own surplus labour. Hence, petty-bourgeois owners treat the income arising from their own labour as divided into "wages" and "profit," and the combined sum of the two is the total value yielded by the labour they perform.[13]

By combining Marx's insight concerning the contradictory character of the petty-bourgeoisie and Carchedi's insight into the contradictory functions of the waged and salaried employees that fall under his rubric of "the new middle class," we have the basis for defining an authentic, albeit relatively small, "intermediate" class that is situated, in contradictory fashion, between capital and wage-labour. Some elements

---

10. Robert Weil, "Contradictory Class Definitions: Petty Bourgeoisie and the 'Classes' of Erik Olin Wright," *Critical Sociology* 21.3 (1995): 13.

11. See also Murray E.G. Smith, *Invisible Leviathan: The Marxist Critique of Market Despotism Beyond Postmodernism* (Toronto: University of Toronto Press, 1994).

12. Weil 15.

13. Weil 11.

of this (highly heterogeneous) class are objectively very close to a working-class structural location, while others stand closer to a capitalist class location.

The existence of such an intermediate class (or classes) is not a matter of dispute, nor is the scientific value of its analysis. But the discursive association of this class (which constitutes a distinct minority within contemporary capitalism) with popular notions of a "middle-class majority" represents an illegitimate adaptation to the ideological structures embedded in popular discourses on class. The persistence of this association within much of the social-scientific literature constitutes a compelling reason for insisting that the term "the middle class" is inherently misleading and therefore that its use ought to be discouraged in any discussion of class that aspires to scientific rigour.

Capitalist development since Marx's day has produced a bewilderingly complex occupational structure that appears at first glance to contradict Marx's prediction of an inexorable process of proletarianization and class polarization. The rapid growth of the industrial proletariat during the era of capitalist industrialization was succeeded in the cradles of Western capitalism by the decline of the "blue-collar" industrial workforce. The twentieth century saw a proliferation of white-collar jobs, many of them "bureaucratic" positions stemming from the separation of head and hand. A huge and growing proportion of wage-labourers in many developed capitalist countries now perform what Marx would have called *unproductive* labour in banks, insurance and real-estate companies, wholesale and retail outlets, as well as in marketing and administration. Such labour may be "socially necessary" to the functioning of the capitalist system, but it is also removed from direct participation in the *production* of goods and services in the commodity form (the form of the product of labour that yields a profit to capital). The long-term expansion of the state in most capitalist countries has also produced a growing number of unproductive wage-labourers who are not in the employ of private capital, but who nevertheless serve the capitalist system as a whole by sustaining its institutional conditions and attenuating its structural contradictions.[14]

None of these trends, however, refutes Marx's prognostications regarding the main developmental tendencies of the capitalist class structure. Indeed, one can argue that Marx's theoretical framework remains indispensable to explaining the proliferation of socially necessary unproductive labour, the bureaucratization of industry and the state, and the decline of the blue-collar industrial workforce. For what is key to the explication of these trends is an adequate analysis of the laws of capital accumulation, the real subordination of labour by capital, the crisis tendencies of advanced capitalism, and the processes of objective socialization that may prefigure, albeit in a distorted form, some of the contours of the future socialist society—an analysis vigorously pursued by Marx in the three volumes of *Capital*.

Marx's main predictions about the evolution of the capitalist class structure have been strikingly confirmed. Marx was quite right to foresee an increasing tendency for

---

14. Smith 196-200.

the direct producers to be separated (alienated) from their means of production and to be transformed into wage-labourers. In a related vein, he was correct to forecast the gradual disappearance of independent commodity producers—the traditional petty-bourgeoisie of small farmers, fishermen, artisans, etc.—as well as small shopkeepers involved in the market circulation and final sale of commodities. Moreover, he was able to foresee accurately the process of concentration and centralization of capital that permits the greater part of the productive resources of society to come under the control of a relatively small number of capitalist enterprises (what nowadays are called transnational corporations and conglomerates). In all of these forecasts Marx has been proven remarkably prescient—indeed, far more prescient than most of his contemporaries. In particular, his prediction of a fundamental division within society between capitalist employers and those who must sell their labour power (intellectual or manual, skilled or unskilled) in order to survive has been completely borne out.

What is questionable, however, for Marxist and non-Marxist theorists alike, is the notion that the obligation to sell one's labour power can be seen as a sufficient criterion for a working-class location on the class map. If it is, then clearly the great mass of people in advanced capitalist societies (perhaps 85 per cent of the population in the US, Canada, Japan, and the European Union) have already been inducted into the ranks of the working class, even though many of them may not realize it. From a Marxist perspective, such an image of modern capitalist societies is attractive, but it is also fraught with major difficulties. For example, how meaningful is it to include within the same class category an assembly line worker at an auto plant and a police constable whose job may be to escort scabs across the autoworkers' picket lines in the midst of a strike? Members of the police force may sell their labour power to make a living, but they are also "hired guns" on behalf of bourgeois property—the enforcers of laws that pre-eminently serve the interests of capital. Within the production process, some wage-labourers may carry out supervisory functions that are of crucial significance to maintaining capitalist domination over the labour process. Such workers may carry out a range of work tasks that are technically necessary to production; but their supervisory tasks define them also as "hired guns" of capital, at least to some degree. The point is simple: the imperative to sell one's labour power to make a living may be a necessary condition for a working-class designation; but the nature of the work performed will serve to situate many wage-labourers in ambiguous categories somewhere "between" the working class and the capitalist class. Such intermediate categories constitute a significant buffer between the two principal classes of advanced capitalist society.

How large is that buffer, how independent can it become from capitalist control, and how significant an obstacle is it to the development of the class struggle that Marx saw as crucial to the transition to socialism? These are some of the questions that shape many of the most important debates regarding "the middle class." As in all such debates, we are obliged to sort out its ideological from its scientific determinants.

From the end of World War II up to the 1970s, most advanced capitalist societies saw a small but real attenuation of income inequalities that conferred some credibility on the notion that "the middle class" was both expanding and becoming increasingly affluent. If the middle class is defined simply as an ensemble of middle-income categories, as it often is in popular discourse, then socioeconomic trends for some three decades provided powerful support to the notion of an emerging "middle-class society." Even today, income distribution graphs for most Western countries display bell-shaped curves. However, humps have been growing at the extremes of the income scales of many of these countries at a rapid rate over the past 20 years. In the United States in particular, the statistical evidence for the decline of the "middle-income" middle class is considerable. The majority of the population may still be clustered close to the median income, but that is cold comfort for the 80 per cent of the workforce whose real wages were at least 18 per cent lower in the mid-1990s than they were in the early 1970s.[15]

In light of recent social trends, the concept of an ascendant and increasingly independent middle class (so integral to conventional, liberal-democratic images of modern capitalism) would seem to be on exceedingly shaky ground. In popular, liberal-democratic discourse, the middle class is seen as a class that owes its pre-eminence not only to an expanding numerical weight but also to the power conferred upon it by a privileged role in social reproduction. Ultimately, the "middle class" can be seen as the defining reality of contemporary society only to the extent that it sheds its "contradictions"—its role in *mediating* between capital and labour—and asserts itself as a dominant class force by transforming capitalist society into a "post-capitalist" society founded upon the traditional petty-bourgeois values of class harmony, meritocracy, and what Marx called "bourgeois right" ("from each according to his ability, to each according to his contribution").[16]

Since World War II, the social-scientific literature has been marked by many attempts to establish the centrality of the "middle class" to "post-capitalist" (or "post-industrial" or "postmodern") society. In the early post-war period, middle-class dominance was celebrated as a triumph of technocratic and meritocratic principles over the inherited privileges of private property ownership. Many social scientists argued that a "managerial revolution" had allayed the spectre of class struggle between socially irresponsible capitalists and socialist-minded workers.

New times, however, bring new ideas—and new twists on old ideological themes. Since the early 1980s, neo-conservatives have revisited and sought to popularize a new take on the thesis of "managerial" or "technocratic" revolution. Far from celebrating it, they have taken to deploring the usurpation of power by a "liberal elite"—and to

---

15. Simon Head, "The New, Ruthless Economy," *The New York Review of Books* XLIII, 29 Feb. 1996.

16. Karl Marx, "Critique of the Gotha Programme," in Karl Marx and F. Engels, *Selected Works*, Vol. 3 (Moscow: Progress Publishers, 1970) 18-19.

blaming "bureaucrats" and "technocrats" for the malaise of contemporary capitalist society.[17] If the idea of a managerial revolution was once deployed to support the notion of a convergence between capitalist and socialist "industrial systems," the dismantling of "actually existing socialism" has lessened the appeal of this idea substantially. The very partial "decommodification" of social relations that was imposed on Western capitalism by the post-war strength of national labour movements and the challenge of Soviet-style "real socialism" is now regarded as a tumour on the underbelly of a crisis-prone capitalism. In this context, as Gary Teeple notes, "contradictory class locations" have begun to disappear for increasing numbers of workers, both in the private and public sectors.[18] It is an old-fashioned capitalism that seems once again to be on the rise, and the champions of this capitalism believe fervently that it can—and must—manage with a substantially smaller buffer between capital and labour than it did during the days of the Cold War. Far from being an ascendant class, what Barbara and John Ehrenreich once called "the professional-managerial class" appears to be falling victim to the sharpening contradictions of a capitalist order in crisis as well as the ideological triumphalism of a capitalist ruling class now convinced that it has finally rid the world of "the specter of communism."[19]

If the "middle class" cannot credibly be seen as an ascendant professional-managerial class, poised to restructure fundamentally the social relations of modern (or postmodern) societies, and if it likewise cannot be conceived as a "majority class" that combines within itself the functions of capital and labour, then the "middle class" must be regarded as an essentially misleading and ideological category. Conceptually, the expression "the middle class" almost inevitably invites a view of class structure as consisting of "upper," "medium," and "lower" categories—categories that lend themselves to arbitrary definition and profound ideological mystification. To be sure, intermediate classes or "class locations" situated between capital and labour certainly exist, and these include professional-managerial elements as well as the traditional, self-employed petty-bourgeoisie (ranging from farmers to accountants). But the unavoidable confusion of these "in between" or "buffer" elements with the "middle-class majority" of popular imagination should oblige social theorists to end their habit of referring to these contradictory class locations as "the middle class," whether "new" or otherwise. To continue the habit is to reinforce a powerful ideological mainstay of the culture of prejudice.

Murray E. G. Smith

---

17. Cf. Barbara Ehrenreich, *Fear of Falling: The Inner Life of the Middle Class* (New York: Harper Collins, 1989).

18. Gary Teeple, *Globalization and the Decline of Social Reform* (Toronto: Garamond Press, 1995) 53.

19. Barbara Ehrenreich and John Ehrenreich, "The Professional Managerial Class," *Between Labor and Capital*, ed. Pat Walker (Montreal: Black Rose Books, 1978); Murray E.G. Smith and K.W. Taylor, "Profitability Crisis and the Erosion of Popular Prosperity," *Studies in Political Economy* 49 (Spring 1996).

suggested readings

Bottomore, Thomas B. *The Socialist Economy: Theory and Practice.* New York: The Guilford Press, 1990.

Ehrenreich, Barbara. *Fear of Falling: The Inner Life of the Middle Class.* New York: HarperPerennial, 1990.

Giddens, Anthony, and David Held, eds. *Classes, Power and Conflict: Classical and Contemporary Debates.* Berkeley: University of California Press, 1982.

Goldstein, Don et al., eds. *The Future of Socialism.* Special issue of the *Review of Radical Political Economics*, 24:3,4, 1992.

Laibman, David, ed. *Socialism: Alternative Visions and Models.* Special issue of *Science and Society*, 56:1, 1992.

Mandel, Ernest. *Marxist Economic Theory.* New York: Monthly Review Press, 1969.

Marx, Karl, and Friedrich Engels. *The Communist Manifesto.* New York: Monthly Review Press, 1998.

McNally, David. *Against the Market: Political Economy, Market Socialism and the Marxist Critique.* London: Verso, 1993.

Nielsen, Kai, and Robert Ware, eds. *Exploitation.* Amherst, NY: Prometheus Books, 2000.

PART SIX

Feminism & the women's movement

CHAPTER 20

"Feminists are just 'male bashers'"

Misogynist notion representing a step up from "bra burners." Better not to be thought of only for denouncing one's underwear

Identifying oneself as a "feminist" is a difficult decision, even for some of the students who enthusiastically participate in Women's Studies courses in colleges and universities. This is curious. You would think women would be very proud to identify themselves with such an important social movement devoted to tearing down one of the central bulwarks of the culture of prejudice. In the sweep of the twentieth century, the gradual increments achieved toward the equality of women are remarkable and represent historically significant social change. If it were not for feminists, none of this would have happened.

If it were not for feminists, women would be legally the property of their fathers or husbands, deprived of property ownership, the right to vote, rights over their own children, rights to education and reproductive rights. Pregnancy outside of marriage would be assumed to be a result of a woman's moral failure or "feeblemindedness." Their husbands would be free to assault and rape them, with no legal consequences. Their social and geographical mobility would be restricted, and their chances of finding meaningful and rewarding employment would be next to none. The list goes on.

The improved status of women today did not "just happen," and it was by no means "historically inevitable." It came about as a result of the bravery, persistence, intelligence, and political acuity of many women, not to mention the hardships and sacrifices some of them had to endure. As a feminist author I am extremely proud to identify myself with the women who worked to right so many wrongs and turn the tide against women being treated as second-class citizens and the property of men.

So how did we end up with all the negative images of the women, the "feminists," who were and continue to be committed to working for the laudable goal of social equality in our democratic societies? It seems like that old law of physics, "For every action there is an equal and opposite reaction," can be roughly applied to forceful social movements that challenge the culture of prejudice. In the case of the women's movement, we can be thankful that the opposite reaction was not quite equal. This is probably because most men want to live with and love women, know that a woman gave birth to them, may have sisters they care about, or can imagine the day they might have daughters and nieces, if they do not have them already. Even if men may hold rather odd ideas about "womankind," most of them have intimate relationships, to some degree or another, with individual women. Thus, even though "slavery" is a metaphor that could be applied to the conditions described in the paragraph above, opposing its reform is not quite the same as, for example, defending one's right to own people of colour, blatantly buy and sell them in an open marketplace, and consider them wholly as commodities, while remaining uncontaminated by feelings of affection or family loyalties.

Nevertheless, the anti-feminist reaction has been effective, and it stretches all the way back to the responses prompted by the suffragists who came up with the novel idea that women should be enfranchised and permitted to cast their votes in democratic jurisdictions. It has been effective in convincing both women and men that feminists are "mannish" and "want to be men" (horrors!), and they are "male bashers" (a strange contradiction here, if they both want to *be* men and yet *hate* them). Although contemporary mainstream propaganda nowadays hesitates to do more than insinuate these absurd ideas, spokespersons for certain right-wing or religious movements have no compunction about calling us all "lesbians." Feminists are "strident" (unwomanly), and they are "bra burners" (silly girls). Given the evidence of feminists' concerns over access to therapeutic abortion and safe birth control, as well as an equal chance for fairly compensated employment outside the home, feminists are portrayed as being "anti-children" and a threat to "family values." (This is a particularly interesting contradiction, since feminists have fought hard to make people understand that women's work in the home is "real" work, and should be acknowledged and valued as such.) Magazine articles take delight in recounting the difficulties women face when trying to juggle career and family responsibilities, especially when the stories involve women who have given up on the former to devote themselves to the latter. Feminists are portrayed as "nags" and "whiners" (just like most women?), but they are also high minded and humourless storm-troopers of "political correctness" (and no one will argue that this is a "womanly" quality). Pat Robertson, leader of the US Christian Coalition, quaintly summed it up in a letter to his supporters in the state of Iowa: "The feminist agenda is about a socialist, anti-family, political movement that encourages women to leave their husbands, kill their children, practice witchcraft, destroy capitalism and become lesbians."[1]

In the face of the onslaught of this kind of propaganda, whether delivered literally or by implication, it is perhaps not surprising that many women are reluctant to call themselves "feminist." No one is going to easily make herself vulnerable by inviting such absurd and unfounded stereotypes of her personality and character, when

---

1. Quoted in the *Guardian Weekly* 6 Sept, 1992: 17.

she can otherwise make it through life just doing her best to feel comfortable and successful as an actor on the stage our foremothers built for us.

This brings us to another rationale for shunning the feminist self-identification: the idea that "feminism is dead." All the battles have been won, women have gained their equality, the work is done—end of conversation. This one is often uttered from the mouths of privileged young women and enthusiastically bandied about in the media. This is indeed tragic, as it demonstrates a blindness to and ignorance of the status of women around our globe. Try telling a physician forbidden to practise medicine in Afghanistan that her battles have been won. Or ask a social worker who is trying to rescue women barely into their teens, or younger, from sexual slavery, whether it be in Southeast Asia or Europe or the streets of the city in which you live. Ask yourself if the world's resources are being wisely expended on the fashion industry, cosmetics, and shoes that do painful and permanent damage to human knees and feet. Ask yourself why women everywhere, but particularly in wartime conditions, are brutalized and sexually assaulted. Ask yourself why women are underrepresented in positions of political power and economic influence, even in "advanced democracies." People who claim that there is no longer a need for the women's movement or who wish to carry on about the demise of feminism are just letting you know that they have not thought the issues through and are demonstrating remarkable narrow-mindedness. Patriarchy is alive and well, even if many people would like us to believe it is not.

So, now that we have discussed the f-word, "feminism," we come down to the p-word, "patriarchy." Feminists use it in various ways, but it has not made its way very far into common language. It is a word like "capitalism" or "colonialism" which tries to capture an enormous range of ideas, concepts, beliefs, ideologies, meanings, and social practices. No two people will probably ever agree on its precise definition. However, it is a useful term to encapsulate the social inequalities between men and women, and how deeply ingrained they are both in social institutions and in ordinary people's lives and minds. As such, it is one of the major pillars supporting the culture of prejudice.

Countless women have talked about, and written about, what has come to be known as "the click." This refers to the moment in time when the world looks very different through the eyes of feminism. Suddenly patriarchy can be seen in the most unexpected places, and it is a shock to think that it would have gone unnoticed before. It might be a newspaper article blathering on at some length about a woman politician's looks, age, and wardrobe while being silent about these details in reporting on her male colleagues. It might be at a wedding, where the father "gives the bride away" to the husband, reflecting patriarchal ownership. It might be when you realize that your parents' home has only your father's name on the title ("A Man's Home is his Castle"), despite your mother's years of financial contributions and her maintenance of the home. Suddenly, there is another insight about what happened to your aunt or your sister, who was enormously successful in her employment, but her promotions just ground to a halt at some point (below the so-called "glass ceiling"). Why did my father offer an apprenticeship in his business to my sister's husband, and not to her or to me? And why was one of my friends ejected from a shopping mall for nursing her baby, when it is taken for granted that men can be naked in public from the waist up, regardless of their sexual or aesthetic attractions?

The "click" normally does not sour personal relationships with the men in women's lives, unless these relationships already contain blatant exploitation or abuse that the man is unwilling to acknowledge. It does not drive women to "male bashing," although women have probably been moaning to each other since prehistoric times about their experiences at the hands of, and under the power of, men. (Presumably, men have been moaning about the women in their lives for just as long.) Nonetheless, the "click" certainly makes for more spirited dinner-table conversations. Of more importance, the "click" does not happen without an understanding of concepts such as systemic discrimination or institutional and social inequalities, as well as an understanding of the way both women and men have been trained to believe these are "normal," the way things are and always have been. In short, it comes with the adoption of a social scientific perspective.

Even in the absence of the "click," there is another, and more personal, reason for women, even those who are deeply concerned about women's issues, to reject the "feminist" label. Once your friends and family know you have declared yourself as a feminist, they tend to confront you with issues or "new facts" and ask everything from "What would your feminist friends say about that, huh?" to "And what would a feminist theoretical analysis of this entail?" It is a challenge for someone to be put on the spot like this, because there are so many faces of feminism.

Indeed, the media often seem to take tasty pleasure in reporting conflicts and debates among women. This is another interesting contradiction. It is taken for granted that male-dominated structures of power and influence will display divisiveness and conflict, but it seems that women's organizations and the women's movement as a whole are expected to function in perfect harmony and without theoretical or programmatic disagreements. It is as if women were not human too, but just clones who united in attaining their goals ("Resistance is Futile!"). Any sensible human being knows that within any organization, whether it is a government bureaucracy, a political party, a labour union, a shop floor, or a grassroots organization, people will come into conflict. Anyone who has raised children or is privileged to have been raised in a secure and supportive family knows that under the best of circumstances there will be conflict. So why should feminists all think alike?

Of course they do not, and although they all share the ultimate goal of gender equality, each person brings to this social reform movement some baggage of her own. She might be a woman who wants to have her voice heard in the boardroom and change the conditions under which the women in her organization work. She might be someone who sincerely believes that until capitalism is replaced by a true social democracy, women will never be granted their rights. She might be someone who has a history of being abused as a child, and cannot stand the thought of another girl or boy being submitted to what she endured. She might feel oppressed, because she is a lesbian in a heterosexist environment. She might be a legal scholar, like Patricia Monture[2] who writes about whether it is more important that her oppression has been derived from being a woman or from being a First Nations person. She might be a postmodern scholar who asks us not to take anything for granted, even the meaning of a single word like "woman." She might be your sister who volunteers at the local food bank and cannot bear to see so many desperate women who cannot feed their children.

There are a number of ways to categorize the various approaches to thinking about feminism, and different authors place different labels on them. However, most people agree that there is a tradition we can call "liberal feminism." These are writers and thinkers who wish to reform patriarchy by working within existing social institutions by, for example, lobbying for political change or opening up opportunities for women in the economy. Socialist feminists bring to their analysis a Marxist theoretical orientation. Not surprisingly, they are concerned about class relations and the exploitation of human labour. One of the most important insights they have brought to feminism is an emphasis on the valuable and essential labour that women do in the home—domestic or reproductive labour—and its contribution to maintaining the productivity of men in the workplace and in raising the next generation of the workforce. "Radical" feminism is a label reserved for those who argue for the overturn of everything smacking of patriarchy or the relations of domination and subordination between the sexes. These writers can be said to be the boldest in their willingness to ask questions about sacred social institutions. Why is heterosexuality compulsory?[3] What if technology relieved women of the burden of bearing children?[4] Radical feminists have worked to create parallel women-focused institutions and services—magazines, websites, bookstores and art galleries, health facilities, sexual assault services, and women's shelters, for example. Cultural feminists, sometimes characterized as an offshoot of radical feminism, are convinced that there are irreconcilable differences between men and women, and distinct policies and institutions are needed to supply women's needs. Indeed, feminist theorists are categorized or categorize themselves in a host of other ways: postmodern feminists, anarchist feminists, lesbian feminists, anti-racist feminists, ecofeminists, and psychoanalytic feminists are a few examples. There are also "standpoint" feminists who argue that women, like colonized or racialized people, have the advantage not only of under-

2. Patricia A.Monture, "I Know My Name: A First Nations Woman Speaks," *Limited Edition: Voices of Women, Voices of Feminism*, ed. Geraldine Flinn (Halifax: Fernwood Publishing, 1993).

3. Adrienne Rich, "Compulsory Heterosexuality and Lesbian Existence," *Signs* 5 (1980): 631-60.

4. Shulamith Firestone, *The Dialectic of Sex* (New York: William Morrow & Co., 1970).

standing their own condition, but also of possessing a keen awareness of the strengths and weaknesses of those who have power over them. This is a necessary survival strategy, and it makes for a more complete comprehension of their social world than that held by their masters.

In my feminist theory classes, I urge students not to try to place themselves in any one of the myriad categories outlined above. These theoretical traditions are overlapping and the taxonomy is imprecise. However, each offers its own perspective and deserves study, because one never knows when it might come in handy. Depending on the problem with which one is struggling, a serious feminist thinker should have access to all the theoretical resources available to provide insight.

I also urge my students to learn to be comfortable about not having all the answers. Perhaps the best illustration of this concerns the fundamental problem of whether women are inferior to men, superior to men, or just about the same.[5] This question drives feminists crazy. It is also the source of constant and continuing stores of research funding for non-feminists; it seems that money is always available for scientists who wish to study the *differences* between women and men.

To analyse the question in broad strokes, if we women are "just the same" as men, we should not be given particular privileges in the public arena for pregnancy, complications of menstruation or menopause, child care, elder care, or any of the other things that used to be thought of as "women's problems" or "women's work." It is an insult to be coddled or given special consideration. We want to compete as equals on an equal playing field. Any concession made to us is an insult to our personhood. We will do the job as well as, or better than, a man.

On the other hand, and again in broad strokes, women are experts in things men "just don't understand," and therefore are both different from and superior to men. With a nod to standpoint feminism, it can be argued that we possess the viewpoints of both men and women. We probably make better doctors, because women spend more time listening to patients rather than processing them. We are probably better managers for the same reason. Along with the folk wisdom that women are better at mediation than confrontation, we can claim to be better at interpersonal communication than at the paranoid power games men tend to play. Women know how to run a tight ship and are better at "multitasking," because they have been trained for that in the domestic sphere all their lives.

We shall not delve into the question of whether women are inferior to men, since this has been taken for granted for centuries and continues to be on the central agenda of many scientific research projects, similar to the ones referred to elsewhere in this book on the differences among "races." Read the Carol Tavris book, cited above, if you wish to pursue this line of inquiry.

---

5. Carol Tavris, *The Mismeasure of Woman: Why Women are Not the Better Sex, the Inferior Sex, or the Opposite Sex* (New York: Simon & Schuster, 1992).

I refuse to come down on either side of the sameness/difference argument. My reason is that I cannot see gender as a clear binomial; I see no black and white. In my opinion, there are shades of "maleness" and "femaleness" in all of us, regardless of the chromosomes that happened to get together at our conception, untold factors impinging on our birthing and childhood, the luck or lack of it visited on us as we moved into adulthood. Gender stereotypes are arbitrary, according to historical era, culture, social class, ethnicity, and so on. It is folly to attempt to compare men and women on any measure of intelligence, ability or worth, just as it is to try ranking "races." We are all runners in the same human race. This part of me, the empirical part, supports the "sameness" argument.

On the other hand, the "romantic" part of me supports the "difference" argument. The "womanly virtues" (empathy, understanding, sisterhood, motherhood, conciliation) are well worth celebrating and are all the more reason why the vast majority of female feminists have no desire whatsoever to model themselves on men. However, what it is to be a "man" or a "woman" is defined by place and time. In our place and time, the definitions are continuing to put women at a disadvantage. It does not matter whether the sexes are more the same than we have been led to believe, or whether they are radically different. The problem is in the inequality. Both women and men should be proud to call themselves feminists in their united desire to abolish gender inequities.

Judith C. Blackwell

CHAPTER 21

"Feminism is no longer relevant"
Delusional statement by people who think women "have it all"

In the first decade of the twenty-first century, many young university students regard the issue of women's rights as an artifact of the 1960s. They assume that women now have all the same rights and opportunities as men do. This view may reflect their own insulated views and limited experience. While many achievements have been won, the emancipation of women globally remains a matter of struggle and, as Susan Faludi[1] has pointed out, many of the achievements of feminists in North America are threatened by a sexist and right-wing counter-attack.

Throughout the world, women consistently work more, earn less, suffer gender-specific forms of violence, and endure severe restrictions imposed by political and religious authorities. Even the briefest glance at the situation of women globally indicates the serious challenges to any notion of women's emancipation. In Afghanistan, the Taliban regime prohibited women from attending schools. In Sudan, women are banned from working in occupations where they may come into contact with men. Throughout the Middle East and much of Africa, women are subjected to genital mutilation that threatens their lives, ruins their health, and interferes with childbirth. In every war and refugee situation, women face all the same dangers as men do, but they also endure gender-specific violence such as rape and other forms of sexual torture and abuse. Women are often subjected to such abuse as a means of humiliating the enemy and terrorizing civilian populations. In East Timor, under Indonesian military occupation, women were sterilized without their knowledge. Many societies emphasize that control over women's personal behaviour is a matter of honour for the family, community, and the state. For example, Turkey recently reinstated virginity tests for women studying in medical high schools. Women who did not pass the test, conducted by police and other agents of the state, were stigmatized as prostitutes and had almost no possibility of marriage or a "respectable" life; several

---

1. Susan Faludi, Backlash: *The Undeclared War against American Women* (New York: Anchor Books, 1991).

young women committed suicide because of such tests.[2] (After international pressure, the Turkish government rescinded the law in February 2002.) Spousal abuse, usually directed at women, is widespread and many societies do not regard such acts of violence as crimes. Many Islamic societies provide lenient sentences for men who kill female relatives to preserve family "honour" related to women's sexual behaviour. In Iran, after construction worker Saeed Hanaei confessed to strangling sixteen prostitutes "for the sake of God and for the protection of my religion," he was hailed as a hero by his neighbours and several fundamentalist newspapers rushed to his defence.[3] Prostitution has become one of Thailand's major industries and thousands of young rural women are deceived or sold by their families into the sex trade. Other Thai women are promised jobs as factory workers or waitresses in Japan, but are then kept as slaves and forced to work as prostitutes.[4] Throughout Africa, women constitute the majority of each country's poor population and their illiteracy rates are consistently higher than those of men. In many societies women cannot own land, have fewer political rights, and are paid less for the work they do. Women's struggle for control over their own bodies in terms of reproduction continues. Despite their increased participation in waged labour, women are still responsible for the majority of housework. One survey found that, among Swedish men, 73 per cent never do laundry, 71 per cent never clean the house, 64 per cent never do dishes, and 52 per cent do not do any grocery shopping.[5] In Canada, women earn only 61 per cent of what men do and approximately 20 per cent of women live in poverty, with far higher rates of impoverishment among Aboriginal women, women of colour, and older women.[6]

Clearly, then, the situation of women reveals profound inequalities around the world. Half the world's population continues to be subordinated and oppressed in a wide variety of ways simply because of gender. Women's emancipation from these conditions and their acquisition of rights that are equal to those of men are fundamental steps toward realizing any concept of social progress.

Yet, while women's emancipation is a necessary preliminary to social progress, it is not in itself a sufficient condition to produce an equitable society. While noting that the numbers of men and women in government positions are nowhere near equal, we can also see that merely having women in positions of power does not guarantee

---

2. "A Matter of Power: State Control of Women's Virginity in Turkey," *Human Rights Watch Report* 6.7 (June 1994).

3. *The Globe and Mail*, 1 Aug. 2001: A9.

4. "Owed Justice: Thai Women Trafficked into Debt Bondage in Japan," *Human Rights Watch*, September, 2000.

5. Lorraine Elliot, "Women, Gender, Feminism and the Environment," *The Gendered New World Order*, ed. Lois Ann Lorentzen and Jennifer Turpin (New York: Routledge, 1996) 19.

6. Centre for Social Justice, *Media Advisory*, Toronto, 27 June 2001.

social justice. For example, former Israeli prime minister Golda Meir sought to dismiss the plight of Palestinian refugees with her notorious claim that Palestinians "did not exist," while former US ambassador Jeanne Kirkpatrick was a staunch defender of Central American dictatorships and death squads. As Britain's prime minister, Margaret Thatcher promoted neo-liberal policies that devastated social programs; former US secretary of state Madeleine Albright declared that the deaths of a half-million Iraqi children were worth the price to achieve US goals in the region. US trade representative Carla Hill vigorously championed corporate domination; US National Security Advisor Condoleeza Rice considered bombing Afghanistan to be an appropriate response to terrorist attacks on New York and Washington. Middle-class women have enthusiastically supported dictatorships such as that of Augusto Pinochet in Chile. Others have joined fascist movements and racist groups and have directly participated in genocidal violence, as in Rwanda.[7] Canadian newspapers provide ample space for the right-wing views of columnists such as Barbara Amiel, Diane Francis, and Margaret Wente. Concentrating only on gender oppression overlooks the significant differences among women based on class and race.

Granted, feminists have challenged gender-based inequalities, but Western feminism has been criticized for its concentration on the concerns of white, middle-class women. Liberal feminists are often preoccupied with issues related to careers for well-educated professional women. In general, they do not concern themselves with the basic structures of power but simply want women to have equal chances to occupy privileged positions within such structures. Radical and cultural feminists accept the idea of an essentialized difference between men and women. Some advocate the idea of matriarchal societies; others argue for organizations for women only and designed to serve the unique needs of women. Socialist feminists usually have a more thorough sociopolitical critique, but they still endorse a strong system of state control, imagining this as the means to liberate women. Anarchist feminists and ecofeminists go beyond these issues to address connections between the oppression of women and the exploitation of the environment and other forms of life.

Anarchism is often misinterpreted as the advocacy of chaos and random violence. In fact, there are many different kinds of anarchists, ranging from those who promote capitalist, individualist societies to those who advocate anti-authoritarian forms of communism and believe that equitable forms of social organization must be organized from below rather than being imposed from above. Unlike Marxists, anarchists do not privilege any particular form of domination as having a special status; their goal is to abolish all forms of hierarchy, not to establish a state controlled by a small elite group of revolutionaries. Anarchist feminists oppose all forms of domination and see all forms of oppression as mutually reinforcing. Thus, as L. Susan Brown notes, a sexist anarchist would be a contradiction in terms: "Not only is

---

7. "Rwanda—Not So Innocent: When Women Become Killers," *African Rights* (August 1995).

anarchism inherently feminist but it also goes beyond feminism in its fundamental opposition to all forms of power, hierarchy, and domination. Anarchism transcends and contains feminism in its critique of power."[8]

A good example of this broader critique of power can be found in the alternative views that feminists propose about defence of animals. (Certainly, not all feminists are alert to these issues and even a work like Maria Mies and Vandana Shiva's *Ecofeminism*[9] makes no mention of animals.) Historically, feminist concerns and concern for animals were linked. Nineteenth-century feminists recognized similarities between oppression of women and of animals and many organized animal-defence and anti-vivisection campaigns because they recognized these as part of the same issue: concern for nature and victimized groups oppressed by patriarchal society. Early twentieth-century animal-protection organizations consisted mainly of women, and it is mainly women who support the animal-rights movement today. These women see similarities between their position and that of animals. Some suggest that because women's roles have emphasized caring and nurturing, they are more compassionate toward animals, while male roles do not conform with such practices and emotions. It is no coincidence that what the animal-rights movement opposes are also so-called "macho" values: cold, emotionless rationality, detachment from the world, domination of nature, the expression of virility through hunting and other forms of violence.

Josephine Donovan[10] finds the work of animal-rights philosophers Peter Singer and Tom Regan valuable but says that ethical treatment of animals must be based on premises that both of these authors overlook or dismiss: sympathy, compassion, and caring. Donovan thinks that animal-rights issues have been dominated by a theoretical bias toward rationality and abstraction rooted in Kant's *Fundamental Principles of Metaphysics of Morals* (1785), which rejects emotion as a basis for ethical action. In contrast, a feminist approach emphasizes individual, contextual, emotional, and political aspects. Donovan believes that Western philosophy has ignored these aspects but thinks that Schopenhauer's emphasis on compassion and sympathy provides a basis of justice and morality. To have sympathy for another being means we recognize that being as an individual and cannot treat that individual as an object, as a means to an end. Sympathy entails respect and equal treatment. Donovan notes that Schopenhauer explicitly includes animals within the moral community, rejecting the idea that animals have no rights as something "revoltingly crude, a barbarism of the West."[11] Donovan finds this alternative philosophical tradition carried over into feminist

8. L. Susan Brown, "Beyond Feminism: Anarchism and Human Freedom," *Reinventing Anarchy Again*, ed. Howard Erlich (San Francisco: AK Press, 1996) 153.

9. Maria Mies and Vandana Shiva, *Ecofeminism* (New York: Zed, 1993).

10. Josephine Donovan, "Animal Rights and Feminist Theory," *Ecofeminism*, ed. Greta Gaard (Philadelphia: Temple University, 1993) 167-94.

11. Donovan 156.

thought, where it is possible to develop ethical treatment of animals from "an emotional and spiritual conversation with nonhuman life forms. Out of a women's relational culture of caring and attentive love, therefore, emerges the basis for a feminist ethic for the treatment of animals. We should not kill, eat, torture and exploit animals because they do not want to be so treated, and we know that. If we listen, we can hear them."[12] However, Gary Francione convincingly argues that "compassion" provides a less adequate foundation for protection of animals' interests than a rights-based approach.[13] Indeed, virtually all who exploit and abuse animals also claim to have "compassion" for them or to treat animals "humanely."

Donovan does acknowledge that compassion must be supplemented by awareness of context; what is needed is not just sympathy for other beings, but also a political analysis of the situation in which they exist. This entails not only care for animals, but awareness, for example, of negative implications of factory farming on environment and health. Donovan says animals are of special concern to feminists. The association of flesh with power is gendered: hunting is a stereotypically male activity. Hunters experience it as an activity that solidifies male identity, reaffirming virility, making them sexier if they can demonstrate their ability to kill. (Some believe anxiety about gender identity causes some men to become hunters; by killing animals, they can demonstrate they are not homosexuals.) Eating flesh is itself identified with stereotyped masculinity ("Real men don't eat quiche"); and while women have been typically relegated to the kitchen, when men do cook, they often prepare flesh, cooking it outdoors on a barbecue. In Victorian England, flesh was not considered appropriate food for women, because it was too strong, too sexual, and might cause nymphomania. Women are also seen as flesh for men's consumption. Both women and animals are linked to the natural world and in the ideology of the West (Christianity, capitalism, patriarchy, mechanistic-rational), the natural world is seen as evil, inferior, something to be dominated.

Ecofeminists have made important contributions by emphasizing the joint oppression of women and nature and showing that the same patriarchal framework that justifies subordination of women also legitimizes exploitation of nonhuman animals and the environment. Lori Gruen[14] argues that the categories of "woman" and "animal" serve the same function in patriarchal society: both are dominated others; their function is to serve, to be used. This connection, constructed by patriarchy and oppression, obligates feminists also to address oppression of nonhuman animals. Gruen outlines some links: medical experiments on animals compared with those performed on women; a hygiene fetish in which cleaning products, deodorants, and cosmetics, all

---

12. Donovan 185.

13. Gary Francione, *Rain Without Thunder* (Philadelphia: Temple University Press, 1996).

14. Lori Gruen, "Dismantling Oppression: An Analysis of the Connection Between Women and Animals," *Ecofeminism*, ed. Greta Gaard (Philadelphia: Temple University, 1993) 60-90.

closely associated with women, are tested on animals; the fur industry that persuades women it is glamorous to wear animal skins; and flesh eating: "women prepare and cook; animals are prepared and cooked."[15] Both women and animals play a subordinate role in the hierarchy of flesh eating, although animals are at the very bottom: slaughtered, packaged, sold, and consumed.

Gruen notes that factory farms exploit female animals in particular ways. The egg industry is based on hen factories in which female birds are confined in small spaces. The dairy industry keeps cows in constant cycles of artificial impregnation, birth, and lactation (infants are removed after three days and confined for veal production). This intense period of pregnancy and hyper-lactation lasts about five years. During this time, cows are pumped with hormones to double normal milk production and are dosed with disinfectants, antibiotics, and hormones. Dairy cows suffer from udder infections and experience intense pain from constant milking by machine. They are fed high-energy concentrates, but cannot absorb them at the same rate they are forced to produce milk; unable to metabolize food at such a high rate, their body tissues begin to break down. Although their natural life span is twenty years, dairy cows burn out after five and are then slaughtered.

Ecofeminists argue that factory-farm systems that produce not only flesh but also eggs and milk (i.e., exploitation of reproduction) have particular implications for women, although men should also be vegetarians. Most ecofeminists argue that one should not only be vegetarian but vegan.[16] Choosing one's diet becomes a political act: one becomes violent by consuming food produced in a violent system. Rejecting flesh, eggs, and milk is part of a rejection of a patriarchal system—although, admittedly, changing that system requires more than a change in diet.

Ecofeminists recognize links between women and animals and oppose oppression of both. Seeking to end all forms of oppression, ecofeminism surpasses the anthropocentrism of other feminist theories which, by failing to critique the elevation of humans above other animals, provide inadequate analysis. Liberal, Marxist, and socialist feminisms either ignore animals and nature or regard these as separate from and inferior to humans. Radical feminists do address a woman/nature connection, but valorize women as caring and nurturing while characterizing men as cold, detached, and divorced from nature; in this analysis, abuse of animals stems from patriarchy and commitment to abstract rational thought. However, Gruen rejects radical feminism because it sees a dichotomy between male/female as inevitable and accepts hierarchy but just reverses it, positing women as superior. Although some ecofeminists tend to essentialize women as closer to nature and overlook the significance of class, others reject dualistic constructions and provide an important critique by emphasizing interconnections of all forms of life. Accepting an expanded concept of a moral

---

15. Gruen 72.

16. Carol J. Adams, *Neither Man Nor Beast* (New York: Continuum, 1994) 89.

community, ecofeminists reject all forms of hierarchy and domination. Thus, struggles for emancipation of women are linked to abolition of all forms of oppression. By refusing to eat flesh, wear leather, and engage in other forms of exploitation, ecofeminists reject the patriarchal system that treats sentient beings as objects for profit. They call for a shift in values away from power, control, and competition.

For over two thousand years, cultures of prejudice have placed humans at the top of a hierarchical system (although humans themselves were ranked within this system according to class, skin colour, gender, and sexuality). This system of thought depicts nature and other living beings as subordinate and expendable, to be exploited for human benefit. These grotesque ideas have profound psychological impact, alienating us from the world, other beings, and ourselves. They have brought oppression, slavery, genocide, and extinction of species and have led us to the brink of global ecological catastrophe. In challenging cultures of prejudice, our task is to oppose these deluded notions and create a world in which social justice will flourish. Ecofeminists make an important contribution by advising that changing our relationship with animals and nature is essential to achieving these goals.

John S. Sorenson

suggested readings

Afshar, Haleh. *Women and Politics in the Third World*. New York: Routledge, 1996.

Briskin, Linda, and Mona Eliasson, eds. *Women's Organizing and Public Policy in Canada and Sweden*. Montreal: McGill-Queen's University Press, 1999.

Donovan, Josephine, and Carol J. Adams, eds. *Beyond Animal Rights: A Feminist Caring Ethic for the Treatment of Animals*. New York: Continuum, 1996.

Engels, Friedrich. *The Origin of the Family, Private Property and the State*. New York: Pathfinder, 1971.

Gaard, Greta, ed. *Ecofeminism*. Philadelphia: Temple University, 1993.

Hamilton, Roberta. *Gendering the Vertical Mosaic: Feminist Perspectives on Canadian Society*. Toronto: Copp Clark Ltd., 1996.

Luxton, Meg, and June Corman. *Getting By In Hard Times: Gendered Labour at Home and on the Job*. Toronto: University of Toronto Press, 2001.

Peters, Julie, and Andrea Wolper, eds. *Women's Rights, Human Rights: International Feminist Perspectives*. New York: Routledge, 1995.

Peterson, V. Spike, and Anne Sisson Runyan. *Global Gender Issues*. Boulder, CO: Westview, 1993.

Sayers, Janet, Mary Evans, and Nanneke Redclift. *Engels Revisited: New Feminist Essays*. London: Tavistock, 1987.

Tavris, Carol. *The Mismeasure of Woman: Why Women are not the Better Sex, the Inferior Sex, or the Opposite Sex*. New York: Simon & Schuster, 1992.

Turpin, Jennifer, and Lois Ann Lorentzen, eds. *The Gendered New World Order: Militarism, Development, and the Environment*. New York: Routledge, 1996.

Vogel, Lise. *Marxism and the Oppression of Women*. New Brunswick, NJ: Rutgers University Press, 1983.

Ward, Kathryn, ed. *Women Workers and Global Restructuring*. Ithaca, NY: Cornell University, 1990.

PART SEVEN

Health, sexuality, & Reproduction

CHAPTER 22

"Doctor Knows Best"
Dubious homespun advice encouraged by medical professionals everywhere

North Americans and Europeans are happy to be living in an age when biological and medical sciences have made remarkable advances. The media regularly report discoveries in medical technology, surgical procedures, and "miracle" drugs. We are gratified to hear that life expectancy is rising and infant mortality rates are falling and that infectious diseases are being controlled or even possibly eradicated. We are encouraged to believe that the medical profession and its related scientific disciplines should be thanked for our good fortune and our good health compared to the generations before us. It is considered regrettable that most of the peoples of the world have not attained our standards of health and disease prevention, but we are told there is hope for them once they develop themselves to the standards of the Western world. Provided our governments make sufficient resources available, we can expect continuing improvements from the genome project, expensive new drugs and medical machinery, research on environmental contaminants, development of prevention programs, and community care. This chapter presents the case that, even when they are taken together, these unquestionably worthy endeavours make only a small contribution to the health of nations. The most important factors accounting for differences in health status among people, cross-culturally or within countries, are located in the culture of prejudice and its cornerstone, social inequality.

SOCIAL SCIENCE IN MEDICINE

The argument presented here relies on research conducted in an important social scientific discipline within medical science: epidemiology. The structure of this word signals that this field of study relates to "epidemics," suggesting plagues and infectious diseases. Its investigative scope, however, is much broader than this, in that it also interests itself in the distribution of a wide range of disabilities and the risk factors associated with them in different populations and geographic areas.[1] In population studies and in large-scale controlled comparisons of people with certain diseases to those who are disease-free, as well as in longitudinal studies that follow samples over time to see what kinds of people develop health problems, epidemiology attempts the complicated tasks of teasing out the variables that may predict disease development and of identifying relationships of use in the design of health policy and preventative programs. Other epidemiological studies identify "hot spots" of certain kinds of cancer or other illnesses, which in turn can prompt investigation into industrial pollutants or other environmental factors that seem to be making people sick. On the downside, when the findings of epidemiological research are interpreted simplistically or blown out of proportion by the media or the food industry, we get such phenomena as "food fads." We are urged to eat oat bran or margarine, for example, and then a few years later find out that the first will not necessarily provide the health benefits promised and the second is poisonous compared to the alternatives. At its best, however, epidemiological research has provided the basis for the argument that social inequality makes people sick. Epidemiology demonstrates that the disadvantaged are more vulnerable to early death, disease, and suffering, no matter where they live on this planet and no matter how sophisticated or effective modern medicine has become.

The impact of social science on modern medicine has led people to question some basic assumptions about medicine's role in advancing the well-being of humanity. Take the case of tuberculosis. There is a beautiful little chart, reprinted countless times, on tuberculosis mortality rates in England and Wales between 1838 and 1970.[2] It begins with a death rate of about 4,000 per million people and then, year by year, the rate relentlessly declines, an almost straight diagonal line from the upper left to the lower right corners of the chart. By 1880, when the bacterium responsible for tuberculosis was identified, the rate had more than halved to less than 2,000 per million. When antibiotics came into use in the late 1940s, it was already below 500. Vaccination appeared in the 1950s, and by 1970 the rate was so low it almost hits the

---

1. A little-known piece of history is that Florence Nightingale was one of the founders of the discipline of epidemiology. She is generally remembered as "The Lady With The Lamp" because, as a result of her work on the battlefields of the Crimean War, she organized what was to become the profession of nursing. Less well known is where her interests turned after she left the war zone and returned to England. Her intellectual curiosity turned to comparative rates of morbidity and mortality in British soldiers and civilian men who lived in poverty, as well as numerous public health policy concerns. She was also a great supporter of the burgeoning field of statistical analysis. In short, Florence Nightingale was influential in introducing social science theory and methodology into the field of medicine. See Lynn McDonald, *The Women Founders of the Social Sciences* (Ottawa: Carleton University Press, 1994).

2. It can be seen as Figure 2 at <www.sigmaxi.org/amsci/articles/01articles/hertzmanp1.html> or in Leonard A. Sagan, *The Health of Nations: True Causes of Sickness and Well-Being* (New York: Basic Books, 1987) 69.

bottom of the chart. Whooping cough and measles death rates in children show a similar pattern, along with other diseases which were virtually consigned to history *before* medical science developed interventions to prevent or cure them.

The only conclusion that can be drawn from this epidemiological evidence is that modern medicine has had only a minor influence on increasing life expectancies and decreasing disease rates. How do epidemiologists explain such dramatic improvements? Clyde Hertzman locates the answer in the broader socioeconomic environment:

> Socioeconomic factors that could be related to improved health include improvements in housing, water supply, pollution control, nutrition, child spacing, working conditions, education and a wide range of psychosocial conditions that are thought to be most hospitable in prosperous, tolerant, democratic societies with strong civic communities.[3]

As for the poorer countries, Hertzman opens his paper by sharing his experiences in the Gilgit region of northern Pakistan. For fifteen years, the region had been undergoing a "revolution in health," after developing new social policies and institutions:

> ... a women's organization for agricultural diversification, economic participation and mutual aid; schooling for girls; a rural sanitation service; and a system of primary health care. The impact of the changes was breathtaking. During this short period the infant mortality rate fell more than four-fifths to approach Western levels. Birth rates were cut in half. The main concerns of village women had become the familiar modern problems of balancing work and home life, since both male *and* female children were now at school and not available to mind younger siblings.[4]

He concludes that the improvements in health status it took Western countries two centuries to complete were accomplished in Gilgit in a mere fifteen years. Of particular note, this achievement did not come about by bringing in the machinery of "modern medicine."

Also notable is the role of women in the miraculous transformation observed in Gilgit. Time and again it has been found that the liberation of women from ignorance, exhausting domestic servitude, continual childbearing, and crippling social conventions precipitates an astounding rush of energy and productivity into cultures and economies. One of the great ironies of human history is that men and boys have traditionally had privileged access to better nutrition, education, and life opportunities, thereby squandering a productive resource capable of producing radical social

---

3. Clyde Hertzman, "Health and Human Society," *American Scientist* 89 (2001): 540.

4. Hertzman 538.

change for the betterment of all. Arguments against the oppression of women typically involve issues of social justice and equity; here, they are buttressed by issues of economics and the health of nations.

HEALTH, WEALTH, AND SOCIAL INEQUALITY

One of the interesting concepts medical epidemiologists have developed is "the socioeconomic gradient." This concept illustrates the observation that health and social class always go hand in hand, no matter what society or culture is studied. Quite simply, people in the upper echelons of the social order are healthier and live longer than those in the middle, who in turn are healthier than those at the bottom. It does not matter how socioeconomic status and health status are measured; this relationship is consistently observed.

If it were all just a matter of economic resources, it would be logical to expect that wealthier countries should have better health status than those less well off. This may have been the case a century ago. However, today there is only a weak relationship in this regard, as there are considerable variations in health status among countries of roughly equivalent economic status.[5] A comparison between the United States and Canada superbly illustrates how the expected relationship turns into its opposite. Until the early 1970s, the two countries spent about the same amount on health *per capita* as a proportion of Gross Domestic Product (GDP).[6] Then Canada began to fall behind in health spending. By 1991, Canada was spending approximately 10 per cent of GDP on health care, whereas over 13 per cent was being allocated in the US. Nevertheless, on the basis of such important health care indicators as infant mortality, infant birthweight, and life expectancy, Canada was ahead of its richer southern neighbour. According to Rachlis and Kushner,

1. The Canadian system costs substantially less than the US system and the difference is getting bigger.

2. Low-income Canadians have much better access to health care services than low-income Americans.

3. For urgent conditions, Canadians and Americans have similar access to high-tech services.

---

5. Measuring wealth by Gross Domestic Product, there is a five-year range in life expectancies among the richest countries of the world (Hertzman 541).

6. Michael Rachlis and Carol Kushner, *Strong Medicine: How to Save Canada's Health Care System* (Toronto: HarperCollins Publishers, 1995) 193.

4. For elective services, upper-income Americans have better access than Canadians.

5. There is little difference in the quality of patient outcomes between the two countries.[7]

This comparison indicates that it is not the *absolute* level of wealth which conveys health advantages to a country, although higher social status groups within countries are at an advantage compared to those of lower status.

In fact, interesting differences have also been found among jurisdictions within the two countries. One study, which Hertzman[8] singles out for its methodological sophistication, measured mortality rates and income inequality in the Canadian provinces and the US states. The researchers were not interested in comparing the gross wealth of these jurisdictions, but rather in comparing its distribution. Income inequality was defined in terms of the proportion of the whole income that went to the poorest half of the population. The study discovered that mortality rates in men of working age were remarkably higher where a lower percentage of income went to the less well-off, and death rates steadily improved as the proportion allotted to them increased. The differences in mortality rates in jurisdictions where the poorer received a larger share and where they received a smaller share were as high as 60 per cent.

Clearly, there are inequalities in health and disease rates among nations. There is also no doubt about the inferior health status of marginalized sub-populations and of the economically disadvantaged within nations, sometimes shockingly so, as in the case of Aboriginal peoples. It is easy to confound these variables, for example by assuming it is simply sheer poverty or the "bad habits" of the poor and uneducated causing this health inequality, rather than acknowledging that social inequality *per se* can explain the health deficits observed. Indeed, a US panel of scientific experts has reported that ethnic and racial minorities receive less adequate health care compared to the white majority, even when their health insurance plans and financial income are equivalent.[9]

A widely reported study casts the spotlight on the importance of placement in social hierarchies and vulnerability to ill health. Michael Marmot and his team of researchers conducted a longitudinal study of health risks and mortality rates among occupational groups within the British civil service.[10] Here we can observe an "occupational gradient," consistent with the socioeconomic gradient discussed above. Of course, class,

---

7. Rachlis and Kushner 207.

8. Hertzman 541.

9. Sheryl Gay Stolberg, "Minorities Get Inferior Care, Even if Insured, Study Finds," *The New York Times* 21 March 2002.

10. A summary of this body of research can be found in Rachlis and Kushner 72-74.

occupational, and income disparities were observed among administrators, professional and executive officers, clerical staff, and the "others" who comprised the bottom category. However, all of those studied were public servants who presumably had some degree of job security and regular incomes. They were not homeless or on social assistance; none of the occupational categories was defined to target the socially marginalized, although undoubtedly the "other" category contained a higher proportion of visible minorities. The study sample appears to have been composed of people who had solid jobs and at least some chance, however remote, to move up the ladder.

As expected, Marmot and his associates discovered that people in the sample were more likely to suffer from heart attacks and die younger if they smoked tobacco, had high blood pressure, high cholesterol levels, and so on. Of more interest were their data on the distribution of mortality among the four occupational groups. The standard health-risk measures counted for little compared to job category. The lower-status workers had the highest mortality rates, the highest-status administrators had the lowest, and the middle categories lined up in the same hierarchical order.[11] The people at the top, if they smoked tobacco, were at increased risk, but not as much as the smokers at the bottom. Everyone's blood pressure went up during the work day, but that of the lower status workers went down only marginally when they were off the job. This research provides a clear demonstration of the occupational gradient.

The studies reported in this chapter are compelling. They form just part of a major research initiative to understand what makes people sick (aside from the obvious) and what helps people to be healthy. New lines of epidemiological research are extending into the areas of personal stress, living in socially limiting and discriminatory environments, social support networks, developmental influences of poverty on children, the frustrations of low status jobs, self-efficacy, and power over one's direction as a human being.[12] Thus, at the heart of modern medicine there is a valuable body of social scientific theory and research demonstrating that, in addition to its other iniquities, the culture of prejudice quite simply makes people sick.

Judith C. Blackwell

---

11. Rachlis and Kushner 75.

12. See, for example, Nancy Adler, Michael Marmot, Bruce McEwer, and Judith Stewart, "Socioeconomic Status and Health in Industrial Nations: Social, Psychological, and Biological Pathways," *Annals of the New York Academy of Sciences* 896, at <www.nyas.org/books/vols/toc896.html>, 11 Nov. 2001.

CHAPTER 23

"Modesty and virtue are the essence of femininity"

who needs genital mutilation, when ideology can cripple sexual fulfillment just as effectively?

It has been argued that the greatest tragedy of patriarchy is the way in which it has robbed women of awareness of their sexuality and the full realization of their desire. Three French feminist thinkers—Luce Irigaray, Hélène Cixous, and Julia Kristeva—have written much about the understanding, liberation, and actualization of women's eroticism. They are confident that women and men differ greatly in this regard. As Luce Irigaray has argued, men's sexuality is phallocentric—focused on and radiating from the penis. On the other hand, "... *woman has sex organs just about everywhere*. She experiences pleasure almost everywhere."[1]

Under the patriarchal model, virtuous young women have been assumed to have *no* erotic desires, or at most to possess latent sexuality that should be awakened only in heterosexual marriage.[2] Thus, young women have been encouraged to wait for the "White Knight" to ride into their lives, the man who would not only bring lifelong financial security, but would also "complete" them, by teaching them to realize their full womanhood. As sexual prey, women have been instructed to behave with modesty and to fend off male predators until "Mr. Right comes along." Even then, their experience of sexual pleasure was to be relegated firmly behind their duty to please in the marriage bed.

In contrast, male passion has always been taken for granted. Men's sexual desire in patriarchal societies is often not only expected and assumed to be part of their nature, but it has also been regarded as a badge of their masculinity. It is celebrated and openly discussed. Although times may be changing, traditionally an unmarried woman's eroticism has been her secret, a source of guilt and shame. Women do not speak of their masturbatory pleasures or their erotic dreams; they shy away from these topics even

---

1. Luce Irigaray, "This sex which is not one," *New French Feminisms*, ed. Elaine Marks and Isabelle de Courtivron (Brighton: Harvester, 1981).

2. In contrast, women not possessing the requisite virtue were assumed to be *consumed* by sexual lust and capable of tempting even the most upright man into the depths of vice and degradation.

with close female friends. They are not encouraged to explore their sensuality and their vast potential for orgasmic experience. They are not to speak about sexual longing, although they may talk much about "love." They may not even realize that what they perceive to be "love" is, in reality, little more than the sexual desire they have been taught to deny.

The stifling of female sexuality is arguably the greatest crime of patriarchy.[3] Western women are appalled when they hear of cultures condoning ritual genital mutilation of girls, the butchery of the sources of their erotic pleasure. What Western women do not realize, however, is the extent to which they too have been crippled, the myriad of ways in which their sexuality has been constrained, confined, and made inaccessible to them. Reclaiming female sexuality, therefore, is seen by some women to be as important for self-realization and individual fulfillment as gaining an equal footing in the workforce or attaining political equality.

Luce Irigaray sees parallels between the suppression of women's sensuality and the suppression of women's words and "truths." She urges women to write, to find their voice and their language, to seek self-knowledge through exploration of the self and with other women:

> Speak just the same. Because your language doesn't follow just one thread, one course, one pattern, we are in luck. You speak from everywhere at the same time. You touch me whole at the same time. In all senses. Why only one song, one discourse, one text at a time? To seduce, satisfy, fill one of my 'holes'? I don't have any with you. We are not voids, lacks which wait for sustenance, fulfillment, or plenitude from another. That our lips make us women does not mean that consuming, consummating, or being filled is what matters to us.[4]

The challenge Irigaray is posing to us is to cast off stereotypes of women and the "nature" of their sexuality—or their presumed lack of it.[5]

---

3. This is not a new idea. The fiction of the American novelist Edith Wharton (1862-1937) reflects recurrent themes about how rigid societal rules constrained people, particularly women, from understanding themselves and finding their own self-fulfillment. Marilyn French describes a letter Wharton wrote to a friend saying, "the 'real unpardonable sin' was the denial of life. And, by life, she meant largely sexual experience, but also an existence created by the self rather than by society." This appears in an introduction to a 1981 reprinting of Wharton's set of novellas, *Old New York* (New York: Berkley Books, 1981) xxiii.

4. Luce Irigaray, "When our lips speak together," *Signs* 6.1 (1980).

5. Perhaps men, too, have sex organs "just about everywhere"? Perhaps they also have been crippled by phallocentrism? Perhaps they are getting tired of their long history of raping, pillaging, and abusing those whom they claim to "love"? These are the sorts of questions asked in research into masculinities.

SEXUAL OBJECTIFICATION

As long as women are defined as sexual *objects* and treated as such, they lose the power to define themselves and follow their own desires; they lose their human and sexual *subjectivity*. Sexual objectification refers to the many ways women are presented as objects of men's desire. Although the standards of beauty and general "attractiveness" change between cultures and over time, a host of social pressures conspire to urge women, from a very young age, to strive to attain whatever current characteristics of being the "desirable object" embody. Thus, women worry about the shape of their bodies, their posture, their composure, their presentation of self, their forms of speech, and even the attitudes and inclinations they express both in conversation and public behaviour. The standards are woven into the fabric of their lives. Self-perceived failure to meet these criteria (because of age, body shape or size, skin colour, and so on), not only erodes self-esteem, but, indirectly or directly, leads them to a false evaluation of their likelihood of attaining self-realization—both as "a woman" and as a person likely to find sexual fulfillment.

As long as women and girls starve themselves, wear constraining and uncomfortable clothes and footwear, worry about the size or shape of their breasts, hips or ankles, and spend fortunes on cosmetics, they can be seen to be tacitly endorsing the primacy of the male gaze and buying into the pernicious idea that a woman's "true worth" is contained in her ability to attract the right kind of masculine attention. To the degree to which a young woman buys into this project, she is distracted from the more important agenda of becoming a healthy, well-rounded adult, with her own goals in life and the self-confidence to pursue them. As sexual object, a woman has no sexual subjectivity; her pleasure is in attracting the right kind of sexual attention, not in exploring her own desires.

There is a terrible contradiction in the expectations imposed on young women. On one hand, cultural forces instruct them to mould themselves into objects of desire. On the other, they are encouraged to be modest and chaste, or at least not allow themselves to be perceived as sexually desirous. In short, they are to be "sexy," but not sexual. This contradiction can be a source of confusion, impeding the development of healthy sexuality and self-understanding. Despite the so-called "sexual liberation" of recent decades, young women are still called "sluts" if they are sexually active, and sometimes even when they are not. Their eroticism is not encouraged or celebrated. Too often, female sexuality is only a source of puzzlement, embarrassment, and shame during the perilous transitions of adolescence.

Furthermore, when all the flurry of heterosexual attraction has sorted itself out and if a woman attains the requisite husband and produces the expected offspring, the sacred state of "motherhood" descends to rob her again of her sexual subjectivity. Although most of us can consider ourselves to be "living proof" that our mothers "did it" at least once, most people do not seem to feel that it is seemly for our mothers to engage in sexual activity beyond what was required to fulfill their duty to have children. Moreover, in our culture, motherhood and female eroticism are perceived as mutually exclusive. In addition, because the idealized sexual object is youthful, there appears to be an assumption that exploration of a woman's sexual subjectivity should concomitantly decline as she moves into middle and, especially, older age.[6] We may assume that our fathers will continue in their randiness ("the old goat") and just hope it will at least be disciplined within conventional limits. For women, however, as "sex objects," as "wives" and as "mothers," their sexual subjectivity has been systematically drained throughout their lives, and anything remaining of its power is systematically poisoned.

None of us can "know" our sexual selves, just as none of us can "know" what a word "really" means. (That is the power of Irigaray's conceptual melding of words and eroticism.) Over the latter half of the twentieth century, much feminist ink was spilled about this human tragedy. More will follow in this century, one assumes. The resolution to this mass larceny of healthy female sexual reality will only come when people cast aside the crippling gender role stereotypes that are so dear to the culture of prejudice and yet so destructive of human fulfillment. Questions about how the media, our churches, our doctors, our friends, teachers, parents, and siblings have dictated and defined women's desire must be pondered. The liberatory program is to do our best to understand ourselves, to question and resist the gendered stereotypical images and ideologies which have bombarded us and to develop strategies for protecting coming generations from being similarly poisoned.

Judith C. Blackwell

---

6. This problem comes into particular focus for women recovering from divorce or widowhood. Needless to say, it is particularly acute for women whose partners have left them for younger women.

CHAPTER 24

"Homosexuality is unnatural"
or, why my orgasm is better than yours

Some years ago, three women hailed a taxi in the Greenwich Village area of New York City. They had just left a bar widely known to be frequented by lesbians. The taxi driver was directed to a Village residence where two of the women lived and then to take the third to her apartment in the Upper West Side. During that lengthy leg of the trip, the taxi driver subjected his passenger to a barrage about how "lezzies" were the "scum of the earth," the lowest of the low and so on. According to him, they were all foul-mouthed drunks and uncouth specimens of perversion, as he well knew from picking up fares in the Village. The passenger arrived home visibly distressed at being subjected to such a tirade of hatred.

After talking over this experience with her friends, she came to the conclusion that it was probably all about power. The cabby was undoubtedly reminded every working day of the many layers of power above him, and at times he was probably treated with rudeness or downright contempt by those who perceived themselves to be his "betters." In reaction, he could permit himself to lash out in hatred at a stratum with even less power than he, namely women with a sexual orientation he perceived to be "deviant." Such bitterness was a frightening experience for the woman on the receiving end of it. On reflection, however, she came to see it as an incident in which the "personal became the political." It was a sad illustration of one strategy of the culture of prejudice, that which pits the powerless against one another, encouraging them to stay busy putting each other down, rather than analysing and combating the unjust power relations that keep them all "in their place."

Since the 1960s, this strategy of "divide and conquer" has been repeatedly challenged, as can be seen in widespread pressures to discourage derogatory remarks and discriminatory policies against minority groups. We are urged not to express racist, sexist, ageist, and other attitudes that demean groups who deviate from what is generally perceived to be "the norm." Outcries are to be heard when public figures use words that are offensive to minority groups, and the mainstream media seem to be especially sensitive to language deemed prejudicial. While many people seem to be trying to fulfill this mandate, many others have opposed it as "political correctness," suggesting, in effect, that a thriving culture of prejudice is an important measure of "freedom of expression." Notwithstanding this controversy, perhaps one of the most difficult prejudicial and discriminatory attitudes to challenge is heterosexism. Gays and lesbians, bisexuals, and transgendered persons are openly harassed and are targeted for violence. Jokes are made about them and often told by people who probably would never consider telling a racist joke. People still use "fag" and "dyke" as epithets of insult.

To clarify terminology, let us consider the difference between "homophobia" and "heterosexism." Although official psychiatric definitions of "phobia" have changed over time, this word generally denotes fear of or revulsion toward some object or activity, whether it be certain insects or animals or driving across bridges, as examples. Accordingly, the label "homophobia" came to be applied to people who become anxious and often angry about homosexuals and anything having to do with their desires or behaviour.[1] The problem with this word, though, is that it pathologizes individuals, drawing attention to their personal dislikes and aversions rather than focusing on the larger social context in which their hatred and revulsion finds expression.

From a social scientific perspective, therefore, "heterosexism" is a more useful word, since it describes social institutions and patterns of attitude and behaviour, without the need to address the rage or intolerance of individuals who act upon homophobia within these social systems. How can we identify a country, or its legal system, or an organization, or a set of policy measures as heterosexist? We can document jurisdictions where homosexual couples do not have the same spousal rights and obligations in family law, in taxation law, and religious canon, compared to heterosexual couples who are not legally married. Does a Charter or Bill of Rights include "sexual orientation" as a category, along with language, religion, gender, and so on? You can ask yourself when was the first time you saw a movie or a television program which at least tried to portray homosexuals as whole human beings, rather than as derogatory stereotypes. The advertising industry recently patted itself on the back for running commercials showing gay couples making decisions about what to buy. It was a cynical stab at establishing a certain market niche, but unlikely to have made much of an impact in changing heterosexist attitudes in general. All of the above open up areas of social inquiry which appear when we begin to think about heterosexist cultures and institutions, rather than in terms of "homophobic" people. Indeed,

---

1. Like all human peculiarities of this nature, however, inconsistencies and irregularities can be observed. For example, as the Canadian National Film Board's *Forbidden Love* documents, in the mid-twentieth century there was a notable upsurge of lesbian pulp fiction. Although it was read by women, some of whom discovered validation of their desires therein, its primary market was, one presumes, "straight" and "homophobic" men. Although it may seem contradictory to the critical observer, there are men who loathe and condemn homosexuality, but would like nothing better than to watch or read about women engaging in sexual behaviour together.

it is in such a context that some social theorists have articulated and discussed the concept of "compulsory heterosexuality."

A culture of heterosexism bears many similarities to the "white bread" culture in which visible minority children had to grow up, when all the children's books depicted white people, as did television, the movies, and the beauty and fashion magazines. Just as Western European and North American cultures have assumed the norm of whiteness, they have even more diligently assumed the norm of heterosexuality. Penalties abound for persons who deviate from this widely held expectation. Conformity is encouraged by pervasive gender stereotypes. Even the faintest suggestion of same-sex desire is ruled out as a potentially normal outcome of psychosexual development. The concept of compulsory heterosexuality counters the notion of assumed heterosexuality and "overturns the common-sense view of heterosexuality as natural and therefore requiring no explanation, unlike lesbian and gay sexuality."[2]

In a culture of compulsory heterosexuality, once one has come to terms with one's sexual orientation and found out it departs from the "norm," there are abundant minefields to cross. Unless one has decided to be visibly "out," everyone is going to assume one's heterosexuality: at work, at school, in the shopping mall, at the car dealership, at the fitness club or in the library. It could be argued that being a visible minority in these situations is less complicated, although not always less distressing. People cannot act as if their skin colour is something it is not, even if they do have to calculate what that might mean to the people they meet and to prepare themselves for their responses. Most lesbian and gay people, though, continually have to make choices about revealing their "deviant" identities in their interactions with family, friends, colleagues, and strangers.

Being forthright about sexual orientation relieves a lot of pressure to prevaricate and pretend, but it brings its own consequences and complications, and another range of decisions. Coming out might eventually make life easier with your parents, but not with your grandmother or one of your siblings. Maybe you know that most people at your workplace would be comfortable with it, but at least one might make your life miserable and jeopardize your hopes for future advancement. The decisions required are as numerous as the sum of one's social relations.

To make matters even more complicated, we live in sexist social systems, as well as heterosexist ones. If you are a woman with "manly" characteristics (athletic, practical, intelligent, and with "no fashion sense") or a man with "womanly" qualities (interested in aesthetics, conciliatory, unassertive), people have probably been looking at you out of the corners of their eyes all your life, wondering about your sexual orientation. By violating gendered behaviour expectations, men and women have brought down upon themselves the burden of sexual orientation specula-

---

2. Sonya Andermahr, Terry Lovell, and Carol Wolkowitz, *A Glossary of Feminist Theory* (New York: Oxford University Press, 2000).

tions. The heterosexist society is also a deeply gendered society. Homosexuality, therefore, can be characterized as an attack on the culture of prejudice on two fronts: as a challenge to dominant gender roles and stereotypes, and as an affront to those who believe they know the "true" demarcation between appropriate and inappropriate sexual and familial relations.[3]

This brings us to the question about why "modern science" has been so doggedly interested in distinguishing differences between men and women in their behaviour and abilities, in tandem with trying to find out why gay men and lesbians are so different from "the rest of us." Women and men, boys and girls, have been compared on their intelligence, spatial perception abilities, cognitive functions, manual dexterity, and on and on. Scientific publications abound on these experiments. Feminist theorists are probably correct in their assumption that research of this nature is motivated, consciously or unconsciously, by the desire to identify significant "differences" which, in turn, will lead to conclusions about the inherent inferiority of culturally defined subordinate groups and what they can or cannot be expected to do with their lives.[4] In this, it is little different from research on differences among the so-called "races."

Research on homosexuals, mostly gay men, in the twentieth century initially involved clinical research (i.e., one doctor's opinion about his or her patients), although it became more experimental over the years. During most of the century, homosexuality was defined and recognized as a "disease," a "mental disorder." Since homosexuals were obviously in need of a "cure," medical and psychiatric science stepped in to try to change pathological sexual orientation by shock therapies, aversion therapies, and worse. In the midst of this medicalization of the "problem" of homosexuality, in the 1950s psychologist Evelyn Hooker became acquainted with a group of gay men in California. She found them to be, in her opinion, perfectly healthy in mind. She arranged to have them tested on the standard mental health measures of the day and had self-declared straight men tested on the same psychological tests. The results were sent off to experts in the testing field, and none of these authorities could distinguish differences that would reliably help them assign individuals to one group or another, beyond chance assignation. This interesting experimental information was not widely disseminated, and homosexuality retained its designation as a "mental disorder."

Eventually, it was social action rather than good scientific methodology that made the difference. In the early 1970s, public protests were held at meetings of the American

---

3. See Chapter 20 for how insinuations of lesbianism have been made about members of the women's movement. Conversely, lesbians have sometimes been assumed to be feminists, and in some contexts (e.g., if they are candidates for administrative or political positions), the latter may be perceived as more dangerous than the former.

4. Carol Tavris, *The Mismeasure of Woman: Why Women are not the Better Sex, the Inferior Sex, or the Opposite Sex* (New York: Simon and Schuster, 1992).

Psychiatric Association (APA), and the protesters were not just "mentally ill" homosexuals, they were also gay psychiatrists.[5] The next declaration from this authoritative body of psychiatric theory and practice, in 1980, was that a homosexual does not have a "mental disorder," unless he or she is unhappy about being attracted to someone of the same sex. It was called "Ego-dystonic Homosexuality," but by 1987 it had disappeared as an APA mental illness category, and the concept itself had been downgraded to an example of a disease category called "Sexual Disorder Not Otherwise Specified."[6] Thus, homosexuals were not certifiably crazy anymore, although more social action and activist organization was needed to make inroads into correcting the discriminatory attitudes of other agencies and institutions.

From a social scientific perspective, it is utter folly even to presume to state that homosexuality is a mental disease, a perversion, a life choice or any other category of humanity. We have no rigorous way to define any of these descriptive categories, but even more seriously we cannot precisely say what criteria define the "homosexual." Do we include the man who followed the gender rules, married, and had children, but who dressed in his wife's clothing or visited public urinals to have swift same-sex relief? Modern scientific taxonomy does not allow for the vast range of human desires and behaviours we can observe. Admittedly, a number of scientific disciplines should be targeting research on people who inflict suffering and harm on others, but why does it keep meddling in the differences between gay and straight men's brains at autopsy, or the shape of lesbians' ears?[7] Why are these people so much more interesting than predatory pedophiles or fathers who violate their sons or daughters?

Why does science care so much about the differences between presumably heterosexual men and women, gays, lesbians, bisexuals, transsexuals, or cross-dressers? Whether the motivation to "prove" inferiority, discussed above, wholly or partially provides an explanation, it must be acknowledged that this line of research has provided the gay and transsexual community with a political mandate. If sexual orientation is coded in our genes, we have a right to be who we are and be treated with respect as equals. This is not simply a lifestyle choice. Let the state fund all the research it can afford to show that some fruit flies are genetically coded to be same-sex attracted. Let the scientific community prove that we are "different," and we were born that way. Considering that some form of homosexuality can be found in any

---

5. Stuart A. Kirk and Herb Kutchins, *The Selling of DSM: The Rhetoric of Science in Psychiatry* (New York: Aldine de Gruyter, 1992).

6. Herb Kutchins and Stuart Kirk, *Making Us Crazy: DSM: The Psychiatric Bible and the Creation of Mental Disorders* (New York: The Free Press, 1997).

7. No kidding! I have misplaced the newspaper clipping where I read about this, but I positively remember reading about a scientific study comparing straight and gay women's ears. Information on a study comparing the finger length of gays and lesbians can be found at <http://www. lds-mormon.com/fingersex.shtml> January, 2002.

culture, it must be a "fact of human nature," and in this sense "natural" for those who have inherited this genetic legacy.[8]

This may be a compelling political argument for defenders of the human rights of people who are not strictly heterosexual, but it is also an example of the dichotomous thinking critical social scientists wish to dismantle. It does not "explain" the nature of bisexuality, nor does it help us understand transsexuals who were not "born gay," but rather have a lifelong conviction that they were born into wrongly-sexed bodies. It glosses over the high rates of homoerotic behaviour in children and adolescents, as well as in sex-segregated adult populations. It cannot account for women who choose lesbian soulmates after decades of being abused by boyfriends and husbands. Claims that people are simply "that way" by nature divert attention from the shades of grey observed in the rich diversity of human behaviour.

So, is homosexuality "unnatural"? A critical social scientist would argue that the modern cultures making such a fuss over it are themselves unnatural. This argument can be based on anthropological research on cultures in which very different attitudes are observed. It can be buttressed by the historical record of Western culture, where "the homosexual" did not exist as a concept until the nineteenth century and took on a life of its own once it was named and deemed to be a problem. The idea that heterosexism is "unnatural" can be analysed within the larger framework of the sexually obsessed and deeply gendered societies in which we live. Indeed, it can be argued that any questions about what is "natural" for humans are stupid questions, considering that not so long ago it was agreed that women who wore trousers or were interested in political debate were "unnatural." Nevertheless, thinking about why human naturalness is such a tenacious contemporary issue is most certainly interesting. It opens up many avenues of social scientific exploration, both empirical and theoretical.

It seems appropriate to close this chapter with the words of a woman who was conceived as a foetus with both an X and a Y chromosome but, because of a 1 in 20,000 chance, was born as a girl instead of as a boy. Because of a little quirk of nature, this developing person converted the male hormones she produced into female ones, and after the age of puberty this led her into numerous medical deceptions and humiliations, as well as profound identity problems. She concludes that "simplistic thinking" invalidates her lived experience:

> People like us have felt so much shame and self-loathing about not being normal. That's tragic, because one of the things that makes the natural world, and humanity, beautiful is the fact that they're filled with surprises, variations and anomalies. It's taken me a long time, ... but

---

8. Although not commonly reported, same-sex liaisons are commonly observed in non-human animals, too.

more and more I'm feeling that it's a privilege, almost a state of grace, to be different.[9]

It would be easy to end this chapter with a sermon about the lack of tolerance of gendered or sexual difference we observe around us, whether these differences be caused by an accidental encounter of two chromosomes, by choice, by social circumstances, by traumatic experiences—by the host of events accounting for human diversity. Rather than preaching about love and understanding, the more important message seems to be this: "Be suspicious of simple questions or answers." Never assume there is just one "cause" of a problem. Never assume you know the breadth nor definition of a problem.[10] Of more importance, critical social scientists must ask themselves, "Where does the problem *really* lie?" More often than not, it can be traced to the heart of the culture of prejudice.

Judith C. Blackwell

---

9. Martha Percival (pseudonym), "Veering off the two-lane gender highway," *The Globe and Mail*, 14 April 1998: A20.

10. This is especially important when behaviours or attitudes are being labelled "unnatural" or "deviant."

CHAPTER 25

"Abortion is murder"

Anti-woman hysterical rhetoric of the anti-abortion movement

Before modern birth-control techniques became widely available, a married woman could look her husband in the eye and say, "I've already made eight children for you, and only three of them have died. You have sons and daughters. I want no more." Thereafter, if he were an understanding man and agreed not to force sexual intercourse on her, the wife could at least trust that she had some degree of control over her own body. She had no more worries about acquiring life-threatening infections, dying in childbirth, or watching another child die in her arms. If her husband were not an understanding man, she most probably would be pregnant again within the year, once more at risk to death and disability. There was little a woman could do in cases of unwanted pregnancies, whether as a result of sexual assault or accident, except to carry the foetus to term and accept the long range responsibilities of nurturing another infant into adulthood, assuming it survived that long.[1]

Women's reproductive duties have, apparently, always been high on the societal agenda. A woman was expected to marry, and pressured to do so if only by the limited range of life opportunities available to unmarried women. She was expected to bear children and had no right to refuse sexual intercourse within the patriarchal institution of marriage. Her rights to take responsibility for her reproductive health and well-being, since recorded time, were virtually non-existent.

Once swift and safe pregnancy termination procedures became available, women experienced a welcome relief. In combination with twentieth-century birth-control methods (none of which can be relied upon completely),[2] women finally could choose

---

1. Means of birth control and pregnancy termination have been available for centuries. The problem has been that states did not permit sensible education on either topic. This did not mean, of course, that socially advantaged women were precluded from access to both. The majority of disadvantaged women, however, were left with unsound methods and unskilled practitioners.

2. One source estimates that 58 per cent of women who had pregnancies terminated in the United States in 1995 had used contraception during the month in which they became pregnant. The Alan Guumacher Institute, <www.agi-usa.org/pubs/fb_induced_abortion/html> October, 2001.

when and if they would bring children into this world. Yet even today, it would be hard to find an individual who could claim to have never known a woman who has experienced an unexpected pregnancy.[3] On this basis alone, one might assume that there should be widespread sympathy and support for women's right to decide to opt for abortion rather than having their lives radically altered by bearing an unwanted child. The women's movement has always focused on the range of choices available to women, whether they be career decisions or other choices concerning how individual women wish to lead their lives. Choice means control and self-efficacy. Gradually and grudgingly, rights to choose have been ceded, by allowing women to become doctors or to vote, for example. Nevertheless, permitting the choice to terminate a pregnancy has been vociferously opposed and continues to be, even in jurisdictions where abortion is legally available. Thus, abortion remains a quintessential feminist issue.

Access to safe birth control and abortion, such fundamental concerns of the women's movement, invite highly controversial and emotionally laden social policy debates, most notably in the United States, where opposition to a "pro-choice" Supreme Court decision in 1973 has continued unabated. (This was the *Roe v. Wade* decision, based on women's constitutionally protected rights.) Opponents to giving women control over their reproductive lives are most certainly not people who understand the deep concerns of feminism or civil libertarian groups. They are often deeply and sincerely motivated by religious principles or political ideologies. Many of them believe in the "traditional" nuclear family structure, although there is no evidence that this concept has any validity. In the passion of these debates, the participants do not see themselves as acting on the stage of the culture of prejudice, but they are. As critical social scientists, we are obligated to step back and analyse the underlying themes appearing in the debate over access to abortion.

This debate leads us into a miasma of ethical dilemmas. The issues raised can be categorized in various ways, but for our purposes here, let us group them under the following topics: the concept of "Right to Life," the consequences of infant adoption, and the rights of women to have reproductive choice and control over their bodies and their lives.

"RIGHT TO LIFE"

Those who are opposed to abortion declare that the rights of the foetus supersede those of the vessel in which it is gestating. They contend that the combination of cells developing within a woman's body have a "Right to Life." My use of the word

---

3. It has been estimated that 43 per cent of women in the United States will have had an abortion by the age of 45. Even if this estimation were reduced by half, it is likely that most people know at least one person who has made a decision to terminate a pregnancy. The Alan Guumacher Institute, <www.agi-usa.org/pubs/fb_induced_abortion/html> October, 2001.

"vessel" is deliberate, because the "right to life" position, in its purest expression, ignores the fact that a woman is a human life form with rights to make her own decisions about such an important life event as giving birth. One observer has likened the "Right to Life" position to saying the acorn is equivalent to the oak tree.[4] In its extreme form, it says that the acorn is *more* important than the oak tree—that the life of the foetus *ipso facto* supersedes any rights its carrier may have had. A woman's opinion on whether or not she is suited to bringing a human being into this world and looking after it for twenty years or more is rendered irrelevant. Through her becoming pregnant, a woman's individuality, responsibility, and citizenship have been wiped clean from the slate of her existence.

The most radical "pro-life" advocates go to shocking extremes in their disregard for the woman who discovers herself with an unwanted pregnancy. The abuses she may have suffered are ignored. For example, at one point the Pope of the Roman Catholic Church declared that Bosnian women who had been raped by marauding militia of other ethnic factions must bring their pregnancies to term, presumably thereafter to do their best to integrate these offspring of the enemy into their communities. To the extremists on this issue, it does not matter if the woman has been impregnated by her father or her brother or one of their family friends; it is of no consequence if she has been "date raped" by a boyfriend she trusted, "gang raped" by an athletic team or attacked by a stranger in a public place. Further, consideration of the woman's personal circumstances and the impact a pregnancy will carry with it are ignored: her age does not matter; nor does her possible need for an education or other promotion of her economic prospects; nor does her poverty, social isolation, experiences of domestic violence, alcohol or other substance use or medical problems which may put both mother and baby at risk. In short, "pro-life" has seemingly no concern for the lives of pregnant women and no compunction about trampling on their rights.

On a philosophical level, Judith Jarvis Thomson asks us to consider a situation in which a woman has been kidnapped and anaesthetized, awakening to find herself in bed with a world-famous violinist, attached to him by tubes. She is informed that he needs her healthy kidneys to survive for the next nine months after which he should be able to function independently. Or perhaps she will be needed indefinitely if his health status does not work out for the best. Are there not interesting parallels here to the situation where a woman is informed that the "person" developing inside of her is of much more importance and value than she?

Of course, it is arrogant to believe one can assess the relative value of a living, breathing woman compared to a cluster of cells with a mere potential to develop into an independent life form. It is self-evident that few of these little masses might become renowned musicians or scientists or anything else of that ilk, if permitted their

---

4. Judith Jarvis Thomson, "A Defence of Abortion," *Bioethics*, ed. John Harris (Oxford: Oxford University Press, 2001) 25-41.

"birthright." What is so interesting about the "pro-life" philosophy is its complete disregard for the fate of those putatively "precious" children who are to be reluctantly brought into this world by women who are not ready to welcome them. We are asked to put aside all ethical concerns about women's rights in favour of potential humans with uncertain futures in a world that privileges few and insures that most are born with a strike or two against them before they even begin the game.

Raising a child is an enormous responsibility, ideally requiring careful planning and preparation if the infant is to develop into a responsible and productive member of society. Obviously, there must be a financial commitment, as well as the willingness to invest a tremendous amount of time and emotional energy into the well-being of the child. These commitments are likely to decline in intensity after two decades or so, but a lifetime obligation remains. It is curious that the "Right to Life" advocates express such deep concern over the unborn but appear to care so little about what might become of them if they were to be born.

This disregard for the fate of the unborn is also a further indication of the "pro-life" disregard for women and their decision-making abilities and human integrity. The very fact that a woman is reluctant to have a baby should send up a red flag to signal that the potential child is already at risk. Admittedly, no one will argue that there has never been a case of an abortion motivated by what many of us would judge to be selfish or silly reasons. However, this is not grounds to argue that the vast majority of women are not perfectly capable of assessing the potential consequences of carrying a pregnancy to term and evaluating the likely lifetime ramifications of doing so on the children and themselves. Indeed, if a pregnant woman were *not* capable of making such a determination, presumably we should question her suitability for motherhood on that basis alone. Is it in the best interests of society to force such women to bear children by withholding access to terminations?

Let us assume that, including ourselves among those who take human rights seriously, the social order grants women the right to balance the pros and cons, to make their own decisions about allowing an unwanted pregnancy to proceed. If the pregnant woman decides motherhood is not a viable life decision for her at that time, we might wish to urge her not to have an abortion, but to have the baby and permit it to be adopted. On the surface, this seems like a straightforward compromise. However, like all seemingly "simple" solutions, it deserves examination.

THE ADOPTION OPTION

As we gather from the news media and other sources, North America in the early twenty-first century is apparently teeming with people who want to adopt children. With loosened restrictions on who qualifies as potential adoptive parents (some jurisdictions including lesbians, gays, and singles), the pool of candidates has increased. It is heartening, too, to hear of people who go abroad to adopt children who might otherwise grow up in extremely deprived circumstances. Among those who wish to adopt within their own country and culture, there seems to be a sizable number who would prefer a healthy infant rather than an older child and who are inclined toward a baby who is not immediately identifiable as a member of a visible minority group. Considering the nature of this demand, an argument could be made for a social policy encouraging women to bring unwanted pregnancies to term, especially if they were likely to supply a product to meet market demand. Metaphorically, this is like asking a woman to stay hooked up to the violinist for nine months and then go on about her life.

Assuming a woman has strong emotional, ethical or religious reasons compelling her to feel responsible for providing sustenance to another life form, her willingness ensures that the adoption option is indeed a reasonable solution to everyone's problems. However, is it an option to be expected of, or urged upon, the majority of women considering abortion?

First, the nine months of gestation deserve consideration. When we read about surrogate mothers who voluntarily have babies for others, they are often quoted as saying that they "love being pregnant." Unfortunately, the physiological state of pregnancy only rarely seems to bring such unadulterated bliss. There is no need to catalogue the discomforts and medical complications that may arise during pregnancy and childbirth, even in women most desirous of producing children. Further, pregnancy puts a woman at risk of a gamut of emotional fluctuations, problems around body image and self-esteem, altered social relations and so on. All of these are only risks, and none will necessarily occur. However, one does not need a medical degree to predict that the adverse risks of any physiological process of this gravity will be lower for a person expecting joyous reward at the end of the process, compared to one anticipating nothing more than getting over it and getting on with her life. Asking a woman to endure pregnancy and childbirth simply for providing a healthy infant of the "right" skin colour to strangers is an extraordinary request.

What would happen if the state were to mandate adoption and forbid therapeutic abortions? In the first place, it would most certainly drive a sizable number of women unwilling to endure a pregnancy to illegal, unregulated, and potentially dangerous abortionists. As in the past, more privileged women would have access to safer abortions, either by appealing to sympathetic friends with medical degrees or travelling to jurisdictions where they are legal. The toll of death and disability would fall on women with fewer resources.

When we look through the lens of population statistics, between 1994 and 1998, Statistics Canada counted over 100,000 therapeutic abortions per year.[5] It is highly

---

5. Statistics Canada, <www.statcan.ca/english/Pgab/Health/health43a.htm> Sept, 2001.

unlikely that there would have been sufficient numbers of people willing to absorb this volume of production into their families. It has been estimated that there were only about 1,200 adoptions *per annum* in Canada in recent years, with a further 2,000 adoptions abroad.[6] Even if the latter families switched to Canadian babies, these figures suggest that tens of thousands of children would become wards of the state each year.

Furthermore, a policy mandating adoption as the result of unwanted pregnancies would fall most heavily on young women. Roughly 80 per cent of therapeutic abortions in Canada are provided to women under the age of 30, precisely in the years when people lay the foundations for their future economic productivity. A social policy aimed at disrupting this development in significant numbers of young women would obviously carry considerable social costs.

In short, the adoption option is, as it should be, available to women who choose to have babies they cannot or wish not to raise. It is not, however, a workable policy solution.

THE RIGHTS OF WOMEN

In 1988, the Supreme Court of Canada struck down the federal law regulating abortion on the grounds that it violated women's human rights under the *Charter of Rights and Freedoms*. There was much discussion at the time about revising the law or drafting new legislation. Nothing ever came of it, which is not surprising. It is difficult to imagine any legislation aimed at satisfying the concerns of the "Right to Life" movement which would not violate one or more of the human rights provisions in the Charter.

Of course, the controversy has not receded. Bitter demonstrations are regularly held outside abortion clinics, and physicians who work there receive death threats, are stalked, and receive life-threatening attacks. In North America over the past decade, seven people were murdered and 17 were victims of attempted murder because they were understood to be willing to help women resolve the problem of an unwanted pregnancy.[7] In this context, "abortion is murder" is a reality indeed.

Unless therapeutic procedures are legally and readily available to women, desperate women around the world will turn to extreme methods or unregulated practitioners for a solution to their problems, as they have done throughout history. Many of them will be mutilated and many will die. It can thus be argued that laws and reg-

---

6. "More than 20,000 await adoption, but most remain wards of the state," *The Toronto Star*, <www.thestar.ca/NASApp/ca> Oct. 2001.

7. National Abortion Federation, "Violence and Disruption Statistics," <http://www.prochoice.org/> Nov. 2001.

ulations which ban or limit access to termination of pregnancy are a *de facto* form of murder, by reason of their deliberate intent to narrow women's choices and drive them to actions that put their health and their lives at risk.

Applying a critical perspective to the abortion debate is a challenge, because it is such an emotionally charged issue. A spokeswoman for the anti-abortion lobby may be featured in the media, declaring that a past decision she made to have an abortion has haunted her all her life. It was a choice she wishes she had never made, and our hearts go out to her. Individual life experiences are very powerful and should be respected as such. Nevertheless, each one of us, as human beings, can most probably remember a regrettable choice we have made, or an action or remark that was cruel or unfair to someone else. However, these are not the experiences upon which to base social policy or make ethical decisions about what other people should or should not do, and they most certainly do not justify recommending the abrogation of the human rights of others. The highly charged debates over abortion are often characterized as matters of morality. From a social scientific perspective, however, the debate is over the restriction of the rights and freedoms of women and the perpetuation of their taken-for-granted status as inferiors within the culture of prejudice.

Judith C. Blackwell

CHAPTER 26

"The family is a haven in a heartless world"

The "family values" myth

In the early 1960s, Betty Friedan wrote a book which was to generate an electrical connection to a certain class of women.[1] Her readers lived in industrialized societies and were largely well-educated (i.e., sent to post-secondary education so at least they could get the degree of "MRS"—married to someone who had "good prospects"). Aside from the economic potential of the men who became their husbands, they did not know what they were getting into. After several years of married life, many of them found themselves feeling depressed and unfulfilled, lacking in intellectual stimulation and prey to self-blame and fears that they were "bad" wives and mothers. The book's title, *The Feminine Mystique*, gave name to the "problem with no name": the fact that many women had been tricked into believing that the roles of wife and mother were all they needed to complete their lives and, if they did not find utter fulfillment in the family, it was all their fault.

Friedan urged these women to engage their intellectual abilities outside the cloister of the home. It was a powerful message to the privileged women who needed to hear it. For these women, it was a call to save themselves from self-blame and chronic depression—to understand themselves as productive human agents, capable of making significant contributions outside of the domestic sphere.

On a global and historical level, however, this fine message is laughably irrelevant, considering the enormous range of profound problems that women's lot has been. Throughout history, most women have made significant contributions to the economic well-being of their families, often with backbreaking work in agricultural or industrial production. However, Friedan was not attempting to do an analysis of *all* women's problems. Even within her own time and culture, she might have expanded her analysis to include "old maids" who were still being treated with pity and derision in the 1960s, or lesbians, or the pregnant teenagers living in ghettoized slums in her own country. At the time she was writing, the concept of "sexual

---

1. Betty Friedan, *The Feminine Mystique* (New York: Dell, 1963).

harassment in the workplace" was unheard of in North America, and the fact that female children in other countries were being subjected to genital mutilation was unknown to the Westernized mind. In retrospect, Friedan's focus was limited, but that is not a fatal criticism. She studied the women who interested her, and she inspired the women who read her book to reimagine themselves.

Of more concern is the way that the culture of prejudice has used Betty Friedan's work as some kind of icon of feminism and continues to brand the women's movement as a "threat to family values." This kind of cant can be heard today. According to this belief, feminists say that women are not fulfilled unless they are in the workforce—they have no personal value if they are not involved as wage-earners. Feminists are said to be scornful of women who choose housework over the combination of waged and domestic work. According to this perspective, women know in their instinctive hearts that their rightful place is in the home with their children. (What they will do with their time after the young ones have gone off into the world on their own is a question unasked.)

The portrayal of the women's movement as "anti-family" could not be further from the truth. Feminists, especially socialist feminists, have been adamant in arguing for recognition of the value to the economy of women's unpaid domestic labour and in pointing out how it has not been acknowledged as "work." Furthermore, feminists have noted the value of "women's work" to the capitalist system insofar as they take care of the current generation of workers, feed and clothe them, and provide an atmosphere in which they can relax and prepare themselves for another hard and productive day on the job. In addition, child-care responsibilities produce the next generation of educated and well-socialized workers for the labour force.[2] Indeed, feminist economists have pointed out that women's considerable contributions to the economy through unwaged labour were not even reflected in Gross National Product indices measuring the productivity of national labour forces. In short, feminists have valorized women's contributions to the family, albeit within the larger criticism of the unequal gendered division of labour it represents.

The vision of the husband earning a "family wage" to support a woman and their children at home is a snapshot of a particularly privileged kind of family. This family form, previously possible only for the wealthier classes, became more widely available to the working classes for only a short period of history, most notably in Western countries in the post-World War II era. This kind of "nuclear" family is a cultural artifact akin to marriage in its representation in the "diamond is forever" advertisements. Historically, women and men and boys and girls have worked together to sustain families. On a global level, women have not only been responsible for child care, exhausting domestic labour and often supplying the household with water, but they have also contributed to the family income through agricultural

2. See the Postscript to this chapter for an elaboration of the value of the family to capitalist economies.

work, selling eggs, doing laundry, sewing and cleaning for other families, taking in boarders—the list goes on.

Today in industrialized countries, with the decline in the vigour of the union movement, with "downsizing" and "outsourcing," there are fewer and fewer occupations that can provide a family wage. As a result, women's participation in the labour force has steadily increased. In 1998, almost 64 per cent of "husband and wife" families, as defined by Statistics Canada, had "dual earner" status. In essence, women are not only doing officially invisible work in their households, but most of them are also officially recorded workers in industrialized state economies.

Feminists are very concerned about opportunities for women to compete on a level playing field in educational institutions, in the workplace, and everywhere else. They are also concerned about the well-being of children and the family environments that will promote their healthy development. They are by no means "antifamily" when they argue that single-parent families, "blended" families, gay and lesbian families, and the whole array of familial patterns we see today are potentially healthy. They just simply do not buy into a romanticized notion of the idealized heterosexual family solely supported by a man, where children are slavishly obedient and wives give way to their husbands' every whim and desire. A "man's home" is most certainly not "his castle," and to the degree patriarchal values convince men that it is, more is the danger for the women and children who live with them. Feminists are keenly aware of the unacceptable rates of violence in spousal and dating relationships, as well as the abuse of children in families.[3] As costly and unjust as non-lethal family violence can be, we also cannot ignore the frequency with which it escalates to murder,[4] a topic to which we will return at the end of this chapter.

PROMOTING "FAMILY VALUES"

No one can deny the societal importance of secure and healthy environments in which to raise children. The ideology of romantic love encourages us to seek life partners with whom to share life's adventures and intimacies; successful relationships of this nature are a joy to behold, especially when they are sustained throughout the stresses and costs of childrearing. As a result, it seems churlish to question the agendas of those who sincerely promote "family values" as an unadulterated societal good.

---

3. Walter DeKeseredy, "Patterns of Family Violence," *Families: Changing Trends in Canada*, 4th ed., ed. Maureen Baker (Toronto: McGraw-Hill Ryerson, 2001) 238-66.

4. DeKeseredy (p.249) reports on an 18-year period in Canada when almost 80 femicides on average were recorded each year. Femicide is defined as "the killing of females by male partners with whom they have, have had, or want to have, a sexual and/or emotional relationship."

Nevertheless, it must be acknowledged that the pro-family agenda is part of a larger political movement which is anti-feminist and deeply conservative.[5] This political momentum, sometimes referred to as "neo-conservatism," advocates *laissez-faire* economics, privatization of public services, restrictions on public spending, and reliance on volunteerism. Instead of government investment in health care, child care and education, not to mention social assistance, this agenda advocates responsibility for these functions to be managed for profit, relegated to the voluntary sector or returned to the "traditional family." Family values spokespersons do not elaborate on which family members will bear the brunt of these policy initiatives. One does not need to be a genius, however, to figure this out. One simply needs to be a woman enmeshed in familial relationships of caring and responsibility.

The bulk of people whose labour will be called upon to look after the ill and injured given early discharge from hospitals, the children whose kindergartens have been closed down, and the elderly will largely be female friends and family members—sisters, wives, daughters, nieces, and grandmothers. Their caregiving will be unwaged and for the most part its important contribution to the social order will be unacknowledged. Meanwhile, an increasing number of families will be relying on the earning power of two adults, except in single-parent families where there is only one wage-earner available. It is heartening to observe the modern masculine exceptions, but until these men are no longer seen as exceptions, be assured that the burdens the state downloads onto families will largely be assumed by women.

Thus, the smug statements of the "traditional family values" contingent are a smoke screen. They say their policies allow women more choice, to permit them to stay at home with their children, for example. In fact, they are consigning modern women not only to the essential demands of breadwinning, but also to the burden of caregiving which could otherwise be provided by trained professionals. They are just as limited in their vision as *The Feminine Mystique* was in appealing to a readership who were privileged enough to have access to a family wage. Furthermore, neo-conservative policies that erode social programs tacitly assume that women, many of whom already carry the "double burden" of both waged work and the bulk of unpaid domestic labour in their own homes, will take up the slack, stepping in where the state has withdrawn social services.

---

5. Meg Luxton, "Feminism and Families: The Challenge of Neo-Conservatism," *Feminism and Families: Critical Policies and Changing Practices*, ed. Meg Luxton (Halifax: Fernwood, 1997) 10-26.

"NO MOTIVE KNOWN": ANOTHER "PROBLEM WITH NO NAME"

A woman in her mid-thirties is stabbed to death, in her own home, and her two children are also found murdered. The man arrested is reported to be the woman's former husband or lover. A counsellor who has been called in to help the dead children's schoolmates says he has no answer to their question, "Why can this happen?" The news report goes on to say that there is "no motive known" for the killings.

Violent crime is quite obviously a cultural fascination; otherwise we would not be exposed to it so regularly in the news, the cinema, fiction and television. Commentators are anxious to create taxonomies of human brutality, to be able to "explain" crimes as "drug-related," "gang-related," "gay bashing," and so on. It is curious, then, that there is no convenient term for the consistently observed pattern of violence against women by men who believe they are "in love" with their victims. Even more curious is how this brutality, when it escalates to murder, is relegated to the category of "senseless" crime, with no motive known.

There is an observable and consistent pattern of male violence against women, leading to their murders and often those of their children, a pattern repeatedly reported in the media. The aggressor is possessive, overly controlling, angry, and incapable of accepting what he perceives to be rejection. These cases often involve stalking and other forms of harassment. The only truly safe solution for the woman who is the target of such an obsession is to take her children far away, completely change her identity, cancel her credit, and sever all ties with family and friends. Why is it that, for an incredible number of women, the family has been the antithesis of a "haven"?

There are a number of sociologically interesting questions that flow from these tragic and all-too-common situations. What do they tell us about gender role socialization and what it means to be a "man" in modern civilization?[6] Why is there a psychiatric diagnosis (Delusional Disorder, Erotomanic Type) for the very rare case of a person, usually a woman, who imagines someone (usually a famous or powerful man) is in love with her, but there is no diagnosis for the more common and more dangerously lethal rejected male husband or lover? Would there be any societal benefit to treating these men as "mad," rather than "bad"? What would be the drawbacks? Considering that so many women and children suffer at the hands of these men, why is *this* still a problem with no name?

To mindlessly decry divorce rates and insist that dysfunctional families should be encouraged to "stay together for the sake of the children" is to ignore a wealth of social scientific evidence revealing the social costs of such policies. The self-righteous supporters of "family values" are complacent in their presumptive cloud of approval for a self-evidently "just" cause. In fact, to oppose access to abortion, same-sex marriages

---

6. Joseph A. Kuypers, ed., *Men and Power* (Halifax: Fernwood, 1999).

or any number of potentially healthy family relationships other than the heterosexual "nuclear" form, is to be a compliant booster of the culture of prejudice.

Judith C. Blackwell

POSTSCRIPT:

In a response to an earlier draft of this chapter, one of my colleagues[7] takes an interesting slant on family values rhetoric. In writing this chapter, I have considered the issue in light of the injustices it visits on women and children. I am in agreement with what Murray Smith has to say, and he has consented to let me quote him in this context. It contains the essence of the chapter on the social institution of the family which *he* would have written for this book, if *I* had not volunteered to take on the topic. This is why I decided to add this Postscript.

Another reason is to illustrate how critical social science does not confine an individual scholar to a particular perspective on any one social issue. What Murray Smith wishes to emphasize is different from my chosen focus, but I consider it to be just as valuable as what I have to say. There are no "party lines" in critical social science.

> You make many good points in the chapter; but if I were writing it, I would make the point that all the nonsense about "family values" is really about reinforcing an archaic institution that is vital to capitalist society because it remains the cheapest way to reproduce wage-labour across generations. No matter that it places the burden for childrearing primarily on the shoulders of unpaid wives/mothers; no matter that it is a means of oppressively regulating sexuality; and no matter that it keeps women and men alike in domestic situations that are frequently unhappy. From the point of view of capital, the family is the ideal institution for reproducing the commodity labour-power—the one significant input to capitalist production that is not itself produced by capitalists or with a view to making a profit.
>
> So why does "family values" rhetoric appeal to the working class itself? Jane Humphries offered an intriguing answer some time ago when she suggested that, from the standpoint of workers, the family is a kind of communist oasis in a capitalist environment. The economist Paul Samuelson also referred to it as a "communist organization." It is the one significant institution in a capitalist society where bonds of personal intimacy rather than considerations of economic exchange are paramount. It is a sphere in which labour is performed out of a sense of

---

7. Murray Smith, personal communication, 27 March 2002.

personal obligation and love (whether child care or care for elderly or sick family members) rather than for a wage. Because it is important that some family members be in a position to provide such "free of charge" services, the working class is attracted to the idea that the "family breadwinner" (typically a man) should be able to earn a "family wage"—a wage sufficient to support a stay-at-home spouse and children. Thus "family wage ideology" militates against the ongoing drive of capital to reduce wages to a level sufficient to the subsistence of the individual worker. It is a normative means of defining the value of labour-power to permit at least one adult member of the household (traditionally the mother/wife) to remain at home or to only work part time, so that she can perform those vital domestic tasks that are so important to meeting the needs of the working-class household. Of course, the reality of a "family wage" has been significantly eroded in recent years, and this is one of the reasons that right-wing "family values" rhetoric resonates so well with working class people. The "nostalgia" for the traditional nuclear family is not primarily about "keeping women in their place"; it is probably much more about preserving living standards and an institutional sphere in which "communalist" rather than pecuniary considerations prevail.

Capital, as usual, wants to have its cake and eat it too. It wants to preserve the traditional nuclear family as the cheapest means of reproducing the commodity labour-power and as a mechanism for "disciplining" the working class and habituating workers to the dull compulsion of capitalist economic relations (not to mention instilling conservative values). At the same time, it wants to change the normative determinants of the value of labour-power in such a way that the average wage is insufficient to support a whole family—that is, it wants to lower the value of labour-power as a means of increasing profits. This contradiction produces a great deal of irrational thought about the value of family life. But the breakdown of the institution is also implied within it. Capitalism needs the family—but it also undermines it, without offering any institutional replacement.

suggested readings

Baker, Maureen, ed. *Families: Changing Trends in Canada*. 4th ed. Toronto: McGraw-Hill Ryerson, 2001.

Coontz, Stephanie. *The Way We Never Were: American Families and the Nostalgia Trap*. New York: BasicBooks, 1992.

Corman, June, and Meg Luxton. *Getting By in Hard Times: Gendered Labour at Home and on the Job*. Toronto: University of Toronto Press, 2001.

Haddad, Tony, ed. *Men and Masculinities: A Critical Anthology*. Toronto: Canadian Scholars' Press, 1993.

Kimmel, Michael S., ed. *Changing Men: New Directions in Research on Men and Masculinity*. Newbury Park, CA: Sage Publications, 1987.

Luxton, Meg, ed. *Feminism and Families: Critical Policies and Changing Practices*. Halifax: Fernwood, 1997.

Roth, Rachel. *Making Women Pay: The Hidden Costs of Fetal Rights*. Ithaca, NY: Cornell University Press, 2000.

Starr, Paul. *The Social Transformation of American Medicine*. New York: BasicBooks, 1982.

Waring, Marilyn. *If Women Counted: Worth and Value in the Global Economy*. San Francisco: Harper & Row, 1988.

PART EIGHT

Policing the culture of prejudice

CHAPTER 27

"Lock 'em up and throw away the key!"

Expensive, inefficient, inhumane, and remarkably simple-minded solution to the modern "crime problem"

The logic of this approach to crime control is simple. There are those among us who break the laws, and the law-abiding are put at risk or directly suffer as a consequence. To reduce this threat, generous resources should be provided to identify the evil-doers. The best way to ensure that those identified do not continue to do harm is to isolate them in secure facilities and hope they will have learned their lesson by the time the system is prepared to release them.

What makes this simple approach complicated? Depriving someone of freedom and citizenship rights is a heavy penalty, so it is necessary to distinguish between those "deserving" it and those who can remain free after receiving less stringent penalties. This discrimination is necessary on humanitarian grounds; it is clearly excessive to lock up a first-time petty shoplifter or a driver exceeding the speed limit, for example. The question is where the state decides to draw the line between those deserving to be deprived of their liberty and those who can be reprimanded in some other way. In addition, the correctional system is extremely costly to run, and no society can afford enough secure facilities to feed and house everyone who has been convicted of a crime. The calculus of incarceration, in short, involves two fundamental considerations: determining how many deserve imprisonment for how long, and gauging the capacity of the prison system to accommodate them.

On the basis of incarceration rates, it is clear that there is considerable variation in how societies determine who deserves imprisonment and who does not. If asked which country in the world has the greatest number of people in prisons, China would probably come to mind, with its vast population and repressive legal system. In fact, the United States has more people incarcerated than any other country in the world. In 1998, the state of California alone had a prison population larger than those of the United Kingdom, France, Germany, Japan, Singapore, and the Netherlands combined.[1] US crime rates are higher than in other countries, but by no means

---

1. Eric Schlosser, "The Prison-Industrial Complex," *The Atlantic Monthly* December 1998: 51-77.

high enough to warrant such disparities when compared to other national jurisdictions. Furthermore, this enormous appetite for imprisoning people is a fairly recent phenomenon in US history, beginning in the mid-1970s and continuing ever since. There were fewer than 400,000 people locked up in 1970, but by 2000 this figure had increased to over 2 million.

That increasing prison populations are not a direct reflection of general lawlessness is nicely illustrated in an article published by *Scientific American*, "Why Do Prisons Grow?"[2] Based on data from the US Bureau of Justice Statistics, in 1999 there were 203 people per 100,000 in Vermont state prisons and local jails, compared to 1,014 per 100,000 in Texas. Why the disparity? How can people who live in Texas be so radically more prone to crime than those who live in Vermont or Maine (220) or Massachusetts (353)? New York State's incarceration rate is over 40 per cent lower than that of Texas, so it cannot be accounted for by urbanization or "big city" crime, despite New York City's reputation as a hotbed of urban criminals.

Along similar lines, Rodger Doyle asks us to consider the comparison between North Carolina and South Carolina.[3] Both states had roughly the same crime-rate statistics, but there was a noticeable difference in the expansion of their prison populations in the late 1980s and early 1990s. Both states had Republican governors in this era, but South Carolina's governor emphasized "law and order" and the state inmate population grew by over 63 per cent in an 8-year period. There was also an increase in North Carolina, but not at all of the same order (25 per cent). This suggests to Doyle that a political atmosphere of "get tough on crime" goes some way toward accounting for new prison construction and overcrowding of existing facilities, and that the local media as well as politicians may be contributors to rising incarceration rates.

Doyle also wonders about the influence of state histories of racial discrimination on imprisonment rates. This is a question made obvious by the colourful Bureau of Justice map illustrating his article, which shows the "red" states (700+ per 100,000) banding the south, and a table provided reporting that 66 per cent of the inmates of state prisons and local jails in all of the states combined are either African-American or Hispanic. Although ethnic variations in local populations may give us some clue, they are unlikely to account for more than a fraction of the distribution observed in prison populations. For example, in 1996 in the province of Saskatchewan, 11 per cent of the population were Aboriginal, yet over 70 per cent of admissions to custody were recorded as such.[4] In Canada as a whole, while Aboriginal people represent 2 per cent of the population, over the past decade they made up roughly 17 per cent of admissions to custody on both the provincial and federal levels. It is simply beyond belief

2. Rodger Doyle, "Why Do Prisons Grow?," *Scientific American* December 2001: 28.

3. Doyle 28.

4. Canadian Centre for Justice Statistics, *Aboriginal Peoples in Canada* <http://www.statcan.ca:80/english/freepub/85F0033MIE/85F0033MIE01001.pdf> (Profile Series no. 85F0033MIE) Dec. 2001.

to conclude that the criminal inclinations of marginalized and racialized minorities account for such disparities.

Sociologists argue that these disparities can be explained by selective law enforcement. The attention of the police is more likely to be drawn to the activities of members of marginalized groups, and they are more likely to patrol their neighbourhoods, looking for trouble. When apprehended, the marginalized are more likely to be arrested than cautioned. They are less likely to receive bail, and at trial are more likely to be found guilty. The sentences they receive are likely to be harsher than those imposed on the more "average" Canadian or American. According to this analysis, it is understandable that prisons contain disproportionate numbers of racialized and marginalized inmates and that this imbalance does not directly reflect rates of lawless activity.

Conversely, there are very few women in prison populations, which leads to another question.

DOES THE PUNISHMENT FIT THE GENDER?

Under criminal law, sometimes women seem to have an advantage over their male counterparts. Traditional gender stereotypes predispose courts, and especially juries, to believe in the fundamental innocence of women. They are also readily convinced of women's vulnerability to be coerced, manipulated, or driven mad by men, and thus subsequently to be led into crime. Women are far less likely than men to become involved in crimes of violence. When they do, are they more likely to "get away with" them?

Before answering that question, an overview of female criminality in Canada is in order. In 1997, there were 357 women and 14,091 men incarcerated in federal facilities.[5] We may assume these represent people convicted of breaking the most serious laws, because those who receive sentences of less than two years are sent to provincial institutions. On the federal level, 2,184 men and 71 women were serving sentences for murder. Almost 25 per cent of the women were convicted for illicit drug offences, compared to less than 10 per cent of the men.

With regard to the larger picture of all Canadian women in trouble with the law, a government report released in 1985 came to an astounding conclusion.[6] Written by a legal scholar, a criminologist, and two practising criminal lawyers, the report first laid out various criteria for identifying criminal behaviour (e.g., serious harm to others, harm to the community, and so on). They then examined the proportions of women who had been charged with theft of little value without violence (40 per

5. Canada, *Basic Facts About Corrections in Canada* (Ottawa: Solicitor General, 1997).

6. Christine L.M. Boyle, Marie-Andrée Bertrand, Céline Lacerte-Lamontagne, and Rebecca Shamai, *A Feminist Review of Criminal Law* (Ottawa: Status of Women Canada, 1985).

cent), alcohol-related offences (25 per cent), marijuana possession (7 per cent) or "breaking bail, disturbing the peace, prostitution, public mischief, and so on." Their conclusion? Fully 80 per cent of the women had been involved in offences that did not meet the criteria to classify them as "criminal."

Furthermore, as we all know, statistics tell us only part of the story. In 1992, Elizabeth Comack conducted in-depth interviews with women housed in a Manitoba correctional institution.[7] Read this book and weep! The life histories of the women interviewed chronicle incest, physical and sexual assault, poverty, racism, and other miseries. The "crimes" for which many of them had been incarcerated are pitiful: a bad cheque passed for bus fare to see an ailing father, driving without a license because there was not enough money for both a taxi and groceries for the children, hitting back at a husband who had been abusive for years. The litany goes on. After reading these stories, one is overwhelmed with the question, "Why on earth are these women in jail?" The next logical question, then, is to ask where the social-service providers were when these "criminals" were in such desperate need, long before they ran into trouble with the law.

Much has been written about the ways in which law and the criminal justice system disadvantage women. Why is persistent soliciting by prostitutes criminalized, whereas similar behaviour in men (persistent harassment on the street or in the workplace) is not? Why is the veracity of accounts of sexual assault doubted, whereas victims of physical assault are believed? Why do courts assume that when a father requests custody of his children, there "must be something wrong with the mother"? Are courts and juries less sympathetic to women who deviate from the traditional "feminine" stereotypes, that is, women of colour, lesbians, or rebellious and independent young women? Why are the facilities and services offered to incarcerated women even less adequate than those provided to incarcerated men? Slowly but surely, some of these problems are being addressed, thanks to pressure from activists and feminist lawyers, not to mention the Legal Education and Action Fund, better known by its acronym LEAF.[8] However, there still is a long way to go.

This brings us to the question posed earlier: does the criminal justice system sometimes advantage women? British researcher Hilary Allen conducted an excellent study on this topic, uncovering gender stereotyping and a certain "chivalry" in the handling of some women in trouble with the law, both of which worked to their advantage.[9] There are bound to be cultural differences between England and Canada, but

7. Elizabeth Comack, *Women in Trouble: Connecting Women's Law Violations to Their Histories of Abuse* (Halifax: Fernwood, 1996).

8. Sherene Razack, *Canadian Feminism and the Law: The Women's Legal Education and Action Fund and the Pursuit of Equality* (Toronto: Second Story Press, 1991).

9. Hilary Allen, *Justice Unbalanced: Gender, Psychiatry and Judicial Decisions* (Milton Keynes: Open University Press, 1987).

it would not be surprising if similar observations could be made in this country. Studying violent female offenders, Allen discovered a stunning transformation could occur. As some women moved through the criminal justice system, they accumulated psychiatrists' and probation officers' reports portraying them as pitiful and helpless victims of an unjust and uncaring society. Indeed, women who were otherwise "respectable" were provided excuses for their violence: they did not intend to do it, they were not aware, they did not understand. In short, they were just "silly girls." As one psychiatric report put it, "It may well be that she was not aware that by putting a plastic bag over [the victim's] head and tying [an electrical cord] around her neck that she was thereby killing her." Being a traditional mother and wife also worked to woman's advantage, keeping her out of prison or a psychiatric facility and redirecting her into community care. In one case, a woman who had been hostile to her baby since she gave birth to it, stabbed the infant in the back. The psychiatrist's report stressed the importance of her return to "normal life," that is, looking after her baby and her husband. The report also noted the father's stress and anxiety in trying to cope with both his job and child-care responsibilities.

Presumably some men, particularly those who can afford skilled legal representation and expert witnesses, can have their misdeeds minimized in the eyes of courts and parole boards. However, the mitigating circumstances are unlikely to be so gender role-specific as we have seen in the above examples. (Can you imagine an argument that a man should be released because of his wife's job and her burden of child care?)

On February 3, 1998, Karla Faye Tucker was executed in Texas for the crime of murder, the first woman to submit to capital punishment in that state since 1863. Her childhood history was as saddening as the stories Elizabeth Comack recorded in Manitoba. She became the focus of worldwide attention by opponents of the death penalty, and even by Texans who normally provide enthusiastic support for it. Why? She was white, attractive, and had found religion in prison, but more important, she was a woman. In any case, she was put to death.

Thus, we can conclude that gender bias in the criminal justice system benefits a *very small minority* of women in trouble with the law. Clearly, reports on violent male offenders could be written, outlining their miserable childhood experiences, the obstacles they faced in life, their struggles to exist in an atmosphere of social injustice and inequality. However, the bulk of those facing trial for criminal offences do not have the resources to hire legal representation and expert witnesses to present complex arguments on their behalf. In general, it is the socially disadvantaged, both male and female, who are highly vulnerable to incarceration if they run into serious trouble with the law.

THE PRISON—INDUSTRIAL COMPLEX

We have examined a number of reasons why some people acquire custodial sentences while others do not, but it is now time to return to the question of why there has been such an incarceration boom in the United States in recent decades. While the unevenness and unfairness in custodial sentencing is a serious matter, if the experience of the US is a harbinger for the future of other countries, a far more frightening ethical problem confronts us: prisoners for profit.

Much of the expansion in the US prison population can be accounted for by the onset of private-enterprise prisons, constructed by entrepreneurs and, rather in the manner of the hotel business, rented out to state governments to house inmates. Eric Schlosser has called this the "prison-industrial complex," and defines it as follows:

> —a set of bureaucratic, political, and economic interests that encourage increased spending on imprisonment, regardless of the actual need. The prison-industrial complex is not a conspiracy, guiding the nation's criminal-justice policy behind closed doors. It is a confluence of special interests that has given prison construction in the United States a seemingly unstoppable momentum. It is composed of politicians, both liberal and conservative, who have used the fear of crime to gain votes; impoverished rural areas where prisons have become a cornerstone of economic development; private companies that regard the roughly $35 billion spent each year on corrections not as a burden on American taxpayers but as a lucrative market; and government officials whose fiefdoms have expanded along with the inmate population. Since 1991 the rate of violent crime in the United States has fallen by about 20 percent, while the number of people in prison or jail has risen by 50 percent.[10]

The Adirondack area of upstate New York is an illuminating example. In 25 years, the number of prisons there grew from two to 19. This was a lifeline for a failing economy, which once had relied upon the mining, logging, and manufacturing industries. Prison construction brought an initial infusion of funds. Once established, these institutions provided recession-proof employment, not only for those who work within their walls but also for food providers and other auxiliary services. Prisons do not pollute the environment, an important consideration in an area of great natural beauty and a lively tourism industry.

Of course, the Adirondack inmates are overwhelmingly imported from Manhattan and its environs, exiled from their families and friends. Schlosser reports on a bus service that runs every Friday, driving north through the night, bringing about 800

---

10. Schlosser 54.

people to Saturday visiting days. They are largely wives, mothers and children, family members who are mostly African American or Hispanic. Although this is an arduous expedition for visitors, at least it is within reach as long as money for the fare can be managed. Other families are simply out of luck. "Bed-brokers" working for private prisons in Texas collect prisoners from across the US, from Utah and Missouri, for example. Inmates are even brought to the mainland from Hawaii to be housed in privatized prisons.

Thus, the incarceration boom is in fact just another all-American booming business. This accounts not only for the overall increase in the prison population, but also for the increasing proportion of non-violent offenders within it. Violent offenders now represent less than half of the US state and local prison population, drug offenders over 20 per cent, and the rest convicted of various property and public-order offences.[11] More and more people who previously would have received non-custodial sentences are being locked up, often geographically remote from their families and friends. Law-and-order frenzy, even in the face of declining crime rates, feeds public funds into the pockets of entrepreneurs. They, in turn, can save on operating expenses by hiring non-unionized correctional officers at low wages and with paltry pensions and benefits, if any.

The privatization of prisons is not simply an American phenomenon. The major players have developed into transnational corporations and have made strong inroads in the United Kingdom, Australia, and South Africa. Its invasion of Canada has already begun. Since prisons are well known as "schools of crime," this does not bode well for the future.

Judith C. Blackwell

---

11. Doyle 28.

CHAPTER 28

"Just say 'no' to Drugs"

or, why my drugs are okay and yours aren't, as propounded by Nancy Reagan, Leading Lady to former actor and US President Ronald, c. 1980s

We all know a lot about drug use, whether we buy psychoactive substances over the counter in drug stores, have them prescribed by our doctors, furtively smoke them with friends, puff them outdoors in chilly climates where tobacco use is forbidden inside buildings, drink them down in the form of beer at sporting events or swallow them and dance the night away at raves. Wherever there are people there will be drugs. Around the world, untold numbers earn their livelihoods in drug manufacture and distribution, hunting down and meting out punishments to drug offenders, or trying to help users who run into trouble. The wealth and power of the international pharmaceutical industry is awe-inspiring. In all countries and cultures, some drugs are socially approved, others tolerated and others prohibited by law. However, there is wide variation in terms of which drugs are placed in which categories, both among jurisdictions and within them, and there are no consistent pharmacological or harm-based criteria for sorting them among categories.

Prohibition of some drugs, but not others, has been the dominant policy approach in most of the world for the better part of a century. Cannabis (marijuana and hashish), cocaine, heroin, and a multitude of psychoactive chemicals are illegal to possess in even tiny amounts in North America and most of Europe. Other criminalized drug-related activities include sharing the drug, giving it away to friends, selling it to friends or strangers, taking any quantity of it across international borders, manufacturing it and, in the case of marijuana and the opium poppy, cultivating the plant from which it is derived. The blanket prohibitions covering personal activities, such as possession and sharing, are actually more stringent than alcohol prohibition was in the United States in the 1920s.

The policy of prohibition is predicated on the assumption that, by criminalizing various drug-related activities, the supply of the drugs will eventually dry up altogether. No drugs, no problem. Sufficient law enforcement resources are all that is needed to accomplish this "supply-side" social policy goal. Implicit in this model is the assumption that once drug supply is reduced or eliminated, the demand for the drug will automatically disappear. Vigorous law enforcement and punishment of offenders will go some way toward deterring users and potential users. However, the ultimate goal is to reduce the supply so dramatically that drugs will be hard to obtain, and what is available will be priced so prohibitively that few would be able to afford to yield to temptation. In recent years, even those who once most vehemently promulgated the supply-side position have had to admit that a century of experience demonstrates that it is not sufficient on its own, and some resources should be directed toward reducing the demand for drugs.

The failure of prohibition to accomplish its goals should really come as no surprise, since the social problems and the social costs of this policy direction were observed early on, in the failed experiment of alcohol prohibition. Furthermore, it is difficult to ignore the obvious: illicit drugs have remained in copious supply,[1] despite generous funding for law enforcement, prisons filled to capacity with populations increasingly composed of drug users, advances in interdiction technologies, international agreements, and so on. No one can claim the policy has failed for lack of trying.

With recently increased fears of international terrorism, we have been made painfully aware of how easy it can be to move people and goods around the world. The sheer volume of international traffic makes it impossible to monitor all but a small proportion of what passes through border crossings. In addition, illicit goods need not even be subjected to these small risks, when one considers the possibilities of remote coastlines and undefended borders. As we observed during alcohol prohibition, the profits to be made by supplying the demand for "bootleg" drugs are such that they encourage the development of criminal trafficking networks of varying degrees of sophistication and complexity. Whether it be the "mob" or motorcycle gangs, public demand for media coverage and fictional representations of their nefarious deeds appears to be inexhaustible, as are the applicants for positions in these organizations. There is never a shortage of people willing to participate in the illicit drug trades, from the lowliest street "pusher" all the way up to the top entrepreneurs whom politicians and the media like to call "drug lords."

Even if we could imagine a world in which international borders were hermetically sealed against the import of illicit substances, the problem of controlling domestic drug supply would not be solved. This is another lesson unheeded from the experience of alcohol prohibition. Domestic cultivation of high-quality marijuana has been a fact of life for decades in North America and has had a significant impact on state and provincial economies as a result. Climate is no barrier, because modern indoor cultivation techniques allow for both quality control and high productivity. Although your grandmother technically could be arrested for the small amounts of opium in

---

1. Only during World War II was there a significant decrease in the supply of illicit drugs in North America, since it was difficult to ship anything anywhere at that time.

her garden-variety ornamental poppies,[2] large-scale poppy cultivation makes more sense in remote and impoverished agricultural areas of the world. Even if these foreign poppy fields could be eradicated, domestic illicit laboratories are capable of producing substances that the average user would find indistinguishable from high-grade heroin. If all the coca plants in the world were to magically disappear, acceptable cocaine substitutes could be produced with relative ease. Only rudimentary training in chemistry is needed to quickly and cheaply manufacture powerful psychoactive substances, using readily available components and information publicly available in scientific journals. Compared to distilling "moonshine," and other relatively bulky alcohol products, synthesizing powders in a laboratory is neat and discreet.

This brings us to the question of drug quality control, another lesson that should have been learned from the era of alcohol prohibition, when drinkers suffered a gamut of health problems, including death from illicitly and improperly manufactured products. If we accept that some people will take drugs, whether we like it or not, is it humane to enforce a social policy that restricts them to products of unpredictable potency and possible contamination? Does it make sense to make access to drug paraphernalia difficult and thus contribute to the spread of HIV and hepatitis C through shared needle use? Is it sensible to ensure that the high cost of illicit drugs encourages some users to further transmit disease risk by their participation in prostitution? This is yet another concern that has encouraged increasing numbers of people to think about the costs of the prohibition model and to develop doubts about the rationality and morality of the "War on Drugs" mentality.

Elevated to the global level, the illicit drug trade wreaks such mass murder and tragedy that it should sound the death knell of prohibitionist policy on humanitarian grounds alone. Although it is glaringly obvious, this concern has not been widely publicized and is usually not considered even by commentators who are highly critical of current drug policies. On an international level, the illicit drug trade is gigantic and highly profitable.[3] It makes a massive contribution to the flood of untaxed and unregulated money that flows around the globe and poses an ongoing threat to the economic futures of all nation states.[4] Ask yourself whether you have ever wondered about the financing of the various "warring tribes," "ethnic factions," and militias of every description involved in armed conflicts around the world, some of which were alluded to in the introduction to this book. How can they afford those guns, bombs, grenades, land mines, and other hardware of warfare? Unregulated money, illicit drugs, and the

---

2. Michael Pollan, "Opium, Made Easy: One Gardener's Encounter with the War on Drugs," *Harper's Magazine* April 1997: 35-58.

3. Profits, it should be noted, which serve as a temptation to the corruption of agents of law enforcement and, in many countries, politicians, the judiciary, and public officials as well.

4. Tom Naylor, *Hot Money and the Politics of Debt* (Toronto: McClelland and Stewart, 1987).

international arms trade combined are a terrible trio interlocked in the production of death and human suffering.[5]

A rare peaceful image in the midst of the 12-year civil war in Lebanon was the Bekaa valley, where all the warring factions coexisted in their common pursuit of growing cannabis and opium. The role of the illicit drug trade in supporting armed conflict has been well documented in the Golden Triangle (Southeast Asia), the Golden Crescent (the border areas of Iran, Afghanistan, and Pakistan)[6] and in Central America.[7] The list is too long to be elaborated upon here, but a common theme runs through these histories: US foreign policy interests have regularly over-ruled US international drug control efforts. After the events of September 11, 2001, and the subsequent war on Afghanistan, it is not surprising that the US turned a blind eye to how the Northern Alliance forces they supported against the Taliban man-aged to arm themselves. Most certainly, they turned a blind eye to how the Taliban themselves financed their ascent to power.

As social scientists, it is incumbent upon us to be concerned about all of the people who are caught up in wars. Historically, those who suffered and died were gen-erally those on the battlefield. As the twentieth century unfolded, civilians increas-ingly became the victims. To whatever extent the global illicit drug trade feeds into the arms trade, more and more "bystanders" will suffer. Ordinary people are tortured or "disappear," civilians starve, children are maimed and killed, women are sexually assaulted, homes are bombed and burned, refugees are set adrift or confined to con-centration camps. In the name of protecting "our" children in the industrialized countries from illicit drugs, one "war on drugs" after another has been proclaimed. In so doing, weapons have been put in the hands of people who inflict far greater suf-fering on innocent and impoverished people than could possibly be imagined if pro-hibitionist policies were abandoned in the rich nations of the world.

For the past century or so, people in "civilized" nations have made great pro-nouncements about the grave dangers of the prohibited drugs, suggesting that anyone who has anything to do with them will come to grief and become a drain on or a threat to the rest of society. Since the 1960s, the widespread incursion of cannabis use into the middle classes has made it difficult to sustain the "Reefer Madness" reputation it had in earlier decades of the century. In the minds of young people considering cannabis use, the risks seem to have boiled down to the possibility of being saddled with a criminal record for the rest of their lives or being asked embarrassing ques-

---

5. Judith Blackwell, "Canada in a Global Setting: Notes on the International Drug Market," *Illicit Drugs in Canada: A Risky Business*, ed. Judith Blackwell and Patricia Erickson (Scarborough: Nelson Canada, 1988) 326-44.

6. Blackwell 331.

7. National Security Archive Electronic Briefing Book No. 2, "The Contras, Cocaine, and Covert Operations" <www.gwu.edu/~nsarchiv/NSAEBB/NSAEBB2/nsaebb2.htm#1> 16 Nov. 2001.

tions if they should decide to run for public office. However, the mass media have continued to parade before us "crack babies" and hollow-eyed junkies in justification for the latest war on drugs. Thus, prohibitionist policies may not have had the intended impact on drug supply, but their proponents continue to seek justification on the basis of claims about the inherent "dangers" of these substances.

THE SEDUCTIVE AND DESTRUCTIVE POWERS OF DRUGS

We all know something about alcohol, even if we do not drink it ourselves. We know people who drink it, maybe drink it to excess, and we see advertisements glamorizing it in the media. We have a range of ideas about how alcohol may be part of our cultures, religious observances, or implicated in some of the social problems we observe around us. If the drug alcohol were illegal, so much secrecy would surround the consumption of this drug that most of us would be considerably more ignorant of drinkers' lives and realities. Let us pursue this scenario.

Suppose all the information that doctors and journalists and the rest of us could glean about alcohol use and the problems accompanying it came from the people who "hit bottom" or were rapidly going in that direction. What if all our information came from "alcoholics," "dipsomaniacs," and "skid row bums"? If we took all our knowledge from their experiences, we would conclude that alcohol is an extremely dangerous substance. Consumers are bound to be seduced by this drug, increase their frequency of use, experience an intense need to drink, sink down into crime and poverty, have terrible health problems, and if they were not at home committing family violence, they would most likely be unemployed and homeless itinerants. Judging from our attempts to get these people on "the straight and narrow," once they were detoxified we would advise them never to touch alcohol again or associate with people who do. The drug is too seductive, and will bring only further depths of deprivation, crime, and violence. If we only heard about the worst cases of alcohol-related problems, it would be reasonable to conclude that alcohol *causes* violence, prostitution, poverty, crime, and just about every social problem that might come to mind. However, we all know better, because we all know people who drink alcohol in moderation and have not suffered any of these terrible fates.

Consider now the people from whom we, over the past century or so, have gathered our information about illicit drugs. They might be young people whose grades have been declining to the dismay of parents and teachers, or they might be school drop-outs. They might be unemployed, or committed to psychiatric care, or incarcerated in correctional facilities. They may be pregnant teenagers, or "street kids" or prostitutes, thieves or abusers of their family members. Doctors and social workers interview them, as do journalists eager to sensationalize their lives. Scientific papers are written about them. Law enforcement officials make pronouncements about them. The upshot, naturally enough, is a substantially distorted picture of the condition of illicit drug users, one that is no less misleading than the one we would form of alcohol users if all of our conclusions about the psychopharmacological effects of their drug of choice were derived from observations of drinkers who have run into the worst kinds of problems life has to offer.

Confusing correlation and causation, it is easy to jump to the conclusion that, just because people with problems are engaged in illicit drug use, the drugs are to blame for their problems. Drugs have seduced them into addiction; addiction has wreaked havoc on their lives. The alternative explanation, that many troubled people have troubled relationships with drugs, receives scant attention. However, critical social scientists do not like easy answers, and they resist the easy assumption that, when social phenomena are observed to occur together, one necessarily causes the other.

After a number of years doing research on drugs, with a particular focus on heroin, I began to be suspicious of the alleged power and seductiveness of the opiates. In the 1970s, based on anecdotal evidence that considerable numbers of people experimented with and recreationally used heroin and related opiates, I launched a research project on this subject. At that time, serious arguments were being made that smoking marijuana "led to" heroin use and that heroin was the most seductive and powerfully destructive drug on the illicit market. My research proposal was couched in terminology acknowledging this conventional wisdom, assuming that people who avoided addiction made rules and set limits on their consumption, and they had to learn to "control" this alluring drug. The accounts of the people who participated in my research provided some startling opposition to these assumptions.[8] Some people made "rules," but these rules did not seem to be much different from deciding that there is only so much of a weekly budget that can be spent on entertainment of any kind, when food and shelter have to be taken into account first. Fully one-third of the sample made no rules at all, because they did not like the effects of heroin all that much compared to other drugs,[9] or because they indulged only with certain friendship groups and not with others. Revelation after revelation led to a re-evaluation of the seductive power of the opiates, and it directed the research focus to social and psychological factors as the determinants surrounding an individual's encounter with a drug.[10] Such surprises are the intellectual delight of social science research.

---

8. Judith Blackwell, "Drifting, Controlling and Overcoming: Opiate Users who Avoid Becoming Chronically Dependent," *Journal of Drug Issues* 13 (1983): 219-35.

9. Judith Blackwell, "Opiate Dependence as a Psychophysical Event: Users' Reports of Subjective Experiences," *Contemporary Drug Problems* 12.3 (1985): 331-50.

10. Judith Blackwell, "Saboteurs of Britain's Opiate Policy: Overprescribing Physicians or American-Style Junkies?", *International Journal of the Addictions* 23.5 (1988): 517-26.

Indeed, as I was to learn from other research as well as my own, many people take "powerful and seductive" drugs simply because they consider it to be a recreational option, like going to a sporting event with friends or putting on a dinner party. They are not "seduced" and they do not become "addicts." Because of their invisibility in attracting the forces of societal reaction (police, medical professionals, etc.), they happily consume illicit substances without problems; or they experiment and then do not continue or they make it into an occasional social ritual. Just as some drinkers run into problems (a conviction for driving over the limit, regrettable drunken behaviour, concern over drinking "too much," and so on), so do illicit drug users. One-third of the people in my research had decided at some point that their heroin use was getting out of hand. Like drinkers who decide they have been "hitting the bottle" too frequently or in excessive amounts, or who realize that drink is getting in the way of other pleasures or responsibilities of life, these opiate users took control of their consumption. They did not avail themselves of psychotherapy or drug treatment programs. It was not always easy, but they established abstinence or a lowered level of consumption and got on with their lives.

It has been estimated that somewhere between 10 and 20 per cent of substance users will run into some kind of trouble, broadly defined, at some time. This includes both licit and illicit drugs, with the sole exception of nicotine. (Depending on the age when you start to smoke, the likelihood of becoming dependent is frighteningly high.) All things considered, this is extremely good news. It is comforting to think that most people, even when confronted with a substance that can make them feel extremely good about themselves and temporarily indifferent to their problems, can imagine the options open to them and can balance the costs and benefits of their behaviour. They have ideas about where they would like to be in the future and invest in a self-image that does not include being thought of by others as drunks or junkies. It would be extremely *bad* news if research confirmed conventional wisdom, and we could envision only a monolithic powerless population of innocents vulnerable to enslavement by drugs.

MYTHMAKING IN THE CULTURE OF PREJUDICE

Like other chapters in this book, this one ends with the sad realization that the culture of prejudice is economical with truth and generous in providing the populace with myths. The logical question that comes to mind is this: "How have all the myths about illicit drugs been perpetuated for all these years?" For the better part of a century, they have worked to sustain prohibitionist policies that not only do not accomplish their goals, but also impose tremendous social costs and inflict untold human suffering.

It is not as though reasoned, scientifically informed and balanced analyses of the benefits and harms of drug laws were unavailable. The wisdom of reputable bodies constituted by governments to study drug policies stretches back to *The Indian Hemp Drugs Commission Report* (1894) and continues on to *The LaGuardia Committee Report* (New York City, 1944), *The Baroness Wootton Report* (United Kingdom, 1967), the report of The Schafer Commission (US, 1973), the Canadian reports leading up to and including the *Final Report of the Commission of Inquiry into the Non-Medical Use of Drugs* (1973) and the *Final Report of the South Australian Royal Commission into the Non-Medical Use of Drugs* (1979), to mention only the most notable. The conclusions of these sober-minded and well-informed bodies are remarkably consistent. They report on the adverse consequences that flow directly from prohibitionist drug policies and recommend changes to drug laws. Unfortunately, what they all have in common is the minimal impact these commissions have made either on legislation or on the "get tough" stance of politicians, no matter where they sit on the left-right political spectrum. The war on drugs mentality has a life of its own.

The average citizen is not made aware of the harmful individual and societal consequences of the war on drugs. Voters do not know of the intimate links between drug profits and the illegal arms trade, and the mass suffering of uncounted victims of the drug wars in very real armed conflicts around the globe. They do not question the logic in the arguments made in support of the drug wars, and the media are not likely to try to enlighten them. The villains at home are the "pushers," full stop. The victims, as they are portrayed to the public, are the underclasses of the urban centres of industrialized nations. Yet these victims are also villains, as they are portrayed as being threatening to social order and the security of respectable citizens. It is not asked whether they are such miserable people because of the countless miserable circumstances they have encountered in their lives. Rather, the message is that illicit drug use has dragged them into these depths, and it is a good idea for us to protect ourselves by cracking down on these predators.

The domestic victims of the war on drugs are scapegoated, stereotyped, and marginalized and most certainly do not form a constituency that can stand up for their rights. On the other hand, over 30 years ago, comedian Lenny Bruce predicted that marijuana would be legalized before long, because by then all of the lawyers would be pot smokers. Exceeding even Mr. Bruce's expectations, a US president admitted he tried it but "didn't inhale," yet still the cannabis laws remained virtually unchanged. A political climate continues in which legislators compete with each other to appear as hard-liners on the drug issue, on the assumption that only this stance will win them votes. The *status quo* is that the laws are tough, and it will be even better when they get tougher. Prosecute suspected dealers, and in the meantime seize and sell off their assets to support the local police, even before there is a finding of guilt in a court of law. Throw families out of public housing, because one of their teenaged relatives was supplying to his friends or made a bad mistake in helping out his or her dealer in some more ambitious transaction. The aggressive strategy works for politicians, because average middle-class people have not taken the time to research the half-truths and mendacities to which they have been exposed, and a vote for an anti-drug candidate makes them feel somehow safe. In fact, they and their children are already protected,[11] because at best police will turn a blind eye to their peccadilloes; at worst, if their children are arrested, the full brunt of the available legal consequences will not descend upon them. The dispossessed, on the other hand, will be subjected to every indignity and punishment the state has designed for offenders. They will crowd the jails and prisons for minor drug violations and will suffer the majority of the adverse consequences of having been processed through the criminal justice system. They will eventually be coughed out by this system, even worse off than they were before.

In short, no one wins in a drug war, except those who make their living fighting on the side of the aggressors and those at the upper levels of the illicit trade. As long as public indifference and misinformation can be sustained, a costly prohibitionist policy can continue, decade after decade, despite the fact that the harm it inflicts far exceeds any benefits it can claim to reap.

Judith C. Blackwell

---

11. It is interesting to speculate about how much (or how little) drug law enforcement takes place in the "gated communities" springing up all over the US or, for that matter, in any "respectable" urban neighbourhood.

"support Your Local Police"

*Popular propaganda of dubious value to protesters of the culture
of prejudice*

Sociologists agree that hegemony is maintained through a combination of force and consent. The Summit of the Americas meetings in Quebec City in April 2001 provide a demonstration of how dissent is controlled and managed in Canadian society. The Summit was designed to extend the *North America Free Trade Agreement* and, in compliance with World Trade Organization dictates, to impose the rule of the "free market" over health care, education, environmental regulation, and labour standards by creating a Free Trade Area of the Americas (FTAA). The outcome of the Summit would have a negative effect on millions of people while strengthening corporate wealth and power.

Long before the meetings took place, corporate-owned media warned of violence from anti-globalization demonstrators. Rather than addressing the many varied and valid concerns of thousands who joined anti-globalization protests around the world, media focused almost exclusively on the potential for street battles between a few protesters and police. This emphasis continued despite the fact that all influential activists who were interviewed emphasized the need for peaceful protest and that hundreds of activists were participating in workshops on non-violence before the Summit began. Nevertheless, corporate media continued to present all members of the public who wished to express their concern about the serious implications of the Summit as lawless and irrational vandals bent on mayhem and social disorder.

It was clear that even non-violent dissent was seen as a threat. On April 2nd in Ottawa, over 80 people were arrested at the Department of Foreign Affairs and International Trade when they demanded – without violence—that the government release the draft text of the FTAA document. The next day in Toronto, armed police on horseback and with clubs and plexiglass shields far outnumbered the demonstrators at a meeting of finance ministers. Fences and concrete blocks were used to seal off the area while a Special Weapons Unit held their riot guns aimed directly at members of the public they ostensibly were mandated to protect. The crowd listened politely to a speech and then dispersed. The only arrest was of a drunk who had nothing to do with the demonstration.

Anticipating further public protest, Toronto police chief Julian Fantino warned that demonstrators would face "swift and severe" police action. Fantino said that the police had conducted extensive consultations with groups who planned to demonstrate, but those groups said police had never spoken to them at all. They also expressed their fear that the police would use tear gas, pepper spray, plastic bullets, truncheons and concussion grenades. Steve Kerr of the Toronto Mobilization for Global Justice argued, "What we have is police declaring war on people's democratic rights." The extent of the threat to public order was exemplified by Mary Gellatly, a community legal worker with the Employment Standards Work Group, who described how their planned demonstration would include skits and a march with balloons.[1]

As the Summit approached, Quebec City was fortified against dissent. A four-kilometre metal and concrete fence was erected to keep protesters away from the Summit meetings and to ensure that their concerns would not be heard by delegates to the meetings; those who worked or lived within the fenced perimeter had to carry security passes. Over 6,000 police, heavily armed, were mobilized, along with over 1,000 armed forces personnel and hundreds of other security agents, the largest police operation in Canadian history. Customs and Immigration officials did their part by turning back international activists at Canada's borders. On February 4, 2001, undercover police arrested three people for distributing leaflets that called the fortifications a civil-rights violation.[2]

Alan Borovoy of the Canadian Civil Liberties Association noted how a double standard was built into the Summit meetings.[3] Wealthy corporations were guaranteed access to the event, while the public was to be kept far away from the proceedings. Further, the demonstrators' legal right to protest would be violated by the wall. Noting that at previous protests it had been the police who had instigated violence and assaulted protesters, Borovoy observed that security-obsessed governments had "done little to assure the public that the police will respect the constitutional and legal rights of the protesters."

The *Globe and Mail* consistently depicted any opposition to the corporate agenda as invalid, running an unprecedented seven-part editorial series attacking the "myths of globalization." Columnist Margaret Wente dismissed protesters as "naïve and privileged college kids."[4] Marcus Gee reprised his earlier appreciation for sweatshops by applauding the largesse of garment factories that pay impoverished Cambodians $90 for a month of sixteen-hour work days because "those workers were even poorer

1. *The Globe and Mail*, 3 April 2001: A3.

2. *Montreal Gazette*, 15 Feb. 2001: A3.

3. *The Globe and Mail*, 3 April 2001: A13.

4. *The Globe and Mail*, 19 April 2001: A8.

before."[5] Colin Freeze contributed what was obviously intended to be an instructive tale, headlined "When the Student Met the Marxist Worker."[6] Freeze used a man collecting scrap metal at the demonstrations to serve as the Ventriloquist's Dummy: "Asked what he thought about the demonstrations, which focused on alleviating poverty, he said, 'It doesn't interest me, really.'" This rhetorical technique is intended to prove that the "privileged college kids" are out of touch with the poor who simply wish to proceed with their individual entrepreneurial tasks while remaining unconcerned with politics.

State officials emphasized the threat of violence and the need for a heavy police presence. Canada's Foreign Affairs Minister, John Manley, expressed his view that order constitutes the basis of democracy, and thousands of police were mobilized to ensure that a specific form of "order" would prevail. Quebec's Public Security Minister, Serge Menardi, advised that "if you want peace, prepare for war."[7] Florent Gagné, Director-General of Quebec's police, warned of "a real threat." [8] On April 17th, former prime minister Brian Mulroney wrote an opinion piece in the *Globe and Mail* warning that "If demonstrators were to prevail over elected officials, mob rule would result.... Violence and mob demonstrations are the antithesis of democracy...."[9] Mulroney airily dismissed the detailed and reasoned arguments of the anti-globalization movement as "those who—in true Luddite fashion—oppose free trade and globalization for no other reason than that they are opposed to it." The *Globe* that day also published a comment by Norman Spector, Mulroney's former chief-of-staff, containing similar dismissals of dissent as "emotion over reason."[10] Prime Minister Jean Chrétien, who had expressed his concern about police brutality at the 1997 Asian Pacific Economic Cooperation (APEC) meetings in Vancouver by joking that "as for me, pepper I put it on my plate," now indicated his appreciation for public opinion by stating that activists were coming to Quebec City "to protest and blah, blah, blah."

On April 19, 2001, the *Globe* ran a front-page story that seemed to justify security measures, with headlines declaring that six people in possession of explosives had been arrested in Quebec City. However, the next day a small article on page 5 noted that the "explosives" were actually training devices that simulated the sound of grenades. It was also acknowledged that police had infiltrated the group much ear-

---

5. *The Globe and Mail*, 19 April 2001. Gee's earlier comments on sweatshops were in *The Globe and Mail*, 19 April 2000: A15.

6. Colin Freeze, "When the Student Met the Marxist Worker," *The Globe and Mail*, 21 April 2001: A2.

7. *The Globe and Mail*, 3 April 2001: A3.

8. *The Globe and Mail*, 7 April 2001: A15.

9. *The Globe and Mail*, 17 April, 2001: A17.

10. *The Globe and Mail*, 17 April, 2001: A19.

lier but had waited until the Summit to arrest them, with the obvious intent of linking them with the anti-globalization protests.

While state officials and media trumpeted the threat posed by the public, the police seemed hardly able to contain their excitement at the thought of violent confrontation. The attitude of police toward demonstrators was captured by RCMP Staff Sergeant Hugh Stewart, who was quoted encouraging his troops with preposterous macho dialogue: "Okay people saddle up…. Let's get ready to rock and roll." (Stewart had become known nationally as "Sgt. Pepper" for his enthusiastic use of pepper spray against peaceful demonstrators at the 1997 APEC meeting, captured on videotape by the CBC.) In Quebec City, police evidently regarded the chance to confront demonstrators as a thrilling moment. Dressed in fascist-fantasy riot gear, they advanced against the public while rhythmically beating their clubs against their shields. While none of the delegates to the Summit was ever in any danger, police fired plastic bullets indiscriminately into the crowd and used tear gas at the rate of a canister every minute; as a result, the city was enclosed in a haze of gas.

Pre-emptive arrests were directed at individuals targeted as key organizers, such as Jaggi Singh. Singh had been previously targeted by the police in this manner at the 1997 APEC meetings; he was thrown to the ground, then shoved into an unmarked car and arrested on the grounds of assault for speaking too loudly through a megaphone. In Quebec, Singh was once again tackled by an undercover squad while standing beside a theatrical-prop catapult that other demonstrators had used to toss teddy bears at the barricade. Although Singh had never been involved in any violent activity, the police treated him as a dangerous terrorist and kept him in prison long after all other demonstrators had been released. At Singh's hearing, Quebec police officer Francois Collin said that the catapult was used to throw Molotov cocktails, but later he admitted that he had never witnessed this. Police also testified that Singh was encouraging violence, but writer Judy Rebick said that he had in fact been telling demonstrators to withdraw and that Judge Yvon Mercier had misrepresented her testimony in order to keep Singh in prison.[11]

After the Summit, the media disclosed that use of lethal force had been authorized.[12] While demonstrators complained that police had been aggressive, the Prime Minister lauded police restraint and media echoed this with near-universal applause for police self-control. Evidence for the excellence of police conduct was found in the observation that no one had actually been killed! (Similar praise for police restraint came from Italian authorities after protests at the Genoa G-8 meetings, even though police there shot a demonstrator and then repeatedly drove a vehicle over his body; in addition, they launched a violent raid on a dormitory where protesters were sleeping.) Serge Menard said, "Quebec can be very proud of the way we han-

---

11. *The Globe and Mail*, 26 April 2001: A11.

12. *The Globe and Mail*, 23 April 2001: A7.

dled the Summit of the Americas" and praised police restraint, accusing demonstrators of taunting the police for sport.

Shortly after the Summit, the report of an inquiry into security control at the 1997 Vancouver APEC meetings was released. At the meetings, the Canadian government had played host to Indonesia's murderous dictator Suharto, ensuring that his sensibilities would not be offended by Canadian citizens raising protest banners, even though his history would not suggest squeamishness. (Suharto had seized power in a coup and presided over the slaughter of perhaps a million people in 1965, as well as the genocidal attack on East Timor.) The police in Vancouver had eagerly pepper-sprayed the public, strip-searched female demonstrators, moved protesters out of sight and generally violated the constitutional rights of citizens. The report indicated not only that the RCMP had overstepped the bounds and violated the civil rights of Canadians, but also that the Prime Minister (who refused to testify and provide important documents) had intervened directly and had urged the police to limit dissent. The report was essentially ignored. Unsurprisingly, corporate media generally regarded it as acceptable that the state would use violent force against the public in order to defend the interests of other corporations and the decorum of foreign despots.

If the public had been complacent about such infringements on civil liberties, many became enthusiastic supporters of even greater limitations of their freedom after the terrorist attack on the World Trade Center and the Pentagon on September 11, 2001. While corporate media swiftly announced that the terrorist attacks would now delegitimize the anti-globalization movement, corporations themselves quickly used the events as a means to undermine protests against their activities. Corporate special-interest groups made fantastic claims as they took advantage of public paranoia to try to block legislation that might interfere with profits. For example, the animal research lobby warned that a federal proposal to increase penalties for cruelty to animals (Bill C15B) would threaten efforts to defend against bioterrorism. University of Western Ontario microbiologist Sally Galsworthy called C15B "dangerous," even though the proposed bill would have no effect on research at all and animal research in Canada is not concerned with antidotes to biological weapons.[13] The Fur Council of Canada went even further and warned that C15B itself was "outright terrorism" launched by animal-rights activists.[14]

Politicians also played to public paranoia, seeking to pass laws that would give police sweeping powers to arrest people without evidence and hold them without trial. Tens of millions of dollars were diverted to the "war against terrorism," much of this going to intelligence services that would spy on the population. In October, the government was fast-tracking anti-terrorist legislation that would vastly increase police powers and

---

13. *The Toronto Star*, 22 Oct. 2001: A12.

14. "Animal Voices," CIUT Radio, 23 Oct. 2001.

expand the definition of terrorism so widely that public protest could be labelled as terrorism for "interfering with or disrupting an essential service, facility or system." Toronto Mayor Mel Lastman epitomized the mood when he called the members of the Ontario Coalition Against Poverty "animals" and "barbarians" for daring to organize a peaceful anti-corporate march on Bay Street on October 16, 2001. When demonstrators arrived from Montreal, police confined them to their buses until they submitted to being videotaped. Although the pre-emptive arrests proposed in the anti-terrorism bill had not been authorized by legislation, they were already being put into practice as demonstrators found to be in possession of spray-paint or goggles were taken into custody; others were arrested for not submitting to a police search.

This brief survey of actions related to the Summit of the Americas meeting shows how government, police, and media presented public dissent as an illegal action warranting extreme police measures. These institutions consistently emphasize the potential of violence on the part of dissidents as a means to avoid coming to terms with their critique. Clearly, neo-liberal regimes do not intend to protect citizens from corporate domination, but prefer to protect themselves from voices of citizens who disagree with their policies. The populace is urged to "Support your local police," but the events recounted here show that they, in turn, have no intention of supporting those who speak up in political protest.

John S. Sorenson

CHAPTER 30

"In America, Justice Is Blind"
Myth of "Equality Before the Law"

"Judge Sabo was discussing the case of Mumia Abu-Jamal. In the course of that conversation, I heard Judge Sabo say: 'Yeah, and I'm going to help them fry the n——r'." (Sworn statement of court stenographer Terri Maurer-Carter in 2001, reporting a discussion she overheard between Sabo and others in a Philadelphia courtroom during the trial of Jamal in 1982.)

In recent years, the campaign to prevent the execution of Mumia Abu-Jamal and either to secure a new trial for him or to free him outright was in the forefront of the broader struggle to abolish America's death penalty and to expose the injustice at the heart of its judicial system. Mumia's case was cutting-edge because it revealed that "American justice" was anything but "blind" to questions of race, class, and political ideology, and that US courts are frequently used to railroad African Americans, lock up political dissidents, and dispatch innocent people to death row. For years, the known facts concerning the case were sufficient to convince many that Mumia had been deprived of a "fair trial" and, quite possibly, that he had been framed for the murder for which he was convicted in 1982. New evidence released in 2001 pointed not only to Mumia's complete innocence, but to a sinister conspiracy on the part of "investigating" officers and prosecutors to make Mumia the "fall guy" for a murder that had been orchestrated from within the Philadelphia police department itself.

The story of the railroading of Mumia began on December 9, 1981, at about 3:30 a.m. near the corner of 13th and Locust Streets in Philadelphia.[1] A police officer had pulled over a vehicle driven by Mumia's brother, Billy Cook. Mumia was driving a taxi through the area at the time, and upon observing the cop beating his brother, he stopped his cab and approached the scene on foot. Moments later, shots rang out,

---

1. Unless otherwise indicated, the information in this chapter was gleaned from the article "Free Mumia Now!" published in the *Class Struggle Defense Notes* publication of the Partisan Defense Committee (No. 26, Winter 1998-99). The PDC is the legal defence arm of the Spartacist League in the US.

and when police arrived on the scene shortly afterward, they found officer Daniel Faulkner fatally wounded on the street and Mumia slumped on the curb with a bullet hole in his chest. The prosecution's case against Mumia rested on three foundations: the testimony of eyewitnesses who identified him as the only person who could have killed Faulkner; the allegation that Mumia confessed to the shooting as he lay bleeding in hospital later that night; and the claim that his gun, which was discovered at the scene, was the murder weapon. Evidence and eyewitness testimony at the Post-Conviction Relief Appeal hearing in the summer of 1995 and at subsequent hearings demolished all three elements of this prosecution case and suggested the likelihood that Mumia was framed, through police coercion of witnesses and the deliberate withholding of key evidence from Mumia's original (and incompetent) court-appointed defence attorney.

At the 1995 hearing, William Singletary testified that he saw another man shoot Faulkner and run away. When he related this same story to detectives prior to Mumia's 1982 trial, Singletary was repeatedly told that his truthful statements were unacceptable to them, and he was warned by a Detective Green "to write what he wanted me to write" or "they would take me to the elevator and beat me up." In the end, he signed a false statement in which he denied witnessing the shooting, and he was never called as a witness at the 1982 trial. Another eyewitness was Robert Chobert, a white cab driver who originally told police that the man who shot Faulkner "ran away." But at Jamal's trial, he changed his story and testified that Jamal was the shooter. Chobert admitted in 1995 that he had perjured himself after having received assurances from the police that he would be permitted to drive his cab without a license (which had been suspended while he was on probation for felony arson in 1981). Three other eyewitnesses also told the police that they saw Faulkner's shooter flee the scene. But only one of these witnesses, Dessie Hightower, actually testified for the defence at Mumia's 1982 trial. He was also the only witness to have been subjected by police to a lie-detector test, which they falsely claimed he had failed. Chobert's perjured testimony was reinforced at the trial by Veronica Jones, a prostitute who testified in 1996 that she had been coerced by police, under threat of prosecution on two serious felony gun charges, into retracting her true account of seeing two shooters fleeing the scene. By 1996, not a single piece of eyewitness testimony supporting the prosecution's case at Mumia's 1982 trial retained a semblance of credibility. Moreover, four witnesses were now prepared to corroborate Dessie Hightower's truthful account of a shooter fleeing from the scene of the murder.

What about the other prosecution evidence? Jamal's supposed "confession" was not even reported until *more than two months* after the shooting. The original official report by Officer Gary Wakshul, who stayed with Jamal for the entire time from his arrest through his initial hospitalization, stated that, "during this time, the negro male made no comments." It was only on the eve of the trial that Wakshul put himself at the service of the prosecution by claiming that he heard Jamal admit to the shooting—a statement that was never corroborated by attending doctors or nurses. The "importance" of this confession had apparently not occurred to Wakshul until he attended a roundtable meeting called by the District Attorney's office to orchestrate police testimony prior to the trial.

What about the discovery of Jamal's .38 calibre gun at the murder scene? Just after the shooting, the medical examiner's report stated that Faulkner was shot with a .44 calibre gun. Neither the bullet found in Faulkner's head nor one found at the scene could be matched to Jamal's gun, and a copper jacket discovered near the shooting could be matched to neither Faulkner's nor Jamal's gun. Indeed, no evidence was ever produced that Jamal's gun was fired at all. Further undermining the credibility of the prosecution's case was the disappearance of one of the bullet fragments removed from the wound in Faulkner's head.

By the mid-1990s, the burden of evidence in the Jamal case pointed unmistakably to his innocence and to serious police and prosecutorial misconduct. Yet repeated efforts on the part of Mumia's defence team, led by Leonard Weinglass, to have the conviction overturned or the case reopened came to naught. Outrageously, Judge Albert Sabo, the original trial judge from 1982, insisted on presiding over the 1995 post-conviction appeal, an appeal that was quite predictably lost amidst openly biased rulings and shameless statements by Sabo. Explaining his brazen attempts at intimidation of the defence team, Sabo offered the opinion that "justice is just an emotional feeling." In 1995, newly elected Republican state governor Tom Ridge signed a death warrant for Mumia. Only the mobilization of Mumia's supporters in sizable protest actions across the United States and internationally stayed the executioner's hand, at least temporarily.

The Mumia defence campaign faced strong, ongoing opposition from the Philadelphia Fraternal Order of Police and a near-total blackout from the American mass media. Very few mainstream politicians dared to associate with it. Internationally, however, the campaign attracted significant support. Thousands rallied in demonstrations in Europe, Australasia, Canada, South Africa, and Latin America, and the case became a *cause célèbre* for many on the political left.[2] The efforts of the Labor Action Committee to Free Mumia led the International Longshore and Warehouse Union to initiate a historic one-day port shutdown on the US west coast in April 1999 in solidarity with Mumia.[3] A solidarity work

---

2. Among the left groups associated with Mumia's defence were the Spartacist League, Refuse and Resist, Socialist Action, Workers World Party, International Socialist Organization, the International Bolshevik Tendency, and the Internationalist Group. International Family and Friends of Mumia Abu-Jamal was also prominent in the campaign, as were a number of celebrities, including actors Ed Asner, Ossie Davis, Mike Farrell, and Whoopie Goldberg and the rock group Rage Against the Machine.

3. "Free Mumia Abu-Jamal," *1917–Journal of the International Bolshevik Tendency* 22 (2000): 3.

stoppage was also called in Brazil by a union representing 150,000 teachers in that same year.[4]

The fact that Mumia's defence was taken up primarily by leftists was no accident. Mumia had long been associated with left-wing black nationalism, having served as the Minister of Information for the Philadelphia chapter of the Black Panther Party in the late 1960s and early 1970s, as an acclaimed freelance radio broadcaster and journalist critical of the racism and corruption infesting the Philadelphia police department, and as a prominent supporter of the MOVE organization in the late 1970s. With passion and eloquence, in both English and Spanish, Jamal spoke of the triumphs and plight of poor and oppressed Black and Hispanic people. He was elected president of the Philadelphia chapter of the Association of Black Journalists at age 26 in 1980.[5]

From the time when, at age 14, he received his first beating from racist cops for his involvement in a 1968 protest against a presidential rally for Alabama governor George "Segregation Forever" Wallace, Mumia had been viewed with enmity by the Philadelphia police. When circumstances allowed them to accuse Mumia of murder following the shooting of Officer Faulkner in December 1981, the police seized the opportunity, and their vendetta against Mumia received the enthusiastic backing of the office of the district attorney. The lead prosecutor at Mumia's trial made it known to the conservative white jury members that Mumia was a black radical who had once quoted Mao Zedong's famous statement that "political power grows out of the barrel of a gun" in an article he had written for *The Black Panther*. To his accusers as well as his defenders, the conviction of Mumia Abu-Jamal had always been at least as much about his radical politics as it had been about the killing of Daniel Faulkner.

As Mumia languished in a high-security Pennsylvania prison, awaiting the signing of a final death warrant, the movement to stop his execution became increasingly divided between his more radical supporters, who demanded "Free Mumia Now," and liberals who called for a new trial. But in 2001, startling new evidence came to light in the wake of Mumia's firing of his long-time attorneys Leonard Weinglass and Daniel Williams. In a bold and controversial move, Mumia's new team of lawyers released the sworn confession of one Arnold Beverly, who admitted to being the real killer of Officer Faulkner. Beverly testified,

> I was hired along with another guy and paid to shoot and kill Faulkner. I had heard that Faulkner was a problem for the mob and corrupt policemen because he interfered with the graft and payoffs made to allow illegal activity including prostitution, gambling, drugs without

4. "Brazilian Workers Mobilize for Freedom for Mumia Abu-Jamal," *The Internationalist* 8 (June 2000): 80.

5. Mumia's exceptional talent as a journalist and commentator is displayed in his book *Live from Death Row* (New York: Avon Books, 1996).

prosecution in the center city area.... I shot Faulkner in the face at close range.

Jamal was shot shortly after that by a uniformed police officer who arrived on the scene.[6]

Together with accompanying declarations by Jamal and his brother Billy Cook, Beverly's testimony is fully consistent with earlier eyewitness testimony, suppressed by the police, that Faulkner's shooter fled from the scene of the killing. Beverly's version of the events is not only in accord with all of the known evidence regarding the shooting; it also serves to explain the remarkable fact that the scene of the crime had been left completely unprotected by the police. (If the police themselves were complicit in the murder of Faulkner, they had every reason not to follow the standard operating procedures for the protection of evidence.)

Despite its compelling character, Mumia's new lawyers were barred from presenting any of this new testimony in court by US Judge William Yohn, who in a July 19, 2001, "memorandum and order" ruled it inadmissible. Effectively, Yohn decided that evidence of Jamal's innocence had no place in a court of law.

For all intents and purposes, Yohn's ruling had been facilitated by the actions of Jamal's own former lawyers, Weinglass and Williams, who had sat on Beverly's confession for over two years, effectively suppressing it. It was precisely over this issue that Partisan Defense Committee counsels Rachel Wolkenstein and Jonathan Piper resigned from Jamal's defence team in 1999, having realized that "lead counsel Weinglass would preclude the necessary steps from being taken to provide a defense for an innocent man."[7] In papers calling for a new state Post-Conviction Relief Appeal hearing based on the new evidence, Jamal's new legal team noted the "effective job" that Weinglass and Williams had done in "trying to undermine the petitioner's case," taking note as well of the publication by Williams of an unauthorized book on the case in which he had cast doubt on the credibility of the Beverly confession.

All this prompts a very important question: why would Mumia's own lawyers betray him in this way? The answer, it seems, is that they were unable to fully accept and confront the truth about the US criminal justice system that Mumia's case illuminates so starkly. In his book, Williams recounts his reaction to the revelation by Wolkenstein and Piper of Beverly's confession:

I was sensitive to the possibility that Mumia's sympathies with MOVE might have prompted law enforcement to jump to a conclusion about

---

6. Beverly's affidavit, together with several others important to the case, can be accessed at the web site of the International Bolshevik Tendency: <www.bolshevik.org> (Mumia Abu-Jamal page).

7. "Affidavit of Rachel Wolkenstein," *Mumia Abu-Jamal is an Innocent Man*, Partisan Defense Committee Pamphlet, Sept. 2001, p. 7

Mumia's guilt. I even believed that law enforcement was willing to fabricate evidence to help in the effort to convict a man they *believed to be guilty*. Rachel and Jon held more extreme views; they were convinced—actually to them, it was sacrilegious to believe otherwise—that law enforcement knew Mumia was innocent, knew that the shooter fled the scene, and relished that a conviction and death sentence would be a terrific coup in the city's war against MOVE. Their view was an article of faith that grew out of their ideological zeal.[8]

If Wolksenstein and Piper, who were supporters of the Trotskyist Spartacist League, were possessed of ideological zeal, it can be said no less certainly that Williams and Weinglass were afflicted with a quite unwarranted faith in the notion that "law enforcement" would never frame up a man they knew to be innocent. As the Partisan Defense Committee noted in their response to Williams' book,

> ... it is simply empirically evident that the Philly cops would knowingly frame up innocent people. Hundreds of convictions based on concocted evidence, coerced confessions, police torture and manipulation of prostitutes to serve as 'witnesses' have been thrown out in the last several years in Philadelphia alone. The whole history of this country is littered with frame-ups of those who have struggled to defend their unions, to fight capitalist injustice or to in any way challenge the rule of capital.[9]

It was this understanding of the role of the agencies of "law enforcement" in a racist, capitalist society that informed the efforts of the PDC, its parent organization the Spartacist League, and some other left groups to oppose the call for a "new trial" and to counterpose the demand "Free Mumia Now" within the broader Mumia defence campaign. It is an understanding rooted not so much in "zeal" as in a rich knowledge of the history of racial oppression, class struggle and political repression in the United States as well as other capitalist countries. Who with any knowledge of the case of boxer Rubin "Hurricane" Carter (whose story was related in a song by Bob Dylan and depicted in a recent Hollywood film), could possibly believe that the police are incapable of knowingly framing an *innocent* man? Who, after investigating the conviction of Geronimo ji Jaga (Pratt), a Black Panther leader framed for murder in 1970 and released in 1997 after 27 years in jail, or of American Indian Movement leader Leonard Peltier, who remains in prison after 25 years, could conclude that "justice" is available in the courtrooms of the capitalist state to those who defy the racism of that state? And who, after learning of the 1999 killing of Amadou Diallo by trigger-

8. Daniel Williams, *Executing Justice* (New York: St. Martin's Press, 2001) 298.

9. Wolkenstein 4.

happy New York cops who pumped 19 bullets into this innocent man as he stood in the doorway of his own home, can doubt that for the front-line agents of US "law enforcement" a black skin all too often is a signal to "open fire."

The case of Mumia Abu-Jamal is only one of many cases in the history of the United States that illustrate the simple truth that the capitalist state and its courts are not "neutral" arbiters of "justice." Rather they are instruments of class domination and racial oppression. In America, justice is not blind, and injustice possesses 20-20 vision.

Murray E. G. Smith

suggested readings

Blackwell, Judith C., and Patricia G.Erickson, eds., *Illicit Drugs in Canada: A Risky Business*. Scarborough, ON: Nelson Canada, 1988.

Brock, Deborah R. *Making Work, Making Trouble: Prostitution as a Social Problem*. Toronto: University of Toronto Press, 1998.

Churchill, Ward, and Jim Vander Wall. *Agents of Repression*. Boston: South End, 1988.

Comack, Elizabeth, and Stephen Brickey, eds. *The Social Basis of Law: Critical Readings in the Sociology of Law*. Toronto: Garamond Press, 1991.

Erickson, Patricia G., Diane M. Riley, Yuet W. Cheung, and Patrick A. O'Hare, eds. *Harm Reduction: A New Direction for Drug Policies and Programs*. Toronto: University of Toronto Press, 1997.

Goodell, Charles. *Political Prisoners in America*. New York: Random House, 1973.

Ratner, Robert, and John McMullan. *State Control: Criminal Justice Politics in Canada*. Vancouver: University of British Columbia Press, 1987.

Reiman, Jeffrey. *The Rich Get Richer and the Poor Get Prison: Ideology, Class, and Criminal Justice*. Toronto: Allyn and Bacon, 2001.

Starr, Amory. *Naming The Enemy: Anti-Corporate Movements Confront Globalization*. New York: Zed, 2000.

Wise, David. *The American Police State: The Government Against the People*. New York: Vintage, 1978.

PART NINE

Ecology &
Animal Liberation

CHAPTER 31

"People come first"
conceits of anthropocentrism

Anthropocentrism is the most fundamental form of prejudice. The assumption that human beings occupy the centre of the universe and that they should take precedence over all other forms of life is not only a self-congratulatory excess but a dangerous delusion that ignores critical findings of scientists and environmentalists who stress the interdependence of all life forms. From this basic assumption of superiority over nature comes an associated complex of other prejudiced attitudes and practices. For example, ideas about dominion over plants and animals are readily applied to other humans, who are seen to be closer to nature, more primitive, childish or criminal-like, and who must either be civilized or destroyed, according to the needs of the moment.

While every individual being is equipped with a drive for survival, modern societies have elevated dominance over nature as the essential aspect of their ideological framework. We assume that humans are superior to every other form of life and that therefore we have the right to dominate the planet. Arrogating this absolute importance to ourselves, it is taken for granted that people must come first in every situation, whether it is the recreational use of neighbourhood parks or the fate of entire rain forests.

Our attitudes toward animals are easily seen in our language. Evil and brutal actions committed by people are deplored as "animal" behaviour. Yet no animal has ever developed violence and cruelty to the level of the human torturer's gruesome craft, as practised in the dungeons of, say, Turkey, Central America or Indonesia. "Animal" passions seem rather tame compared to our pornography industries, sexualized advertising campaigns, and levels of rape and child abuse.

We classify animals according to the functions we assign to them and treat them accordingly: millions of domesticated animals are imprisoned in ghastly conditions to be slaughtered so that we may consume their flesh, while "wild" animals are killed for entertainment. Those animals we regard as "pets" are turned into commodities that can be easily disposed of and are often abused. Despite claims that an excess of sentimentality leads us to overindulge our pets, it is clear that even these animals we supposedly cherish are subject to severe legal restrictions based on extreme phobias. For example, in Canada, dogs are barred from most shops, offices, restaurants, and pubs and must be leashed almost constantly; some cities even ban leashed dogs from parks. Fines for walking an unleashed dog even in a deserted park are higher than fines imposed on those convicted of torturing animals. Even organizations that ostensibly help animals encourage paranoid attitudes. For example, in 2001 the Humane Society of Canada ran a billboard campaign depicting a child's sutured arm and captioned, "How many more days before a child is bitten by a dog?" The organization's web site warned that someone is bitten by a dog every 60 seconds in Canada, but when asked to provide evidence for this claim, a representative of the Society admitted to me that no study had ever been done in Canada, and the Society had merely extrapolated figures from a US report that it could not name. Such hostility toward and obsession with policing even the animal known as "man's best friend" suggest that the attitudes toward other animals are even more aggressive.

Animals are viewed as commodities. Seen as objects rather than autonomous entities, they become status symbols and representations of their owners' fantasies, such as the urban "gangsta" who purchases a pit-bull to complete his MTV-mediated identity. Beings are changed into property, just as under slavery. They can be bought and sold and can be easily disposed of when they become inconvenient. So-called animal "shelters" are actually extermination centres where millions of unwanted animals are killed. The rationale is that "euthanasia" prevents suffering, but the effect is to normalize killing.

Convinced that all other species must be subordinated to our needs and desires, no matter how irrational, people assume that they have a right to control, manipulate, torture and kill non-human animals if it is in their own interests. (This conviction about the absolute precedence of human interests is applied selectively, of course, and the interests of one's own group are assumed to be more valid than those of others.) The basic immorality of such an attitude should be apparent. This anthropocentric approach to nature has religious, philosophical, and economic dimensions.

Most religions promote anthropocentric attitudes but they are carried to extremes by the dominant monotheistic ideologies. For example, this attitude grows out of Christianity's emphasis on an opposition between physical and spiritual worlds and the conviction that the latter is superior. Christianity assumes that humans are a special creation, the main interest of a supernatural being who has placed them in a position of dominance over nature and animals. According to this worldview, plants and animals exist only to serve human beings, according to a supernatural plan. The most important task of humans is to maintain good relations with this supernatural boss, while nature is to be used pretty much as we wish. Despite a few minor exceptions, Christianity has displayed a remarkable hatred of the physical world, including the human body, animals, and the natural environment. This is exemplified in

Christianity's emphasis on abstinence from sensual pleasures and its long history of misogyny and repressive practices focused on sexuality and reproduction. This obsessive hatred of sexuality was linked with ideas about "race" and about animals. Certain groups of people were more "natural," more animal-like, and more sexual, all of which indicated their inferior status. Just as the natural world was to be conquered, so were these other societies. Other monotheistic religions display similar attitudes about renunciation of the physical world and antipathy toward nature.

Even many of those who are not religious subscribe to similar views. A rigidly anthropocentric view of the world is central to Western civilization. Rather than understanding an organic whole, philosophers such as Descartes promoted a mechanistic view of the universe which considered animals merely as machines but awarded humans a superior status. The scientific method advocated by Sir Francis Bacon emphasized a quantitative and fragmented approach that would effect the conquest and domination of nature. Social Darwinists emphasized ideas of competition, struggle, and progress, projecting the values of their own society onto nature.

Production of genetically modified organisms is but the latest step in this arrogant determination to subdue nature entirely. In a quantum leap from traditional methods of plant breeding, many scientists are now engaged in the genetic manipulation of plants to make them resistant to diseases or to modify certain features. Others have participated in the cloning of animals such as "Dolly" the sheep or the genetic modification of pigs so that they can serve as little biological factories to produce human organs for transplanting into people. The dangers of xenotransplantation are not slight and include the possibility of an uncontrollable spread of mutated viruses that could extinguish much of the world's population. These risky procedures are undertaken at the cost of extensive suffering and death of animals. Corporations such as Monsanto spend vast amounts on public relations campaigns to convince us that biotechnology will provide benefits to all of humanity by feeding the hungry and curing disease. While presenting themselves as saviours of humanity, biotechnology corporations actually seek total control over life itself by patenting the control of genetic material and claiming these genetically engineered crops as private property.

The economic consequences of an anthropocentric worldview have had a profound impact upon the environment. For most of human history, we lived in small-scale societies with limited numbers and in some cases achieved ecologically sustainable patterns of life. The growth and recent triumph of "market" or capitalist societies have had a corresponding and devastating environmental impact that has included massive extinctions.

Capitalism, which places profit above all else, encourages a view of the natural world as something that can be exploited for profit. Animals and the environment are viewed as resources and commodities, not as entities with their own value. Despite their opposition to capitalism, Marxists also share the attitude that nature is simply a resource to be exploited for human ends; many have promoted unlimited industrial development and rejected the significance of environmentalist and animal-rights arguments. Since value is determined only on the basis of human labour, nature is not valued in itself but only as a resource for humans to exploit. Armed with such convictions, many of the so-called socialist states were able to distinguish themselves among the most badly polluted places on earth. Eastern Europe is an environmental disaster area, full of dead rivers and lakes, dying forests, and foul air. The 1986 nuclear accident at Chernobyl in Ukraine spread a radioactive cloud over much of Western Europe, caused cancer in tens of thousands of people, and rendered a huge area uninhabitable.

Under the mantra of "economic growth," industries have permission to keep on polluting even though the environmental effects are devastating. Acid rain, linked to fossil fuel use and iron ore smelting, is eating away at stone buildings, devastating rivers and lakes, and causing extinction of many fish populations. Automobile use is rendering the atmosphere unbreathable, but manufacturers continue to seek new markets while investment in public transportation is virtually ignored. Forests are razed to create golf courses for vacationing corporate executives, while obsessed suburbanites saturate their biologically inappropriate lawns with carcinogenic pesticides and chemical fertilizers. The oceans are used as toxic waste dumps, and other hazardous material is shipped from industrialized nations to impoverished Third World states. Production of synthetic chemicals, plastics and pesticides, along with accidents, oil spills, improper use and storage have resulted in large residues of toxic materials in our food and water.

Convinced of the absolute priority of humans over all other forms of life and refusing to see that human population growth must be limited if the planet is to survive, the world's religions promote unrestricted reproduction and condemn as sinful various forms of birth control and abortion. Now, human overpopulation threatens the survival of countless other species. Nearly six billion people are consuming the world as if it were an unlimited resource, creating a virtual war against nature. Our anthropocentric beliefs, combined with the conviction that economic growth in itself is always good and that wealth is a goal to be pursued, have now brought the entire world to the edge of catastrophe.

The conviction that human beings are the crown of creation, coupled with the unbridled greed and self-interest of capitalist cultures that see the natural world as something to be exploited without consequence, has created a crisis for the entire planet through global warming, while species are being driven to extinction at unprecedented rates, their habitats destroyed by pollution, deforestation, and desertification. These are not simply the regrettable consequences of our drive to consume the world's resources. Rather, this arrogant and prejudiced attitude toward the natural world is the whole basis of our social life.

John S. Sorenson

CHAPTER 32

"Eating meat is natural"
Preference defined as inevitability

Most North Americans regularly encounter non-human animals as corpses on their dinner plates. Since eating these corpses is considered natural, challenging such ghoulish practices is difficult. Corpse-eaters are defensive or hostile about their diet, dismissing objections as foolish or refusing even to discuss the topic. However, eating flesh is not "natural"; even at the most obvious level, we do not tear off bloody hunks of flesh and swallow them raw as carnivores do, but instead we process flesh in various culturally accepted ways. Eating flesh is a practice overlaid with symbolic meanings, codes, and obfuscations, part of a highly –mechanized, multi-billion-dollar industry with devastating environmental effects. Killing animals to eat their flesh is not a simple matter of taste or personal choice. It is wrong, in the same way that racism and sexism are wrong. Far from being a trivial or peripheral matter, the slaughter and consumption of animals is the very foundation on which cultures of prejudice are created and maintained. Our attitudes toward animals and the natural world are the essential basis for other forms of exploitation.

Profound ambivalence surrounds killing and eating non-human animals. Many children are shocked to discover what's on their plates; they may refuse to eat flesh and must be forced to do so. They are socialized to think of flesh as meat, an abstract thing, not part of a creature who once lived.[1] Despite our early indoctrination into flesh eating, ambivalence persists; thus modern Western society attempts to distance the killing, conducting this in special warehouses, concealed from public view. Industrial culture kills non-human animals in a streamlined mechanical process, much like the bureaucratic death-machine created by the Nazis. This automated process in which animals are mere units of production not only became a metaphor for capitalism in works by Upton Sinclair and Bertolt Brecht, it was a model for the dismemberment and fragmentation of work itself: Henry Ford developed the

---

1. Carol Adams, *The Sexual Politics of Meat* (New York: Continuum, 2000).

automobile assembly line after visiting Chicago slaughterhouses.[2] The process attempts to disguise its real nature: what emerges from the slaughterhouse is called beef or pork rather than cow or pig; products may be de-boned, divided into portions, moulded into geometrical shapes and wrapped in plastic. Butcher shops try to mask the horror; they advertise dancing pigs, not scenes of death. Yet our childhood repugnance at such practices is not completely subdued: many are uneasy handling uncooked flesh or recoil from the sight of blood. Eating raw flesh seems horrifying, so it must be cooked and disguised: it is re-shaped, coated with breadcrumbs, and heads, tails, and feet are removed before serving. Consuming flesh is an expression of power over other animals, but it is disturbing if this is too obvious.

Attempts to conceal these horrors have serious social and psychological consequences for people, but the impact on non-human animals is more direct and staggering. Huge numbers of animals are killed for food. In the US alone, over 100 million mammals and 5 billion birds are slaughtered each year. In contemporary Western societies, flesh is produced within the logic of capitalism and industrialized food production, which mandates raising as many animals as possible in the smallest amount of space to maximize profit. Animals are completely objectified; they are imprisoned, disabled and mutilated, isolated in crates, and kept motionless or crowded into wire cages. They experience lives of deprivation, frustration, fear, anxiety, boredom, pain, and insanity.

Although such treatment violates ethical and moral principles that we generally feel we should observe (such as to avoid causing unnecessary suffering, confinement and killing of sentient beings), we regard violations of these principles as acceptable in relation to non-human animals. We find it normal to imprison, torture, and kill them because we consider ourselves superior. Such treatment not only reflects the logic of capitalism but also indicates deeply rooted ideas about animals and nature. These ideas are central to colonialism, racism, sexism, and environmental crises. Concern for animal rights and ethical treatment of other species is not a peripheral matter but in fact is the essential foundation for critical thinking and social justice.

Many seek to justify mistreatment of animals on the grounds that it is a natural tendency ("it's natural to eat meat" or "other animals kill and eat meat, so it's natural for us to do so"). The selectivity of this argument is readily apparent: it is seldom extended to advocate consumption of other animal products such as feces, despite the fact that one may observe dogs "naturally" doing so (although unhygienic practices in corporate reprocessing of animal flesh means that corpse-eaters do regularly consume fecal matter, along with other contaminants). In fact, it is not at all clear that it is natural for us to eat flesh. Often, what seems "natural" is in reality socially constructed, reflecting political objectives and cultural values. Although some animals are predators who kill for food, most are not. It is unclear why we should

2. Adams 52.

select predators as models for our behaviour, especially when our closest animal relatives are exclusively or primarily vegetarians. Unlike carnivorous animals who need flesh to survive, we are omnivorous and can live without it. The inconsistency of flesh-eating arguments is apparent, as the suggestion "we should eat meat because other animals do" conflicts with efforts to defend an absolute separation between humans and other animals. On the one hand, exploitation is defended because of our similarity with animals, while on the other it is defended because of our differences.

The global, mechanized flesh system is certainly not natural. Most North Americans do not obtain flesh "naturally" by killing animals with their bare hands but instead procure corpses from factories. Other species do not breed, enslave, and execute animals for their flesh or torture them for trivial purposes (cosmetics testing, etc.). Furthermore, we are moral beings who can make choices. Arguments in support of exploitation based on claims that "it's only natural" suggest a natural order or hierarchy: just as big fish eat little ones, we are Kings of the Jungle, at the top of the food chain.[3] But other "natural" hierarchies have been suggested: Aristotle thought men were superior to women, European colonizers saw themselves as superior to savages, Nazis thought Aryans were superior to Jews. We reject such hierarchies and see it as moral progress to accept egalitarian treatment of others; our principles of justice involve notions of defending the weak against the strong, so why not extend this to animals?

Concern for animals is often dismissed on the "obvious" grounds that we are completely distinct from animals, justifying a different ethical code. The same arguments were used by Nazis who found Jews obviously subhuman, or by white supremacists in South Africa for whom it was self-evident that black people were inferior. Many of us see those distinctions as arbitrary and selfish and reject them, but we are reluctant to do so when it comes to distinctions between ourselves and other animals. In each case, the distinction is capricious, based on self-interest and power and designed to permit exploitation without guilt or shame. If we try to draw absolute distinctions between humans and other animals on some other basis than self-interest, problems arise: What separates humans from animals? Language, reason, emotions, social organization, use of tools, the capacity to feel pain—all have been suggested, but all have been questioned. No matter which criterion one chooses, it is impossible to make a division that includes all humans and excludes all other animals. For example, in terms of mental development, a dog may have a more complex intellectual life than a severely brain-damaged person or an infant. As philosopher Peter Singer says, in order to include all humans, one must set the common denominator at a very low level. Thus, one can always find some animal that shares the relevant characteristic. It is impossible to specify what makes humans special and one can only make vague appeals to "intrinsic worth," "human dignity," and

---

3. Steve F. Sapontzis, *Morals Reason and Animals* (Philadelphia: Temple University Press, 1987).

so on. We like to think in these terms because it flatters us (e.g., we are created in the image of a god, the crown of creation).

Attempts to distance ourselves from other animals overlook the fact that we share numerous physical and behavioural characteristics. Animals care for their young, think, act, and love. They have the capacity to feel pain and suffer. Researchers have found that higher animals are intelligent, possessing some type of moral sense, and are able to experience joy, sorrow, and anxiety. They may experience these emotions to a greater degree than some humans. Studies show that chimpanzees are the intellectual equals of young humans and that the mental capacity of apes is far above that of some mentally disabled people. Animals may have greater ability to communicate than severely mentally disabled people, some of whom lack distinctively human qualities and may be completely cut off from others, "vegetables" incapable of communication or interaction. Thus some people lack abilities that we consider human, while higher animals do possess such qualities. Yet we allow painful and lethal research on intelligent animals while not permitting experiments on mentally disabled people. To argue that severely mentally disabled people should be included in a special category of "humans" while intelligent animals are excluded is to discriminate against these animals without valid reason and to argue for equality only on the basis of membership in homo sapiens. Richard Ryder terms this "speciesism" and compares it to racism and sexism.[4] The argument is not that rights should be denied to mentally disabled people but rather that rights should be extended to other species.

A search for an absolute distinction between humans and animals is futile because it is misconceived. All living things are linked in a chain of genetic relationships. In the nineteenth century, Darwin acknowledged that no fundamental differences exist between humans and the higher mammals in terms of mental facilities. Humans *are* animals, so properly we should refer to other beings as non-human animals. Specifically, we are mammals, belonging to the order of primates (a group that includes apes and monkeys). Primates share various physical characteristics: we have hair, flat fingernails, an opposable thumb and four fingers, a penis not attached to the abdomen, and we nurse our offspring. Our closest relatives are gorillas and chimpanzees.

As Jared Diamond has demonstrated, molecular biology, the study of molecular changes associated with genetic mutation and DNA, indicates how close this association is. We share 93 per cent of our DNA with monkeys and apes, and differences are even smaller between apes and humans: gorillas and humans differ by 2.3 per cent, and humans differ from chimpanzees by 1.6 per cent. How significant are such differences? The DNA difference between common and pygmy chimpanzees is 0.7 per cent; the two look so similar they were only distinguished as separate species in 1929. The genetic distance between humans and chimpanzees is only double that sepa-

---

4. Richard D. Ryder, *Animal Revolution* (New York: Berg, 2000).

rating these two almost indistinguishable species of chimpanzees and is less than that separating certain bird species that are distinguished only by eye-colour. We share 98.4 per cent of our DNA with chimpanzees; the genetic distance between gorillas and chimpanzees and humans together (2.3%) is greater than that between humans and chimpanzees (1.6%). This means that making a sharp distinction between humans and apes misrepresents the facts: basically humans are a third species of chimpanzee.[5] To recognize ourselves as animals and to acknowledge our relationships with other living creatures entails a fundamental reassessment of our place in the world.

Central to this is the practice of killing other animals. Although some derive pleasure from it, others find that killing brings regret, shame, and disgust. Profound ambivalence about killing has led to efforts at justifying the practice. In foraging cultures, animals used as food were studied closely, but knowledge created a sense of kinship with animals and caused stress and guilt about killing them. To show respect and gratitude, to ask forgiveness and to appease spirits of the animals, many societies developed rituals associated with killing. Similarly, in ancient state societies, animals were often slaughtered at temples and ceremonial aspects emphasized sacrifice, debt to the animals, and efforts to placate their spirits. In Western societies, reverence for animals disappeared but ambivalence remained, and it was necessary to create religious and philosophical explanations to justify violence.

Many religions provide a rationale for killing animals, but Judeo-Christian ideology does so by elevating humans above all other forms of life. In Christian mythology, a supernatural being gave humans dominion over other animals. In a dualistic system that valorized spiritual life, the natural world was to be conquered and subdued. Exploitation was justified by suggesting that the whole world existed for human use and corpse-eaters found convenient supernatural sanctions for their desires. For example, in 1653 Henry More asserted that cattle and sheep "were only given life in the first place so as to keep their meat fresh 'til we shall have need to eat them.'"[6]

This hierarchy of value also constructed a scale of human beings. Elaborate mythologies of racist thought selected visible markers of difference (such as skin colour) to identify those who could legitimately be enslaved. Just as animals were seen as inferior to humans, some people were identified as sub-human. Just as animals were imprisoned, so it was "natural" to put Africans in chains. Both animals and humans became property. Such ideas were instrumental to the development of industrial society, and increasing industrial production seemed to prove that these theories were correct. Ideas about domination of nature were central to colonial conquest of the non-European world. Indigenous people were identified with nature, and nature was evil. Wilderness was something to be tamed, a zone of fierce beasts and demons; indigenous inhabitants were equated with both as Europeans debated whether

---

5. Jared Diamond, *The Third Chimpanzee* (New York: Harper Collins, 1992).

6. Keith Thomas, *Man and the Natural World* (London: Allen Lane, 1983) 20.

Indians were really human: in sixteenth-century Spain, Juan Gines de Sepulveda argued that because Indians were less than human, it was legitimate to enslave them. Racist doctrines equated non-European people with animals: all were to be conquered, dominated, exploited or exterminated.

Western religion and philosophy characterized the natural world as existing for human use. Spurred by such ideas, we raise animals in appalling conditions and kill them to obtain their flesh. Although it is not necessary for our survival, we cause pain, suffering, and death to sensitive creatures simply to satisfy our cravings. As Peter Singer notes, the process of raising animals and then killing them to consume their flesh clearly subordinates their most vital interests to our trivial desires. In order to avoid speciesism, we are morally obligated to stop supporting such actions.[7]

Objections to killing and eating animals are often dismissed as absurd and sentimental. Concern for the environment generally is devalued ("tree-huggers") and, similarly, concern for human rights is disparaged as foolish and weak ("bleeding-heart liberals"). In cultures of prejudice, feelings of compassion, solidarity, commitment, and concern for social justice are held up to ridicule. In the name of realism, we are trained to crush our own decency and to take pride in the accomplishment.

Those who have accomplished these tasks resort to standardized rhetoric to convince others. A typical response to criticism of corpse eating is to declare, "if you were starving, you'd eat a cow." But if one were starving, one might also eat other people, a course rarely recommended as a dietary staple. Although poverty and malnutrition are increasing, most North Americans (unlike some other people) do not face actual starvation on a regular basis, so this argument misrepresents an extreme and unlikely situation as normal and then offers it as justification for murder. Furthermore, if we are really concerned about starvation (not our own hypothetical starvation but the actual starvation of masses of people in the Third World), then we must reconsider the whole agribusiness system in which the flesh industry plays a significant role. Eating flesh is not simply a personal choice but a political one, making one complicit not only in the overwhelming brutality and terror of the slaughterhouse but also in environmental degradation and world hunger. Our food habits—our tastes—cause the suffering and death not only of millions of animals but of millions of people as well (see chapter 7 on colonialism).

Eating flesh not only is unnecessary for our survival and health but is actually unhealthy. Consumption of flesh-derived fat and protein is linked to breast, colon, and ovarian cancer, heart attacks, diabetes, gallstones, osteoporosis, hypertension, kidney disease, high blood pressure, premature aging, and impotence. Unhygienic death factories spread food poisoning, salmonella, E. coli, and parasites. Health risks arise not only from flesh itself but also from poisonous chemical residues left in animal flesh due to the character of factory farming. The drive for profit results in wide-

7. Peter Singer, "All Animals Are Equal," *Ethical Vegetarianism*, eds. Kerry S. Walters and Lisa Portness (Albany: State University of New York, 1999) 173.

spread use of chemicals—disinfectants, hormones, antibiotics—to maximize production. These toxins are passed on to those who eat the corpses. Antibiotics given to animals create immunity to these drugs in humans. More recently, health risks from factory farming were revealed in outbreaks of bovine spongiform encephalopathy ("mad cow disease") in humans. Some suggest that an animal-flesh diet is linked to negative emotional states, increased aggression, and cruelty.

Despite this evidence, eating flesh is promoted as normal and healthy, while vegetarianism is presented as unnatural, subversive, and ridiculous. Huge agribusiness corporations promote such ideas through massive indoctrination campaigns, depicting flesh consumption as natural, essential, and healthy. Those who oppose eating flesh are branded as kooks; for example, the flesh industry attacked popular Canadian singer k.d. lang for her statement that "meat stinks." Huge corporations such as McDonald's use lawsuits to silence ordinary citizens who speak out on the health and environmental consequences of the hamburger business.

But it's not only these corporations that promote eating flesh as natural. Our whole culture (the culture of capitalism) embraces an ideology in which flesh plays a forceful symbolic role: an ideology of domination, hierarchy, competition, and power. Doctrines such as Social Darwinism projected the moral economy of capitalism onto the natural world, using Darwin's ideas of evolution to assure rich people that natural selection had ensured their dominance over poor people. Capitalism presents itself as natural but actually invents the natural world in its own image. Similarly, colonial domination demonstrated superiority: just as humans had power over animals, so Europeans had power over non-European people, who were regularly described as animals (wild beasts, parasites, vermin) and whose status as human was questioned. This ideological system construes power, domination, and control of nature as positive, and eating flesh embodies these values. Killing and eating animals are presented as "facts of life" or "laws of nature." This reaffirms a particular view of the world: a world of hierarchy and competition, where life is harsh and cruel and one must struggle to stay on top. Clearly this offers benefits: if it is "natural" to be selfish, one's own selfishness is excused.

John S. Sorenson

CHAPTER 33

"Hunting is part of human nature"
"Human nature" as a rationalization for the inhumane

While some flesh-eaters seek to conceal from themselves the implications of their actions, others revel in pain and gore. They regard killing non-human animals as sport, a recreational activity. Historically, we find many examples of animals tortured and killed for entertainment. The ancient Romans killed thousands of animals in public spectacles; in the Middle Ages people amused themselves by impaling cats or setting them on fire; today, bullfights continue to draw crowds in Spain. Some people spend huge amounts of money to hunt non-human animals, especially large, rare ones, justifying this as an expression of primal human nature.

Such ideas are based on distorted images of our evolutionary heritage. Early hominids are described as "killer apes," and prehistoric people (and more contemporary foraging societies) are conceptualized within a "Man the Hunter" framework. In fact, early hominid forms such as Australopithecus that evolved 4 million years ago primarily ate vegetables. About 2.5 million years ago, flesh did become more important to hominids, but these were scavengers, not hunters: they ate corpses of animals that died or were left by other animals. Eventually, they developed enough skill to distract predators and steal their food. Hunting skills gradually developed with later forms of homo erectus (who died out 400,000 years ago). Modern homo sapiens of 45,000 years ago did show an ability to hunt large animals, but their diet was largely vegetables obtained by foraging. In contemporary foraging societies, hunting plays a relatively small role: 85 per cent of food is vegetable, provided by women. Although women's work is more important to survival, accounts tend to focus on men's activities. With women providing most of the staple food supply, images of the past and of contemporary foraging societies should emphasize not "Man the Hunter" but "Woman the Gatherer."

In contrast to a view that hunting is natural and that it places us in touch with our true primeval selves, we can see that killing animals for sport has long been a cultural demonstration of political power. Assyrian carvings in the British Museum depict the lion hunt as a princely sport. As one cultural marker of class, English aristocrats still entertain themselves by fox hunting on horseback, accompanied by packs of dogs. Hunting also served as a demonstration of imperial power. European colonialists took up hunting as a sport appropriate to their status. When Great White Hunters went on safari, they were accompanied by dozens of local people to carry things (sometimes the natives even carried the Great White Hunters themselves). Surrounded by servants, the Great White Hunters lived in big tents, wore distinctive costumes for killing, and dressed formally for dinner. The safari was another act in imperialist theatre, demonstrating wealth, power, and control over nature. These displays were not only intended to impress the natives but to solidify self-images of superiority. Leading inferior people into the wilderness to kill big animals, the Great White Hunter on safari played out a symbolic drama with moral and political lessons.

Hunting demonstrated power over animals, land, and people. For example, this was embodied in US president Teddy Roosevelt, racist, imperialist and big game hunter, who slaughtered huge numbers of animals on trips around the world, even shocking other hunters with his taste for killing. Roosevelt also liked killing indigenous peoples, whom he described as "beasts of prey." His *Winning of the West* applauds slaughter of Native Americans as "the most ultimately righteous of all wars."[1] In Roosevelt, ideas of white supremacy merged with those of manly virtue through conquest of animals and inferior "races."

Killing indigenous people and animals was part of the same process. For example, in the genocidal campaigns of the nineteenth century, when the object was to clear indigenous people from the plains, the US Army shifted strategy in 1870. Instead of continuing to attack villages and shoot Indians directly, the army decided to starve them into submission and slaughtered millions of bison, with effective results. Responding to proposed legislation to protect remaining bison (nearing extinction), General Sheridan suggested that a medal be struck and given to bison hunters: one side would feature a dead bison, the other, a defeated and demoralized Indian.[2]

Killing animals for sport is pathological, a manifestation of depravity, corruption, and insanity. The pleasure derived from tormenting other creatures is not only an expression of individual sickness but indicates the deranged ideology at the core of our culture of prejudice. The pathological character of hunting is demonstrated in statements made by hunters who express a love of nature and the animals they kill. Romanticizing slaughter, they speak of the passion and mystery of hunting, of communion or even erotic engagement with animals they murder. Similar sentiments arise in statements by serial killers of humans; for example, Jeffrey Dahmer (who killed his male lovers and ate their bodies) spoke of loving and possessing his victims.

---

1. Quoted in Noam Chomsky, *Turning the Tide* (Montreal: Black Rose, 1986) 87.

2. Ward Churchill, *A Little Matter of Genocide* (San Francisco: City Lights, 1997) 260, n118.

Typically, such serial killers are found to have first practised their craft on animals. The aggression celebrated in paeans to hunting is the same impulse as that which created death camps, genocide, war, and threats of nuclear destruction.

Further evidence of our joy in destroying animals and dominating the natural world is provided by other crude and savage forms of entertainment. Just as hunting and bullfighting are rituals of domination of nature expressed in slaughter of animals, we derive pleasure from other rituals involving power over animals. Rodeos, for example, celebrate individualism and competition, stoic suffering, and singular forms of sexuality. The cowboy, symbol of macho Western individualism, is expected to return to the ring even with broken bones, to wrestle, rope, and tie down large animals.[3] In these deeply fetishized spectacles of pain, bondage, and discipline, bizarrely costumed men engage in a "male cult of sadomasochism" celebrating supremacy over nature.[4] Another spectacle of power is the circus, notorious for mistreatment of animals (lack of food, water, and exercise, confinement, isolation, beatings). Although some circuses have abandoned abuse of animals for public entertainment, others still put them in ridiculous costumes and force them to perform tricks, and engage in highly controlled and orchestrated behaviour for our amusement. Reinforcing myths about the violence of animals and humiliating them in rituals of domination, the circus demonstrates human power and the inferiority of animals, reaffirming our belief that we are masters of the world.

While domination of nature and hatred of animals have been consistent and dominant themes throughout the history of Western societies, the notion that non-Western societies are characterized by respect for animals may be an exaggeration. It is often argued that in indigenous societies animals are treated as kin, part of a network of family. However, the "respect" that hunters say they have for animals they kill may be simply a means to justify the killing of animals and assuage their guilt. In many indigenous societies, animals have been sacrificed, with the objective of obtaining benefits from some supernatural power. Often these sacrifices were carried out in such a way as to prolong the animal's suffering. The suggestion that non-Western societies lived in harmony with nature with little impact on the environment may be exaggerated as well. The movement of Siberian hunters into North and South America twelve thousand years ago was followed by the extinction of many species of mammals and birds, and the archaeological record demonstrates that hunting societies often killed large numbers of animals.

Of course, the impact is even greater today as animals' habitats are reduced by oil fields and golf courses and indigenous peoples themselves are pushed into more marginal areas. In Central and West Africa, for example, the slaughter of primates for "bush meat" threatens the extinction of several species. Commercial hunting of

3. Elizabeth Atwood Lawrence, *Rodeo* (Chicago: University of Chicago Press, 1982).

4. Jim Mason, *An Unnatural Order* (New York: Continuum, 1997) 249.

primates in these areas has become a billion-dollar business. In the past some hunting of primates did occur, but human population growth and habitat destruction have increased this. As life becomes more desperate for impoverished humans, attitudes toward nature have become more utilitarian, and wildlife comes to be seen as a resource to be exploited for money. Lack of enforced regulations, availability of guns, and the profit imperative of timber companies have created a crisis. Timber companies run their own hunting camps and see primates as a cheap source of food for workers, but the "bush meat" trade extends far beyond the logging camps to the finest restaurants of African cities and beyond, where elites pay high prices to eat rare and exotic delicacies.

The assumption that humans have the right to dominate the planet has led to a rate of mass extinctions unprecedented since the dinosaurs went extinct 65 million years ago. As many as half the planet's species may be affected. Furthermore, contemporary extinctions are not the result of species being unsuited to their environments but are caused by the destruction of habitat and the hunting of species that are well adapted to their environments. These attitudes constitute a virtual war against the environment and animals. In Indonesia and Madagascar, virtually all forests have been razed, and almost all the world's primates are endangered. In India, human population growth and industrialization are reducing habitat for all animals. Dumping of sewage, agricultural and industrial waste, and oil spills in the Black Sea have depleted oxygen in the water to the point where oxygen-dependent animals and plants can no longer survive. On an even broader scale, fossil fuel use and deforestation increase carbon dioxide, which traps heat and creates the greenhouse effect responsible for global warming and large-scale climate disruptions. Some species have already become extinct and others will surely follow because of this rapid and unprecedented alteration of the planet's climate.

As Ponting[5] shows, European colonialism not only oppressed millions of people around the world but also constituted a devastating attack on other species, who were slaughtered for their flesh, skins, feathers, tusks and oil. Animals were seen merely as a resource, leading to disaster in every case, as industries competed to derive the maximum profit with no thought of conservation. Many, like the dodo and the passenger pigeon, were driven to extinction; the beaver population and the great bison herds of North America were decimated. Use of fur as a status symbol in Europe also led to the near extinction of many species of seals.

Europeans started fishing cod off eastern North America around 1500, but with the introduction of factory trawler technology in the 1950s, stocks rapidly declined. Politicians, biologists, and fishers all insisted they knew what they were doing and that the industry could be managed. However, intense competition from North American and European fishers drained cod in the Grand Banks, and Canada

5. Clive Ponting, *A Green History of the World* (New York: Penguin, 1992).

announced a moratorium in 1992 that led to thousands of job losses. Most whaling industries have collapsed because of near-extinction of many species, but the International Whaling Commission opposed the imposition of quotas even when presented with irrefutable evidence of the crisis; even when a moratorium was finally established, Japan, Norway and Iceland continued to kill whales under the guise of scientific research.

In every case, industries have claimed to be able to manage animal populations in sustainable fashion. Yet the record shows the same pattern: competition and exploitation to the point of extinction or decimation. Anthropocentrism, self-interest, and the belief in inevitable progress and a free market are the ideological pillars of our society. Self-interest and economic calculation dictate that resources be maximized, overlooking the fact that these animal "resources" do not exist in endless quantities and that under these conditions of ruthless competition their numbers will soon be depleted. Those who praise economic growth fail to see the consequences of exploiting finite populations. As the natural world is transformed from environment to commodity, the moral issues of exploiting animals are rarely even raised, and the idea that these "resources" have value in themselves goes unrecognized.

John S. Sorenson

suggested readings

DeGrazia, David. *Taking Animals Seriously*. Cambridge: Cambridge University, 1996.

Foster, John Bellamy. *The Vulnerable Planet: A Short Economic History of the Environment*. New York: Monthly Review Press, 1999.

Francione, Gary L. *Introduction to Animal Rights*. Philadelphia: Temple University, 2000.

Noske, Barbara. *Beyond Boundaries: Humans and Animals*. Montreal: Black Rose, 1997.

Marcus, Erik. *Vegan: The New Ethics of Eating*. Ithaca, NY: McBooks, 1998.

Mason, Jim. *An Unnatural Order: Why We Are Destroying the Planet and Each Other*. New York: Continuum, 1997.

Montgomery, Charlotte. *Blood Relations: Animals, Humans, and Politics*. Toronto: Between the Lines, 2000.

Ponting, Clive. *A Green History of the World: Nature, Pollution, and the Collapse of Societies*. London: Sinclair-Stevenson Ltd., 1991

Rifkin, Jeremy. *Beyond Beef: The Rise and Fall of the Cattle Culture*. New York: Penguin, 1993.

Ryder, Richard D. *Animal Revolution: Changing Attitudes Towards Speciesism*. Oxford: Berg, 2000.

Singer, Peter. *Animal Liberation*. New York: Avon, 1990.

PART TEN

the economy

"when corporations win, everyone wins"

or, why big business is our saviour, as explained in a letter to the editor, the st. catharines standard, August 9, 1997

Let us begin by defining the key terms of this upbeat aphorism, something our letter-writer did not bother to do. What are "corporations" and who, exactly, is "everyone"?

A corporation may be defined as a formal organization whose activity is directed toward the production of goods and services with the aim of realizing a profit. Most business enterprises of consequence in a capitalist economy are legally incorporated and therefore qualify as corporations, but the term "corporation" is usually reserved for large-scale companies that sell stock to the public. Such companies embrace a variety of constituents: corporate executive officers and high-level managers; production workers; middle- and low-level managers who supervise the activity of the workforce; stock-owners who earn corporate dividends but who may have little to do with the day-to-day operations of the firm; and a myriad of individuals involved in administration, accounting, marketing, and other non-production activities.

"Everyone," for the purposes of our argument, can be defined as the whole of humanity—the six billion people who populate the Earth and who depend for their livelihood upon the appropriation and transformation through human effort and ingenuity of the planet's natural resources. Some of these people are employed by large-scale corporations; most are not. A very small percentage have a significant stake in the ownership of corporations; a large majority lack an ownership stake in even small-scale productive property such as farms. In the last analysis, the economic activity of all productive enterprises, large and small, depends upon the demand for products that satisfy specific human needs or desires. Yet, because corporations operate as part of a capitalist economic system, they will continue productive activity to meet those needs only so long as they remain economically viable in *capitalist* terms—that is to say, only so long as they remain profitable, and therefore only so long as the demand for their products is backed by real "purchasing power," i.e., by money. In sum, corporations are capitalist institutions that serve the needs of "everyone" (humanity) only to the extent that the satisfaction of those needs coincides with the imperative to make a monetary profit for the owners of corporate assets. With these definitions in mind, let us return now to the proposition under consideration: "When corporations win, everyone wins."

The empirical evidence is clear on one point: the big corporations are definitely "winning"—winning in their efforts to monopolize the productive assets of the global economy, to dominate the most profitable branches of national economies, to make their operations less and less dependent upon the employment of large numbers of workers, to weaken or eliminate the resistance of trade unions, to exploit the biosphere in ways that maximize short-term profits while depleting non-renewable natural resources and damaging ecosystems, to eliminate barriers to capital mobility across national lines, and to subordinate all aspects of human existence to the principles of "free market" exchange and production for private profit. But does all this mean that those of us who derive our income primarily from wages and salaries, and not from corporate dividends or corporate stock appreciation, are "winning" too? Are *we* benefitting from these "victories" of the corporate giants? Let us consider some of the factual evidence.

According to the Institute for Policy Studies in Washington, D.C., the annual sales earnings of the world's 200 largest corporations are only slightly less than half the amount earned collectively by the poorest 4.5 billion people on Earth—some 80 per cent of humanity.[1] The IPS reports, "Two hundred giant corporations, most of them larger than many national economies, now control well over a quarter of the world's economic activity." Furthermore, the income of these corporations is growing faster than the value of the world's combined Gross Domestic Product (GDP). In 1982, global GDP was $12.6 trillion, while sales of the top 200 corporations equalled a little less than 25 per cent of this. By 1995, global GDP had doubled to $25.2 trillion, and the sales of the top 200 had increased to more than 28 per cent of global GDP. In 1995, there were 191 countries in the world, but only 21 of these had a GDP that exceeded the sales of the world's largest corporation, Mitsubishi of Japan. Mitsubishi had sales that year of $184.5 billion, an amount that is greater than the GDP of Indonesia, the world's fourth most populous nation. Of the 100 largest "economies" in the world, 51 were corporations, and only 49 were countries.

Since the leading 200 corporations account for about 28 per cent of the world's economic activity in marketed goods and services, one might expect that these corporations would employ a comparable share of the world's waged and salaried workforce. But that would add up to approximately 650 million people, according to United Nations estimates of the current size of the employed segment of the global workforce. In reality, the top 200 corporations employed fewer than 19 million in 1995, less than one per cent of the global workforce.

---

1. Sarah Anderson and John Cavanagh, *The Top 200: The Rise of Global Corporate Power* (Washington: Institute of Policy Studies, 1997). For updates, see <www.ips-dc.org/reports/top200.htm>.

The staggering disproportion between the magnitude of economic activity dominated by the largest transnational corporations and the amount of employment directly generated by that activity casts considerable doubt on the proposition that "when corporations win, everyone wins." Still, it might be thought that the activity of these corporations has *indirectly* beneficial effects on the livelihoods of those who are not in their direct employ. To arrive at a more complete picture, therefore, we need to examine the situation confronting the great mass of humanity who make up the global workforce: the 2.5 billion men, women, and children who have no choice but to sell their ability to work on the "free" labour market—overwhelmingly to small or medium-sized businesses lacking the assets, market shares, and profit margins enjoyed by the top 200. Indeed, as the economic life of the planet has become increasingly dominated by giant corporations driven by the quest for profit, the question is urgently posed: Are the living standards and economic security of these workers and their dependents improving? While the upper 10 to 20 per cent of that workforce have witnessed an appreciable gain in their individual incomes over the past quarter century, the great majority have seen a decline in their incomes, general living standards, and job security. The bottom 80 per cent of the global population—on a world scale as well as within individual countries—now includes large numbers of unemployed and part-time workers; and even those with full-time jobs have, as a rule, seen a decline in their *real* wages (wages adjusted for inflation) and a deterioration in their working conditions over the last quarter century.

In 1996, according to the UN's International Labour Organization, over one billion people worldwide were either unemployed or underemployed, about thirty per cent of the world's total (employed and unemployed) workforce.[2] This represented an increase of 180 million people over 1994. Moreover, even those countries with low *official* unemployment rates, such as the United States, have demonstrated an inability in recent years to create full-time jobs that are adequate to support a family for more than a minority of their workforces. Meanwhile, the growth of GDP per capita (the value of GDP divided by population) on a global scale remains sluggish. For the industrialized capitalist nations, GDP per capita has grown at an annual average rate of about 2.0 per cent since 1973, compared to an average rate of 3.6 per cent in the period from 1950 to 1973. These figures might suggest that the living standards of most people are slowly improving in the industrialized capitalist core of the world economy, yet such is not the case. Spiralling class inequalities have meant that income gains have been almost entirely monopolized by the top 20 per cent (and particularly the top 1 per cent) of the population. On a world scale, "more than 85 per cent of the world's population received only 15 per cent of its income" and "the net worth of the 358 richest people, the dollar

---

2. International Labour Office, *World Employment 1996/97: National Policies in a Global Context* (International Labour Organization, United Nations, 1996).

billionaires, is equal to the combined income of the poorest 45 per cent of the world population—2.3 billion people."[3]

While the effects of growing class inequality are most pronounced in the "Third World," stagnant or declining real wages and/or high levels of unemployment are features of much of the developed world as well. In Canada, for example, non-supervisory workers have seen a decline in their real after-tax wages of about 1 per cent per year on average since 1975; at the same time, average (official) unemployment rates for the Canadian workforce have risen in every decade since the end of World War II, from 2.9 per cent in 1945-54 to almost 10 per cent in 1985-94. David Gordon reports that for non-supervisory production workers in the US, the "average annual growth of real spendable hourly earnings reached 2.1 per cent a year from 1948 to 1966, slowed to 1.4 per cent between 1966 and 1973, and then dropped with gathering speed at a shade less than *minus* one per cent per year from 1973 to 1989."[4] During the 1990s, no real increase in average wage levels occurred until 1996.

In 1991, the sociologist Francois Moreau suggested that one way to evaluate the trajectory of the capitalist world economy as a whole would be to examine the performance of one of its more typical national components, Mexico: "With an estimated GDP per capita of $4,624, adjusted for purchasing power, [Mexico] actually stands very close to the world average of $4684 for capitalism as a whole, as computed by the [United Nations Development Program]. Mexico is, in fact, one of the richest third-world countries, with a per capita product 21 times higher than the lowest one ..." Moreau reported that the cumulative loss in real wages experienced by the Mexican working class between 1976 and 1991 exceeded 60 per cent, with real industrial wages in 1991 "barely higher than the lowest level reached in 1952, and below their 1939 level."[5] The Mexican debt crisis, the peso devaluation and other "structural adjustments" that followed Mexico's entry into the North American Free Trade Agreement a few years later produced a further collapse in real wage levels. Thus, by 1997, "the average minimum daily salary [equalled] 24.50 pesos, which is the equivalent of approximately $3.00 [US] (about 40 cents per hour); seventeen million of the thirty-three million gainfully employed persons earn an income around the minimum wage. Whereas 10 per cent of all families have annual incomes of at least $100,000, 50 per cent of the population finds itself immersed in profound misery, subsisting on a salary mass equal to 10 per cent of the GNP."[6]

3. United Nations Development Program, *Human Development Report, 1996* (New York, 1996) 94.

4. David Gordon, *Fat and Mean: The Corporate Squeeze of Working Americans and the Myth of Managerial Downsizing* (New York: The Free Press, 1996) 20.

5. Francois Moreau, "The Condition of the Working Class under Capitalism Today: The Mexican Case," *Socialist Alternatives* 1:1 (1991): 142-45.

6. Richard Roman and Edur Velasco Arregui, "Zapatismo and the Workers Movement in Mexico at the End of the Century," *Monthly Review* 49:3 (July-August 1997): 101-02.

The overall picture is disturbingly clear. Despite the continuous development of sophisticated labour-saving technologies and productivity levels unprecedented in human history, the corporate-dominated global economy is not functioning in such a way as to raise living standards or to secure productive employment for the great majority of humanity. On the contrary, it is *squandering* the productive capacities of at least a billion of the world's inhabitants, while continuously reproducing conditions that are favorable to the dominance of several hundred giant transnational corporations and their major stockholders. As tens of millions of people die annually from starvation or from easily treated disease, the world system of corporate capitalism remains governed by the logic of profit maximization—a logic that requires that the continued enrichment of the few must be accompanied by, and accomplished through, the impoverishment of the many.

DOES LABOUR "NEED" CAPITAL?

Those who lived in North America during the 1950s and 1960s may remember a popular adage of the period: "What's good for GM is good for America." While never entirely uncontested, this sentiment captured the dominant mood of the immediate post-war era. The health of the largest corporations was widely considered to be *the* key measure of the well-being of North American society as a whole. A generalized "popular prosperity" was thought to be an inevitable by-product of the expansion and growing productivity of the major corporations—a prosperity manifested in rising real wages, low unemployment, affordable housing, and unprecedented access to health and educational services on the part of "ordinary" working people (many of whom, under these new conditions, came to see themselves as members of the "middle class").

Why has this adage lost its popularity? One reason might be that General Motors Corporation no longer commands the pre-eminent market share that it once held in the North American economy. But that is only a small part of the story. A more important factor is that the popular prosperity of the 1950s and 1960s has been substantially eroded, replaced by economic malaise, austerity, and falling living standards. At the same time, the movement of GM's operations to Mexico and other countries has undermined the notion of a clear identity of interests between this giant transnational corporation and the American and Canadian workforces that built up its assets. Those born after 1960, especially those who have seen Michael Moore's acerbic film *Roger and Me* (a documentary that exposes the utter indifference of GM's corporate leadership to the social effects of the closing of its historic plants in Flint, Michigan), might well be astonished that anyone could ever have believed that what's good for GM is good for *everyone* in America. And yet the will to believe that a fundamental unity of interests exists between those who own and control the world's largest corporations and "everyone else" remains surprisingly strong, as evidenced by our letter-writer's credo, "when corporations win, everyone wins."

At bottom, this credo expresses a faith in a "community of interests" between major corporate share-holders and "the rest of us" that is rooted in an unquestioning acceptance of the institutional arrangements and class relations that have allowed a few hundred corporations to so completely dominate the world economy. With this in mind, let us consider another argument from our letter-writer: "Even if the employers and fat-cat shareholders did use the money they obtained on 'the bent backs of the proletariat', solely to build country estates, buy jewels, limousines and yachts, aren't they creating employment for union brother and sister workers in those industries?" There is, without doubt, an element of truth in this argument, but it is a very *partial* truth—and one presented in a way that conceals much larger truths. The basic message appears to be that "union brother and sister workers" should be grateful for the employment generated by the conspicuous consumption of those who obtain their money "on the bent backs of the proletariat"—that is, through the exploitation of other people's labour. Without the investment and consumptive activities of the rich, ordinary working people would find themselves unemployed and longing for the opportunity to "bend their backs" to make money for others and thereby a wage for themselves. In short, the message is "labour needs capital."

Yet is this really the case? The answer is yes *and* no. Certainly, so long as the ownership of the productive assets of society remains concentrated in the hands of a small minority of the population, workers will only be able to obtain a livelihood by selling their ability to work to those who need their labour to set the wheels of industry and commerce in motion. But does this mean that, in all conceivable social orders, "labour needs capital"? Not at all. As Abraham Lincoln noted: "Labour is prior to, and independent of, capital. Capital is only the fruit of labour, and could never have existed if labour had not first existed."[7] In other words, "capital" is not synonymous with either the natural "conditions" of production nor with the "means of production" that are themselves the product of human labour. Rather, capital is a social relation between people that is specific to a particular historical period and form of society. The theorist who upheld this truth and explored its far-reaching implications most fully was Karl Marx.

According to Marx, "Capital is not a thing, it is definite social relation of production pertaining to a particular historical social formation, which simply takes the form of a thing and gives this thing a specific social character.... [Capital] is the means of production monopolized by a particular section of society...."[8] In other words, when the means of production become the exclusive property of a small minority

---

7. Abraham Lincoln, Message to Congress, 3 Dec. 1861.

8. Karl Marx, *Capital Volume Two* (New York: Vintage, 1981) 953-54.

of the population (the bourgeoisie or capitalist class), these means of production then become forms of "capital"—a social relation involving the class exploitation of "living labour." Elsewhere Marx describes capital aptly as "value in process, money in process."[9]

It was on the basis of this understanding of capital that Marx developed an analysis of the "laws of motion" of the capitalist mode of production that yielded certain predictions about the course of capitalist development. Many of these predictions have stood the test of time remarkably well, despite the efforts of critics who reject Marx's socialist politics to ridicule and distort his analytic contributions. As it happens, one of his most famous predictions was precisely that capital was subject to a long-term process of "concentration and centralization."

According to Marx, the "primitive accumulation of capital" begins with the separation of the "direct producer" from the ownership or effective possession of the means of production—a class monopolization of the productive assets of society, which is the structural precondition for the exploitation of wage-earners by capitalists. In addition to exploitation, however, capitalism also involves the competitive interaction of many individual capitals, and this process leads to winners and losers in the global struggle for profits and market shares. The periodic crises of capitalist production (manifested in recessions and depressions) drive many business enterprises into bankruptcy, making it possible for other firms to acquire additional productive assets at relatively low prices. Through buyouts and mergers, the more successful corporations "concentrate" capital, dominating markets and earning monopoly profits. At the same time, the growth of financial institutions and the diffusion of stock ownership make it possible for the most powerful stock-holders (individual or institutional) to "centralize" decision-making regarding the disposition of capital. Major capitalists sit on the boards of directors of many different industrial corporations and financial institutions, ensuring an interlocking of individual corporations into larger corporate conglomerates and networks.

Marx believed that this inexorable process of concentration and centralization of capital, and the attendant growth of massive corporations controlling a growing share of the world's resources, pointed to an "objective socialization" of production. The interdependence of giant corporate interests, in the larger context of inter-capitalist competition and capital-labour antagonism, would oblige the corporate conglomerates to engage in large-scale planning. And indeed this is precisely what has come to pass. "Free market" enthusiasts who today scoff at the socialist idea of a planned economy should consider that the top 200 transnational corporations, along with many others, are *de facto* "transnational planned economies"—larger, as we have seen, than many national economies and more resistant today than most governments to the idea that they should submit to the blind forces of the market. While corporate

---

9. Karl Marx, *Capital Volume One* (New York: Vintage, 1977) 256.

leaders counsel working people and governments to put their faith in the divine workings of free-market forces, corporations collude to limit competition, combine to dominate the most lucrative economic activities, and pressure governments to curb controls on capital mobility—controls that in the past gave governments some minimal ability to plan to meet social needs, but that are now considered to be "unreasonable" impediments on the corporate pursuit of profit.

Given the reality of the objective socialization of production, does it seem reasonable that such enormous economic power—including control over the allocation of productive assets upon which the whole of humanity depends—should continue to remain in the hands of a tiny fraction of humanity bent on "planning" the global economy in ways that ensure *their* continued dominance, *their* power, *their* private wealth, and the supremacy of *their* interests? Was Marx wrong to believe that the objective socialization of production brought about by capitalist development itself needs to be supplanted by a fully conscious socialization in which the productive assets of the global economy would be brought under social ownership and subjected to a democratic plan geared toward the satisfaction of human needs rather than private profit? The contradictions inherent in the process of objective socialization under capitalism are reaching unprecedented intensity—and may yet, as they have in the past, manifest themselves in a global struggle for markets leading to world war. Can we any longer turn a blind eye to them in the belief that the right of the few to remain fabulously wealthy and inordinately powerful outweighs the rights of billions of people around the world to employment, decent living standards, and a peaceful and cooperative world community? Those who continue to argue "when corporations win, everyone wins" are not only sanitizing some very ugly global realities, they are purveying the ancient and outmoded *prejudice* that the extravagant privileges of the few should take precedence over the most basic needs of the many.

Murray E. G. Smith

"unions are too powerful; they are detrimental to the economy"
Anti-labour sentiment in a world dominated by big capital

Union "density"—the proportion of the labour force that belongs to trade unions—has fallen precipitously in the United States in recent years. From a post-war high of over 30 per cent in the 1950s, it has plummeted to less than 15 per cent. Union density in the private sector has fallen still more sharply, with manufacturing seeing a decline from 38.9 per cent in 1973 to 17.6 per cent in 1995.[1] In the private sector as a whole, union density stood at a mere 10 per cent in 1998. Probably at no time since the 1920s has the influence of organized labour in American society been felt less than in the recent past. And yet many still complain of the power of "Big Labor" and "union bosses," insisting that unions have a negative impact on the economy and that union political campaign contributions have an undue influence on politicians and legislation. From a global perspective, such attitudes appear to be not only strangely misplaced, but altogether out of touch with reality. American conservatives are known for baiting mildly "pro-labour" and "pro-welfare" liberals as "class warriors"; but the fact is that the conservative offensive that began in the 1980s was a remarkably one-sided "class war" in which anti-labour Republicans and Democrats played "hardball" against labour and the poor, while the labour movement responded with astonishing passivity. Such is the strength of anti-union prejudice in American culture, however, that, despite this, significant sentiment persists that organized labour remains altogether too powerful and that the American economy would perform better if it were completely union free.

In Europe, where union density is generally much higher than in the United States, anti-union sentiment exists, but it tends to be confined to the propertied classes. In the Scandinavian countries in particular, union density is extremely high—between 60 per cent and 80 per cent, and even relatively privileged professionals in countries such as Sweden and Norway not only belong to unions but are also often supportive of a strong labour movement.

---

1. Fernando Gapasin and Michael Yates, "Organizing the Unorganized: Will Promises Become Practices?" *Monthly Review* 49:3 (July-August, 1997): 47.

Canada presents a situation that is midway between that of Europe and the USA. With union density of over 30 per cent, Canada has one of the stronger labour movements in the world. At the same time, however, anti-union sentiment seems to be almost as strong in Canada as in the United States.

Various suggestions have been made as to why North American society remains more resistant to trade unions than other parts of the world, and in particular Europe. The fact that both the United States and Canada had "open frontiers" until relatively recently is cited to explain the pervasiveness of an ethos of "rugged individualism." True, the social basis for such an ethos has been largely destroyed in the course of twentieth-century capitalist development. Even so, ideas, cultural attitudes, and their accompanying prejudices are known to persist long after the conditions that nurtured them have disappeared. Many North Americans are only one or two generations removed from the traditional "petty-bourgeoisie"—the class of self-employed small-property owners that operated farms and small businesses and that comprised a majority of the North American population just a few generations ago. Even though the petty-bourgeoisie has dwindled to about 10 per cent of the population, many people still dream of starting their own businesses and becoming their own bosses. "Big government" and "big labour" are often mistakenly perceived by such people as the driving forces behind changes in the economy and social structure that have made such aspirations difficult to realize.

A strong resistance to "collectivism" is also rooted in this "petty-bourgeois" legacy of North American society, and it accounts for the extreme and irrational forms of anti-socialism and anti-communism that characterize much of its political culture. Such cultural influences pose a problem to the labour movement for a variety of reasons. Where private property rights are consecrated and considered absolute, the rights of workers to organize and bargain collectively with their employers are perceived as a threat to individual liberty. The collective withholding of labour during a strike—the most fundamental weapon of working people seeking redress for their grievances—is depicted as a form of blackmail directed against propertied interests and as a "monopolistic" impediment to the optimal functioning of labour markets. Faced with the intransigence of business interests to negotiate "fairly" with an atomized workforce, however, such notions have been firmly rejected by the great majority of wage-earners employed by large corporations and governments. The principle of free collective bargaining is one that capital and the state have had to acknowledge, however grudgingly, despite the strength of cultural currents that promote nostalgia for a community of small farmers and business owners.

Nevertheless, cultural factors that tend to reinforce the myth of free enterprise have undoubtedly discouraged the labour movement from playing an independent role in the political arena, and this, in turn, has prevented organized labour from developing a more comprehensive program that can speak to the interests and concerns of broader sectors of the population, including those who are not unionized. An important difference between the Canadian and American labour movements is that the former—through the labour-based New Democratic Party—has been involved in a project of "independent labour political action" for the past forty years, while the latter has remained tied to the twin parties of American big business, and in particular the Democratic Party. An understudied factor in the decline of the American labour movement over the past twenty years has been the unwillingness of the union officialdom to break in any substantive way with the parties of Big Business, in particular the Democratic Party. As the novelist Gore Vidal has noted, only one significant political party exists in the United States, the Property Party, and it has two right wings. By refusing to break politically with the Property Party of Democrats and Republicans, the leadership of the American labour movement reveals its commitment to a program of class-collaboration, not class struggle. In particular, the support that the labour movement gave to America's global crusade against "communism" during the Cold War was undoubtedly a major factor accounting for its inability to wage a serious fight for working-class interests on the home front.

The upshot is that American unions have remained much more tied to a narrowly "sectoralist" vision of their role in society than have Canadian or European unions. To the extent that the American labour movement involves itself in political life, its outlook is formally class-collaborationist, super-patriotic, and often unsympathetic to demands for social justice raised by African-Americans, women, Hispanics, and other oppressed groups. The tendency of the manufacturing sector unions to advocate a policy of trade protectionism to "save jobs" illustrates just how willing the trade union bureaucracy is to deflect attention away from the need for militant action against the anti-labour offensive of the big corporations and the state by blaming foreign workers. This "business unionism" —one is tempted to call it "pro-business unionism"—has hobbled and handicapped American workers as they have faced a concerted drive by the capitalist class to roll back many of the hard-won past gains of the labour movement.

Business unionism is, to a certain extent, endemic to the labour movement of all capitalist countries—for at the core of all trade unionism is the attempt to improve the terms and conditions of the sale of labour power for workers in particular firms or industries *within the framework of the capitalist system.* Its credo was summed up by pioneer American union leader Samuel Gompers who, when asked what labour wanted, answered with the single word "More." Fundamentally, business unionism accepts the framework of capitalist class relations and seeks primarily to improve the wages, benefits, and working conditions of those sectors of the working class that are organized into unions.

The narrowness of the business unionist outlook was always most obvious with the "craft unions." Organized on the basis of craft or skill specialization, the craft unions, while making demands upon the employers for better wages and working conditions, sought also to preserve the privileges of their skilled members against unorganized and unskilled workers. Indeed, "craft consciousness" not class consciousness was what originally motivated the unionization of many of the "skilled trades." The organization of industrial unions—which embraced all non-managerial employees within a particular industry, regardless of skill or occupational differences—created the potential for a more "class-conscious" and politicized unionism. But as the leadership of the industrial unions thrown up by the tumultuous class battles of the 1930s and 1940s passed to more conservative elements who wielded the strike weapon in an economic environment of post-war prosperity, many of the lessons of North American labour history were swept under the rug, forgotten, or, in the case of a new generation of workers, never learned at all. With the change in economic climate in the 1970s and 1980s, and a renewed offensive by capital against labour to restore higher levels of profitability, unions were confronted with the need to "rediscover" the social vision that had played such a key role in labour's forward march a generation earlier. By then, however, they were saddled with conservative bureaucratic leaderships and apparatuses that were not at all inclined to adopt the militant tactics (such as plant occupations and solidarity strikes) that had allowed for the rise of industrial unions in the first place. Leo Panitch and Donald Swartz's observations about the Canadian labour movement in this connection apply with equal if not greater force to the American scene:

> During the 1960s and early 1970s, union leaders occasionally joined their members in defying the law as it applied to a given dispute, but they very rarely questioned the general framework of legal regulation. This conservatism must be attributed in part to the effects of the Cold War on the labour movement.... The anti-communist crusade after World War II was directed against socialist ideas and militant rank-and-file struggle, as much as at members of the Communist Party who then symbolized, albeit imperfectly and not exclusively, that tradition. As a result, control of the labor movement was assumed by people who were characterized, as David Lewis delicately put it, 'by the absence of a sense of idealism.'[2]

Long-time AFL-CIO president George Meany actually *boasted* that he had never walked on a strike picket line!

The result of the bureaucratic conservatism of the trade-union leadership was that a number of key strikes were lost in the United States in the 1980s; unions made significant concessions on wages and benefits in return for promises (often later broken)

---

2. Leo Panitch and Donald Swartz, *The Assault on Trade Union Freedoms* (Toronto: Garamond Press, 1988) 26.

of "job security"; and the labour movement became paralyzed in the face of corporate downsizings that decimated its ranks in many key industries. The "restructuring" of unionized firms and the failure of most unions even to defend the past gains of their members, much less fight for new ones, combined with governmental assaults on trade-union rights and a concerted effort by employers to block the organization of new unions and "bust" established ones. Given all this it is hardly surprising that union density in the United States has fallen as far as it has.

While conservative anti-union forces celebrate this decline, however, more sober analysts are voicing the concern that it spells trouble for the long-term health and stability of American capitalist society. In a comprehensive review of the literature on the impact of unionization on working life and the economy in the US, Richard Freeman concluded that unions reduce the probability that workers will quit their jobs, thereby increasing the tenure of workers with firms; alter the compensation package toward "fringe benefits," particularly deferred benefits such as pensions; reduce the inequality of wages among workers with measurably similar skills; and promote the operation of workplaces under explicit and well-defined rules. Freeman also concluded that the view that unions harm productivity is erroneous, and that to blame unionism for national macroeconomic problems, such as wage inflation or aggregate unemployment, is unwarranted. Indeed unionized firms introduce technological innovations at least as rapidly as non-union firms, while union pension plans are a major form of savings among blue-collar workers and a substantial contributor to the overall national savings rate.[3]

But if all this is true, what accounts for the strong hostility toward unionism on the part of propertied interests in the United States? Freeman identifies the reason, but fails to give it the attention it deserves: "Union wage gains reduce the rate of profit of unionized firms, motivating considerable anti-union activity by employers." Like many liberals, Freeman fails to recognize that, within a capitalist economy, the average rate of profit is the fundamental regulator of economic growth and investment. He is therefore unable to recognize that capitalist hostility toward unions stems from the fact that they are a potential obstacle to the *reduction* of real wages as a "solution" to problems of low profitability. Such profitability problems are rarely the result of wage rates that are growing faster than productivity; rather, they are rooted in the competitive dynamic between capitalist firms and in the displacement of living labour from production through technical innovation—that is to say, in the irrational and anarchic nature of capitalist production.[4]

3. Richard Freeman, "Is Declining Unionization of the U.S. Good, Bad or Irrelevant?" *The Sociology of Labour Markets: Efficiency, Equity, Security*, ed. A. Van Den Berg and J. Smucker (Scarborough: Prentice-Hall, 1997) 203–04. See also Richard Freeman and J. Medoff, *What Do Unions Do?* (New York: Basic Books, 1984).

4. See Chapter 14 above.

The American experience provides an illuminating case study in the limits of business unionism. Indeed it shows that the more tenaciously a labour movement is committed to a narrow "bread and butter unionism" the less prepared it is to defend its positions during a period of economic crisis and restructuring. The "social unionism" that tends to typify the outlook and practice of Canadian and many European unions involves an attempt to present the labour movement as the champion of all sectors of society that are victimized by large corporations and pro-business governments. By projecting an alternative vision to the so-called "corporate agenda" and insisting upon the need for labour political action that is independent of the parties of capital, social unionism wins allies for the labour movement even among those who are not presently organized into unions. Even so, there are many signs today that even social unionism—which, after all, is committed merely to the reform of the existing capitalist system and not its replacement by socialism—is running up against many unforeseen obstacles. The destruction of the Soviet bloc, the economic dislocations and crises of the past quarter-century, and intensified trade rivalries between the major capitalist powers—all in the context of ongoing "globalization"—have combined to undermine the post-war settlement between capital and labour that gave "social unionism" and a reformist form of independent labour political action their temporary viability. Arguing from a left socialist perspective, Canadian labour historian Bryan Palmer has made the following trenchant case against contemporary social unionism:

> Social unionism ... might be seen as simply a progressive facade behind which a wing of the labour hierarchy adroitly masks its traditional business unionist refusal to use and extend the class power of the unions to launch a struggle for social change. It actually understates working-class power by accepting the current conventional wisdom that class as the central agent of socio-economic transformation has been undermined, and new social movements of women, ecologists, and peace advocates are more potent than class because they can more easily mobilize masses of supporters.... A real social unionism would indeed link up with these sectors, but it would rightly stress the extent to which only mobilizations led by the working class and backed by the working-class capacity to stop the productive forces of advanced capitalist society in their tracks have the actual power to transform social relations. Yet this is precisely *not* what the much-vaunted current social unionism is about. The call for social unionism and the promotion of progressive coalition-building thus demands putting class politics at the centre of such mobilization, confronting, at the same time, the troubling issue of leadership.[5]

---

5. Bryan D. Palmer, *Working Class Experience*, 2nd ed. (Toronto: McClelland and Stewart, 1992) 372, 415.

As capital presses its demands for higher rates of profit at the expense of working-class living standards, the labour movement will soon be confronted everywhere with the need to rediscover the principles of *class-struggle unionism* that inspired some of the movement's greatest victories. These principles, however, are inseparable from a vision of building a new social order free of exploitation and of all class antagonisms. So long as the trade unions are saddled with bureaucratic leaderships that refuse to consider any policies, demands or tactics that pose a significant challenge to the existing system, the labour movement's decline can only continue. Yet in presiding over the decline of the very movement that provides its material basis, the trade union bureaucracy is undermining itself as well, and inviting the emergence of militant alternative leaderships that, consciously or unconsciously, will put the interests of working people ahead of respect for the economic, political, and juridical framework of capitalist society. It was the presence of such a breed of new labour leaders—typically socialists, Communists, and Trotskyists—during the labour upsurge of the 1930s and 1940s that ensured the success of North American industrial unionism and that forced even some of the more politically conservative union leaders to strike a militant pose. It remains to be seen if history will repeat itself in this respect.

Murray E. G. Smith

suggested readings

Brenner, Robert. *The Economics of Global Turbulence*. Special Issue of *New Left Review*, No. 229, 1998.

Imperialism, the "Global Economy" and Labor Reformism. New York: Spartacist Publishing, 1999.

Levitt, Martin Jay. *Confessions of a Union Buster*. New York: Crown, 1993.

Marx, Karl. *Readings from Karl Marx*. Ed. Derek Sayer. London: Routledge, 1989.

Moody, Kim. *Labor in a Lean World*. New York: Verso, 1997.

Palmer, Bryan D. *Working Class Experience: Rethinking the History of Canadian Labour, 1800-1991*. Toronto: McClelland and Stewart, 1992.

Preiss, Art. *Labor's Giant Step: Twenty Years of the CIO*. New York: Pioneer, 1964.

Smith, Murray E.G. *Invisible Leviathan: The Marxist Critique of Market Despotism beyond Postmodernism*. Toronto: University of Toronto Press, 1994.

——. "The Necessity of Value Theory: Brenner's Analysis of the 'Long Downturn' and Marx's Theory of Crisis." *Historical Materialism* 4 (1999).

Smith, Tony. *Technology and Capital in the Age of Lean Production*. Albany: State University of New York Press, 2000.

Trotsky, Leon. *The Transitional Program*. Ed. International Bolshevik Tendency. London-Toronto: Bolshevik Publications, 1998.

Webber, Michael J., and David L. Rigby. *The Golden Age Illusion: Rethinking Postwar Capitalism*. New York: The Guilford Press, 1996.

PART ELEVEN

politics & ideology

CHAPTER 36

"He who says organization says oligarchy"
The anti-democratic prejudices of Robert Michels

Robert Michels' thesis is a favourite of those who wish to believe that complex industrial or post-industrial societies can only be administered from the top down and that the direct rule of the majority is an unrealizable utopia. To be sure, oligarchy—the rule of the few over the many—is a ubiquitous phenomenon in even the most ostensibly democratic of contemporary capitalist societies. In the realm of mainstream politics, it is a particularly apparent fact of life—expressed through the dominance of big business interests over governmental policy and the centralization of decision-making powers in the hands of the leading bodies of political parties. Moreover, oligarchy also finds expression through the bureaucratic structures that pervade corporations, state apparatuses, and such institutions of civil society as trade unions, universities, and churches. The sheer pervasiveness of bureaucratic modes of organization and of institutional control by "elites" seems to powerfully confirm the enduring truth of Michels' proposition. To leave the matter there, however, would be to surrender far too quickly to the complacent prejudice that humanity is condemned to a ceaseless cycle of elite domination.

Radical critics of oligarchy insist that to acknowledge the general empirical accuracy of Michels' observation in relation to modern capitalist societies need not involve accepting his so-called "iron law of oligarchy," according to which the rule of the few over the many is rooted in some unalterable features of the human condition. Indeed, there are satisfactory and even compelling ways of understanding elite dominance and bureaucratic organization which do not require that we see either phenomenon as an "inevitable" result of complex social organization or technological complexity.

Robert Michels elaborated his argument in a book entitled *Political Parties: A Sociological Study of the Oligarchical Tendencies of Modern Democracies*, published in 1911.[1] A case study of the German Social Democratic Party (SPD), of which Michels himself had been a member, it was intended as a contribution to the refutation of

---

1. Robert Michels, *Political Parties: A Sociological Study of the Oligarchical Tendencies of Modern Democracies* (New York: Free Press, 1949, 1962).

Marxian socialism. He argued that Marx and his followers had failed to see that "democracy leads to oligarchy, and necessarily contains an oligarchical nucleus." This is so because of the nature of human beings ("man's inherent nature to crave power and once having attained it, to seek to perpetuate it"), as well as the nature of "political struggles" and of organizations themselves. However, the sub-title of Michels' book suggests an idea that runs counter to the "iron law" that he lays down in the text of the book. Indeed, while Michels is quite successful in exposing the strong "tendencies" toward oligarchy that are so common in modern organizations (even in those formally committed to the broadest possible democratization of society, like the German Social Democratic Party of his era), he is unable to prove either that the rule of the few over the many is a *necessary* condition of organizational life or that truly democratic governance is unobtainable. While tendencies toward oligarchy are very powerful (especially in the type of society that is the context of his case study), Michels notes that "the democratic currents of history ... are ever renewed." Is it unreasonable to suppose that these democratic currents are no less deeply rooted in the "nature of human beings" than the desire of some individuals to "hoard" power and to dominate others? Even if we agree with Michels that humans "crave power" and seek to hold onto it once it has been attained, why should this "craving" only assert itself as the impulse of individuals to dominate other human beings or as the imperative of wealthy minorities to rule over majorities? Why could the human appetite for power not find an even more powerful expression through the efforts of human beings to bring under a *collective* control the natural and social forces that have hitherto thwarted the satisfaction of the needs of the great majority?

A lot hinges on how we choose to define "power." The school of conservative "elite theory" to which Michels belonged viewed power as something that necessarily involves the domination of some social actors over others. This notion was shared by the German sociologist Max Weber, who was a major influence on Michels and who himself was influenced by the "will to power" theme that was a cornerstone of the cynical philosophy of Friedrich Nietzsche. Weber assumed that all societies must be marked by an unequal distribution of power, defined most generally as the capacity to achieve goals against the will of others.[2] At the same time, he recognized that power, in modern capitalist societies, is exercised through bureaucratic organizations that are, in fact, *instruments* of those who possess significant property in the means of production, distribution, and exchange. Yet Weber also argued that bureaucracy was the most efficient way of performing the routinized tasks associated with the production and distribution of goods and services. A top-down hierarchy, involving a detailed and well-defined allocation of duties to different "offices"

---

2. Unlike Michels, however, Weber did not regard the modern democratic order as a complete sham. The rise of parliamentary democracy has an undeniable "levelling" effect, and indeed, processes of bureaucratization and democratization tend to be parallel in the modern capitalist state.

within the bureaucratic structure, was indispensable, he thought, to optimizing productivity, limiting waste, and satisfying the demands of the market. As he stated, "The fully developed bureaucratic apparatus compares with other organizations exactly as does the machine with the non-technical modes of production. Precision, speed, unambiguity, knowledge of the files, continuity, discretion, unity, strict subordination, reduction of friction, and of material and personal costs—these are raised to the optimum point in the strictly bureaucratic organization...."[3]

There is an unmistakable sleight-of-hand involved in Weber's argument. On the one side, Weber argues that centralized power, as represented by bureaucratic organizations, is necessary to "getting the job done" in an optimal fashion. The implication is that if we want to enhance productivity and ensure the creation and distribution of as much wealth as possible, we have no choice but to resign ourselves to top-down—and undemocratic—forms of administration. On the other side, however, Weber argues, quite correctly, that the main locus of power in modern society is property ownership, and that bureaucratic modes of administration are tailored, above all, to serve propertied interests. Perhaps because he regarded private property in the means of production, distribution, and exchange as the natural order of things, he was unable to entertain the possibility that the administration of economic and political institutions could be subject to a collective, democratic control "from below" that would produce no less "optimal" results than those produced by bureaucratic administration under conditions of capitalist domination. Even if some of the elements of bureaucracy that he identified are always and everywhere necessary to maximize efficiency and productivity, this would in no way preclude the possibility of radically democratizing the structures of administration, provided that power is effectively transferred to the working population through the collectivization/socialization of the productive assets of society and the creation of appropriate organs of self-administration.

Michels and Weber suggest that oligarchy and bureaucracy are the only possible outcomes of an increasingly complex technical division of labour; however, they overlook the fact that this division of labour has grown up in the context of *class* division, *class* exploitation and *class* domination. In such a context, it is hardly surprising that organizational forms are tailored to promote the specific interest of a property-holding minority to hoard power and maintain its control over the decisively important institutions of society.

The real essence of bureaucracy, which is never brought out clearly by Weber, is the division of mental and manual labour, a division that permits knowledge to be centralized in the hands of a few. Bureaucratic tendencies are always strongest where social conflict is most acute and where the powerful are most in need of monopolizing knowledge to defend—and justify—their dominance. Moreover, an antagonistic class structure necessarily involves a struggle over access to and control

---

3.   Max Weber, "Bureaucracy," *From Max Weber: Essays in Sociology*, ed. Hans Gerth and C. Wright Mills (New York: Oxford University Press, 1958) 214.

over knowledge regarding "how to get things done." Where the working-class majority has access to such knowledge, they are in a position to more effectively challenge the power, wealth, and privileges of the capitalist minority that owns and controls the major productive assets of society. The history of capitalist industry over the past century has been one of transferring knowledge of the production process away from the general workforce and into a special managerial stratum (sometimes called "scientific managers") whose members are in reality the "hired guns" of the property-owners in the ongoing battle between capital and wage-labour.[4] From this perspective, modern bureaucracy must be regarded as an organizational form that is tied up with the social phenomena of wage labour, the division of mental and manual labour, and private ownership of the means of production, distribution, and exchange. It exists not to optimize the production of wealth and the satisfaction of human needs, but to strengthen the hand of the capitalist class against the working class.

The attentive reader might object that this argument, while plausible, does not address the points made by Michels in his study of the German labour movement. If bureaucracy and oligarchy are linked to private property ownership, how then can we explain the bureaucratization of an ostensibly socialist political party (the SPD) and its trade-union adjuncts—organizations that were not based on the institution of private property and that were even hostile to that institution? Furthermore, how can we explain the rise to power of a privileged bureaucratic oligarchy under the leadership of Joseph Stalin in the years following Russia's socialist revolution and the creation of the Soviet workers' state?

The answer is that, in these cases, the existence of a bureaucratic oligarchy stems not from the *direct* requirements of a property-owning class, but rather from the *general social conditions* produced by a class-antagonistic society and by the pressures of a class-antagonistic world system.[5] The complete overcoming of the division of mental and manual labour—the real basis of bureaucracy—is a task that can be seriously confronted only by a society that is committed to the eradication of class domination and that is already deploying significant resources to raise the cultural and scientific capacities of the mass of the working population. It must also have achieved such a high level of development of the productive forces that it is able to radically reduce the duration of the average working day and thereby free up the time of ordinary citizens for ongoing education and administrative tasks. The conditions under which the German labour movement of Michels' time

4. For an elaboration of these arguments, see "The Roots of Bureaucracy" in Isaac Deutscher, *Marxism, Wars and Revolutions* (London: Verso, 1984); and Murray E.G. Smith, *Invisible Leviathan* (Toronto: University of Toronto Press, 1994) 201–05. The development of bureaucracy within capitalist industry is addressed by Harry Braverman, *Labor and Monopoly Capital* (New York: Monthly Review Press, 1974); Richard Edwards, *Contested Terrain* (New York: Basic Books, 1979); and Dan Clawson, *Bureaucracy and the Labor Process* (New York: Monthly Review Press, 1980).

5. For a discussion of the Soviet case, see Chapter 18.

developed were still conditions in which most ordinary workers received little education and were obliged to work long hours in physically demanding jobs. Small wonder, then, that the SPD, a self-styled "party of the whole of the working class," was a party marked by a thoroughgoing division between a rather passive "base" and a "top" consisting of functionaries, intellectuals, and professional politicians. This division produced the bureaucratic conservatism that Michels described in his case study and encouraged the evolution of the party away from its most radical goals.

Ernest Mandel has described the conservatization of bureaucratized workers' parties and unions as a product of the "dialectic of partial conquests." As some gains are won by mass organizations of the working class, the leaderships of those organizations become preoccupied with safeguarding those gains and with preserving their own positions and privileges. Consequently, they gradually abandon the more ambitious original goals of the movement, in the belief either that the gains already realized are sufficient or that these gains will be placed at risk by a struggle for the party's "full program."[6] There are no easy answers to how this insidious process of bureaucratization can be countered within the workers' movement at large in a capitalist society. Clearly the creation of new organizational forms emphasizing the responsibility of the rank-and-file to hold their leaderships to account and embodying the idea that short-term organizational concerns are secondary to questions of political principle is vital to any anti-bureaucratic strategy.

Do we have any good reason to believe that "ordinary working people" can take the tasks of administering the economy and the state into their own hands? In fact we do: the experience of productive cooperatives for over two hundred years; the involvement of large numbers of workers in self-managing enterprises in the former Yugoslavia and in Mondragon, Spain; the system of workers' control of production that existed for the first few years of the Soviet Republic. These and many other historical experiences have illustrated the capacity of working people to exercise a form of "power" that is not driven by individualist, elitist or oligarchical appetites, and to exercise it in such a way as to enhance, rather than compromise, the productivity and efficiency of modern industry. Moreover, modern science and technology are creating conditions that are objectively far more favourable to the flowering of a "workers' democracy" than those that have existed anywhere in the past. As I have argued elsewhere,

> [The] bureaucratic organization of the production process is not an inexorable concomitant of labour-saving technological innovation. To the contrary, the displacement of living labour from production and the spread of automation, robotics, and computers should *undermine* any purely 'technicist' rationale for bureaucratic relations of authority, while

6. See Ernest Mandel, *Power and Money: A Marxist Theory of Bureaucracy* (London: Verso, 1992).

liberating the social time required to educate and involve the associated producers as a whole in the management of industry—and of society as a whole.[7]

Murray E. G. Smith

---

7. Smith 204.

CHAPTER 37

"Radicalism of the Left and Right are Equally Deplorable"

The "golden mean" prejudice

> The streets of our country are in turmoil. The universities are filled with students rebelling and rioting. Communists are seeking to destroy our country. Russia is threatening us with her might. And the republic is in danger. Yes! Danger from within and without. We need law and order! Without law and order our nation cannot survive. (A Harvard law student addressing parents and alumni in the 1960s. After the prolonged applause died down, the student quietly informed his audience: "These words were spoken in 1932 by Adolf Hitler.")

"Radicalism" is the target of routine and almost ritualistic condemnation by those who fancy themselves to be part of the political centre—the so-called "mainstream." Whether conservative, liberal or social-democratic in their political sympathies, centrist critics of radicalism (a concept often mistakenly confused with "extremism") pride themselves on their moderation, pragmatism, and good sense in resisting the slogans and nostrums of political creeds, whether of the "radical left" or the "radical right," that they consider irrational and even downright evil. For such centrists, radicalism of any sort is a pathological and wholly illegitimate departure from a "golden mean" that has been carefully and assiduously cultivated by generations of men and women possessed of sober political judgment and unimpeachable moral rectitude. Radicals are, on this definition, the "fringe" elements who wish to overturn the golden mean and plunge society into unnecessary conflict and turmoil, whether between classes, races, ethnic and religious groups, or whole nations.

In mainstream political discourse, to characterize an individual or group as radical, and especially as "extremist," is to cast aspersions on both the goals and the methods of the individual or group in question. Radicals are often accused of embracing the morally suspect notion that "the end justifies the means," the implication being that they are prepared to use *any* means, however violent and nefarious, to further their goals. It seldom occurs to the centrist critic that the means of achieving a particular goal are often intimately related to the very nature of that goal—and that therefore not just any means will do in realizing a particular end. It is also seldom acknowledged that politicians of the centrist stripe routinely practise the principle that "the end justifies the means." If it was not with reference to the goal of ending World War II in the Pacific (and terrifying the US's wartime Soviet ally), then how exactly *did* American president Harry Truman justify his decision to drop atomic bombs on the civilian populations of Hiroshima and Nagasaki in August 1945?

According to centrists, both the "radical left" and the "radical right" seek to effect dangerously fundamental changes—and their programs, while different, are equally deplorable. But this is a tendentious claim, and one motivated by a basic satisfaction with the *status quo*. Moreover, the very notion of a "radical right" is an oxymoron—a contradiction in terms—because, far from seeking fundamental social change, the extreme right seeks to strengthen the existing capitalist social order, albeit through recourse to the most odious of methods.[1]

A generation ago, during the Cold War, the American political scientist William Ebenstein gave expression to the centrist worldview with an illustration that depicts the political spectrum as a great circle. At the apex (or north pole) of this circle is liberal democratic capitalism, which implicitly constitutes the golden mean. As we move to the right or to the left away from the golden mean, we encounter various forms of right-wing or left-wing "authoritarianism"; but as we continue the journey south around the circle we encounter fascism and communism, which, while ostensibly on the far right and far left of the spectrum, are actually variants of "totalitarianism." In other words, as we move to the "radical left" or the "radical right" we paradoxically arrive at the same unpleasant place: a political system characterized by Draconian state repression, a disregard for civil liberties, and a hostility toward both "democracy" and the "free market." (Entirely absent from the political universe depicted by Ebenstein was an array of political currents, marginal to twentieth-century *Realpolitik*, from "libertarian capitalism" on the right to anarchism and Trotskyist communism on the left.)

The self-righteousness of the pundits who identify with the liberal-democratic and pro-capitalist "golden mean," while inveighing against "radicalism" and equating fascism and communism as twin evils, is one of the most chemically pure prejudices of our era. The apostles of the liberal-democratic golden mean are, at bottom, defenders of the global *status quo*. While they may advocate a few changes here and there in the ways that the global political economy is structured, they are actually far more concerned with maintaining its "stability." But is such a stance morally balanced, moderate, or rational?

---

1. The sponsorship of fascist movements by big capital is an inconvenient fact for those centrists who make the absurd claim that Hitler and Mussolini were proponents of a form of "socialism." See Daniel Guerin, *Fascism and Big Business* (New York: Pathfinder Press, 1973) and Michael Parenti, *Blackshirts and Reds* (San Francisco: City Lights Books, 1997).

Let us recall a few facts about the present world order. Ten million or more people die every year from starvation. Many millions more die from easily preventable disease. Over any given decade of the past century, more people died from starvation, malnutrition, and illnesses caused by a lack of public sanitation than from all the wars and revolutions of the modern era. The global North, with 20 per cent of the world's population, uses up 80 per cent of world's resources and has an average per capita income that is 15 times higher than that of the global South. During the five decades following World War II, world income increased sevenfold in terms of real Gross Domestic Product, and income per person more than tripled. But this gain was spread so unequally that by the 1990s the share of world income for the richest 20 per cent of the global population had reached 85 per cent, while the share for the poorest 20 per cent had declined to 1.4 per cent.[2]

The global *status quo* is one in which more than three billion people subsist on less than $2 (US) per day; in which 200 transnational corporations, employing fewer than 0.5 per cent of the global labour force, account for 28 per cent of global output; in which military expenditures represent an average of around 20 per cent of governmental expenditures worldwide; and in which over one billion people are unemployed or underemployed. Moreover, historical statistics indicate that the trend on a global scale has been toward increasing inequality over the past century; that the existence of nominally socialist countries moderated but did not reverse that trend; and that the collapse of the former Soviet bloc and its re-absorption into the capitalist world has accelerated the dynamic toward increasing global inequality.

By what perverse logic do centrist defenders of the capitalist world order presume to lecture so-called "left-wing radicals" that they abjure moderation when they declare that these global realities are unacceptable and that fundamental change is desperately needed? How is it possible for defenders of such *extreme inequality* to posture as "moderates"? Is it not plainly obvious that the real "extremists" are those who consider the extreme inequalities and irrationalities of the global political-economic order as "normal," "natural," and even "just"?

To begin to think clearly about some of these questions we should recall the historic meaning of the "left-right" distinction. It goes back to the French Revolution. To be on the "left" means that one is troubled, to one degree or another, by the material inequalities between people in society, whereas to be on the right means that one supports the institutional arrangements that sustain and perpetuate those inequalities. Of course, many centrists would now have us believe that the left-right distinction is no longer an important one. Since there is now supposedly "no alternative" to capitalism, the critique of class-based inequality has become passé and irrelevant. Sensible people must turn their energies toward making the existing system function as smoothly and humanely as possible. However, this line of argument is simply

---

2. Holly Sklar, "Economics for Everyone," *Z Magazine*, July-August 1995: 44.

the latest funeral oration for a political outlook that has resisted final burial time and time again: the *egalitarian* outlook that has long inspired the socialist tradition. True, the egalitarian-socialist project has suffered terrible setbacks in recent decades, but history demonstrates that it always finds a way of reviving itself.

Those who situate themselves in the political centre (or even more fashionably, if absurdly, in the "radical centre") regard themselves as sober-minded critics of a left-socialist radicalism that seeks to achieve social equality through the elimination of private property in the productive assets of society and therewith class divisions. In addition, these centrists fancy themselves to be champions of a kind of "formal equality" between all members of society.[3] To be sure, they are often in favour of eliminating overt discrimination against women, visible minorities, gays and lesbians, and immigrants. They denounce the racism, sexism, homophobia, and xenophobia of the "extreme (fascist) right"—and to this degree they seem to embrace many of the enlightened values professed by the left. But their tolerance for the *material* inequalities that are inevitably engendered by *class exploitation* means that they share a fundamental family resemblance with the far right. Contrary to William Ebenstein's schema, the political centre is really far closer to the "extreme right" than is the "radical left"—for, like the extreme right, political centrists are in the business of defending the massive material inequalities that are the seedbed of all manner of social antagonisms, both domestically and globally.

Vladimir Ilyich Lenin, the principal leader of the Russian socialist revolution of 1917 and one of the founders of the Soviet state, was reported to have once said that "One can never be radical enough; that is, one must always try to be as radical as reality itself."[4] Lenin believed that the existing state of the world was fundamentally flawed and that bold action was urgently needed to transform it. His outlook and commitment were "radical" in that he sought to get to the root of the problems of the contemporary world and to bring about the fundamental changes required to banish all forms of exploitation and social oppression.

Lenin has long been vilified in the West because he led the first and only successful workers' revolution in human history. A recent profile of him by an American critic illuminates the hypocrisy and dishonesty of the centrist critique of the radical left. Writing in a special issue of *Time* magazine devoted to "Leaders and Revolutionaries of the 20th Century," David Remnick quotes the following assessment of Lenin written by former Soviet dissident Andrei Sinyavsky:

> The incomprehensibility of Lenin is precisely [his] all-consuming intellectuality—the fact that from his calculations, from his neat pen, flowed

---

3. It was this "formal equality" that Anatole France had in mind when he wrote famously of the "majestic egalitarianism of the law, which forbids rich and poor alike to sleep under bridges, to be in the streets, and to steal bread."

4. Cited in Alexander Cockburn, *The Golden Age Is In Us* (London: Verso, 1995) 225.

seas of blood, whereas by nature this was not an evil person. On the contrary, Vladimir Ilyich was a rather kind person whose cruelty was stipulated by science and incontrovertible historical laws. As were his love of power and his political intolerance.[5]

Remnick goes on to comment,

It is, perhaps, impossible to calculate just how many tens of millions of murders 'flowed' from Leninism.... Very few of Stalin's policies were without roots in Leninism: it was Lenin who built the first camps; Lenin who set off artificial famine as a political weapon; Lenin who disbanded the last vestige of democratic government, the Constituent Assembly, and devised the Communist Party as the apex of a totalitarian structure; Lenin who first waged war on the intelligentsia and on religious believers, wiping out any traces of civil liberty and a free press.

Remnick provides little evidence to support these sweeping accusations. But as an example of Lenin's "cruelty" he does cite a 1918 letter by Lenin, recently unearthed from Soviet archives, in which he supposedly exhorts "Bolshevik leaders to attack peasant leaders who did not accept the revolution." Lenin wrote, "Comrades! ... Hang (hang without fail, so that people will see) no fewer than one hundred known kulaks, rich men, bloodsuckers.... Do it in such a way that for hundreds of versts around, the people will see, tremble, know, shout: 'They are strangling and will strangle to death the bloodsucker kulaks.' ... Yours, Lenin."

As is characteristic of anti-communist ideologues, Remnick does not bother to inform the reader that when Lenin penned those "cruel" words the young Soviet workers' republic was engulfed in a bitter civil war, and the rich peasants (whom Remnick prefers to call "peasant leaders who did not accept the revolution") were backing the White armies of the old order in their determined efforts to crush the Bolshevik government and undo the revolutionary victory of 1917. The impression given by Remnick is that Lenin was already presiding over an "all-powerful" regime by 1918 and that his call to hang one hundred Kulaks was an act of gratuitous bloodthirstiness. He does not inform the reader that the counter-revolutionary White armies, with the strong backing of the most powerful capitalist countries in the world, were waging a campaign of mass terror in the countryside to dissuade poor peasants from supporting the Red Army and the Bolshevik government, or that most historians of the Russian Civil War concede that the "cruelty" of the

---

5. Cited in David Remnick, "Vladimir Ilyich Lenin," *Time* 13 April 1998: 56.

counter-revolutionary forces far exceeded that of Lenin's followers.[6] The reader is also left in the dark concerning the fact that the Civil War raged for over three years, costing millions of lives and devastating a society and an economy already reeling from the blows of World War I.

There is no acknowledgment that Lenin's commitment to a pluralistic socialist democracy was sorely tested by these conditions of civil war, or that, faced with far less dire circumstances, President Abraham Lincoln had suspended "freedom of the press" during the US Civil War of 1861-65. Remnick accuses Lenin of setting up "camps"—but what government on earth has failed to set up detention camps for prisoners of war and other perceived foes under comparable conditions of war? He accuses Lenin of creating the "totalitarian structure" later dominated by the truly murderous Joseph Stalin. But, unlike Stalin, Lenin regarded "one-party rule" as a *temporary measure* to save the Soviet republic during the first years of its existence and never as a "principle of Leninism."[7] To equate Lenin and Stalin, as Remnick does, is to equate a revolutionary internationalist, whose "last struggle" was precisely to block the growing bureaucratization of the Communist party and the Soviet government, with the tyrant who was the personification of the nationalist, venal, and conservative bureaucracy that usurped power in the Soviet Union in the name of "building socialism in one country."[8] As early as the 1930s, Leon Trotsky, co-leader with Lenin of the Bolshevik Revolution and implacable foe of the Stalinist regime, demolished the canard that Bolshevik-Leninism had led "logically" to Stalinism:

---

6. W. Bruce Lincoln, hardly a pro-Bolshevik historian, writes, "... the enemies of Bolshevism committed some of the most brutal acts of persecution in the modern history of the Western world." He quotes White Army General Denikin: "The greater the terror, the greater our victories.... We must save Russia even if we have to set fire to half of it and shed the blood of three-fourths of all the Russians." *Red Victory: A History of the Russian Civil War* (New York: Touchstone, 1989) 317 and 85-86.

7. The idea that Lenin was always committed to a political monopoly of the Communist Party is belied by the fact that the Bolsheviks formed a coalition government with another party, the Left Social Revolutionaries (LSR), immediately following the October 1917 insurrection. This coalition fell apart when the LSRs refused to support the Treaty of Brest-Litovsk that ended Russia's war with Germany. Marxists, including those sympathetic to Bolshevism, do not always agree in their assessments concerning many of Lenin's policies between 1918 and his death in early 1924. See for example the debate in *International Socialism*, Nos. 52 (1991) and 55 (1992) involving John Rees, Robert Service, Robin Blackburn, and Sam Farber. But even Lenin's harsher Marxist critics acknowledge that the objective conditions confronting the fledgling Bolshevik regime necessitated a "repressive policy." The implicit stance of David Remnick and his ilk is that Lenin and the Bolsheviks should have simply committed suicide and abandoned their working-class base to the tender mercies of the Whites. The progenitor of this style of criticism of Leninism was the historian Leonard Schapiro, who did more to promote the idea that "Leninism led to Stalinism" than any other twentieth-century scholar. For a devastating critique of Schapiro's dishonest arguments, see "Leonard Schapiro: Lawyer for Counterrevolution," *Spartacist* 43/44 (Summer 1989): 32-43.

8. Moshe Lewin, *Lenin's Last Struggle* (New York: Random House, 1968); V.I. Lenin and Leon Trotsky, *Lenin's Fight Against Stalinism*, ed. Russell Block (New York: Pathfinder Press, 1975).

The state built up by the Bolsheviks [reflected] not only the thought and will of Bolshevism but also the cultural level of the country, the social composition of the population, the pressure of a barbaric past and no less barbaric world imperialism. To represent the process of degeneration of the Soviet state as the evolution of pure Bolshevism is to ignore social reality in the name of one of its elements, isolated by pure logic.... [C]ertainly, Stalinism 'grew out' of Bolshevism, not logically, however, but dialectically; not as a revolutionary affirmation but as a Thermidorian negation.[9]

Of course, such materialist arguments are not likely to sway such profound thinkers as Andrei Sinyavsky and David Remnick, for whom "seas of blood" flowed from Lenin's "pen." They would prefer to believe that the millions who died under Stalinism (in China, no less than in the Soviet Union) were the victims of a "bad idea"—Lenin's alleged attempt to "create a new model of human nature and behaviour through social engineering of the most radical kind."[10] Yet, as heinous as many aspects of the Stalinist record of "socialist construction" really was, the fact remains that it involved both a break from many of Lenin's own most fundamental principles and a flawed but successful attempt to modernize and industrialize backward countries at breakneck speed, under the pressure of an aggressively hostile capitalist world. If the "primitive socialist accumulation" carried out by Stalin's and Mao's regimes cost millions of lives (many quite unnecessarily), the "primitive accumulation of capital" that permitted the industrialization of Great Britain and Western Europe produced a death toll that was at least ten times greater. Consider the millions of African slaves who died en route to the Americas or who were worked to death on New World plantations, and the tens of millions of Aboriginal peoples in the Americas, Polynesia, and Australasia who perished as a result of the spread of European colonialism. Consider the ten million Africans massacred by the Belgian colonists in the Congo in the 1890s, or the untold number of Chinese who died in the Opium Wars that Britain initiated in order to open China's market to opium imports from India.

For all the undoubted horrors of the Stalinist experience of "socialist construction," the undeniable fact remains that the bureaucratized workers states of Russia, China, Cuba, and Eastern Europe were able to achieve levels of "human development" unmatched in most of the capitalist-dominated world. Their "planned economies" produced astonishing advances, despite the bureaucratic mismanagement that plagued them. Analyzing the United Nations "Human Development Index" (HDI) data for 1987, shortly before the re-absorption of the Soviet bloc countries into world capitalism, the Canadian sociologist Francois Moreau calculated that the

9. Leon Trotsky, *Stalinism and Bolshevism* (New York: Pathfinder Press, 1970) 3 and 15.

10. Remnick 57.

HDI for the capitalist world as a whole (including its industrialized core and Third World periphery) was 629, while the HDI for the nominally socialist "transitional societies" of Eastern Europe, China, South-East Asia, and Cuba was 764. Moreau concluded, "What the UNDP analysis shows, no doubt without consciously intending to do so, is that transitional societies have actually achieved a higher level of 'human development' for a given level of economic development than capitalist countries."[11] Much of this progress was soon to be undone, as the forces of capitalist restoration triumphed throughout the former Soviet bloc. During the 1990s, the HDI index plummeted in many Eastern European countries, most dramatically in the lands of the former Soviet Union.

A true measure of the moderation of centrist critics of radical socialism is the equanimity with which they have witnessed the catastrophic decline of living standards in Russia and Ukraine as these countries returned to the fold of what Russian president Boris Yeltsin called "normal civilization." We do not find David Remnick and his ilk writing articles about how the mass of the former Soviet population has been sacrificed on the altar of capitalist restoration. On the contrary, we find them celebrating this "victory over Communism," seemingly oblivious to its human costs. For them, apparently, the scales of human history have been re-balanced; the golden mean secured. And that is all that really matters.

The centrist balance sheet on twentieth-century Communism is seldom challenged, but it certainly deserves to be. For it is constructed not out of objective historical analysis, but almost wholly out of myopic ideology and the crudest of prejudices. Another view is possible, one to which I gave expression in an article entitled "Revisiting Trotsky":

> In the long view of history, the twentieth century may well be remembered as a time when socialist construction was attempted under conditions virtually guaranteed to ensure its failure and the (temporary) ideological rearmament of world capitalism…. The recipe: create conditions in which it is all but impossible for the more backward sectors of the world to achieve economic and social development *except* by breaking away from the world capitalist system and 'socializing' their economies; then encircle the countries that take this 'socialist road', blackmail them, invade them, force them into arms races they manifestly cannot afford, deny them access to technological innovations through trade embargoes, and do everything possible to force upon them the conclusion that reintegration into the capitalist-dominated world is their best option short of thermonuclear star wars. Having crippled them, hold

---

11. Francois Moreau, "The Condition of the Working Class Under Capitalism Today: The Mexican Case," *Socialist Alternatives* 1:1 (Fall 1991): 141.

them up as examples of communism and as the inevitable product of class-struggle socialism and anti-imperialism; then very simply declare that, however good socialism looks in theory, it can't hold a candle to capitalism in practice.[12]

Some will dismiss this as the jaundiced view of a radical whose ideals have been thoroughly discredited; but a reasoned refutation of the argument it embodies is not likely to be forthcoming any time soon. For in the realm of ideas, as in so many other human domains, "might makes right"—especially for those, like David Remnick, who choose to make their living as ideologues for the mighty.

Murray E. G. Smith

---

12. Murray E.G.Smith, "Revisiting Trotsky: Reflections on the Stalinist Debacle and Trotskyism as Alternative," *Rethinking Marxism* 9:3 (1996/97):. 43-44.

"vote for the candidate of your choice, but vote"
The "democratic" prejudice

Here is a slogan that is frequently repeated during election campaigns in Western democratic countries, one often accompanied by the message, "If you don't vote, you have no right to complain about government policy."

Why are politicians, mass media pundits, educators, and other purveyors of conventional wisdom so eager to convince everyone—including large numbers of people who have little knowledge of or interest in politics—that they must "exercise their franchise"? At some level, no doubt, the eagerness is motivated by a sincere belief that every citizen has a sacred civic *duty* to vote. We are brought up to believe that the right to vote should never be taken for granted; that people have fought and died to win or defend this right over the past century; and that widespread indifference to the electoral process could lead to an erosion of all our democratic rights and freedoms. From this mainstream perspective, voting is not only a way of affirming a preference for one or another candidate or party in an election; it is a way of safeguarding and signalling support for prevailing "democratic institutions."

There is, however, another important reason why the opinion-makers in Western societies bend every effort to "get out the vote." The reason is that a low voter turnout may call into question the popular mandate of a government. As is well known, a party can easily form a government with well under 50 per cent of the vote, if that vote has been split among several parties. Indeed, a candidate or party can even win an election with fewer popular votes than those received by an electoral rival, as the US presidential election in 2000 demonstrated. Low voter turnout *compounds* this problem by allowing the possibility that a government could be formed by candidates or parties who have received the support of as little as 20 to 30 per cent of the *potential* electorate (as was certainly the case in the election of George W. Bush in 2000). Clearly, opponents of an unpopular government can more persuasively argue that it does not have a mandate for its policies if it has received the active electoral backing of only a quarter of adult citizens than if it has received the backing of 40 or 50 per cent of those citizens.

What is at stake, then, is nothing less than the *perceived legitimacy* of a government and its policies. Can it be said with a reasonable degree of plausibility that a particular government policy expresses the "will of the people" if the party implementing that policy won election with the backing of a relatively small minority of voting-age citizens? If a government pursuing an unpopular policy can claim to have received only 25 per cent of the potential vote, does not the "democratic principle" demand that the policy in question be vigorously questioned and even actively opposed? The perceived *illegitimacy* of a government creates a real opportunity for large numbers of ordinary people to mobilize against its policies and even to engage in acts of resistance.[1] In other words, it provides an opportunity to *politicize* a population that might otherwise remain passive, apathetic, and paralyzed by the idea that the government has a "right" to implement unpopular policies on the grounds that it was "elected by the people" and possesses a mandate. The active participation of large numbers of people in politics—in questioning, challenging, and resisting government policies—is the last thing that the guardians of the *status quo* want to encourage; far better to "get out the vote" so that the victor in an election has a clear mandate to carry out policies which, almost inevitably in a capitalist society, will run counter to the interests of the majority. Some "democracy"!

Radical critics of capitalist democracy sometimes counter the conventional mantras with the aphorism, "If elections could change anything they'd be illegal." Of course, this is an overstatement in some respects. Elections can bring about important changes, not only by putting a different party in power, but also by changing the political climate and the "balance of forces" in a country, province or state. Nevertheless, this saying expresses an important truth: elections alone cannot bring about a *fundamental* change in the social, economic, and political order. The early twentieth-century fears of elitist critics of democracy, such as Vilfredo Pareto and Gaetano Mosca, as well as the hopes of socialist critics of modern capitalism that the extension of the right to vote to working-class people would lead inevitably to the election of governments committed to the eradication of social inequality, have proven to be misplaced. Arguably, the universal franchise, in the long run, has had a basically conservative effect on the dynamics of social change by drawing into nominal political decision-making whole layers of the population who are as likely to base their votes on prejudice, fear or superficial impressions as they are on a rational calculation of their own interests. The participation of "all citizens" in the selection of a government confers legitimacy on the forms of domination imposed by it, as the German sociologist Max Weber recognized. From the point of view of dominant class interests, the beauty of representative democracy, whether in parliamentary or other forms, is that it permits real decision-making to remain in the hands of a tiny minority. Meanwhile, mass actions

---

1. For a stimulating discussion of general problems of legitimacy in advanced capitalist societies, see Jurgen Habermas, *Legitimation Crisis* (Boston: Beacon Press, 1976).

on behalf of majority interests can be portrayed as lacking the popular legitimacy that a "duly elected government" has acquired by winning a mandate from "the people."

The Austrian economist Joseph Schumpeter once wrote that democracy is "that institutional arrangement for arriving at political decisions in which individuals acquire the power to decide by means of a competitive struggle for the people's vote." In such a definition of democracy, which is actually the prevailing definition within Western capitalist societies, the original democratic idea of "rule by the people" disappears. The idea of majority rule is effectively replaced by the concept of *rule by a minority with the consent of the majority*. However, the credibility of this concept is severely undermined when large numbers of people express their disdain for, or disinterest in, the electoral charade by not voting, for this tacitly calls into question the illusion of "majority consent." Just as "voting for the sake of voting" (whether or not the voter approves of any of the candidates or understands any of the issues) affirms support for institutions based on the concept of "minority rule with the consent of the majority," the act of not voting subverts the notion that citizens have a "duty" to confer legitimacy upon "duly elected governments" in circumstances where those citizens do not approve of the policies of any of the major parties and where they lack confidence in the existing political structures, however nominally "democratic," to represent their interests.

Substantial grounds exist for viewing the kinds of representative democracy that prevail in capitalist societies as little more than a shell game: a choice between twee-dle-dum, and tweedle-dee. The policy choices available to any government that has come to power through a conventional electoral process are severely constrained. Even if that government is formed by a political party that has strong ties to organized labour (like the British Labour Party or the New Democratic Party in Canada) and even if that party had been elected on the basis of a platform calling for the socialization of the economy under workers' control (a platform that no mass social-democratic labour party anywhere has advanced in decades), radical change is an unlikely outcome. First, to the extent that such a government is committed to playing by the rules of existing constitutions (which everywhere permit only exceedingly gradual change), the measures taken to bring about socialism would inevitably lead to capital flight, massive resistance from the business classes, and a general disorganization and paralysis of the existing (still-capitalist) economy. Not only would the active agents of capital do everything in their power to block incremental moves toward the "socialization of the economy," the very "structures" and "logic" of the economy would tend to force a reformist socialist government to water down its program and transform itself into a "responsible administrator" of the capitalist order.[2] This has been the fate of social-

---

2. For an elaboration of "structuralist" and "capital-logic" approaches to a Marxist theory of the state, see Nicos Poulantzas, *Political Power and Social Classes* (London: New Left Books, 1973); Bob Jessop, *The Capitalist State* (Oxford: Martin Robertson, 1982); and John Holloway and Sol Piccioto, eds., *State and Capital: A Marxist Debate* (Austin: University of Texas, 1978). Elements of such approaches are also suggested in Vladimir Ilyich Lenin, *The State and Revolution* (Moscow: Progress Publishers, 1969).

democratic parties almost everywhere that have been able to form governments. Not surprisingly, the "maximum program" of social-democratic parties around the world is no longer the abolition of capitalism and the socialist transformation of society; it has become "the administering of a capitalism with a human face"—and even this modest goal has proven to be beyond the reach of most social-democratic regimes.

The second reason that even an ostensibly socialist government committed to abiding by existing constitutional arrangements is not likely to bring about radical change is that such a government would necessarily preside over a pre-existing state apparatus—including a civil-service bureaucracy, a judiciary, a standing army, and a police force—that has been consciously shaped to serve the interests of capital, not labour.[3] To the extent that such a government would make serious inroads into the power and the prerogatives of the propertied classes, it would almost certainly invite resistance and sabotage from various branches of the state. When the Popular Unity government of Salvador Allende sought to implement a program of nationalizing foreign-owned multinational corporations in Chile in the early 1970s, while leaving more than 90 per cent of other firms in private hands, even this essentially left-nationalist program was too much for the top officers of the Chilean military. Under the leadership of General Augusto Pinochet, and with the connivance of the US government, these officers staged a brutal coup in 1973, murdering Allende and thousands of other Chilean leftists and destroying the organized labour movement in Chile for a generation.

All this points to the real limits of "democracy" under capitalism. Democracy is something that is tolerated and even valued by the ruling class of a capitalist society—so long as it poses no serious threat to its long-term class interests. If those interests are seriously imperiled, however, the "democratic" capitalists are quite prepared to resort to authoritarian methods to maintain their property, their power and their dominance. They will back a Hitler, a Franco, a Suharto, or a Pinochet as the last line of defence of their social order.

Representative democracy is nevertheless the *preferred* political form of governance in wealthy capitalist countries. This is true for a number of reasons. First, such countries can afford to make the kinds of material concessions to its working populations that is a necessary consequence of a multi-party competition for the "people's vote." These concessions typically include government programs aimed at promoting "social welfare," such as health, education, unemployment, and social assistance programs. Such concessions have the effect of politically stabilizing societies that are otherwise characterized by extreme forms of material inequality. In particular, they tend to attenuate class conflict. In the absence of a multi-party system and the forms of representative government, capitalist societies display a tendency toward extreme forms of plutocracy (undisguised rule by the wealthy). In a sense, representative government and the

---

3. This more "instrumentalist" approach to a theory of the state is associated with Lenin's *The State and Revolution*, as well as Ralph Miliband's *The State in Capitalist Society* (New York: Basic Books, 1969).

universal franchise *disciplines* the capitalist class to subordinate its short-term drive to maximize profits to its longer-term interest in safeguarding social cohesion and perpetuating its social order.

The second reason that representative democracy is the preferred form of governance is that it encourages the masses of people to *identify* with the state and to view the existing social order as just. Those lacking significant property or wealth in a capitalist society understand quite viscerally that "he who pays the piper calls the tune" and that economic clout is easily converted into political influence and power. In the absence of the forms of representative democracy, it is all too easy for the poor, the working-class and middle-class strata to conclude that the state is controlled by the rich and serves only their interests. The presence of "democratic institutions" modifies this perception to an important degree. Ordinary people are persuaded to believe that the state is funded by their tax dollars, and that as "taxpayers" with the right to vote they can exercise at least some influence on government officials, even when those officials remain beholden to various "special interests." In other words, representative democracy encourages people to believe that political influence and power are "plural" and diffuse, not concentrated or class-based. The state can then more effectively present itself as the mediator of contending interests in society and as an institution that "stands above" class divisions, promoting an overarching "national interest."[4]

This brings us to a third consideration. Democratic forms of rule in capitalist societies encourage the inculcation of nationalist ideology—the idea that what distinguishes the population of a given country in terms of class, race, gender or age is less important than the "national interest" and "common values" uniting that population. Not only does nationalism discourage working people from pursuing independent forms of political action (especially of an explicitly anti-capitalist sort) and from recognizing that their fundamental interests are identical to those of workers in far off lands, it also makes it easier to mobilize their support for the foreign policy and military adventures of their own ruling class. Chest-thumping about how "our democratic way of life" was threatened by "totalitarian" governments was an effective means to rally mass support for a "hard line" against "communism" both at home and abroad during the Cold War. Today, with rivalries heating up between the United States and China, many would-be "democrats" and "human rights" activists, including many active in the "anti-globalization movement," seek to pressure their "democratic" governments to take a strong stand against the neo-Stalinist rulers of China. In so doing, however, they may actually be helping prepare public opinion for a future military confrontation between the West and China—one that almost certainly would be waged under the banners of "democracy" and "human rights" even though its real aims would be the neo-colonial subjugation of China by the dominant capitalist powers.

---

4. For a theoretical elaboration of the mainstream "pluralist" theory of political power and the state in a capitalist society, see the many works of the American political scientist Robert Dahl.

For all their avowed anti-capitalism, anti-globalization activists who urge sanctions against China and other "human rights violators" sow enormous illusions in the moral and democratic rectitude of the advanced capitalist countries. Yet even a rhetorical commitment to "human rights" is something that most of these states have come to only quite recently, while the real practice of these democracies, both at home and abroad, remains one of defending a brutally unjust social order. Human rights activists should understand that the democracies of the capitalist West are not merely "hypocritical" on the question of human rights; they are the mainstays and chief beneficiaries of a world order that perpetuates the misery, oppression, and exploitation of billions of people. It is sobering to recall, for example, that the "democratic" United States of America has been responsible for spilling more blood on the soil of foreign lands than any other country since the end of World War II. Its direct military interventions in Korea, Southeast Asia, and the Persian Gulf (Iraq) have claimed the lives of at least five million people. Furthermore, America's Central Intelligence Agency was instrumental in the overthrow of nationalist regimes perceived to be "too left wing" in Iran, Iraq, the Dominican Republic, Indonesia, Chile, Nicaragua, and Afghanistan, resulting in the loss of many more lives as well as the ascendancy of viciously reactionary and anti-democratic regimes. The US State Department has poured huge amounts of money into subverting elections wherever and whenever "communists" seemed likely to form or participate in governments, including the Italian election of 1948 and the Russian election of 1996. It is remarkable—and a striking testament to the power of ideology—that, despite this record, most Americans persist in believing that the United States is a force for good in the world. How could it be otherwise? America, after all, is a "democracy"—as well as the "land of the free" and the "beacon of liberty"!

The fourth reason that representative democracy serves ruling class interests so well is that it deflects attention away from the operations of a crisis-prone and exploitative economic system to the "policies" of governments. Governments in capitalist societies routinely take credit for "prosperity" and are just as routinely blamed for any downturn in the economy. The illusion is cultivated that the performance of a capitalist economy depends primarily on how well it is administered by a particular governing party (a notion that absurdly exaggerates the capacity of the state to "plan" a capitalist economy). This encourages people to blame politicians for economic bad news rather than to see the contradictions and irrationalities of the capitalist mode of production as the underlying cause of unemployment, economic insecurity, falling living standards, and poverty.

Are other forms of democracy possible? In the English-speaking democracies, some on the political left have sought to popularize the idea of a system of proportional representation, whereby political parties would receive seats in parliament or other legislative bodies based on the percentage of the popular vote they received.[5] This

---

5. See Michael Dummett, "Toward a More Representative Voting System: *The Plant Report*," *New Left Review* 194 (1992); Judy Rebick, *Imagining Democracy* (Toronto: Stoddart Publishing, 2000).

would allow even very small parties, with as little as three to five per cent of the popular vote, to be represented in legislative assemblies, to publicize their policies, and even to participate in coalition governments. In countries where such a system is already in operation, voter turnouts tend to be higher because a vote for a "fringe party" is not perceived to be a "wasted vote." Such a system has both advantages and disadvantages from the point of view of the capitalist ruling class. On the negative side, it can lead to considerable political instability, with shifting alliances between parties producing a succession of short-lived coalition governments that are unable to pursue a consistent and effective policy over the medium to long term. On the positive side, however, it can reinforce faith in the institutions of "representative democracy" among segments of the population seeking radical change, while pressuring small parties of the left to participate in broader coalitions ("popular fronts") that may include "progressive" capitalist parties. Participation in governmental coalitions (whether formally or informally) makes it virtually impossible for radical parties of the left to pursue a consistently anti-capitalist policy. The larger the constituency for anti-capitalist change is in a country, the more useful the system of proportional representation could be in diverting parties on the "far left" from leading serious struggles against the existing social order, by "co-opting" them into the parliamentary process.

Ultimately, a truly democratic form of governance is impossible to envision within the framework of a capitalist society. On the other hand, a vibrant system of socialist self-administration, based on council democracy and a socialized economy, is quite easy to imagine (if not to achieve). In a society where the means of production and distribution are collectively owned and where no huge inequalities in material wealth are present, people would exercise political influence only through rational persuasion, and not through economic clout, intimidation or privileged access to the mass media or policy-makers. Citizens would not vote every few years in "general elections" designed to confer legitimacy on the arbitrary decision-making powers of the party sufficiently well-funded, cunning or lucky to win election. They would exercise their right to vote as one aspect of their participation in deliberative bodies (councils) that would address a range of concrete issues and problems of economic and social planning. Indeed, active participation in the deliberations of work-based and community-based councils would be a prerequisite for being able to vote at all. Under such conditions, the ancient ideal of democracy—that is, of *rule by the people* —could at last be fully realized.[6]

Murray E. G. Smith

---

6. The hollowness of capitalist democracy is no more plainly revealed than in the fact that it does not even allow for a discussion of alternatives to it. Many "blueprints" for a socialist democracy have been elaborated, and some in great detail. Yet most people are unaware of their existence due to the deliberate efforts of the mass media, conventional politicians, and the educational system to ignore, conceal, and divert attention from them.

suggested readings

Albo, Greg, David Langille, and Leo Panitch, eds. *A Different Kind of State? Popular Power and Democratic Administration*. Toronto: Oxford University Press, 1993.

Bottomore, Thomas B. *Elites and Society*. New York: Basic Books, 1964.

Braverman, Harry. *Labor and Monopoly Capitalism*. New York: Monthly Review Press, 1974.

Clawson, Dan. *Bureaucracy and the Labor Process*. New York: Monthly Review Press, 1980.

Clegg, Stewart R. *Modern Organizations*. London: Sage Publications, 1990.

Deutscher, Isaac. *Marxism, Wars and Revolutions: Essays from Four Decades*. London: Verso, 1984.

Macpherson, C.B. *The Life and Times of Liberal Democracy*. London: Oxford University Press, 1977.

Miliband, Ralph. *Socialism for a Sceptical Age*. London: Verso, 1995.

Parenti, Michael. *Blackshirts and Reds: Rational Fascism and the Overthrow of Communism*. San Francisco: City Lights, 1997.

Perrow, Charles. *Complex Organizations: A Critical Essay*. New York: Random House, 1986.

Przeworski, Adam. *Capitalism and Social Democracy*. Cambridge: Cambridge University Press, 1985.

Smith, Murray E.G. "Political Economy and the Canadian Working Class: Marxism or Nationalist Reformism?" *Labour/Le Travail* 46 (Fall, 2000).

——. "Revisiting Trotsky: Reflections on the Stalinist Debacle and Trotskyism as Alternative." *Rethinking Marxism* 9:3 (1996/97).

Trotsky, Leon. *The Transitional Program*. Ed. International Bolshevik Tendency London-Toronto: Bolshevik Publications, 1998.

Wood, Ellen Meiksins. *Democracy Against Capitalism: Renewing Historical Materialism*. Cambridge: Cambridge University Press, 1995.

"Black September" and the culture of prejudice

The greater part of this book was completed in the fall of 2001, a few months following what has been described as the "defining event" of a new global era. That event was the September 11th terrorist attack on the United States, which claimed an estimated 3,000 lives. For many the attack was traumatic, signifying as it did an end to a longstanding and widespread belief that the inhabitants of North America were shielded from the wider conflicts of a persistently troubled world. For those who held an uncritical view of the "North American way of life," secure in the idea that it stands as a model for the rest of the world, the hatred manifested by the attack was entirely incomprehensible and utterly inexpressible. Unsurprisingly, our "leaders" gave disingenuous expression to a sentiment of "lost innocence" by declaring that those responsible could have been animated only by pure "evil."

Horrific and tragic though it was, the September 11th attack was unique and unprecedented only in the *nationality* of the majority of its victims. As it happens, September 2001 also marked the anniversary of two other episodes of barbaric brutality, each of which claimed many more lives. On September 11, 1973, the Chilean military, with the active support of the United States government, overthrew the democratically elected Popular Unity government headed by President Salvador Allende, murdering at least 7,000 left-wing political activists and driving thousands more into long-term exile. Three years earlier, an even bloodier episode was to set in motion a series of events with a more direct connection to September 11, 2001: the Jordanian civil war in which more than 10,000 Palestinian refugees were massacred at the decree of the Hashemite monarch King Hussein. The state terror unleashed by Hussein against the Palestinians was the conflagration that led to the creation of "Black September," the infamous terrorist group that assassinated a number of Jordanian officials and murdered twelve Israelis at the Munich Olympic Games in 1972. Why did Black September target Israelis for vengeance? No doubt because they regarded the mass displacement of Palestinians from their homeland by the Israeli state as the root cause of their plight. The violence that Hussein inflicted on the Palestine Liberation Organization (PLO) was ghastly, but it was also the sort of action that might be expected from a monarch straining to preserve his power and authority in the face of a perceived threat from an armed guerrilla movement that was using Jordan as a base of attack against Israel. More to the point, the Palestinians would not have been in Jordan in such large numbers in the first place had the Zionists not expelled them from their homeland in the late 1940s, and the PLO would not have posed such a threat to King Hussein had the Jordanian West Bank not been occupied by the Israelis in the aftermath of the 1967 Arab-Israeli War.

One thing leads to another. Osama bin Laden and his al Qaeda terrorist organization presented three conditions for ending their "holy war" against the United States both before and after the events of September 11, 2001: first, that Israel retreat from the territories that it occupied in 1967 and that an autonomous Palestinian state be recognized; second, that the trade sanctions imposed upon Iraq that have cost the lives of over one and a half million people, most of them children, over the last decade be lifted; and third, that United States military bases established in Saudi Arabia during the Persian Gulf War of 1991 be closed. An overwhelming majority of humankind would likely sympathize with these demands, even as they would condemn bin Laden's methods and reject his program of establishing repressive, fundamentalist theocratic states throughout the "Islamic world." At the same time, most inhabitants of the Third World—and a great many people elsewhere—would consider the terrorist methods of al Qaeda no more "evil" (to use President George W. Bush's favoured term) than the methods employed by the US and other major powers in maintaining a global order that serves the interests of huge transnational corporations while perpetuating the grinding poverty of billions of people.

US FOREIGN POLICY AND "BLOWBACK"

Time and time again, the US government and its military and intelligence establishments have intervened on foreign soil in the name of defending the "vital national interests" of America. For over forty years, this was done under the banner of the Cold War—the global fight against Communism. No regime or movement was too authoritarian or too repressive to be refused the friendship and support of the United States so long as it enlisted in the global anti-Communist crusade. In East Asia, the US was the main foreign combatant in the Korean and Vietnam wars that cost millions of lives. In the Western hemisphere, the US was involved in toppling governments that were not to their liking in the Dominican Republic, Brazil, Guatemala, Chile, Nicaragua, Panama, and Grenada; in propping up unpopular right-wing regimes throughout Central and South America; and in maintaining a crippling trade blockade on Cuba.

In the "Islamic world," the United States repeatedly sided with forces opposing movements for democracy, social justice, and socialism. In 1965, the US Central Intelligence Agency (CIA) helped to engineer a military coup in Indonesia that claimed the lives of as many as one million Communists, trade unionists, peasant organizers, and ethnic Chinese, placing General Suharto in power. Ten years later, when Suharto invaded and annexed East Timor, the United States and its Western allies looked on benignly. In Iran, the CIA was instrumental in toppling the left-nationalist government of Muhammad Mossadegh in 1953 and restoring the brutally dictatorial and deeply unpopular monarchy of Shah Pahlavi, thereby paving the way for the Islamic Revolution of 1978. In Iraq in 1963, the United States supported the seizure of power by the quasi-fascist Ba'ath party, which unleashed a reign of terror against the Communist-led workers movement in that country and subsequently vaulted Saddam Hussein into power in 1979, positioning him to wage a ten-year proxy war against Iran. Above all, in Afghanistan, the United States backed the struggle of the feudal landlords, money-lenders, and Islamic clerics against the modernizing government of the People's Democratic Party of Afghanistan (PDPA) and its Soviet backers. The CIA armed and equipped the Islamic fundamentalist zealots who sought to reverse PDPA policies of giving land to the tillers, educating women, and reforming the anti-woman ("bridal price") marriage laws. The United States was also instrumental in organizing an "international brigade" of thousands of Islamic fundamentalist reactionaries to fight the Soviets in Afghanistan—a gang that included one Osama bin Laden, a scion of the Saudi ruling class who made common cause with the Afghan *mujahedin* and their American patrons against the Soviet intervention.

As early as 1950, US Secretary of State John Foster Dulles noted a "common bond" between the United States and "the religions of the East" in fighting communism. By the 1990s, with the spectre of communism seemingly exorcized, some of the Islamic forces that the US and the West had cultivated as useful Cold War allies turned violently on their imperialist patrons. In the case of al Qaeda, the Frankenstein monster took a torch to the castle of its creator in September 2001. US intelligence agencies had long anticipated such a "blowback" on American soil; the audacity and scale of the terrorist offensive, however, took even them by surprise. A new "Black September," indeed.

In keeping with the larger theme of this book, its three Canadian authors are perhaps obliged to state clearly that our critical view of the role of the US in the world does not stem from "anti-Americanism" and still less from the notion that Canada's (or Europe's or Japan's) role is in any sense more "progressive." A focus on the crimes of American imperial power is warranted here because the United States is the *leading* capitalist power and principal *gendarme* of the existing world order. As such, it is also the lightning rod for the anger of billions of people around the world. At the same time, the US is by no means a monolith. Rather, it is a deeply class-divided and racially-torn society in which an overwhelming majority has a compelling interest in joining with the exploited and oppressed of the rest of the world in challenging the power of ruling classes everywhere. Recognizing this, we reject the view shared both by America's leaders and by Osama bin Laden, according to which *entire peoples* should be blamed and punished for the crimes of their rulers. From our perspective, it makes no sense at all for ordinary working people in the United States—or elsewhere—to "unite" with George W. Bush against bin Laden when it was Bush's predecessors (including his father) who were instrumental in setting up bin Laden's operation in Afghanistan in the first place. Instead of making common cause with Bush, ordinary Americans have every reason to blame him and his ilk for creating conditions that made it a virtual certainty that they would be exposed to terrorist attack.

"DON'T CONFUSE US WITH THE FACTS"

Ruling classes tailor history to their current requirements and hate to be reminded of inconvenient historical facts. They seek to portray themselves as forces for good in the world—and even as crusaders for "enduring freedom." In the wake of the September 11th tragedy, George W. Bush declared that everyone in the world must take a side—"either you're with us or you're with the terrorists." According to the US president, "America's war on terrorism" was, quite simply, a war on "evil-doers." To compromise the "unity" of all those opposed to terrorism was to give aid and comfort to the forces of evil. History lessons soon became subversive, and anyone who suggested that the September 11th events might be regarded as a case of "the chickens coming home to roost" was denounced for condoning terrorism. Even to question the official characterization of the kamikaze-like airplane hijackers as "cowardly" was to invite opprobrium. Very few commentators were prepared to observe that the best way to combat terrorism—and the social and geopolitical conditions that spawn it—is to challenge the forces that preside over a monstrously unjust world order and that mobilize any and every backward sentiment and prejudice to perpetuate it.

In Canada, a University of British Columbia professor and former president of the National Action Committee on the Status of Women, Sunera Thobani, spoke at a conference in early October 2001. After condemning the attack, Thobani noted that "from Chile to El Salvador, to Nicaragua to Iraq, the path of US foreign policy is soaked in blood." Her statement was factually accurate and similar to many others made by those unwilling to enlist in President Bush's "war on terrorism." However, the forces of righteousness and prejudice know a vulnerable target when they see one.

Thobani is a left-leaning feminist of East Indian descent who immigrated to Canada from East Africa. "Right-thinking" politicians and media pundits seized upon her remark and howled for retribution. The premier of British Columbia, Gordon Campbell, called for her dismissal from her faculty position, and one irate citizen made a formal complaint to the police, insisting that she be charged under Canada's "hate" laws. In the end, Thobani was neither fired from her job nor charged with fomenting "hatred" against America. However, the furor over her indisputably accurate remark starkly revealed the degree of irrationality and intolerance that a society shot through with prejudices is capable of generating.

"AMERICA STRIKES BACK"

The treatment accorded to Thobani was innocuous compared to that meted out to over 1,300 non-citizen residents of the United States, who were summarily arrested and held without access to lawyers or their families. Soon after this roundup, Attorney-General John Ashcroft pushed through a "USA-Patriot Act 2001" to permit preventive detentions of non-citizens for seven days without charges and indefinitely once charges were laid, to legalize FBI break-ins, and to authorize the CIA to engage in domestic spying. Effectively, the Act defined a "terrorist" as just about anybody deemed to be an opponent of the government, thus opening the way to heavy-handed repression of anti-globalization protesters, labour organizers, environmental activists, leftists, and anyone prepared to engage in acts of civil disobedience.

In the days following September 11th, a bipartisan consensus emerged within the US government to treat the terrorist atrocity as a pretext for clamping down on democratic rights and civil liberties, whipping up a patriotic frenzy, and demanding that working people "tighten their belts" in response to an economic downturn that was already well underway but that could now be blamed conveniently on Osama bin Laden. The Bush administration also created special military tribunals to try, convict, and even execute suspected terrorists, while dispensing with normal constitutional guarantees and rules of evidence. At present, US citizens are still to be exempted, but citizens of any other country can fall victim to these kangaroo courts. Meanwhile in Canada, the federal government also passed new anti-terrorism legislation that amounted to a blank cheque for the authorities to prosecute anyone they choose. Many other Western "democracies" have followed suit.

Less than a month after terrorism was visited on the United States, its military began raining down cruise missiles and bombs on Afghanistan—a country that had already endured over 20 years of civil war. There was *no* evidence pointing to the involvement of *Afghan* nationals in the events of September 11th, but the unwillingness of the Taliban regime to "hand over" Osama bin Laden was sufficient to place it in the cross-hairs of imperial vengeance. It mattered little to the US government and its allies that the pursuit of bin Laden and al Qaeda members and the ouster of the Taliban regime would cost many thousands of innocent Afghan lives through "collateral" military damage, mass flight, and the disruption of relief efforts. The paramount concern was to avenge the insult to US imperial power and seize the opportunity to display the military might of the planet's sole remaining "super-power."

To win popular support for the attack on Afghanistan, both at home and abroad, Bush and Co. knew they had to package it as attractively as possible. Although the US state department had welcomed the Taliban's ascension to power in 1996 and had provided the regime with considerable financial assistance only months before, President Bush and Secretary of State Colin Powell now professed concern for the plight of women under Mullah Omar's rule. The war on Afghanistan was justified not only as self-defence against terrorists and those who "harbour" them, but also as a war to liberate Afghan women from the oppressive rule of anti-woman fundamentalists. Once again, only a few voices pointed out that the US had long supported reactionary Afghan forces whose *main complaint* against the pro-Soviet regime of the People's Democratic Party of Afghanistan had been that it sought to liberate Afghan women from oppressive traditional customs and to teach little girls how to read!

THE CLASH OF BARBARISMS

Black September 2001—its causes, consequences and aftermath—is a particularly poignant case study of what we have called the "culture of prejudice." Nationalism, religious obscurantism, misogyny, racism, xenophobia, anti-communism, ethno-centrism, and neo-colonialist paternalism have all been important ingredients in the unfolding story. At the same time, the response to the terrorist attacks has also demonstrated how powerful groups cynically exploit the raw emotions and the understandable, but often misdirected, anger of ordinary people in order to galvanize mass support for reprehensible policies.

After concluding its aggression on Afghanistan and installing an unstable but temporarily pro-Western regime, the Bush administration has continued to employ its "war on terrorism" as an all-purpose pretext for strengthening US hegemony and pursuing its enemies throughout the world. The "Bush doctrine" has defined Iraq, Iran, and North Korea as an "axis of evil" on the grounds that their regimes are either producing "weapons of mass destruction" or sponsoring terrorist activities that run counter to US strategic interests. The multilateral orientation pursued by previous American administrations to counter communism during the Cold War is now being replaced by an imperial unilateralism and an explicit policy of blocking any country (whether ostensible friend or foe) from achieving anything close to military parity with the United States. According to the "good versus evil" worldview of America's leadership, the US has an unlimited right to stockpile nuclear, chemical, and biological weapons, as well as to project its power on a global scale, while regimes that refuse to bend to its will must be forced to disarm or face the prospect of invasion.

Shortly after the terrorist bombing in Bali in the fall of 2002 (an apparent message to Westerners that they are a target not only at home but even when abroad on vacation), the United States launched a missile attack on an alleged al Qaeda cell in Yemen, claiming an unconditional "right" to pursue terrorists within the geographical confines of "failed states" and without the consent of local authorities. As this book goes to press, United Nations weapons inspectors have been dispatched to Iraq once again in search of "weapons of mass destruction"—a likely prelude to an invasion that could well lead to an extended US military occupation of that country to secure American control over Near East oil fields. With the Cold War a fading memory, a surprisingly old-fashioned colonialist mind-set seems to be making a comeback, as cultures of prejudice collide and feed off one another in increasingly frenzied fashion. Samuel Huntington has referred to this collision, rather absurdly, as a "clash of civilizations" (see Chapter 6). We think it is more aptly described as a clash of barbarisms.

The mortal enemy of these new barbarisms and of the cultures of prejudice that sustain them is the human capacity to rise above primitive passions and recurrent cycles of hatred and violence—to embrace a rational, critical, and egalitarian worldview that is informed by the best that social science has to offer. We hope that this book will contribute to a strengthening of that vital capacity.

The Authors
November, 2002

335

GLOSSARY

ANARCHISM: A philosophy that rejects externally-imposed authority, hierarchy, and domination and seeks the creation of a free, self-regulating society in which all people can realize their full potential.

ANIMAL RIGHTS: A philosophy that suggests that non-human animals have their own inherent value and interests and are not simply the property of humans.

ANTHROPOCENTRISM: A belief that humans are the most significant beings in the universe and that everything else is subordinate to them.

BLENDED FAMILY: A family in which children from previous marriages of their parents live in the same household with children of the current marriage.

BUSINESS UNIONISM: A conservative form of trade unionism that seeks a "better deal" for particular segments of the workforce while eschewing serious class struggle, broad social reform, or revolutionary transformation.

CAPITAL: A social relation involving the expansion of economic value through the exploitation of wage-labour.

CAPITALISM: Despite the "ism," this refers not to an ideology or economic doctrine, but to a definite, historically specific mode of production and form of economy. The capitalist mode of production is characterized by the private ownership of the productive assets of society and by *generalized* commodity production, in which more and more of the total pool of social labour is drawn into the production of goods and services with the aim of realizing a *profit* on the market. This profit-oriented economic system relies on the transformation of the mass of direct producers into wage-labourers whose very capacity to work (their labour-power) is treated as a commodity like any other and whose performance of surplus labour is the basis of capitalist profit.

CAPITALIST CLASS: The social class whose members own and control the most profitable economic assets of a capitalist society (the means of production, distribution, and exchange) and who employ and exploit waged and salaried workers who are excluded from significant property ownership.

CIVIL SOCIETY: A contested concept referring to the part of society that is distinguishable from the state and para-state agencies and institutions as well as from domestic households. It encompasses privately owned businesses, trade unions, churches, charitable organizations, and non-governmental organizations involved in social movements of various kinds.

CLASS COLLABORATION: Practices that promote cooperation and harmonious relations between antagonistic social classes and their political representatives, almost always to the advantage of the ruling class.

CLASS STRUGGLE: An advanced form of conflict between social classes pointing toward and ultimately involving a struggle over political power.

COMMODITY: Any good or service that is produced by human labour in order to be sold (exchanged) on the market, rather than for immediate consumption by its producer(s). (A narrower definition often found in the business press limits the concept to "primary" products, such as foodstuffs and minerals.)

COMMUNISM: Both the theory and practice of revolutionary Marxism, and the name given to a future society, to be created by the working class, in which the economy is collectively owned and administered, social classes have disappeared, economic abundance has been achieved, and the prevailing principle is "from each according to his/her ability, to each according to his/her needs." The identification of the term with Stalinism, throughout most of the past century, served the interests of the capitalists and the Stalinists alike, but was nevertheless completely wrong.

CONTRADICTORY CLASS LOCATION: A position within the class structure that combines the characteristics of more than one social class.

CORPORATE MEDIA: Mass media controlled, owned, and operated by profit-oriented private business enterprises.

COUNCIL DEMOCRACY: A form of democratic governance that permits direct participation by all working members of a particular enterprise, neighbourhood or community in decision-making processes that are of concern to them, and that involves the election of representatives (delegates or deputies) who are subject to immediate recall by their electors. Different models of council democracy have

been proposed and attempted in practice. Some involve a democratically centralized and hierarchical structure, while others involve a decentralized and federative one; some are compatible with the idea of a centrally planned economy, while others presuppose a system of enterprise self-management in a "socialist market economy." The Russian term for council is "Soviet." The democratic content of the Soviet system disappeared soon after the revolution of 1917, with Stalinism retaining the *form* of a centralized structure of popular councils, but investing it with the *content* of one-party, bureaucratic rule.

DEMOCRACY: A contested term that literally means rule by the people.

DISCRIMINATION: Behaviours and practices of a dominant group that have negative effects on the members of a subordinate group.

DOMESTIC LABOUR: Unwaged work involving housework, nurturing the young, feeding and clothing the family, caring for the disabled and elderly, yard work and/or home maintenance among other responsibilities.

DOUBLE BURDEN: The combination of paid work and unpaid domestic labour.

DOWNSIZING: Reducing the labour force by systematic attrition and lay-offs.

ECOFEMINISM: A theoretical perspective premised on the idea that the liberation of women is inseparable from the liberation of nature.

ETHNOCIDE: Cultural genocide; the attempt to eradicate a group through destruction of its language, religious practices, forced relocation of children, etc.

EXPLOITATION: To make use of something in order to achieve a particular end (as in the human exploitation of natural resources). As a social relation between people, it refers to processes whereby some human individuals systematically take advantage of others in order to better the conditions of their own existence. Marx's concept of the exploitation of labour refers to the processes through which a dominant class of appropriators (whether slave-owners, feudal lords, or capitalists) extract "surplus labour" from a class of direct producers (whether chattel slaves, feudal serfs, or wage-labourers) and thereby enrich and empower themselves.

FAMILY WAGE: An income sufficient to support a worker, spouse, and children.

FASCISM: A political movement and form of governance committed above all to preventing the working class from organizing independently to promote its own interests against capital. Fascist movements and regimes are violently hostile to independent trade unions and to labour-based socialist and communist parties, and are prepared to mobilize racist, xenophobic, and nationalist sentiments to win mass support and to establish a highly authoritarian one-party state, often as a prelude to military conquest. Fascists usually rely on the backing of big business, but once in power they often disregard the short- to medium-term interests of big capital in the pursuit of their goals.

FORCES OF PRODUCTION: The human capacities including labour power and means of production that are deployed in transforming nature and satisfying human needs through the production of objects of utility (use-values). These include productively relevant technology and skills, together with the knowledge embodied in them.

FREE MARKET ECONOMY: A euphemism for a capitalist economy relatively "unburdened" by state regulation, obstacles to foreign trade or a well-developed "welfare state."

FREE TRADE: Trade between countries that is unimpeded by tariffs and other measures to "protect" domestic markets and industries from the competition of foreign-produced commodities.

FUNCTIONALIST STRATIFICATION THEORY: A perspective that regards socioeconomic inequalities both as an inevitable consequence of an increasingly complex social division of labour and as necessary to the optimal functioning of modern societies. In short, it treats inequities as "normal" and "beneficial."

FUNDAMENTALISM: A form of religious fanaticism in which mystical beliefs form the basis for political action.

GENITAL MUTILATION: A practice in some cultures, also known as "female circumcision," which dictates butchery of the genitals of girls. This may involve surgical removal of the clitoris (a woman's major source of sexual pleasure) and/or stitching of the vaginal opening (to ensure virginity before marriage). These atrocities are frequently performed by non-professionals in non-sterile settings, and became a source of particular concern in the Western world when it was discovered that they are performed in immigrant communities.

GENOCIDE: The attempt to physically eradicate a particular group of human beings on the basis of "racial," cultural or other criteria.

GLOBALIZATION: A vague term; in this book it designates a worldwide system of unregulated corporate power.

HEGEMONY: Traditionally associated with the dominance of one country or ruler over others, this concept, as extended by Antonio Gramsci, is used by social scientists to refer to the organizing processes and principles through which one class maintains its rule over others by winning the allegiance of the mass of the population, both through influencing the way people think and through measures, compromises and accommodations in which the interests of different groups are addressed. In short, the word refers to the ability of the powerful to persuade the less powerful to see and participate in the social world in the way the dominant class wants them to, while at the same time remaining unaware that by accepting this world view as "commonsense," they are participating in and perpetuating their own subordination.

IDEOLOGY: A system of ideas that defends and promotes the interests of a dominant social group or class. See the Introduction to this book for further elaboration.

INDEPENDENT COMMODITY PRODUCTION: A form of commodity production which does not result in the accumulation of capital or significant profit making, but whose purpose is to allow the commodity producer (for example, a farmer) to obtain money on the market in order to buy other useful commodities for personal consumption.

LABOUR MOVEMENT: The ensemble of organizations and institutions built up to defend and promote the interests of the working class. In different times and places, it may include trade unions, labour-based political parties, workers cooperatives, credit unions, and organizations committed to socialism and communism.

LABOUR POWER: The capacity of a worker to perform physical and/or intellectual labour.

LABOUR PRODUCTIVITY: The material output of production in relation to the amount of labour required to create that output.

LABOUR-VALUE, LAW OF: The law through which, in a capitalist society, the allocation of resources and the (unconscious) articulation of a society-wide division of labour is regulated. Its main postulates are 1) living labour is the sole source of new value (including the value embodied in profits and wages); and 2) value exists as a definite quantitative magnitude at the level of the economy as a whole, limiting the growth of both wages and profits.

LENINISM: The ideas associated with Russian revolutionary leader Vladimir Lenin's attempt to extend and enrich the theory and practice of revolutionary Marxism in what he called the epoch of imperialism (the highest, and most decadent, stage of capitalist development). These included the concept of a revolutionary vanguard party and of a workers state (dictatorship of the proletariat) based on workers councils.

MANAGERIAL REVOLUTION THESIS: The idea that, with the rise of the joint-stock company and the dispersion of stock ownership in an advanced capitalist economy, real control over corporations and the economy is no longer exercised by capitalist owners motivated above all by short-term profit maximization but by a new class of managers and technocrats whose expertise and education permit them to take a longer and broader view of what is beneficial to society as a whole.

MAQUILADORAS: Factories that enable production to be moved out of developed nations and into poorer ones, where worker safety regulations are rare and wages are often exploitatively low, for example, the factories established in Mexico to take advantage of the North American Free Trade Agreement.

MEANS OF PRODUCTION: The land, tools, technology, physical plant, machinery and other equipment, as well as the raw materials and fuel/energy, that are employed in the process of producing objects of utility. Means of production are distinct from human labour and labour power.

MEAT: Euphemism used to describe the flesh of dead animals.

MONOPOLY: A situation in which the market for a particular good or service is dominated by a single firm or a small number of firms.

NATIONALISM: An ideology that proposes a shared identity among members of a national group and, usually, a commitment to the retention or acquisition of a distinct territory.

NATURAL LIMITS: The idea that the expansion of human wealth and well-being is limited by natural constraints, especially the availability of cultivable land and other natural resources.

OLIGOPOLY: A situation in which the market for a particular good or service is dominated by just a few large firms.

OUTSOURCING: Replacing the traditional employer-employee relationship with contractual services provided by agencies outside the company; finding workers, usually non-unionized, in poor geographical areas or foreign countries who will work for low wages.

PATRIARCHY: A social structure that privileges men over women; a system of domination based on the valorization of what are assumed to be "masculine" traits and subordination of those considered "feminine."

PETTY-BOURGEOISIE: The social class within capitalist society that derives its income neither from the sale of labour power nor through the exploitation of the labour of others. With access to small-scale means of production or other economic assets, the petty-bourgeois is self-employed, typically as a farmer, independent contractor, or shopkeeper.

PLANNED ECONOMY: An economy in which the allocation of resources is determined primarily through conscious planning by a central authority rather than through the operation of unconscious market forces.

POLITICAL CORRECTNESS: A popular propaganda term used to marginalize any dissenting opinion by portraying it as part of a dominant orthodoxy imposed by an all-powerful cabal of anarchists, communists, feminists, homosexuals, postmodernists, etc.

PRIMITIVE ACCUMULATION OF CAPITAL: The process whereby direct producers (such as peasants) are separated from the ownership or effective possession of means of production (especially land) and whereby these means of production become the exclusive property of a capitalist class. Historically, the primitive accumulation of capital refers also to the various ways in which the capitalist class acquired the wealth necessary to consolidate its economic dominance (for example, through land enclosures, colonial pillage, and the exploitation of slave labour in the New World) and thereby financed the Industrial Revolution.

PROLETARIANIZATION: The process of transforming non-working-class members of society (especially the petty-bourgeoisie) into wage-labourers.

PROXY WAR: Process in which imperial powers arm and direct local regimes to defend their interests. Violence may be directed at local agents of rival imperial powers or at inconvenient civilian populations.

RACE: A system of ideas and a form of social power in which people are categorized according to any mixture of real or imagined physical or cultural characteristics.

RACISM: A system of ideas and a form of social power in which people are categorized according to any mixture of real or imagined physical or cultural characteristics. Racist ideology is based on the false assumption that there are biological differences among groups of human beings such that they can be categorized hierarchically, with some "races" accorded superiority over others.

RADICALISM: A political orientation that seeks fundamental change by uprooting long-standing social institutions and replacing them with new ones.

REFERENCE GROUP DYNAMICS: The processes through which individuals come to define their worldviews, and even their own identities, by referring to the situations of people with whom they interact.

REVOLUTION: A social upheaval that brings about major transformations in the political and/or social and economic institutions of a country.

RULING CLASS: The social class whose material interests predominate in an antagonistically class-divided society and whose direct representatives usually, though not always, administer its state apparatus.

SOCIAL RELATIONS OF PRODUCTION: The social relations between people that frame and provide an institutional context for production and the division of labour within particular forms of society (e.g., market exchange, class relations, state economic planning, competition, exploitation, co-operation, etc.). Under capitalism, the most important social relations of production are the exploitation of wage-labour by the owners of capital, and the mutual competition of individual capitals for market share and profits.

SOCIALISM: A form of social organization in which the major means of production and distribution are socially owned and in which the allocation of resources and the articulation of a social division of labour are based on conscious planning rather than the workings of market forces. Socialism represents a qualitative rupture with capitalism and is described by Marx as the "lower stage" of communism. Many people mistakenly identify socialism with the welfare state under capitalism.

SPECIESISM: A bias toward the interests of one's own species over those of other species; analogous to racism and sexism.

STALINISM: The social phenomenon of bureaucratic rule on the basis of collectivized (or socialized) property forms (nationalized industry, centrally planned economy, etc.). At the ideological level, Stalinism is associated with the nationalist concept of building "socialism in one country" and a rejection of revolutionary working-class struggle against world capitalism.

STATE: The ensemble of institutions entrusted with preserving and perpetuating the dominance of a ruling class, above all the armed forces, the police, and the judiciary, but also governmental and administrative apparatuses charged with promoting social cohesion, social "welfare," and the "national interest." Under capitalism, the state safeguards the long-term interests of "capital-in-general," or "the social capital," and this sometimes involves sacrificing the interests of particular, individual capitalists.

SUBJECTIVIST CLASS THEORY: The view that social class is not a matter of objective location with respect to property relations and the social division of labour, but rather a matter of what one believes about one's status or position within a social hierarchy.

SURPLUS LABOUR: The labour performed by those directly involved in production above and beyond the "necessary labour" required to meet their own needs. Surplus labour creates the surplus product that is appropriated by dominant, propertied classes.

SURPLUS POPULATION: That part of the working population that is *in excess* of what is required for the optimal functioning of a capitalist labour market. An optimally functioning labour market requires employed workers, underemployed workers, and a "reserve army" of unemployed workers, who are drawn into paid employment or laid off according to the needs of capital.

SURPLUS VALUE: The economic value that is created by wage-labourers beyond the value that is represented in their wages and that is appropriated by capitalists in the form of profit, rent, and interest. Surplus value is the difference between what the capitalist must pay for the commodity labour-power (the worker's capacity to labour) and the actual value created by the worker through the performance of labour. Accordingly, the wage-worker does not sell his or her "labour" to the capitalist, but only an *ability to work*.

TECHNOCRACY: A mode of social control and governance in which decision-making is dominated by scientists, engineers, and other technical "experts."

TECHNOLOGICAL DETERMINISM: The view that social phenomena and outcomes are decisively shaped by the requirements of a technology that stands above particular social interests.

THEOCRACY: A form of government in which a supernatural being is considered supreme ruler. Religious authorities claim to interpret the supernatural being's wishes and exercise power over state and civil society.

TRADE UNIONISM: The project of organizing workers to collectively negotiate and fight for improvements in the terms and conditions of the sale of their labour power under capitalism.

TRANSNATIONAL CORPORATIONS: Corporations that operate in a number of countries, effecting transfers of capital and resources across national borders. The extent to which such corporations have become freed from particular national identities, loyalties, and nation-state regulatory regimes is a matter of some controversy amongst both their defenders and their critics.

TROTSKYISM: The body of theory and program associated with Leon Trotsky's struggle to preserve the continuity of revolutionary Marxism (in particular, Bolshevik-Leninism) in opposition to the bureaucratic (Stalinist) degeneration of the Russian Revolution. Major themes of Trotskyism include a rejection of class collaboration, a commitment to a "council" form of socialist democracy, and a rejection of the Stalinist conception of building "socialism in one country" in favour of an internationalist program of world revolution.

UNDEREMPLOYMENT: A condition describing individuals who are unable to find permanent and/or full-time employment despite their desire for such employment.

UNEMPLOYMENT RATE: The ratio of the number of unemployed individuals to the total number of individuals in the workforce.

UNEQUAL EXCHANGE: A process of market exchange in which surplus value is transferred across national lines, to the advantage of developed countries and to the disadvantage of underdeveloped ones, through an "undervaluing" of certain types of commodities.

UNPRODUCTIVE LABOUR: Labour that is not directly involved in the production of surplus value for capitalists. Some labour in the employ of capital (for example, the labour of retail clerks) is unproductive because it is solely involved in the circulation rather than the production of commodities. Conversely, some labour that produces useful things or effects is nevertheless unproductive because it is not employed by capital and yields no surplus value for capital.

VALUE: A social relation between people involving the articulation of a social division of labour based on the private production of commodities for a market. Individual commodity values represent a definite fraction of the total "social labour" expended in the production of all commodities. As such, they constitute the centres of gravity around which the market prices of commodities oscillate.

VEGAN: One who eats no animal products.

VEGETARIAN: One who eschews the flesh of animals; some vegetarians continue to eat other animal products, such as milk and eggs.

VIVISECTION: Mutilation and torture of living beings, justified on the basis of obtaining scientific knowledge, but typically yielding redundant and misleading results.

WELFARE STATE: An ensemble of government policies, programs, and regulations aimed ostensibly at maintaining basic living standards and "equality of opportunity" for all inhabitants (and especially citizens) of a nation. These may include social assistance programs, universal health care and pension systems, and public education.

WORKFARE: Public assistance programs that require workforce participation as a condition for social assistance.

WORKING CLASS: Within capitalist societies, the social class whose members must sell their labour power for wages or salaries in order to obtain a livelihood. Labour power is typically sold to private capitalists who own the means of production, distribution, and exchange, but it is also sold to state and para-state agencies of the "social capital."

XENOTRANSPLANTATION: A form of vivisection in which organs are transferred across species boundaries.

ZIONISM: Form of colonialism based on nineteenth-century plans to create a homeland for European Jews.

index

Argentina, 36, 89
Aristotle, 38, 273
Aryan Nations, 41
Aryan Republican Army, 42
Asia, 80, 88
Asian Pacific Economic
  Cooperation (APEC) in
  Vancouver
  security control, 253, 255
Asiatic Exclusion League, 54
assimilation, 54, 122, 126
Australia, 55, 81, 98

Bacon, Sir Francis, 269
Banfield, Edward, 113–14
Barbie, Klaus, 89
The Baroness Wootton report,
  248
The Bell Curve (Hernstein
  and Murray), 43–45
Beothuk, 126
Berg, Alan, 42
Beverly, Arnold, 260–61
bias, 20–22. See also prejudice;
  propaganda, "value free"
  social science
  definition, 20
  gender (criminal justice), 237
  partisan scholarship, 25
bigotry. See prejudice
Bill C15B, 255
Bin Laden, Osama, 70, 72–73,
  330–33
biotechnology, 269
bioterrorism, 255
birth control, 180, 215, 270
  education of women and, 111
bisexuality, 208, 212
Bishop, Anne, 51
The Black Panther, 260
Black Panther Party, 40, 260
Black September (terrorist
  group), 329
Blackwell, Judith C., 23, 246n,
  264
blaming the victim, 137
"bleeding-heart liberals," 276
"blended family," 225
Bolivia, 89
Bolshevik Revolution. See
  Russian Revolution

Borovoy, Alan, 252
Bosnia, 33, 35
bourgeoisie or capitalist class,
  152, 163, 166, 168, 293
  bourgeois right, 173
  petty-bourgeoisie, 169–70,
  172, 174, 296
  values, 173
Brazil, 36, 330
Brecht, Bertolt, 271
Britain. See United Kingdom
British Labour Party, 323
Brown, L. Susan, 189
Bruce, Lenny, 248
bureaucratic organizations,
  174, 305, 308, 328
  conservatism, 309
  division of labour, 307, 309
  technocrats, 174
Bush, George W., 49, 62n,
  70, 73, 93, 330, 332, 334
  Axis of Evil, 62n
  election, 321
bush meat, 281–82
Business Council on National
  Issues, 119
business press. See media
Business Roundtable, 95
business unionism, 297, 300
Butler, Richard, 41

Cambodia, 92
Campbell, Gordon, 334
Canada, 48, 96
  Aboriginal rights, 125
  abortion, 220
  anti-terrorism legislation, 333
  anti-union sentiment, 296
  churches, 61
  control of dissent, 251
  female criminality, 235
  health spending, 200
  immigration policies, 53–55
  indigenous people, 121–26
  industrialization, 117
  institutionalized racism, 40
  labour movement, 297–98
  policy of assimilation, 122
  poverty, 107–08
    child poverty, 111–12
  prison population, 234

religious affiliation, 61
self-employment, 131
support for free-trade, 95
unemployment, 130, 290
union density, 296
use of WTO, 99
women's earnings, 188
Canadian Alliance, 40
Canadian Human Rights
  Commission, 125
Canadian Liberties
  Association, 252
cannabis, 241–42, 246
  middle classes, 244
capital, 134–35, 154, 156, 166, 170,
  172, 291–94, 295, 300, 301
Capital (Marx), 155, 171
capitalism, 32, 57, 138, 145, 148,
  161, 302. See also free
  enterprise
  class-antagonistic, 24, 166
  class domination and, 15,
  134, 263
  concentration of capital, 293
  corporate, 287, 291
  crisis tendencies, 17, 135, 140,
  157, 171, 174, 293, 326
  democratic, 165, 312, 324
  European, 81
  exploitation of natural
  world, 191, 269
  failure of, 137
  and "family values," 229
  and flesh eating, 277
  global, 92, 317
  hostility toward unions, 299
  Marx on, 162–63, 292–93
  objective socialization
  under, 294
  primitive accumulation of
  capital, 317
  racial oppression, 263
  reconstruction, European
  and Japanese, 90
  restoration of in Russia and
  Ukraine, 318
  rules of game, 152–54
  scientific managers, 308
  unemployment, 130, 132
capitalist class, 152, 163, 166,
  168, 293

neo-Nazis, 68, 89–90
neem tree, 100
neo-colonialism, 140, 325, 334
neo-conservatism, 39, 173, 226,
227
laissez-faire economics, 226
neo-fascism, 39
neo-liberalism, 56, 102, 114, 256
neutrality, 24–25
New Dark Age, 39
resurgent interest in race, 37
New Democratic Party, 297,
323
New People's Army, 59, 91
Newsweek, 44
Nicaragua, 69–70, 89, 92, 326,
330
Nietzsche, Friedrich, 306
Nightingale, Florence, 198n
non-human animals. *See*
animals
North American Free Trade
Agreement (NAFTA),
95–96, 251, 290
Northern Alliance, 63, 72
nuclear family, 224

Oklahoma bombing, 41, 68
oligarchy, 161, 305–06, 308
oligopoly, 128
Ontario Coalition Against
Poverty, 256
"Operation Infinite Justice,"
70
opiates, 246
Opium wars, 317
Order (Christian Identity
Group), 42
organized labour. *See* labour
movement; unions
Origin of Species (Darwin),
109–10
Osborne, Helen Betty, 123
Oslo Peace 1993, 34
"outsourcing," 225
overpopulation. *See under*
population

Pahlavi, Shah, 331
Pakistan, 199, 244
Palestine, 34, 74, 330

Palestine Liberation
Organization (PLO), 330
Palestinian suicide
bombers, 34
Palmer, Bryan, 300
Panama, 92, 330
Panitch, Leo, 298
Pareto, Vilfredo, 160, 322
Partisan Defense Committee,
257n, 261n
patriarchy, 35, 43, 181, 183,
190–91, 193. *See also*
masculinity
flesh, eggs and milk as part
of, 192
spousal and child abuse, 225
suppression of female
sexuality, 203–04
patriotism, 16
Peltier, Leonard, 40, 262
People's Democratic Party of
Afghanistan (PDPA), 331,
334
Persian Gulf, 326
petty-bourgeoisie. *See under*
bourgeoisie
Philippines, 59, 91
Phineas Priesthood, 42
Pierce, William, 42
Pinochet, General Augusto,
324
Pioneer Fund, 44
Piper, Jonathan, 261–62
planned economy, 24, 160,
293–94, 317
plutocracy, 324
police, 55, 89, 172, 251, 258
attitude toward
demonstrators, 254
brutality, 253–54
framing the innocent, 262
New York police, 263
Philadelphia police, 260
powers under anti-terrorist
legislation, 255
preemptive arrests, 148
Quebec police, 253–54
racism, 40
RCMP, 123–24, 254–55
Toronto police, 252
use of pepper-spray, 255

political correctness, 14, 17–18,
44, 180, 208
media attacks on, 45
Political Parties (Michels), 305
Ponting, Clive, 282
Poor Laws, 115–16
population
birth rate, 53, 111
control, 139
growth, 137, 139
Malthus' natural law, 137
overpopulation, 140, 270
and poverty, 139–40
surplus population, 130
Posse Comitatus, 41
post-industrial societies, 173,
305
postmodernism, 15
Potlach, 82, 122, 147
poverty, 56, 60, 79, 166, 276,
330. *See also* wealth
"culture of," 114
destruction of subsistence
agriculture and, 110
feminization of, 141
global, 140
homeless people, 36, 111
inequitable food
distribution, 138, 276
negative attitudes to, 111–12,
113–19
and overpopulation, 137,
139–40
Social Darwinism and,
110–12
Third World, 79, 85
"undeserving poor," 115, 117,
119
as unwillingness to work, 114
workfare and, 118
Powell, Colin, 70, 334
Precautionary Principle, 98
pregnancy termination. *See*
abortion
prejudice, 20, 22, 27, 140. *See
also* bias
definition, 13, 19–21
myths supporting, 23
religious ideology, 60
primitive accumulation of
capital, 293